Diva

Diva

Feminism and Fierceness from Pop to Hip-Hop

Kirsty Fairclough, Benjamin Halligan, Nicole Hodges Persley and Shara Rambarran

BLOOMSBURY ACADEMIC
NEW YORK • LONDON • OXFORD • NEW DELHI • SYDNEY

BLOOMSBURY ACADEMIC

Bloomsbury Publishing Inc, 1385 Broadway, New York, NY 10018, USA
Bloomsbury Publishing Plc, 50 Bedford Square, London, WC1B 3DP, UK
Bloomsbury Publishing Ireland, 29 Earlsfort Terrace, Dublin 2, D02 AY28, Ireland

BLOOMSBURY, BLOOMSBURY ACADEMIC and the Diana logo
are trademarks of Bloomsbury Publishing Plc

First published in the United States of America 2023
This paperback edition published 2025

Copyright © Kirsty Fairclough, Benjamin Halligan, Nicole Hodges Persley and
Shara Rambarran, 2023
Each chapter copyright © by the contributor, 2023

For legal purposes the Acknowledgements on p. viii constitute
an extension of this copyright page.

Cover design by Louise Dugdale
Cover image: Photographer, Carlo Allegri / REUTERS / Alamy Stock Photo

All rights reserved. No part of this publication may be: i) reproduced or transmitted in any form, electronic or mechanical, including photocopying, recording or by means of any information storage or retrieval system without prior permission in writing from the publishers; or ii) used or reproduced in any way for the training, development or operation of artificial intelligence (AI) technologies, including generative AI technologies. The rights holders expressly reserve this publication from the text and data mining exception as per Article 4(3) of the Digital Single Market Directive (EU) 2019/790.

Bloomsbury Publishing Inc does not have any control over, or responsibility for, any third-party websites referred to or in this book. All internet addresses given in this book were correct at the time of going to press. The author and publisher regret any inconvenience caused if addresses have changed or sites have ceased to exist, but can accept no responsibility for any such changes.

While every effort has been made to locate copyright holders the publishers would be grateful to hear from any person(s) not here acknowledged.

Library of Congress Cataloging-in-Publication Data
Names: Fairclough, Kirsty, editor. | Halligan, Benjamin, editor. | Hodges Persley, Nicole, 1969- editor. | Rambarran, Shara, editor.
Title: Diva : feminism and fierceness from pop to hip-hop / [edited by] Kirsty Fairclough, Benjamin Halligan, Nicole Hodges Persley, and Shara Rambarran.
Description: [1.] | New York : Bloomsbury Academic, 2023. | Includes bibliographical references and index. | Summary: "The first academic engagement with "divas," including a discussion of their roots, evolutions, functions, and appropriations. Channelling the ideas and strategies of feminism, empowerment, intersectionality, identity politics, and more to create this key popular culture figure"–Provided by publisher.
Identifiers: LCCN 2023005459 | ISBN 9781501368257 (hardback) | ISBN 9781501369667 (paperback) | ISBN 9781501368264 (ebook) | ISBN 9781501368271 (adobe pdf)
Subjects: LCSH: Women singers. | Popular music–History and criticism. | Feminism and music. | Women in popular culture.
Classification: LCC ML82 .D58 2023 | DDC 780.82–dc23/eng/20230207
LC record available at https://lccn.loc.gov/2023005459

ISBN: HB: 978-1-5013-6825-7
PB: 978-1-5013-6966-7
ePDF: 978-1-5013-6827-1
eBook: 978-1-5013-6826-4

Typeset by Deanta Global Publishing Services, Chennai, India

For product safety related questions contact productsafety@bloomsbury.com.

To find out more about our authors and books visit www.bloomsbury.com
and sign up for our newsletters.

Contents

List of figures — vii
Acknowledgements — viii

Introduction: Y'all! the diva and us *Kirsty Fairclough, Benjamin Halligan, Nicole Hodges Persley, Shara Rambarran* — 1

Section one the rise to power

1 'Proceed with Caution': Mariah Carey – the ultimate diva in popular music and culture? *Shara Rambarran* — 25
2 Performing creative labour: Whitney Houston metanarratives on MTV, 1985–8 *Gwynne George* — 42
3 A girl of many colours: Dolly Parton's image evolution: 1967–2022 *James Reeves* — 56
4 A fondness for shock: The celebrated outburst of Grace Jones *Mark Duffett* — 70

Section two the diva and our times

5 Aaliyah's voice and after *Benjamin Halligan* — 97
6 'Suck On My Balls, Bitch!': #MeToo and Beyoncé – A paradigm shift *Hannah M. Strong* — 113
7 Amuro Namie: Japan's diva in the postmodern era? *Dorothy Finan* — 127
8 Reconstructing the American Dream: Janelle Monáe's Afrofuturist performances *Timmia Hearn DeRoy* — 141
9 'WAP': Erotic revolutionary hip-hop by Cardi B and Megan Thee Stallion *Shawna Shipley-Gates* — 160
10 Putting divas back in their place: Controversy and backlash at the 2020 Super Bowl Halftime Show *Gina Sandí Díaz* — 176
11 Simultaneously Black: Drake and Nicki Minaj and the performance of hip-hop cosmopolitanisms *Nicole Hodges Persley* — 190

Section three diva cultures

12	Curating the diva *Harriet Reed*	213
13	A Diva on the Iranian stage: Ali Akbar Alizad's remix of Jean Genet's *The Maids* *Rana Esfandiary*	230
14	Recasting diva culture: Performative strategies of fourth wave Black feminist stand-up comedy *Rachel E. Blackburn*	247
15	Independent women: The impact of pop divas on stand-up comedy *Ellie Tomsett and Nathalie Weidhase*	262

List of contributors 277
Index 282

Figures

1.1	The opening of Mariah Carey's 'Obsessed' Video	35
1.2	Mariah Carey as the Stalker	36
5.1–5.3	From a live Instagram stream: Ashanti emcees with a small club crowd and DJs with a laptop; December 2021	106
5.4–5.7	Return to the industrial setting, with cage, fence and lattice designs, and light bleeding across the image	107
5.8–5.10	Amerie emceeing live at the Milton Club in 2017, with social media advert	109
6.1	Beyoncé performs 'Sorry' at Coachella	122
7.1	Screengrab of Amuro Namie in the music video for 'a walk in the park' (1996)	130
7.2	Screengrab of Amuro Namie in the music video for 'Hero' (2016)	135
12.1	Spice Girls items from the *Spice Up Manchester* exhibition	215
12.2	Catwalk costume display, from *Kylie – The Exhibition*	219
12.3	Destiny's Child costumes on display, for *The Supremes – From the Mary Wilson Collection*	222
12.4	Installation image of *The House of Annie Lennox* (house model interior)	224
13.1	Photo by Siavash Tasaodian	231
13.2	Photo by Ehsan Zivaralam	238
13.3	Photo by Ehsan Zivaralam	238
13.4	Photo by Ehsan Zivaralam	244

Acknowledgements

A number of the contributors to this book spoke at the conference 'Diva: Hip-Hop, Feminism and Fierceness', which was convened by Benjamin Halligan for the Centre for Film, Media, Discourse and Culture in the Faculty of Arts, Business and Social Sciences at the University of Wolverhampton on 17 July 2019. The co-editors wish to thank the Centre, Faculty and University for their support. The conference included a rare screening of Pogus Caesar's 1995 documentary *Aaliyah Live in Amsterdam*, followed by Pogus in conversation with Natalie Graham. We wish to extend our special thanks to them too since this closing event offered a particular, and energising, orientation to this book.

Rana Esfandiary's chapter also appears in her book *Performing Persia* and is included here with the kind permission of the Taylor & Francis group.

From Kirsty: I would like to thank my brilliant co-editors for their patience and support, my son Evan for putting up with Beyoncé on repeat and of course all the divas who inspired our book.

From Ben: My thanks to Amerie and the Milton Club, our colleagues at Bloomsbury (past and present), Pogus Caesar, Amrit Chodda, Phil Dearden, Richard Glover, Silke Machold, Fran Pheasant-Kelly, Kwame Phillips, Aliyah Rawat, Ellie Tomsett, Christopher Weedman and my co-editors.

I would like to note a dedication to an outstanding researcher, whose assessment and PhD award coincided with the final months of the preparation of this book, and whose company I was privileged to have at that time: Dr Richard Ekpedekumo (1959–2022).

From Nicole: Thanks to my fellow editors, for inviting me to be a part of this amazing project. I truly appreciate the critical generosity shared in the collaboration process. We created this volume with the tragic bookmarks of a global pandemic and the death by police violence of George Floyd. The empathy, concern and sincerity of these colleagues over the course of editing this volume is a testimony to the resilience of the human spirit and our collective desire to make scholarship that draws attention to the need for art to help sustain, support and guide us to a better version of ourselves in times of crises that impact us all.

For more on critical generosity see: Román, D. (1998), *Acts of Intervention: Performance, Gay Culture, and AIDS*, Indiana University Press; Dolan, J. (2013),

'Critical Generosity', *Public: A Journal of Imagining America*, 1 (1–2). Available online: https://public.imaginingamerica.org/blog/article/critical-generosity-2/ (accessed 6 November 2022)

From Shara: I would like to thank my co-editors, Bloomsbury, friends and family.

Introduction

Y'all! the diva and us

Kirsty Fairclough, Benjamin Halligan,
Nicole Hodges Persley, Shara Rambarran

Definitions and delineations

The figure of the singer diva became prominent in the wider Western cultural landscape in the late 1990s – as effecting an entry into the mainstream, and then positioned as central to, or indeed the zenith of and, in turn, transformative to, pop cultures. The *VH1 Divas* series was a particular marker in this, and the first divas concert, on 14 April 1998, curated a line-up that mixed long-established divas (Aretha Franklin, Carole King) with the relatively recently established (Gloria Estefan, Mariah Carey). The setting was plush: orchestra and conductor, choreographed entrances and award ceremony-like lighting, as if working to dispel lingering prejudices in respect to Black culture (explored in this book in relation to the 'hood' by Nicole Hodges Persley, and the 'welfare queen' by Gwynne George). And such a mise-en-scène, which can be considered with respect to a neoliberal framing of music and stardom (which invariably showcased wealth) is diametrically opposite to Black music events of the previous generation, such as the Los Angeles 'Black Woodstock' – Wattstax of 1972, organized by Stax Records – which arose from, and reflected, its context of mass poverty, disenfranchisement and (literal) ashes:

> 'Charcoal Alley' – 103rd Street, seven miles south of the [LA Memorial] Coliseum, remained in ashes, and some of the main streets around the stadium, especially Vermont Avenue and Broadway, also still had deep scars at sites that had been torched in August 1965 [during the Watts Riots].

> So the first requirement of the Wattstax festival was that the LAPD [Los Angeles Police Department] wouldn't be allowed inside the Coliseum . . . and that the security force inside had to be all Black – and unarmed.
>
> (Davis and Wiener 2020: 625)

The appearance of Isaac Hayes for the Wattstax finale, striding on stage to the 'Theme from *Shaft*' (1971) – becaped, his bare chest bound in gold chains, and sporting tight orange trousers, shades and a shaven head, while asking/singing 'who's the Black private dick that's a sex machine to all the chicks?' – could be said to anticipate a post-Wattstax, post-1968 capitalist strategy for Black popular music, with a trajectory through Motown's 'Black Capitalism' phase, elements of the commercial phase of disco, aspirational content for MTV music videos, the materialist turn in rap, and then on to VH1's divas.[1] Hayes was introduced by Jesse Jackson, signalling a new Black power, and its alliances, for the 1970s – just as *VH1 Divas*, in its duets and collaborations, signalled alliances and potentials for the coming 2000s. Wattstax Black power for the 1970s (via Hayes and Jackson) can be read in political, community, creative and even sexual terms. Black power for the millennium (via, say, Carey duetting with Aretha Franklin) prompts different sets of readings – the task of those who have contributed to this book.[2]

Likewise, the 2000 *VH1 Divas* event, a tribute to Diana Ross, took in music from both the Supremes and Ross herself, and Donna Summer, Destiny's Child and RuPaul. In this, a renewal or renaissance of the diva figure seemed to be occurring, with contemporary hip-hop and pop positioned as in a direct continuum with (and so gaining something of the respectability and traction of) soul, rhythm and blues, and even 1970s women singer-songwriters. This occurred at the point of 'a radical reshaping of the landscape of popular music', away from buying and owning physical media and towards the live experience: 'the meeting of a demand for the actual presence of the global superstar in the global suburbs' (Edgar et al. 2015: 1).

Writing in 2001, Linda Lister sought to delineate three types of divas: Prima Divas (related back to the operatic prima donna: those with exceptional vocal abilities, with Barbra Streisand as an exemplar); late-twentieth-century innovators (with Madonna as exemplar); and a third category identified with 'the singer/songwriter/artist' (with the Lilith Fair Festival as exemplar, and hence 'Liliths') (2001: 2, 7). Lister concludes that a process of 'divafication' – enacted by both star and 'dutifully lip-synch[ing]' fans (8) – had effectively removed the negative connotations formerly associated with the word 'diva,' thus diminishing the lexicon of misogynistic terminology. In retrospect, and with the diva considered as particular to hip-hop, divafication has since taken on something not so apparent in this earlier consideration: the patina of the fabulous, the notion of the event and the idea (explored extensively in the chapters of this book) of cultural resistance. That is: the diva themselves had arrived, in person – electrifying, glamourizing and possessed of an attitude. An indicator of the substantial cultural significance of this phenomenon, with respect to its potential or emergent politics, is apparent in bell hooks's measured but incendiary words when she referred to prima diva Beyoncé as a 'terrorist' and 'slave' ('especially in terms of the impact on young girls'; cited in Gay 2014) – and indeed the condemnatory response from Cooper in respect to hooks's 'antifeminist' intervention into 'the momentous generational shifts of this moment' (2017: 234). That shift had occurred in a way that was outside the oppositional political imaginings of the 1960s and 1970s: glamour, which was then considered as the hubris or delusions of a decaying establishment, had now been reconceptualized as a matter of individual empowerment, and self-determination. This is recognized in the appropriation or reworking of diva and diva performative/behavioural tropes (which our contributors identify as 'divadoms') in trans cultures. The diva brought or renewed exceptional senses of superstardom, of glamour, of occasion, of live performance, of being fabulous, of emotional empathy and of a toughness born of struggle – that is, after the Stonewall Riots of 1969, and on to the goals of individual empowerment associated with third wave feminism: of being able, and more than willing, to answer back.[3] That toughness seems proactive and, as per the activism that is read as typifying fourth wave feminism (see Chamberlain 2017; Rivers 2017), utilizes social media to call-out behaviours, and then not blanching from delivering those kinds of full-blooded criticisms in person too, as the opportunity arises (and with this appetite for confrontation identified as the modus operandi, even of the very young; see Retallack, Ringrose and Lawrence 2016). Such proactive toughness, and desire to assert a position, aligns with the concept of 'fierceness' – something often attributed to divas. And we see a parallel of this fierceness in work on the idea of the feminist killjoy (Ahmed 2017): fourth wave feminists, with a renewed sense of a collective sisterhood (something that had given way to the individualism of third wave feminism), are more than willing to stop the party in order to call attention to micro-aggressions, structural oppressions and gaslighting.

Indeed, the 2008 Beyoncé album *I Am . . . Sasha Fierce*, named after the then-stage persona of the singer, included two singles that were notable in their conception of fierceness. For 'If I Were A Boy' (2008), the singer imagines relationship difficulties from the privileged male perspective – a role switch that both highlights power dynamic disparities between genders, in a righteous, outspoken way, and recalls the mid-1990s third wave feminism (or postfeminism) moment in which some women were understood to unapologetically adopt male behavioural traits (as with British 'ladettes' – see Whiteley 2010). And, for 'Single Ladies (Put A Ring On It)' (2008), the singer celebrates a new-found freedom, post-relationship split, while chastizing her ex-partner, who is seemingly stung by witnessing this exercise of this new-found freedom, for their failure to commit to the relationship when they had the chance. In this respect, a fierce embrace of a regained and fierce autonomy is both empowerment and progress, revenge and a moral or ethical lesson for those left in its wake.[4] Fierceness, then, seems to hold the potential to catch the unreconstructed in the cross-fire: those who have not aligned themselves with the programme (of contemporary feminist-informed emancipation) have seemingly been left behind for good – ditched as part of the problem rather than part of a solution. Fierceness does not seem to be anger which, as per punk and post-punk, had its place and efficacy in popular music – albeit, as Springer argues, not necessarily for people of colour, whose anger has been historically read in different ways (2007). Rather, fierceness seems to be an absolute certainty and self-belief, along with a hair-trigger rapidity in dismissing those who do not support such hard-earned emancipation.

Many of the chapters in this volume track just such skirmishes, and note the ways in which divas continually (thrillingly, disappointingly, bafflingly) wrongfoot expectations, and in doing so come into their own. Consequently, the very definition, and then use, of the term 'diva' remains tantalizingly unsettled (and so we have been happy to present differing definitions from our authors). Even the diva status seems ontologically ambiguous. Peter Howe, in his writing on the work and experiences of paparazzi (2005), identifies three case study divas (Elizabeth Taylor, Jacqueline Kennedy Onassis, and Princess Diana) as figures who 'transcended their roles to radiate an irresistible allure' (2005: 106). But that allure requires the boost of media construction:

> Ask any photographer who shot them, and [sic] he'll tell you that photographing them was a two-way affair: they may have reacted at times with anger and

frustration at the constant attention, but they all flirted with the camera and understood its power.

(2005: 106)

Such a dynamic is familiar from Federico Fellini's *La Dolce Vita* (1960) – a foundational text to an understanding of the links between post-war urban regeneration and the rise of a new celebrity or media class, complete with the aspirational idea which Catherine Hakim would define as 'erotic capital' (2011) for the secular age. The diva herself (played by Anita Ekberg) is first cast as a visiting Goddess, then the centre of a press scrum, then courted by journalists and pursued by paparazzi for unending photoshoots, then subject to strategies of seduction by others – and finally seen to be subject to an unhappy marriage and domestic violence and, arguably and consequently, suffering from mental instability. Ekberg's Sylvia seems blessed by God (or cursed by the devil) to simply be born to be a diva, dragging the hordes and their cameras in her wake. Andy Warhol's superstars, in a comparable way, seemed to arise across the confusing or contradictory matrices of both happenstance (the everyday-ness of his stars) and the possession of some kind of one-in-a-million ineffable X-factor, that fuels Howe's allure. The case of Edie Sedgwick is particularly telling in this respect: someone who seemed to drift into the Warhol environs, only to be placed before the camera with little to no direction – other than to be herself – and is enhanced by the osmosis that occurs within a company of stars. In this respect, the superstar, as with Edie, for Danny Fields, seems to have accidentally become a pathbreaker for feminism ('a kind of early form of women's liberation'), a muse for poets, and someone whose beauty transcends sexual preferences, but also a helpless ingénue (Fields, quoted in Stein and Plimpton 2006: 225, 228). Stephen Koch writes, in an early study of Warhol called *Stargazer*, that Sedgwick

> like all denizens of the [Warhol] Factory, both male and female ... glows with absolutely self-absorbed narcissism, and, God knows, she played the game of posturing chic everyone else around her played. For a few glittering months, the razor-cut cap of streaked blond hair, the thick eyebrows and lavish but meticulous eye make-up, the huge loop earrings, were *le dernier cri* [i.e. the latest word in fashion]. But there was also something else residing in that face, that carriage of her frail body – perhaps a certain rich girl's self-confidence, a certain unshakable attention to the real, a certain belief in the truths of her presence as a woman.
>
> ([1973] 1991: 67)

And indeed the unhappy comeuppance for Sedgwick, as per the trajectory of *La Dolce Vita*, existed too: the film *Ciao! Manhattan* (John Palmer and

David Weisman, 1972), released posthumously, seemed to chart her downfall and distress. Fields notes, of Sedgwick, a kind of star energy that may, siren-like, lure admirers to their fates: of Edie and other Warhol stars, '. . . they were very destructive people – self-destructive and other-people-destructive. They were riding the whirlwind' (Fields, quoted in Stein and Plimpton 2006: 226).[5] Indeed, this type became part of the mythology of these times: Russ Meyer's *Beyond the Valley of the Dolls* (1970) spoofs the superstar diva, with Ashley St. Ives (Edy Williams) pursued by aspirant lovers and Svengalis. And Betty Davis's 'He Was a Big Freak' (1974) lists the ways in which the singer revels in her erotic powers over men: now a 'turquoise chain' has replaced Hayes's blingy chains of gold, and is used by the singer, she boasts, for sexual domination. (Hannah M. Strong, Gina Sandí Díaz and Shawna Shipley-Gates all engage, in this volume, with contemporary ideas of revolutionary eroticism as empowerment.)

So to call someone a 'diva' can be an acknowledgement of their unique stardom, but it can also be a slight or a warning. That 'diva' description could mean criticism of 'diva-like behaviour' (and, in our context, this is an important point: advice not to book a performer for a concert further to anecdotes about their backstage interactions with others, or elaborate or finicky refreshment demands in riders – anecdotes that can riff off a variety of prejudices), or it could just be a bit of humorous side-eye, further to one-off moments. Even divas themselves seem confused:

> [Duchess of Sussex Meghan] Markle used the word 'diva' of [Mariah] Carey, and Mariah replied that Meghan had her own diva moments . . . 'It stopped me in my tracks, when she called me a diva,' Markle said, with great urgency, [and] you can almost hear her leaning forwards. 'I started to sweat a little bit. I started squirming in my chair in this quiet revolt. Why would you say that? My mind was spinning with what nonsense had she read or clicked on that made her think that about me.' OK, so clearly Mariah Carey thinks of the word as positive or neutral, while Meghan Markle thinks it is pejorative.
>
> (Williams 2022)

One commonality then, across positive, neutral or pejorative understandings, is that the diva is a singular and stand-out presence – worthy of debate, impressively tough, unavoidably fierce.

All these qualities were arguably intrinsic to the survival of the diva singer figure in the post-war years of cultural marginalization in the West: we think of the vamping and centrality of female guest vocalists in jazz bands of the 1950s (as with Anita O'Day, and with some of the endlessly touring greats of Dixieland, and Swing, such as Louis Armstrong), rather than just decorating album covers; the rapturous receptions, as met and matched by their performances, of the female singers in the concerts of the Harlem Cultural Festival in the late 1960s; the domestic violence suffered by Tina Turner at the hands of her mentor and collaborator Ike in the 1970s, even as her star rose; more generally, the precarious and dangerous positions that even famous divas have historically found themselves in, as explored by Whiteley (2005); or the ways in which the New York voguing scene transformed street hustlers and rent boys into downtown ballroom stars in the 1980s, as documented in *Paris is Burning* (Jennie Livingstone, 1990).[6] In all this resilience and survival, something quite different to Warhol's conception of superstardom seems to have been in operation: the maxim that anyone or everyone can be a star for a finite period in the media age (for Warhol, euphemistically: fifteen minutes), or that star quality can be plucked and curated by Warhol and his associates from the most unlikely of places or walks of life, does not apply to the diva. These divas seem to need to be born with talent, nurture it even in adversity, and practice and work without stopping. For Afrika Bambaataa, on hip-hop, '[i]t's about survival, economics, and keeping our people moving on' (cited in Hebdige 2004: 223). From this vantage point, Warhol's modus operandi seems one of an apolitical white privilege.

Prior to this rise of the diva, around the millennium, the diva figure often existed, and was germinated, in pop cultures parallel to the mainstream. Studies of MTV in the 1980s, understood to be the catalyst in terms of pop culture of the last few generations, invariably need to grapple with the operative hierarchy of promotion, with non-white performers mostly absent or offered 'specialist' spaces, aligned with music not identified with whiteness, and with something of the same marginalization for non-heterosexual, or even non-male, artists.[7] The movement from the margins to the mainstream has occurred in parallel, over the last two decades, for two groups that now jointly exert a central influence over contemporary culture and politics: female r'n'b and hip-hop artists, and feminist thinkers and activists. The coming together of these two groups and sensibilities has redefined contemporary popular music (in all senses of music of Black origin), and wider culture and politics, in the West. And this ascendency has also occurred at the point of the multimediaization or cross-platforming of the star, for

> a more diffuse and complex celebrity culture, [for which the] new modes of analysis needed have had to expand their scope and extend their range and, it should be added, enhance their methodologies. The impact of developments such as gossip blogging, the emergence of reality television, and the increased power, influence and reach of the paparazzi have all come to function as central concerns . . . Celebrity culture, now no longer confined to the realms of down-market gossip magazines, is to be found as fully embedded within all spheres of popular media.
>
> (Edgar, Fairclough and Halligan 2013: 16)

And, in or across this, and as flooding out via social media platforms, comes a counter-strategy from the diva. This is the movement towards (as indicated by Sasha Fierce – but it is a tendency that characterized David Bowie's career) 'a more subtle aesthetic blend of "person" and persona', as Manghani and McDonald identify in relation to Kylie Minogue's media presence (2013: 233). In this, the diva superstar quotient remains undiminished, constantly refreshing their mythical persona, but this is now offset by gestures towards homely authenticity, a 'realness', and an intimacy with fans. And for every upwards construction of this story (from bedroom wannabe singer to global diva) seems to come a downward collapse (the global diva revealed to be less than the sum of their parts as the façade crumbles – a particularly contemporary morality tale that was explored, to the horror of many, in Paul Verhoeven's 1995 film *Showgirls*; see Nayman 2014). And yet both types of stories illustrate the way in which there has been an emboldening and centring of the female singer figure.

Contemporary feminisms

This emboldening and centring of the female singer figure is often found in sound mixing and vocal delivery: singing so as to, at times, cut across the musical backing, even dwarfing it in the mix, and with imperfections or human inflexions included, as if marks of an impetuous attitude towards professional delivery, or marks of fierceness or asides, or evidencing a shared intimacy. This is described as

> a seeming anarchic disregard for the structure of the song: during 'Gotta Work' (in [Amerie's] album version, from *Because I Love It*, 2007) the lyrics of the verse crash into and then across (to the point of almost three bars) the chorus, as if

too much needs to be said, and too urgently, to cut the discourse in deference to the chorus. The inclusion of extraneous, personal material (such as Taylor Swift's giggle, after the lyric 'I go on too many dates', for the 2014 single 'Shake It Off' but there is a laugh on 'Gotta Work' as well), can be read in just such a way too.

(Halligan 2015: 296)

Such a propensity may then be aligned with third wave feminism, which meshed an emboldening with an unapologetic, sometimes party-oriented attitude, coupled with a tendency to loudness (in both senses).

By the early/mid-1990s, the notion of a third wave of feminism had not yet fully formed or was still a matter of some confusion or debate. This was an intermezzo moment, as it were, between understood periods of feminism.[8] Or, at least, third wave feminism had not yet come to be understood in the ways that it has been since the mid-2000s. When a critical mass was achieved, third wave feminism was typically read as a matter of straight empowerment (and with the trajectories and goals of empowerment then becoming the foundation of tensions between second and third wave feminists) – as per the outspoken 'gobbiness' of the Spice Girls, whose six singles of 1996–7 established such an attitude, branded 'Girl Power'. That is: six singles and five Spice Girls – totalling thirty female articulations on constant radio airplay across twenty-four months, from petulant, sexualized aspiration ('Wannabe' of 1996) to the sassy weaponization of sexuality to achieve ambitions ('Who Do You Think You Are' of 1997), in a way that anticipated or maybe even in part prompted Catherine Hakim's theorization of 'erotic capital' – divisive in the debated transition from second to third wave feminism – as the very potential (in the sense of intrinsic power) of contemporary woman (2011). Either side of the intermezzo, at least in terms of media stereotypes, are the superfeminine: exponents of erotic capital (one thinks of TLC's *CrazySexyCool* of 1994, complete with booty-call sampled audio), 'rock chicks' (Lister's 'Liliths' figures, often modelled on Stevie Nicks of Fleetwood Mac; 2001), 'virtual idols' (such as Hatsune Miku and Lil Miquela; see Conner 2016, Zaborowski 2016, and Rambarran 2021), 'K-pop' girl groups (such as Blackpink and Red Velvet), or post-punk singers (particularly in Riot Grrrl, but seen too in 1990s 'indie' figures such as Alanis Morissette, Courtney Love or Sophie B. Hawkins). This indie category nearly included Mariah Carey too, who recorded a 'secret' 'alt-rock' album, *Someone's Ugly Daughter* in 1995 (see Monroe 2022). But prior to this, and indeed to the present, the visual presentation of Carey was invariably of the superfeminine template: LP gatefolds effectively reworked as soft porn centrefolds.

Academic writing around the emergence of third wave feminism typically articulates the movement away from concerns that were understood to be confined to the margins (of second wave feminist cultures), and often focusing on strategies of living, to a cultural war to be waged in the mainstream (third wave feminism). It is worth briefly reviewing the perceptions on this 'shifting ... terrain' (Rivers 2017: 3) at this point, around the period of the postfeminist intermezzo. An early key text, *Third Wave Agenda: Being Feminist, Doing Feminism* (Heywood and Drake 1997), devotes one of its four sections to 'Youth Music Culture' and, as can be expected, mostly concerns the progressive gender politics associated with punk and then traces a development into the music associated with Riot Grrrl in the 1990s, with a critique of the gender politics of mainstream rock and variants of rap, via bell hooks, ending the collection (Niesel 1997). By 2004, the concern with 'Politics and Popular Culture' (for *Third Wave Feminism: A Critical Exploration*; Gillis, Howie and Munford [2004] 2007) is disconcertingly mainstream, with a scope that takes in video games, women's fashion/lifestyle magazines, fantasy television series, pop music charts and romcoms. In this context, the British girl group Girls Aloud are found wanting when considered in relation to the Spice Girls – the former noted as self-identifying as 'girl's girls', so that '[n]ot even the "nod" to a feminist inheritance imparted by the Spice Girls' can be detected (Munford 2007: 267). Rebecca Munford's discussion is structured by a consideration of the fatal potentials of 'postfeminism' within 'third wave feminism'. In Munford's conceptualization, third wave feminism is a legitimate outgrowth of second wave feminism, and is apparent, in its subversive operations and unapologetic in-your-face presences, in Riot Grrrl in the early 1990s. On the other hand, the sexed-up 'girly' variant of feminist empowerment is associated with the Spice Girls, with Girls Aloud as their lesser acolytes and with various other media, particularly the magazine *BUST* (self-announced as 'that shared set of female experiences that includes Barbies and blowjobs, sexism and shoplifting'; quoted in Munford 2007: 266) – and this unavoidable occurrence in the mainstream is one that 'opens up a space for patriarchal recuperation as girl power emerges as the site of that dangerous and deceptive slippage between third wave feminism and post-feminism' (2007: 276). So for Munford, third wave feminism holds the promise of a continuum with the rich radicalism of the second wave – providing that an apolitical and apathetic postfeminist current does not derail the development.[9] The Spice Girls' 'Girl Power', however, despite or even because of its zesty presence in the mainstream, is manageable and marketable, and is a faux-feminism, de-fanged by the male éminence grise – a defeat of female liberatory politics through a process labelled postfeminism. Such a transformation needs the basic category error: the passage from one culture to the next, with (ideological) baggage jettisoned at the border – a process which Munford also sees as a crossing when she writes, '[t]he alacrity with which the media has embraced "girl power" and its icons indicates the precarious boundary between the "(re)fashioning" of feminism proposed by the third wave Girlies and the "fashionable" (post-)feminism propounded by the Spice Girls . . .' (2007: 274).

Arguably the issue in the late 1990s cultural landscape was that previous generation's iterations of the sexually upfront and empowered female singer had represented a sequential calibration of these two attributes: she was empowered, and from a position of empowerment 'flaunted' sexuality in everyday situations. One thinks of the album covers of Carly Simon's 1972 *No Secrets* or Linda Ronstadt's 1976 *Hasten Down the Wind*: both singers bra-less, photographed as if caught mid-conversation (Simon perhaps stepping out of a house, Ronstadt at a beach party), their erect nipples visibly pressing through the thin gauze of their tops. The stripper-like performance of Girls Aloud, in their dancing and striking of poses for the 2003 'No Good Advice' video (which included the classic podium move of reaching down to the client, levelling cleavage to his face), merges the two: the flaunting of sexuality *is* (indeed, as per Hakim) empowerment.

However, scholars of hip-hop have historically looked with despair at such sexualization since the yin to this yang is an aggressive, at times repulsive, reassertion of patriarchy and boosting that which Moya Bailey identifies as 'misogynoir'. (2021) And this issue, and the damage associated with it, seems the first port of call for those who have written about hip-hop. For Pough:

> Many would question the subtitle of [my] article – 'Tapping the Potential in Hip-Hop' – specifically the notion that there is indeed any potential to tap in Hip-Hop. Those people would list *ad nauseam* the numerous instances of violence, sexism, and misogyny as well as the glorification of drug use and drug sales described in contemporary rap music. They would list certain rappers who have been arrested for these acts and the recent deaths of young Black male rappers as reason enough to surmise that there is indeed no potential to tap in Hip-Hop. Those same people would probably tell us that this entire generation of young people is a lost cause because of reasons ranging from apathy to selfishness.
>
> (2004: 283)

For Neal, even a semi-apologetic contextualization of such problematic attitudes cannot absolve the musicians, whose stances also function to the ends of the exclusion of women hip-hop artists on their own terms:

> Rap music and hip-hop culture have often been singularly cited for the transmission and reproduction of sexism and misogyny in American society . . . [a]s sexism and misogyny are largely extensions of normative patriarchal privilege, their reproduction in the music of male hip-hop artists speaks more powerfully to the extent that these young men (particularly young black men) are invested in that privilege than it does to any evidence that they are solely responsible for its reproduction . . . But there is also no denying the fact that hip-hop's grip on American youth allows for the circulation of sexist and misogynistic narratives in a decidedly uncritical fashion.
>
> The embrace of patriarchal privilege by some male hip-hop artists partly explains the marginalization of women among hip-hop artists, particularly when those women don't conform to the normative roles assigned to women within hip-hip (the chicken-head groupie, oversexualized rhyme-splitter, baggy-clothed desexualized mic-fiend are prime examples).
>
> (Neal 2004: 247)

Pough and Neal both consider the rebarbative aspects of this culture to be, in part, media spin, as does Rose – citing Chuck D's maxim: 'Don't believe the hype!' (2004: 291) But negotiating this culture, with respect to being a feminist, has itself generated writing that has sought to consider empowerment within these meshes. This is most notable in the writing of Joan Morgan (1999), self-described as a 'hip-hop feminist', who tends to reject the 'victim' label, and subverts the idea of the submissiveness of the 'chicken head' (i.e. serial fellator). But, in this context, the appeal of Riot Grrrl to feminist academics is quite clear. Riot Grrrl was a point of entry into feminist consciousness for a certain generation of female punk singers, often with frictions around a censorious late phase of second wave feminism,[10] which had equipped the Grrrls with the tools of critique, emboldened them to speak – or shout/scream – out, and conceptualized the idea of anger as a vector for speaking up, and performance, and public persona (Marcus 2010: 122–3). This made for a very particular type: as with Kathleen Hanna's dancing, grimacing and appearance in Sonic Youth's 'Bull in the Heather' (1994) – grotesque, cutesy, infantile, aggressive. Tellingly, then, Sini Anderson's 2013 documentary on Hanna, *The Punk Singer*, begins with a 1991 spoken-word performance in which a young Hanna, if not performing as a character, is then seemingly reliving the trauma of being sexually abused – possibly by a family member, possibly as a child, intoning 'I'm going to tell everyone what you did to me.' That 'telling' is presented as the raison d'être and indeed political strategy of Riot Grrrl, which remained radical, avenging and oppositional, and forged from trauma – a considerable distance from, if not another universe altogether to, the allure of Girl Power, or the allotted functions of the groupie.

By the 2020s, and with apologies to Munford, we need to dispense with the optimism invested in the nascent third wave idea. Munford's idea of postfeminism came to subsume Munford's idea of third wave feminism, and so third wave feminism came to denote the depoliticized, un-sisterly, self-empowering offshoot/degeneration of second wave feminism. This idea of or hope for a legitimate second to third wave development gave way to a generational split between the two. But third wave feminism, nevertheless, represented a form of striving for gain whereas the issue with the term 'postfeminist' was that it suggested that the basis of equality had been achieved, at least in terms of women in the workplace, legal protections, the shatterings of glass ceilings and so on. The assumption of postfeminism is one of achieved privilege and that striving was over. That is: the generation of (white) women born in the West in the 1960s/1970s had then come of age in a moment of historical enlightenment, and could readily claim a bounty comparable to their male counterparts. The postfeminist condition is one that presupposes that the potentials of privilege are realizable – if indeed they have not already been entirely realized. To be clear: we have no wish to be critical in terms of what would then be considered, in terms of intersectionality, as an unthinking failure to question or interrogate one's privilege ('positionality') or hold the realization of this privilege up as a goal for the still-oppressed. In the work of innumerable feminists who have grappled with questions of representations and role models, it is apparent both that privileged layers need to be considered in tandem with the less privileged, and that privilege is in itself no safeguard against male violence (as per the Everyday Sexism Project, #MeToo and related campaigns from 2017 onwards). Fourth wave feminism then needs to be considered in this context: taking the fight back to the oppressors, often using social media for internet activism – to mount public critiques, of both individuals and institutions, and achieving something too familiar from the second wave, for Blevins (2018): 'consciousness-raising'. The chapters in this collection track and reflect on just such occurrences, and sometimes use them as raw data for analysis in respect to the diva, the diva's detractors and new identifications of forms of oppression – such as misogynoir. In so doing, this work offers a definition to the newly emergent fourth wave.

Writing about divas

For these reasons, and in this context, we have encouraged personal, subjective writing from some of our contributors, as a way of offering, in part, case studies of particular lines of empathy or appreciation. The resultant writing, within the constellation of fourth wave feminism, has evidenced patterns of (in the best sense) sloganeering: pithy calls-to-action and sound-bite foundations for wider and often impassioned critiques, rather than the construction of layers of reasoning that deepen through ever-further-nuanced lines of argument. Elsewhere, we have asked contributors to consider the multimedia elements of the diva presence: not just recorded music, and not just live music, but an infinite number of interventions – on social media and on broadcast media before that. For this reason, we have ensured that an expansion of diva culture occurs in this book – into fields of comedy and theatre, and even broadcast sports events – so as to scope and assess the wider hinterland of divadom, or the persistence of the diva across contemporary popular culture, and to break the cultural tendency out of the confines of popular musicology.

The first section of this book looks at key moments in the rise to power of the contemporary diva. The four figures discussed are each distinguished by their particular contributions to diva culture. Mariah Carey, for Shara Rambarran, is positioned as, effectively, the diva template across the turn of the millennium – but her fabulousness does not exclude the legacies of a difficult childhood, the experiences of the erasure of her creative work (and even ethnic identity), the sexism visited upon her, and the ways in which she has addressed these challenges in respect to their impacts on her well-being. Whitney Houston, for Gwynne George, offers a parallel exemplar: a figure who displayed her labour as part of her creativity, considered in the context of the persistence of damaging racial stereotypes concerning women of colour. Dolly Parton, for James Reeves, offers lessons for the long haul: a singer and presence who seems adept at change and self-reinvention and has utilized as much to attain creative independence, and her iconographic status, but who seemingly remains true to herself across all such phases (which Reeves periodizes). Mark Duffett's consideration of Grace Jones ends this section: the diva perceived as a contrarian and live wire – but who, Duffett argues in the case of Jones, needs to be interpreted in a global rather than local context, with 'being a diva' read in respect to resisting structural racism and aligned to economic power in the new celebrity economy.

Our second section addresses the contemporary diva and presents a series of snapshots of key figures accordingly. Benjamin Halligan considers the bridging figure of Aaliyah – whom he posits as central to the elevation of the diva into the starry firmament of popular culture beyond the turn of the millennium. But Halligan addresses an issue at the outset which is far from unusual: that the life of this late diva is now inextricably entwined with stories of coercion and abuse. Consequently, Halligan seeks to extract or free Aaliyah's music from this context in order to restore to it the acclaim that, he argues, it deserves. Beyond this, Halligan considers the use of the aesthetics of religious iconography by the diva, including via social media and, for an encounter with Amerie, in the live context. Halligan notes that the maximal presentation of Aaliyah's voice, when coupled with the forthright sexual nature of her later lyrics, seemed shocking – even to a comical degree. Hannah M. Strong's engagement with Beyoncé checks back on as much, but now in the context of #MeToo activism, and the way in which her live performance at Coachella in 2018 provocatively usurped and reversed gender dynamics. For Strong, this is an important marker with respect to the way in which #MeToo politically radicalized pop culture and with a figure such as Beyoncé lending heft and legitimation to this through her global reach. Nonetheless, paradoxes are apparent, in the combination of 'flashy feminist messages flanked by heteronormative and male-centred imagery'. For Dorothy Finan, the career of Amuro Namie contains comparable tensions: the transition from teen pop star to adult r'n'b and hip-hop diva, via looking to and reworking (at times problematically), for her Japanese fans, African American music culture. This is read as denoting a coming into a (postfeminist) maturity on the part of this diva and Finan considers Amuro as, eventually, an establishment figure – performing at high-profile national events, such as the twenty-sixth G8 summit of 2000 for example – further cementing her iconographic status, and boosting her 'epocal charisma'. The latter is contextualized with respect to a postmodern reading of Japanese society with Amuro's fandom read as a way of negotiating social and political changes.

Timmia Hearn DeRoy considers Janelle Monáe's re-enactments of histories of enslavement, via Afrofuturist aesthetics. DeRoy details the complicated layers of meaning apparent in Monáe performances and personae, as read to the ends of deconstructing and reconstructing a vision of the future, and the American Dream, beyond white bourgeois power. A similar liberatory impulse informs Shawna Shipley-Gates's reading of Cardi B and Megan Thee Stallion: to discuss the revolutionary potentials of eroticism in Black female hip-hop – in their unabashed and unapologetic expressions of, or channelling of, sexual exuberance. This intervention situates their music as within, and yet critical of, the patriarchal apparatus and arrangements of historical hip-hop traditions. One such realized potential of this hip-hop eroticism is a reclaiming of female autonomy: to author one's own persona, to eroticize one's own body (irrespective of its conforming or otherwise to received 'norms') and speak with one's own voice, as thrillingly enhanced by the kinds of explicit details that even, say, Aaliyah at her most sexualized had parleyed into euphemisms. Thus vaginal lubrication becomes, for Cardi B and Megan Thee Stallion, an affective matter: to talk of their biological evidence of liberation and taking back control of sexuality and desire on the part of the vagina-owner. And yet Gates notes some distance between feminism per se, and hip-hop feminism, with the latter galvanizing practitioners to engage in elements of hypersexualized self-presentation that would traditionally have come under fire from second wave feminists. This discussion in itself offers solace to those who have found the often backward sexual politics of hip-hop enough to remove the culture from any sense of progressive art.

Gina Sandí Díaz turns to the controversy that greeted the performances from Jennifer Lopez and Shakira for the 2020 Super Bowl Halftime Show, tracking the biases and prejudices apparent in the rhetoric of critics (both professional and denizens of social media). The offence, in this reading, is the way in which two global majority (and middle-aged) women so spectacularly occupied a space typically understood to function to extoll or celebrate values coded as geographically specific (to North America), and as white and politically conformist. Díaz deftly splices intersectional theory into ideas of divadom in order to identify and delineate affective, everyday oppressions, in a continuum with some of the darkest moments of colonialism. Thereafter, Nicole Hodges Persley explores what is effectively a postcolonial position of cosmopolitanism with respect to the work (and media presences) of Drake and Nicki Minaj. Persley argues that they intentionally manipulate the simultaneously Black transnational contexts that their bodies occupy, subverting racial and gender norms associated with the global concept of diva culture. In so doing, they effectively capitalize on, and advance, the ontological status of being a diva.

The final section in this collection considers the diva in contexts outside popular music. Harriet Reed turns to the relatively new phenomenon of museum and gallery curation around acclaimed (but popular) musicians – particularly with respect to the ways in which this has upset or revised received notions of artistic worth. Rana Esfandiary considers the figure of the diva in the charged political context of a production of Jean Genet's *The Maids* in Iran, tracing connections between assumed interpersonal power dynamics and the performative aspect of the diva figure. Rachel E. Blackburn, Ellie Tomsett and Nathalie Weidhase, in the final two chapters, consider the diva in respect to stand-up comedy – that is, the ways in which these figures, noted earlier as exemplars and templates, are imagined (or reimagined) in other areas of emboldened outspokenness, and the often comic distance that is established between the glamour of the diva, and the relatable everyday experiences of the comic. Two different tensions are explored: for Blackburn, the racial undertones of the reception of diasporic figures, for Tomsett and Weidhase, the gendered and raced dynamics of the inclusion of diva figures in the discourse of stand-up.

In these respects, in or through the gallery, theatre or in stand-up, the diva addresses us, or the diva's presence imposes itself on us, all – or, from the diva's exalted perspective, you all, or, as per the emcee or DJ cry or invitation: 'Y'all!' We find ourselves continually in the presence of the diva when thinking about contemporary popular music and wider culture: a condition of 'the diva and us'.

Notes

1 Hayes's music at this point – particularly on the Stax released *Hot Buttered Soul* (1969) – was also suitably epic: very lengthy tracks, building steadily to their climaxes, and often covers that were subject to Hayes's unique, eroticized soul-ification. In 1971 Hayes had presented himself as the titular *Black Moses* – presumably offering to lead his people to a promised land, away from persecution. Jackson introduced Hayes by slowly pulling back the hood of his cape – revealing the star to the Wattstax audience as they cheered wildly.

    On the Watts Riots, see Horne (1995), and on the concert, see Phillips (2014); on neoliberal pop and wealth, see Halligan (2017); on Motown's politics, see Smith (1999).

2 The writer and producer of the 1998 *VH1 Divas* was Martin Lewis, who had co-created and co-produced another music- and entertainment-based event with political ideals: the *Secret Policeman's Ball* series of benefit shows, for Amnesty International. The human rights cause of the organization was particularly pointed and, in the context of the times, oppositional – as resoundingly apparent in Peter Gabriel's performance of 'Biko' for the 1987 event, with its invitation to the audience to join in, and militant gestures of international solidarity with the struggle against apartheid-era South Africa.

3. On trans activism and the Stonewall riots, and particularly the figure of Sylvia Rivera, see Feinberg (1998). In terms of our discussion of divas, We move away from cis-gendered assumptions to a non-binary framing. Nonetheless, it is necessary to reserve the right to talk of the 'female', particularly in historical contexts, in respect to acknowledging how the idea of the 'female singer' was itself an important intervention into musical cultures.
4. Beyoncé's particular feminism, in terms of its efficacy and even orthodoxy, remains a wider matter of debate, as per hooks, but see too Weidhase (2015).
5. Fields was an associate of Warhol's and a friend of Sedgwick's, and a manager, writer and publicist.
6. On Turner, see Turner (2018); on *Paris is Burning*, see Hilderbrand (2013).
7. For a discussion of MTV's attempts to right this balance, by the early 1990s, see Goldstein (1996: 262–79).
8. On this 'intermezzo', see Lotz (2007: 73) or, for the 'shifting . . . terrain' of feminist ideas at this juncture, see Rivers (2017: 3).
9. Munford articulates this position with reference to Germaine Greer and Susan Faludi; (2007: 267).
10. See Marcus (2010: 41–2) for Bikini Kill's Kathleen Hanna on Faludi, and arguing with Andrea Dworkin.

Reference

Ahmed, S. (2017), *Living a Feminist Life*, Durham: Duke University Press.

Bailey, M. (2021), *Misogynoir Transformed: Black Women's Digital Resistance*, New York: New York University Press.

Blevins, K. (2018), 'bell hooks and Consciousness-Raising: Argument for a Fourth Wave of Feminism', in J. Vickery and T. Everbach (eds), *Mediating Misogyny*, 91–108, London: Palgrave Macmillan.

Chamberlain, P. (2017), *The Feminist Fourth Wave: Affective Temporality*, London: Palgrave-Macmillan.

Conner, T. (2016), 'Hatsune Miku, 2.0pac, and Beyond', in S. Whiteley and S. Rambarran (eds), *The Oxford Handbook of Music and Virtuality*, 129–47, New York: Oxford University Press.

Cooper, B. C. (2017), 'On bell, Beyoncé and Bullshit', in B. C. Cooper, S. M. Morris and R. M. Boylorn, *The Crunk Feminist Collection*, 230–5, New York: Feminist Press at the City University of New York.

Davis, M. and J. Wiener (2020), *Set the Night on Fire: L.A. in the Sixties*, London: Verso.

Edgar, R., K. Fairclough and B. Halligan (2013), 'Music Seen: The Formats and Functions of the Music Documentary', in R. Edgar, K. Fairclough and B. Halligan (eds), *The Music Documentary: Acid Rock to Electropop*, 1–21, London: Routledge.

Edgar, R., K. Fairclough, B. Halligan and N. Spelman (2015), 'A Stately Pleasure-Dome?' in R. Edgar, K. Fairclough, B. Halligan and N. Spelman (eds), *The Arena Concert: Music, Media and Mass Entertainment*, 1–12, London and New York: Bloomsbury.

Feinberg, L. (1998), *Trans Liberation: Beyond Pink or Blue*, Boston: Beacon Press.

Gay, R. (2014), 'Beyoncé's Control of Her Own Images Belies the bell hooks "slave" Critique', *The Guardian*, 12 May. Available online: https://www.theguardian.com /commentisfree/2014/may/12/beyonce-bell-hooks-slave-terrrorist (accessed 22 September 2022).

Gillis, S., G. Howie and R. Munford ([2004] 2007), *Third Wave Feminism: A Critical Exploration*, expanded second ed., London: Palgrave Macmillan.

Goldstein, L. (1996), 'Revamping MTV: Passing for Queer Culture in the Video Closet', in B. Beemyn and M. Eliason (eds), *Queer Studies: A Lesbian, Gay, Bisexual and Transgender Anthology*, 262–79, New York and London: New York University Press.

Hakim, C. (2011), *Honey Money: The Power of Erotic Capital*, London: Penguin.

Halligan, B. (2015), 'Intimate Live Girls', in R. Edgar, K. Fairclough, B. Halligan and N. Spelman (eds), *The Arena Concert: Music, Media and Mass Entertainment*, 291–307, London and New York: Bloomsbury.

Halligan, B. (2017), 'Liquidities for the Essex Man: The Monetarist Eroticism of British Yacht Pop', in G. Arnold, D. Cookney, K. Fairclough and M. Goddard (eds), *Music / Video: Histories, Aesthetics, Media*, 97–108, London: Bloomsbury Academic.

Hebdige, D. (2004), 'Rap and Hip-Hop: The New York Connection', in M. Forman and M. A. Neal (eds), *That's the Joint! The Hip-Hop Studies Reader*, 223–32, New York and London: Routledge.

Heywood, L. and J. Drake, eds (1997), *Third Wave Agenda: Being Feminist, Doing Feminism*, Minneapolis and London: University of Minnesota Press.

Hilderbrand, L. (2013), *Paris is Burning: A Queer Film Classic*, Vancouver: Arsenal Pulp Press.

Horne, G. (1995), *Fire This Time: The Watts Uprising and the 1960s*, Charlottesville: University Press of Virginia.

Howe, P. (2005), *Paparazzi*, New York: Artisan.

Koch, S. ([1973] 1991), *Stargazer: The Life, World & Films of Andy Warhol*, revised and updated version, London and New York: Marion Boyars.

Lister, L. (2001), 'Divafication: The Deification of Modern Female Pop Stars', *Popular Music and Society*, 25 (3–4): 1–10.

Lotz, A. D. (2007), 'Theorising the Intermezzo: The Contributions of Postfeminism and Third Wave Feminism', in S. Gillis, G. Howie and R. Munford (eds), *Third Wave Feminism: A Critical Exploration*, expanded second ed., 71–85, London: Palgrave Macmillan.

Manghani, S. and K. McDonald (2013), 'Desperately Seeking Kylie! Critical Reflections on William Baker's *White Diamond*', in R. Edgar, K. Fairclough and B. Halligan (eds), *The Music Documentary: Acid Rock to Electropop*, 219–34, London: Routledge.

Marcus, S. (2010), *Girls to the Front: The True Story of the Riot Grrrl Revolution*, New York: HarperCollins.

Monroe, J. (2022), 'Mariah Carey Hints At Release For Secret 1995 Alt-Rock Album', *Pitchfork*, 19 September. Available online: https://pitchfork.com/news/mariah-carey-hints-at-release-for-secret-1995-alt-rock-album/ (accessed 22 September 2022).

Morgan, J. (1999), *When Chickenheads Come Home To Roost*, New York: Simon and Schuster.

Munford, R. (2007), '"Wake Up and Smell the Lipgloss": Gender, Generation and the (A)politics of Girl Power', in S. Gillis, G. Howie and R. Munford, *Third Wave Feminism: A Critical Exploration*, expanded second ed., 266–79, London: Palgrave Macmillan.

Nayman, A. (2014), *It Doesn't Suck: Showgirls*, Ontario: ECW Press.

Neal, M. A. (2004), I'll Be Nina Simone Defecating on Your Microphone: Hip-Hop and Gender', in M. Forman and M. A. Neal (eds), *That's the Joint! A Hip-Hop Studies Reader*, 247–50, New York: Routledge.

Niesel, J. (1997), 'Hip-Hop Matters: Rewriting the Sexual Politics of Rap Music', in L. Heywood and J. Drake (eds), *Third Wave Agenda: Being Feminist, Doing Feminism*, 239–53, Minneapolis and London: University of Minnesota Press.

Phillips, M. (2014), '"Rated R Because it's Real": Discourses of Authenticity in *Wattstax*', in N. Lawrence (ed.), *Documenting the Black Experience: Essays on African American History, Culture and Identity in Nonfiction Films*, 132–52, Jefferson: McFarland and Company.

Pough, G. D. (2004), 'Seeds and Legacies: Tapping the Potential in Hip-Hop', in M. Forman and M. A. Neal (eds), *That's the Joint! A Hip-Hop Studies Reader*, 283–89, New York: Routledge.

Rambarran, S. (2021), *Virtual Music: Sound, Music, and Image in the Digital Era*, New York: Bloomsbury.

Retallack, H., J. Ringrose and E. Lawrence (2016), '"Fuck Your Body Image": Teen Girls' Twitter and Instagram Feminism in and Around School', in J. Coffey, S. Budgeon and H. Cahill (eds), *Learning Bodies: The Body in Youth and Childhood Studies*, 85–103, Singapore: Springer.

Rivers, N. (2017), *Postfeminism(s) and the Arrival of the Fourth Wave: Turning Tides*, London: Palgrave Macmillan.

Rose, T. (2004), 'Never Trust a Big Butt and a Smile', in M. Forman and M. A. Neal (eds), *That's the Joint! A Hip-Hop Studies Reader*, 291–306, New York: Routledge.

Smith, S. E. (1999), *Dancing in the Street: Motown and the Cultural Politics of Detroit*, Cambridge, MA: Harvard University Press.

Springer, K. (2007), 'Divas, Evil Black Bitches, and Bitter Black Women: African American Women in Postfeminist and Post-Civil Rights Popular Culture', in D. Negra and Y. Tasker (eds), *Interrogating Postfeminism*, 249–76, Durham: Duke University Press.

Stein, J. with G. Plimpton (2006), *Edie: An American Biography*, London: Pimlico.

Turner, T. (2018), *My Love Story: A Memoir*, New York: Atria Books.

Weidhase, N. (2015), '"Beyoncé feminism" and the Contestation of the Black Feminist Body', *Celebrity Studies*, 6 (1): 128–31.

Whiteley, S. (2005), *Too Much Too Young: Popular Music, Age and Gender*, London: Routledge.

Whiteley, S. (2010), 'Trainspotting: The Gendered History of Britpop', in A. Bennett and J. Stratton (eds), *Britpop and the English Music Tradition*, 55–70, Surrey: Ashgate.

Williams, Z. (2022), 'You Give Me Diva: Meghan Markle Shies Away from a Word Worth Reclaiming', *The Guardian*, 3 September. Available online: https://www.theguardian.com/uk-news/2022/sep/03/meghan-markle-word-diva-celebrate-sheer-excellence (accessed 22 September 2022).

Zaborowski, R. (2016), 'Hatsune Miku and Japanese Virtual Idols', in S. Whiteley and S. Rambarran (eds), *The Oxford Handbook of Music and Virtuality*, 111–28, New York: Oxford University Press.

Section one

The rise to power

1

'Proceed with Caution'

Mariah Carey – the ultimate diva in popular music and culture?

Shara Rambarran

Introduction

It has always been challenging for female artists/music divas to write about their subjective experiences in life, including the sexist attitudes and harassment they may face in the male-dominated music industry (Strong and Raine 2019; Whiteley 2000; Wolfe 2020). As Sheila Whiteley argues: 'there is a comparability with the broader struggle against sexism that characterizes second wave feminism in aspects like the emphasis on practicality and pragmatism – equality in law, equal work, control over body and image, and access to the production of knowledge, culture and so forth' (2000: 1–2). We may be reminded of divas in music, such as Marie Lloyd (Scott 2008), Josephine Baker (Bennetta 2007), Patti Labelle (Bertei 2021) and Grace Jones (Rambarran 2021; and also discussed in the present volume), for whom their private lives and appearances were more, or tried to be, exposed by the media. There is also the music creative process to consider, where female artists are routinely faced with a variety of challenges, and a lack of equality and respect, when working in the recording studio or other work situations. In a 2018 report on diversity in popular music, 'Inclusion in the Recording Studio?', Smith, Choueiti and Pieper (2018) argue that there is still a need to confront gender equality issues since women, in particular, remain mostly prohibited from the creative process. While Smith et al. specifically focus on the lack of recognition for women who work in the recording studio environment (whether as producers, engineers, songwriters, etc.), their intervention confirms that there are still outstanding issues that need to be addressed. Progress remains slow in the creative industries in terms of advocating for equality, opportunities, respect and support for women, and it is clear that more action is required, and awareness needs to be constantly reviewed and discussed. Take Mariah Carey, for example, who has rightfully earned her recognition as a singer, songwriter and performer. For Mariah to 'make it' in the industry involved both determination and hard work; she experienced first-hand that the 'music business is designed to confuse and control the artist' (Carey and Davis 2020: 115), as discussed at length in her autobiography. This pernicious situation was evident in the early years of her career: she was 'ripped off' by publishing deals, experienced a lack of control in her artistry and creativity, and was not fully acknowledged for her role as a music producer – something which still remains overlooked, and is seldom discussed. While Carey is forthright in respect to her experience in the business – 'I think if you are a woman . . . your musicianship always gets underplayed' (2020: 303) – it is apparent that she and fellow female creatives need the recognition they deserve, and to achieve a greater visibility in popular music. This chapter, in highlighting the challenges faced by Mariah Carey, explores how, nonetheless, she remains able to assert diva qualities through her music.

I know her: Mariah Carey

Mariah Carey – a pop, r'n'b and hip-hop artist, and music producer – rose to stardom during the early 1990s. Her renowned live performance on *MTV Unplugged* (1992), and her constant visual presence in the media, signalled that Carey was a figure who could be read as having excelled in her music career. Take her acclaimed 1992 *MTV Unplugged* performance, for example. After the success of her first two albums, and performing live on popular television shows such as *The Arsenio Hall Show* and *The Oprah Winfrey Show*, some critics momentarily forgot about (or ignored) Carey's achievements and have criticized her for not performing live in front of an audience, so proving her singing ability. Carey proved her critics wrong by appearing on the popular intimate music show, *MTV Unplugged*, which was a unique opportunity to showcase her singing skills.[1] The successful *Unplugged* series proved to be a welcomed addition to MTV (Music Television), as the cable channel is (or was) mainly known for broadcasting mainstream rock and pop music. However, as Rischar argues, from the 1990s onwards, there were 'some singers who could utilize the vocal and production style of mainstream pop, but these crossover singers started to ornament the melody more' (2004: 408), with Carey being a perfect example of as much. While *Unplugged* served as a platform for charting artists, such as Carey, this was also their moment to demonstrate their authenticity as musicians and performers in front of a live audience, by showcasing or showing off their skills, their dedicated musical styles (other than mainstream pop) and to become personal with the audience. Other significant and remarkable *Unplugged* performances include Lauryn Hill (2001) (see La Marr 2012) and the key grunge groups of that moment: Nirvana, Pearl Jam and Alice in Chains (see Rossetti 2022). Carey stunned the audience, media and, arguably more significantly, the critics, by proving that she can sing by parading her five-octave range and *bel canto* singing on seven songs including 'Emotions', 'If it's Over' and a memorable duet with Trey Lorenz for a cover version of Jackson 5's 'I'll be There'. Not only did this critically acclaimed event mark Carey's musical status as a diva, but the extended play album recording of the show sold at least 2.7 million copies and stayed in the US Billboard charts for fifty-seven weeks (Bowenbank 2022).

Carey's collaborative work further verified her centrality to this moment in music culture, through collaborations with some of the hip-hop greats from the mid-1990s onwards – and with her 1995 single 'Fantasy' (and its extensive number of remixes) as a prime example of such an integration of other voices and artists, even those (in the case of Ol' Dirty Bastard) that one would not naturally associate with Carey. Further collaborations followed: to date, with Jermaine Dupri, Jay-Z, Nas, Nate Dogg, Snoop Dogg, Fatman Scoop, Nelly, Missy E, Bow Wow, Bone Thugs-n-Harmony, and the Neptunes. However, the media's response to her musical progression and persona, and even the nature of her presence in the public eye, has not always been kind, let alone one of admiration. Rather than an expected focus on Carey's musical talents (with the exception of her vocals that are always and rightfully championed), the media has historically captured her 'infamous' public antics, pruriently tracked her intimate life, and questioned her behaviour in live performances and even press interviews. But Carey, outwardly at least, deftly lives up to the media scrutiny and scandal with her diva attitude, performance, identity, and music.

After all, Carey has every reason to showcase her flair and celebrate her achievements in the public eye: at the time of writing, she has scored six number-one albums, nineteen number-one singles on the US Billboard charts (Billboard, no date), and won five Grammys. Furthermore, Carey is famously known for her five-octave vocal range and her flageolet singing (also known as the flute or whistle register, which is normally associated with the highest female singing voices; see Miller and Schutte 1993). From a critical perspective, and via the critical apparatus of Star Theory (associated with Dyer 1979), Carey could be described as both the 'ordinary' and 'extraordinary' star models. In that 'ordinary' sense, Carey associates herself with fans and 'regular' people, and hails from 'a less-privileged social background' (Kooijman 2008: 27) – and I will elaborate on this later. What makes Carey 'extraordinary' though is that she carries exceptional qualities that distinguish her from others and, more significantly, as noted by Kooijman, 'enabling fans to admire them' (2008). It is this ordinary/extraordinary dynamic that is the central concern of this chapter. But to understand Carey and her music, and so identify the exceptional in oeuvre and persona, we need to first address her backstory.

Mariah Carey was born in 1969, in New York, to an African American and Venezuelan father, and Irish American mother (who was an opera singer). She had a turbulent childhood due to her parents' divorce. Her escape from this troubled reality, which was also an exposure to racism and poverty, was through music (O'Brien 2012; Carey and Davis 2020). She began writing songs as a teenager (Carey and Davis 2020: 101), heavily influenced by r'n'b and soul artists, such as her queen, the late Aretha Franklin and her adopted 'Godmother', Patti Labelle. During her teenage years, Carey worked semi-professionally as a singer/backing singer, and songwriter, and made demos in the recording studio, working with Gavin Christopher. She became a backing singer for Brenda K. Starr and was signed by Sony's record executive, Tommy Mottola. He was impressed with her five-octave vocal range, and they eventually married too. Carey recalls the hardships of working in the music industry:

> My earliest memory is wanting to be a professional singer. I've been working toward this goal since I was 12 years old, working with different studio musicians. I went out on my own when I was 17 . . . and did all the things that people do who are trying to 'make it' in show business. After I'd waitressed, at one or two in the morning, I'd work in the studio 'til eight o'clock in the morning writing songs and doing demos with Ben Margulies, my [then, albeit short-lived] writing partner. I condensed about ten years of hard work into about four.
>
> (Cited in Sholin 1991)

Carey produced her self-titled debut album in 1990. And yet her status as a producer was overlooked: she is only credited (as a producer) for one album track alone. She did, however, win a Grammy as Best New Artist in 1990. Further bestselling albums followed, such as *Emotions* (1991) and *Music Box* (1993), yielding number-one chart hits ('Emotions' of 1991 and 'Hero' of 1993). These songs were mainly based on Mottola's vision of Carey's music: 'wholesome, sweet and full of vocal pyrotechnics' (O'Brien 2012: 381). Eventually artistic work reached the point where Carey wanted to experiment with her music and explore more of her cultural heritage and identity in and through her music. She secretly recorded an alternative rock album, *Someone's Ugly Daughter*, with her friend Clarissa Dane in 1995 (under the pseudonym 'Chick'). This was a therapy album for Carey as she felt suffocated in her marriage to Mottola and now needed to express her frustrations and anger through music (Carey and Davis 2020: 166). Mottola, however, did not welcome Carey's evolving creative vision (seemingly either as husband or producer); they divorced in 1998.[2] Unsurprisingly, Carey later revealed that the divorce was not chiefly due to creative differences, but more in relation to the belief that Mottola was controlling her – both in terms of her musical development, and seemingly in terms of her freedom of movement, as detailed in her autobiography (Carey and Davis 2020: particularly 97–8). While she wanted to experiment with her music and image, Mottola wanted her to remain a ballad singer. Carey reflects on this dislocating experience of not being in control as akin to a wider confusion as to her ethnic heritage, in her appearance: 'When I was a kid I felt like a misfit and an outcast because of my heritage and the way people made me feel about it . . . in the days when I was being told what to do . . . it tore me up' (cited in Boucher 2005).

In 1997 Carey released her post-separation album, *Butterfly*. This was a ground-breaking album in that, in a postmodern fashion, it fused different styles, drawn from r'n'b and hip-hop. And, along with her music, Carey's image changed too. She now transitioned from wearing semi-fully clothed outfits to – to the amazement of her fans of this moment – skin-tight tops and fitting jeans. As a sign of her 'grown up' image and exploring or flaunting her sexuality, her music videos also underwent a 'glow up': dancing, flirting, revelling in freedom, and a celebratory, infectious, 'having a good time'. However, post-divorce life and hectic work schedules proved to be overwhelming, seemingly evidenced in Carey's unusual behaviour in public appearances. Further to the infamous MTV episode of *TRL* (*Total Request Live*, 19 July 2001) for instance, she was criticized by the press (including the television host) for being drunk and seemingly having a public meltdown. Carey confirmed in her autobiography that her appearance was an impulsive publicity stunt to promote her musical drama film *Glitter* (Vondie Curtis Hall, 2001), which did not go the way she planned because she was exhausted (Carey and Davis 2020: 235–6). Further incidents followed including a physical and mental breakdown that resulted in her hospitalization, after which she was diagnosed with bipolarity (Cagle 2018). After establishing support systems for this bipolarity, she further explored her freedom, image and music with a diversification of roles. More albums followed and also many television and film appearances, including, MTV's *Cribs* (2002), becoming a *Pop Idol* judge, having her own Reality Television show, *Mariah's World* (E! 2016–17), and her acclaimed acting role as a decidedly unglamorous social worker, Mrs Weiss, in the film *Precious* (Lee Daniels, 2009).

Even without recourse to further life details (which, indeed, are outlined in her autobiography; Carey and Davis 2020), we (in the sense of Carey's public) can see that she has had an eventful life. Despite the struggles she has faced, her music has been and remains her catharsis: 'Music was my whole life – so much of my belief system, my survival, was entwined in my songs' (Carey and Davis 2020: 113). Nor have her struggles detracted from or lessened her musicianship: she is not afraid to publicly display antics, or be intimate in her songs or interviews. For example, she has become more open about her mental health: 'I put positive people around me and I got back to doing what I love – writing songs and making music' (cited in Cagle 2018), allowing her to be expressive with her life experiences and identity.

Another pointed example of the obstructions Carey encountered concerns race. Throughout her life and career, Carey has always struggled with a sense of societal acceptance of her mixed racial background. She stresses that every time she experiences racism, 'a piece of purity was ripped from my being. [It l]eft behind a spreading stain . . . I've never been able to completely scrub it out. Not with time, not with fame or wealth, not even with love' (Carey and Davis 2020: 34). And racism has impacted her mental health; negative experiences arose from

> a combination of being biracial and experiencing that side of life. My mom experienced a lot of racism as an opera singer because she was married to a Black man . . . I felt so different from everybody else growing up, because I was biracial, because I was so ambiguous-looking and because we didn't have the money to escape whatever the everyday realities were.
>
> (Cited in Hattenstone 2018)

So, despite being a celebrated music artist, Carey is still judged via her racial identity – described by *Playboy* in 1990 as a 'white girl who can sing', and Australia's *Herald Sun*, as 'the new white US soul singer with a reputed [*sic*] eight-octave range' (both cited in Lynch 2015). Carey's articulate response was: 'it seems that most people don't know much about interracial children' (cited in Lynch 2015). Her racial identity was flagged up again in 2018 when she posted an image of the football quarterback player Colin Kaepernick on Instagram.[3] For this, she received unsupportive comments on her Instagram page from her so-called 'Lambs' (a term used to describe Mariah Carey fans), and outright trolls, with undesirable comments such as: 'what does she know, she's white' and 'OMG noo [*sic*] Mariah . . . you were one of my favorites'. Carey responded by saying 'This is how many years later? That ignorance level. When you have a Black father and then people are calling you white, and then people are like "But her father is Black," it's really difficult' (cited in Frank 2018). Carey addressed her experiences with racism early on, in songs such as 'Close My Eyes' (1997) and 'Outside' (1997) and, reflecting this as an ongoing issue, '8th Grade' (2018). In these songs, she reflects on her life, racism, bullying, hardships and remorsefully sings that there is no resolution. For 'Outside', for example, she intimately reflects on her childhood, and then attempts to release her pain through despair and anger in the bridge section – making the listener more drawn to her vocals than the music. Towards the end of the song, Carey surrenders – gives up on hope – and sorrowfully sings that she will always be 'somewhere on the outside . . . '

'Outside' was well received by her Lambily[4] and, in particular, by the LGBTQIA+ community. Carey states: 'I'd like to leave that song open so people can relate it to their own lives, and a lot of fans tell me, "this song helped me through having to talk about being gay with my family and with my friends" . . . there are other songs too, because I kind of come from that place of feeling different or not accepted . . . ' (cited in Azzopardi 2016). As an icon (and so an exemplar of how to live in the world, and deal with and process such obstacles), Carey is able to effectively repurpose her music in this embracing way, through the powerful lyrics and vocal performances that resonate with her fans, pushing home the importance of articulating her feelings about her experiences. In 2016, she won the GLAAD (The Gay and Lesbian Alliance Against Defamation) Media award for her achievements and her support to those communities. In this way, the diva functions to translate personal negative experiences into more universalized articulations of marginalization that are recognized, and warmly received, by other groups too – and contribute, empathetically, to a wider culture of support.

Mariah Carey: The diva

Carey demonstrates an 'ordinary' persona as a star by sharing her personal experiences involving race, social class, trauma, mental health and sexuality through her music. What makes her 'extraordinary' is that over the years, we have witnessed Carey's eccentric antics as a performer and celebrity. Carey essentially plays along with the diva image. In her performances and when in the public eye, she is outspoken, confident and theatrical. Take most of her music videos, for example, where there are regular 'Mariah' themes involving a grand entrance, close-up shots of her desirably smiling at the camera, wearing memorable or distinctive clothing (stylists include Nicolas Bru and DiAndre Tristan), displaying minimal but tantalizing dance moves, putting lip gloss on, lying on the bed or sitting down for a considerable amount of time and the classic trope of wind blowing through her hair. Her actions exude confidence, and viewers are reminded of her performance ownership in these visuals. But Carey also practices being, or seeming to be, a diva in her personal life too, as observed through her social media: exercising while wearing high heels and welcoming the actual birth of her twins with her 'Fantasy' song playing in the background (as told on the LIVE Kelly and Ryan Show, 2018). While Carey may be seen as over-the-top, she tempers this with her comical side, displaying something which may be seen then as her real personality, even when this is passed off as her alter-ago, 'Bianca', or exists via her fondness for orchestrating prank telephone calls. Another diva moment was seen in her attempt to trademark herself as the 'The Queen of Christmas' (Maishman 2022), further to that subgenre of festive Christmas pop music, with her 1994 song 'All I Want For Christmas is You'. Through this song, seemingly 'timeless' and 'classic' in the way in which it is so deeply embedded in popular culture during the festive season (it even seems to signal or herald the onset of the Christmas season) Carey also seems to strive to embody an 'ideology' of Christmas: it is cheerful in manner, of romantic nostalgia and given over to fantasy and fairy tales – conforming to those Christmas tropes identified by Whiteley (2008: 9). But Christmas here is Mariah-ified too in the glamming- and sexing-up of Christmas, with her extravagant festive-fuelled performances and music videos and wearing sexy Christmas-themed outfits on Christmas day.

'Obsessed' with Mariah Carey

In order to focus on Carey as a diva, this chapter will now explore the 2009 song and music video 'Obsessed'. This was written by Mariah Carey, Christopher Stewart and Terius Nash and produced by Carey, Tricky Stewart and The-Dream (Terius Nash). The song's narrative concerns someone who has claimed to have had a relationship with Carey. There are strong rumours that the song is a response to the hip-hop artist, Eminem, who claimed they had an affair in 2001 – something which Carey strongly denies (Complex 2008).[5] The song's theme also suggests sexual harassment (which I will discuss later) and contains Carey 'dissing' Eminem, or the subject of the song, in a classy and diva manner.

The song is a combination of hip-hop, trap, r'n'b and pop.[6] This could be said to be a postmodern track in that it carries musical codings that set the foundation and theme of the song. To elaborate: every musical layer throughout the track is memorable with catchy internal and external hooks – as typical in classic pop music production. In the introduction section, there are multiple (recorded) voices of Carey, signalling senses of a chaotic fixation, perhaps musically intended to sound hypnotic or indeed create a sense of obsession with the song and Carey herself. The instrumentation is fairly minimal, consisting only of programmed drums (Roland TR 808) and synthesizers, serving as the accompaniment and delivering catchy melodies and rhythms – reminiscent of early Tamla Motown music. The deep bass sound has particular importance here since it carries two musical roles: the *tenuto* (held) bass part and rhythm (along with the kick/bass drum). The bass also signifies trap music, as it is played with a detached snare/clap, along with synthesized brass and strings, resulting in a dejected sound. Furthermore, the track is musically shaped as hip-hop (and so possibly a nod to Eminem's music producer, Dr. Dre), hinting once again that the song is about Eminem. Here, the song displays signs of Dr. Dre's musical trademarks of pizzicato high-pitched strings, brass stabs and detached piano riffs.[7]

Carey quotes from the famous film, *Mean Girls* (Mark Waters, 2004): 'Why are you so obsessed with me?'[8] A skit is then heard when the 'MC' shouts out: 'Will the Real MC please . . . step to the mic . . . .' Knowingly, the letters MC are not just a reference to 'Master of Ceremonies' but also to Mariah Carey. However, those familiar with Eminem's works will know that this snippet is an interpolation of the lyrics of his 'The Real Slim Shady' (1999). Carey's voice sounds disembodied because (or as if) from a use of autotune; it seems that she is not in control of her vocal performance (and indeed when creating her own vocal arrangements is one of many Carey's noted musical skills). The music production, however, gives the illusion that Carey's vocals are in control and showing musical signs of her diva persona. For example, the classy diss to the person in question is clear to hear in verse one, from her innocent and lingering tone on the words 'bar', 'are' and 'car', to the confrontational words, 'lame', 'name' and 'E'. The diss leads to the chorus where the words 'why are you obsessed with me', 'sexing me', and 'upset with me' are technically enhanced, and echoed words such as 'obsessed' and 'me' at the end of each line sound very hypnotic and alluring, inviting the listener to be *obsessed* with Mariah. For the accuser, however, all this will sound like a personal confrontation – and they would feel further challenged, and uncomfortable, in the second part of the chorus once Carey stands up to them, singing 'you're delusional, you're losing your mind ...' An anthem-based bridge follows before the second verse, where Carey invites the 'ladies' and 'girls' to join her and affirm the word 'obsessed', as a way of sending a strong message to the culprits in question. Overall, the digitally enhanced vocals are a very provocative spoof, because the inversion of Carey's vocality, including expressions and emotions, are mostly controlled and accentuated by the digital technology. Carey does not let the listener down, however; at the end of 'Obsessed', the 'real' voice of Carey is finally featured, and the listener can feel her frustration and so empathize with the song. To justify Carey's frustration, an arrangement of her vocals, including her trademark high-pitched whistle sounds, throw a mixture of vexing and disoriented emotions which are subtly, or coincidentally, purposely or indeed sonically surveying the music of Black origin of the late 1990s and early 2000s,[9] musically referencing a Dr. Dre-esque high-pitched detached piano riff (as reminiscent of 2Pac's 'California Love' of 1995, 'Still D.R.E' by Dr. Dre and Snoop Dogg, and Eminem's 'The Real Slim Shady', both of 1999, and Mary J. Blige's 'Family Affair' of 2001). While it seems that the song points to Eminem, the track successfully creates an obsessive atmosphere with its lyrics, direct musical digs at the wrong-doer, and an intense but memorable vocal arrangement. The diva presence of Carey is heard throughout – after all, the word 'obsessed' is heard at least twenty-five times, hooking the listener to the song, and Carey.

The accompanying music video, directed by Brett Ratner, is light-hearted in manner. Carey has three main roles: the performer, the pop star/celebrity and the stalker. Interestingly (and to be taken in a comical manner), Carey plays her

Figure 1.1 The opening of Mariah Carey's 'Obsessed' Video. (Screengrab from the music video).

own male stalker, making the viewer think that she is imitating Eminem as the attire and body moves are suspiciously similar to his.[10]

In the opening scene, Carey is already displaying one of her visual trademarks of lying down. She asks: 'Why are you so obsessed with me?' And this quickly leads to the main setting of the video: the Plaza Hotel in New York. The stalker (i.e. Carey) is watching every move of 'his' favourite singer, going as far as inveighing his way into being her bellboy and personal assistant in her photo shoot, by serving as the operator of the 'wind machine', which is actually just a hair dryer. While also acting as the performer (and narrator of the song), and pop star, Carey maintains her diva looks in the video: making a grand entrance (stepping out of the Rolls-Royce Phantom car), hair blowing, minimal but tantalizing dance moves (on the chaize lounge), lying down, and with the classic close-up of the 'Mariah' look, where she smiles directly at the camera. In typical diva mode, Carey is oblivious to the fact that she has a stalker (though in one scene she senses someone is following her and tries to run away from 'him'/herself) – oblivious even during the photo shoot, when the stalker tries to edge closer to her, with the hairdryer. While Carey herself is seen to be too busy performing obsessively with the camera, her second role as the stalker actually dominates the video. While Carey-the-stalker may come across as novelty to the viewer – who would expect Carey to disguise herself as a man? – there are comical visual references to Eminem, and particularly to his film *8 Mile* (Curtis Hanson, 2002) and the related Eminem song 'Lose Yourself' (2002). As well as sporting similar attire to Eminem in that film, the stalker also lives in a bleak bedsit – though this particular bedsit is decorated with Carey memorabilia. Here, the stalker (or indeed Carey!) obsesses about her(self)

Figure 1.2 Mariah Carey as the Stalker. (Screengrab from the music video).

and watches her (own) videos. Furthermore, throughout the photo shoot, the stalker deliberately tries to get closer to Carey by blocking the photographer (played by the late French fashion photographer Patrick Demarchelier). The stalker narrative drastically ends when 'he' gets hit by a bus while desperately trying to take a photo of Carey.

Queen Mariah and the Third Meaning

While 'Obsessed' may imply that the song and video is aimed at Eminem, as argued, and as was hinted at in the media at the time too, Carey has made no such confirmation, and the matter is absent from her autobiography. The song and video, therefore, generate multiple meanings, leaving the listener/viewer to compose their own interpretation of 'Obsessed'. From a theoretical perspective, it is useful to deploy Roland Barthes's concept of the 'Third Meaning' (Barthes 1977: 52-68), where multiple meanings of texts are dissected to reveal the author's likely intention. This identifies the text as consisting of three levels. The first is described as the informational level – that is, obtaining an instant interpretation, as based on the information, delivered on its 'surface' (i.e. the song is about a sinister person who is obsessed with Carey). The second level meaning, termed the symbolic, offers hints: the most suggestive or obvious semi-hidden intention of the text (i.e. in this case, that the song is about Eminem). The third level meaning, termed the signified, is presented as the feasible intention of the text, and that may not be directly communicated due to its emotional and sociocultural settings. This third element suits the context of 'Obsessed': while Carey has not confirmed that the song is about Eminem, it becomes clear that the theme and message are addressing the matter of sexual harassment and misogyny (which I discuss later).

Carey delivers the third level of meaning in the music video. Drawing on Barthes's 1957 essay on 'The Face of Garbo' (Barthes 2000), his case study of the film *Queen Christina* (Rouben Mamoulian, 1933), Barthes argues that Greta Garbo, who portrays the life of Queen Christina of Sweden, performs different gender personas in the story (i.e. man, woman, king, queen), all without abandoning her true identity (i.e. herself). Barthes: 'Garbo does not perform in it any feat of transvestism; she is always herself . . . ' (2000: 56). This concept applies too to Carey: she is performing and using her body, in tandem with the use of camera techniques, lighting, costumes and make-up. She 'successfully' portrays the male character but, underneath it all, we or the viewer know that this is still Mariah Carey. Arguably, this concatenation of Mariahs could be considered to be a crass marketing tactic or gimmick (we know Carey is talented in many areas, including as a brand and celebrity, and this video conception then gives a number of these to us . . . but also allows Carey to be presented in different ways in one sole video). She is to resort to and repurpose Barthes's description: 'the Divine . . . [who has] descended from heaven where all things are formed and perfected under the clearest light' (56-57). Barthes's Divine signals Carey's diva-ism, in its centrality to her creative vision: it is as if she alone takes charge of the video performance as every scene and every move is presented and performed by her, and herself only. This thematic obsessiveness and visual multiplicity of Mariahs then suggests that divadom is something that can be infinitely evolved – but this does not split or dilute the one-star presence: the 'Divine' Mariah herself, who is ubiquitous, the focus or foci of obsessive gazes, and both protean and yet (as per Barthes's Garbo) true to her known persona. Indeed, 'Obsessed' was the lead single from the album *Confessions of an Imperfect Angel* (2009) – the cover of which features three Mariahs in a row.

Conclusion

Eminem responded to Carey's song and video with 'The Warning' (2009), in a sexist, threatening and offensive manner, and by critiquing 'Obsessed', and making explicit references to their so-called or alleged affair. In the content of lyrics from Eminem here, included the advice that he would not 'fight with you over some slut bitch cunt' since he has 'put up with her psycho ass over six months and [had] only spread her legs to let me hit once . . .', the song 'Obsessed' fittingly serves as a confrontation against and protest to male predators and bullies. The song is a reminder of the challenges that women face – not only in the creative industries but in life and in culture in general. In this respect, I would argue, the song could be said to act as a precursor to the #MeToo movement (see Chandra and Erlingsdóttir 2021) – a movement that Carey has supported since she has experienced sexual harassment, rendering her – despite her star status – cautious and vulnerable: 'When you have to control your own emotions constantly and be aware of every move you make and pretty much ask permission to exist, it affects your life' (cited in Hattenstone 2018). This brings us back to the earlier discussion of women in popular music and creative industries. While changes are being made to promote gender equality and diversity, statistics collected or presented by pressure groups invariably continue to illustrate that the creative industries (and indeed so many other work situations) remain mostly male-dominated; see, for example, and most recently, Bain (2022). It is in this distorted context that misogynists may use their power to damage a woman's career and life. While it is clear that this tendency has negatively affected Carey in various ways, she has nonetheless successfully retaliated with or via her songs and music, and is not fazed by the backlash she received: 'my true fans stick with me and the rest of the people will get over it . . . ' (cited in Herndon 2019).

Carey, then, has demonstrated a determination to excel in her music career despite facing obstacles along the way. Her life, experiences, struggles, roles and her music resonate with her fans and followers – and have now done so across more than three decades. And yet, as argued, she is theatrical, glamorous, eccentric and fun. Is Mariah Carey, then, the ultimate diva in popular music and culture of the moment? Along with other greats, such as Grace Jones, Madonna, Diana Ross and Beyoncé, Carey, certainly belongs in the diva elite squad. And what is revealed from this exalted vantage point? In her autobiography, Mariah Carey offers a dictionary definition of the term diva, followed by her own persuasive definition: 'A distinguished and celebrated female singer; a woman of outstanding talent in the world of opera (usually soprano) and by extension in theater, cinema, and popular music. My definition of diva is the classic one.' (Carey and Davis 2020: 303)

Notes

1 To comply with the musical intimacy of the show, the music on 'Unplugged', as the name suggests, was mostly acoustic versions of the performing artists'

songs (Williams 2013: 213). Carey's *Unplugged* consisted of a mixture of acoustic (including classical) and jazz/pop instrumentation. While there were many performers on stage, the stage setting was small, and the music was mellow and intimate. The show occurred on 16 March 1992 at the Astoria Studios in New York, and was released as an EP that year.
2. Her marriage to the Sony executive was considered controversial at the outset, with an age difference of two decades and a clearly problematic power dynamic.
3. The NFL player became a controversial figure in 2016 after kneeling during the NFL's pre-game national anthem. This 'taking the knee' was a silent protest against police brutality and injustices towards people of colour.
4. The name Lambily is a combination of the words 'Lamb' (Mariah's fans) and family.
5. Eminem wrote a song about their 'relationship' called 'Bagpipes from Baghdad' (2009).
6. Special thanks to Michail Exarchos for assisting me with some parts of the musical analysis.
7. Examples include: Dr. Dre featuring Eminem, 'Forget about Dre' (1999), and 50 Cent, 'In Da Club' (2003).
8. One of Carey's favourite films is *Mean Girls*, which concerns a former home schooled girl trying to fit in at a new high school – marked as well by her family's return to the US from a generic 'Africa'. This film has been spoofed and referenced in popular culture, as with Ariana Grande's 'Thank U Next' (2018) music video, and K-Pop singer SUNMI's (of the Wonder Girls) 'You Can't Sit With Us' (2021).
9. Special thanks to Benjamin Halligan for this observation.
10. The director said he based the video on the 1983 Martin Scorsese film *The King of Comedy* (see Vena 2009). This is not the first time Carey played two different characters in one music video: in 'Heartbreaker' (1999) she plays her alter-ego, Bianca, the bad (dark-haired) girlfriend, and herself as the cute/sweet (blonde) girlfriend.

Reference

Azzopardi, C. (2016), 'The Heroism of Mariah Carey', *The Rainbow Times*, 22 August. Available online: http://www.therainbowtimesmass.com/heroism-of-mariah-carey/ (accessed 8 June 2019).

Bain, K. (2022), 'Women Still Vastly Underrepresented in Music Creation Process, New Study Finds', *Billboard*, 31 March. Available online: https://www.billboard.com/music/music-news/women-in-music-study-annenberg-gender-inequality-1235052876/ (accessed 10 October 2022).

Barthes, R. (1977), *Image Music Text*, trans. S. Heath, London: Fontana Press.
Barthes, R. (2000), *Mythologies*, trans. A. Lavers, London: Vintage.
Bennetta, J.-R. (2007), *Josephine Baker in Art and Life: The Icon and the Image*, Urbana and Chicago: University of Illinois Press.
Bertei, A. (2021), *Why Labelle Matters*, Austin: University of Texas Press.
Billboard (no date), 'Mariah Carey – Chart History'. Available online: https://www.billboard.com/artist/mariah-carey/chart-history/tlp/ (accessed 29 December 2021).
Boucher, G. (2005), 'After Hard Fall Mariah Carey Bounces Back', *Chicago Tribune*, 11 December. Available online: https://www.chicagotribune.com/news/ct-xpm-2005-12-11-0512110447-story.html (accessed 8 June 2019).
Bowenbank, S. (2022), 'Mariah Carey Celebrates the 30th Anniversary of Her "MTV Unplugged" Performance: "I Truly Feel Blessed"', 2 June. Available online: https://www.billboard.com/music/pop/mariah-carey-30th-anniversary-mtv-unplugged-1235080821/ (accessed 3 August 2022).
Cagle, J. (2018), 'Mariah Carey: My Battle with Bipolar Disorder', *People*, 11 April. Available online: https://people.com/music/mariah-carey-bipolar-disorder-diagnosis-exclusive/ (accessed 4 October 2021).
Carey, M. and M. A. Davis (2020), *The Meaning of Mariah Carey*, London: Macmillan.
Chandra, G. and I. Erlingsdóttir, eds (2021), *The Routledge Handbook of the Politics of the #MeToo Movement*, New York: Routledge.
Complex (2008), 'A History of Eminem and Mariah Carey's Relationship', *Complex*, 1 August. Available online: https://www.complex.com/music/2009/08/a-history-of-eminem-and-mariah-careys-relationship/ (accessed 8 June 2019).
Dyer, R. (1979), *Stars*, London: British Film Institute.
Frank, A. (2018), 'Forever Mariah: An Interview with an Icon', *Pitchfork*, 28 November. Available online: https://pitchfork.com/features/interview/forever-mariah-an-interview-with-an-icon/ (accessed 8 June 2019).
Hattenstone, S. (2018), '"I Bathe in Milk": Mariah Carey on Bossiness, Breakups and being Bipolar', *The Guardian*, 4 June. Available online: https://www.theguardian.com/music/2018/jun/04/mariah-carey-bossiness-breakups-bipolar-interview (accessed 8 June 2019).
Herndon, J. (2019), 'Mariah Carey Goes There on Sex, Shade, and the Stories Behind those Epic Memes', *Cosmopolitan*, 9 July. Available online: https://www.cosmopolitan.com/entertainment/celebs/a28137694/mariah-carey-profile-cover-cosmo-interview-sex-shade-memes/ (accessed 8 June 2019).
Kooijman, J. (2008), *Fabricating the Absolute Fake: America in Contemporary Pop Culture*, Amsterdam: Amsterdam University Press.
La Marr, J. B. (2012), 'The People Inside my Head, too: Madness, Black Womanhood, and the Racial Performance of Lauryn Hill', *African American Review*, 45 (3): 371–89.
LIVE Kelly and Ryan (2018), 'Mariah Carey's Kids Have Been Listening to Her Music Since Birth', 21 November. Available online: https://www.youtube.com/watch?v=rtbSIesdD0Q (accessed 8 June 2019).

Lynch, J. (2015), 'Mariah Carey in 1990: Critics Loved Her, Thought She Was White', *Billboard*, 16 September. Available online: https://www.billboard.com/music/rb-hip-hop/mariah-carey-1990-critics-white-6699720/ (accessed 8 June 2019).

Maishman, E. (2022), 'Mariah Carey "Queen of Christmas" Trademark Attempt Prompts Backlash', *BBC News*, 16 August. Available online: https://www.bbc.co.uk/news/world-us-canada-62564327 (accessed 25 August 2022).

Miller, D. G. and H. K. Schutte (1993), 'Physical Definition of the "Flageolet Register"', *Journal of Voice: Official Journal of the Voice Foundation*, 7 (3): 206–12.

O'Brien, L. (2012), *She Bop: The Definitive History of Women in Popular Music*, London: Jawbone Press.

Rambarran, S. (2021), *Virtual Music: Sound, Music, and Image in the Digital Era*, New York: Bloomsbury.

Rischar, R. (2004), 'A Vision of Love: An Etiquette of Vocal Ornamentation in African-American Popular Ballads of the Early 1990s', *American Music*, 22: 407–43.

Rossetti, F. (2022), 'Distorsions of Authenticity: Grunge According to MTV Unplugged Between Performance, Resistance, and Memory', *Cinergie – Il Cinema E Le Altre Arti*, 11 (21): 197–214.

Scott, D. B. (2008), *Sounds of the Metropolis: The Nineteenth-Century Popular Music Revolution in London, New York, Paris and Vienna*, New York: Oxford University Press.

Sholin, D. (1991), 'Mariah Carey', The Gavin Report, 8 February. Available online: http://www.mariahcareynetwork.com/print/articles/1991-tgr.html (accessed 8 June 2019).

Smith, S., M. Choueiti and K. Pieper (2018), 'Inclusion in the Recording Studio? Gender and Race/Ethnicity of Artists, Songwriters and Producers across 600 Popular Songs from 2012–2017', University of Southern California: Annenberg Inclusion Initiative. Available online: https://assets.uscannenberg.org/docs/aii-inclusion-recording-studio-20200117.pdf (accessed 8 June 2019).

Strong, C. and S. Raine, eds (2019), *Towards Gender Equality in the Music Industry: Education, Practice and Strategies for Change*, New York: Bloomsbury Academic.

Vena, J. (2009), 'Mariah Carey's "Obsessed" Video "Not About Eminem," Director Says', *MTV News*, 16 July. Available online: https://www.mtv.com/news/huffqz/mariah-careys-obsessed-video-not-about-eminem-director-says (accessed 8 June 2019).

Whiteley, S. (2000), *Women and Popular Music: Sexuality, Identity and Subjectivity*, New York: Routledge.

Whiteley, S., ed. (2008), *Christmas, Ideology, and Popular Culture*, Edinburgh: Edinburgh University Press.

Williams, J. A. (2013), *Rhymin' and Stealin': Musical Borrowing in Hip-Hop*, Michigan: University of Michigan Press.

Wolfe, P. (2020), *Women in the Studio: Creativity, Control and Gender in Popular Music Sound Production*, New York: Routledge.

2

Performing creative labour
Whitney Houston metanarratives on MTV, 1985–8

Gwynne George

This chapter considers the ways in which, across her early music videos, Whitney Houston used self-conscious stagings of creative labour in the forging of her iconic star brand – in particular, the ways in which these stagings interacted with pop-cultural trends and sociopolitical discourses of the 1980s. Houston rose to prominence within the first five years of MTV, which, following its launch in August 1981, quickly became an essential avenue for the promotion of popular music artists. Upon her debut, Houston soon became one of the station's most popular stars and, in this respect, was among the preeminent divas of the early music video age. Yet, despite her success – and its inherent significance, given the dearth of Black women representation on MTV – Houston seldom features in scholarly discussions of MTV. In an effort to correct this critical and scholarly marginalization and neglect, this chapter reads Houston's music videos with a view to understanding their implications on the building of her iconic star brand.

As scholars such as Jason King have noted, while music videos can be studied at 'face value' – encompassing their narratives, lyrics and visual images – they should primarily be examined for how they 'construct, support, or negotiate an artist's metanarrative identity' (1999: 88), in order to be most comprehensively understood. For Houston, her music-televisual texts allowed her to foreground her professionalism, by repeatedly showcasing and insisting upon her artistic labour as a Black creative professional. All but one of Houston's early music videos incorporate the idea of creative labour – whether rehearsing with backing singers, recording in the studio or performing onstage, her professionalism was repeatedly foregrounded. These repeated, self-conscious stagings of her professionalism contrasted discursively with the frequent mobilization of the racialized trope of the welfare queen, which was coined by the Reagan Administration (1981–9) and constituted a new way to pathologize the Black family, and Black women in particular, to drum up support for the dismantling of government welfare programmes. As I will explore, Houston's repeated insistence on her creative labour struck discursive blows to contemporary denigrations of Black women's labour and served as implicit rejoinders to white supremacist scripts of Black dysfunction.

Moreover, Houston's music-televisual performances of spectacular creative labour cohered with emerging depictions of 'working girls' as a cultural archetype in Hollywood in the 1980s, wherein women were shown conspicuously moving into the workplace and enjoying their roles as professionals – thus allowing for certain forms of empowerment, albeit curtailed, in the workplace (Brunsdon 1997; McRobbie 2009). While scholarship on the working girl has tended to read this figure as archetypically white, Houston arguably embodied certain elements of this model, by leveraging her performance capital as an assertive Black woman professional working in the mainstream. As I will explore, these performances netted positive results, by rewarding her with fame and popularity within the videos' diegetic worlds, as well as imbuing her metanarrative of stardom with notions of prestige and professionalism. As a result, I join other scholars to suggest that studies of postfeminism can – and should – broaden their analysis to allow for a consideration of the ways in which Black women feature among its tropes.

I begin this chapter by establishing Houston's blockbuster success on MTV in the 1980s. I then explore the ways in which Houston used presentations of creative labour in her music videos to leverage her performance capital with spectacular results. Finally, by offering brief summaries of the Reagan-era working girl archetype, as well as contemporary white supremacist constructions of Black dysfunction via the trope of the welfare queen, I consider the ways in which Houston's self-presentation as an assertive working girl has ramifications on studies of postfeminism and popular culture, as well as the ways in which it invites readings of Houston's music videos as Black feminist spaces. Overall, I argue that in her early career, Houston spectacularly and complexly engaged interlocking race, gender and class discourses of the 1980s, leading to her charismatic star power. In this respect, Houston played a key role in the conceptualization of the contemporary diva figure.

Whitney Houston and the televisual context of MTV

With the release of her debut album, *Whitney Houston*, on Valentine's Day 1985, Houston soon became one of the most prominent stars of the 1980s and remains one of the most commercially successful popular music artists of all time. Houston's emergence came within the first five years of MTV, which had launched on 1 August 1981. The network quickly became an essential avenue for the promotion of popular music artists: by the end of 1982, it was reported that artists featured on MTV immediately experienced a 10 to 15 per cent increase in record sales (Sanjek 1988: 640), while other data suggested that artists who had little radio airplay in certain markets enjoyed brisk album sales in areas serviced by MTV, further indicating the station's importance (Dwyer 2015: 122–3). Music videos thus added a new way for performers to promote themselves and became a key site of star image construction. As Houston remembered in 2001:

> The image was starting to become very image-y, you know? It was the look, it was the hair, it was the makeup, it was the way you moved, the way you danced, the way your mouth sang a song [. . .] the way your head moved. All those little gestures and things became very important for video purposes. [. . .] They said 'Video Killed the Radio Star' – well, it kind of happened. [. . .] We had to be visual, and MTV made us be visual. So we had to pull it off.
>
> (MTV News 2001)[1]

Houston's first entry into MTV playlists came in January 1986, when 'How Will I Know' (1985) was placed in medium rotation.[2] Between 1985 and 1988, Houston would release eight music videos, of which five would enter MTV's heavy rotation playlist – a category described in *Billboard* magazine in 1984 as 'a home for the big hits to be played without the bells and whistles, just getting the depth of exposure their popularity demands' (Seideman 1984: 44). As well as through watching MTV, fans could access Houston's videos via VHS releases, such as *Whitney Houston: The #1 Video Hits* (1987), which was the fifth bestselling music VHS tape of 1987 – further demonstrating the popularity of her music-televisual texts (Billboard 1990: V26).

Houston's success on MTV was significant, given the relative paucity of Black women stars on MTV in its early years.[3] Indeed, when asked about her memories of the early days of MTV in a 2001 interview, Houston responded:

> I remember that I couldn't get on. I remember that it was a major breakthrough for African American entertainers to be on MTV, because it was solely for rock

artists. [. . .] I do remember the hassle of introducing Black artists to MTV, because – let's face it – it was solely for white artists at that point.

(MTV News 2001)

In contrast to what is sometimes erroneously claimed, Houston was not the first Black artist to enter heavy rotation on MTV. By the time of her debut, breakthroughs had occurred for both Black artists and women artists – as well as artists existing at the intersection of Blackness and womanhood – who had previously been excluded from its playlists.[4] Nevertheless, Houston undoubtedly became one of the most iconic MTV stars of the 1980s. In addition to frequently appearing in the station's heavy rotation playlist, her videos were ranked highly in retrospective lists: for example, in a 1989 *Top 100 Videos of the 1980s* countdown, MTV placed 'How Will I Know' and 'I Wanna Dance with Somebody (Who Loves Me)' (1987) at #15 and #36, respectively.[5]

Despite their contemporary critical dismissal – for example, Keith L. Thomas of the *Atlanta Journal-Constitution* described 'How Will I Know' as 'unimaginative' and 'Greatest Love of All' (1986) as 'hokey' (1986a, 1986b) – I argue that Houston's early music videos performed important symbolic work. As I will explore later, Houston used the performance of creative labour as an integral element of her screen star image in shaping her star-text. Her sustained presentation of assertive Black female professionalism, through her videos' repeated insistence on her creative labour in her music videos, cohered with other contemporary cultural trends amid the contradictory contours of the era of Ronald Reagan. In particular, Houston's embodiment of an empowered working girl allowed her music videos to become transgressive spaces, creating empowered models of Black female professionalism that studies of postfeminism have heretofore neglected.

Performing creative labour on MTV

Across her pop-cultural texts and publicity image, Houston repeatedly insisted on the ideas of creative labour and professionalism. Consider, for example, contemporary interview remarks from Houston, wherein she made direct reference to her own hard work: 'I am [. . .] a perfectionist and my own worst critic. I believe that God is responsible for everything that has happened to me. At the same time, it all goes to show that hard work does pay off,' Houston told the *New York Times* in 1985 (Holden 1985: C13). As I will explore in this section, Houston's spectacular creative labour was a frequent trope of her early music videos, through repeated emphasis on her singing, recording, rehearsing and performing.

First, Houston's music videos drew explicit attention to the sheer work behind her star brand through her repeated use of performance videos. Of Houston's first eight music videos, four incorporate sequences of her appearing on the concert stage. Of these four, only one was genuine concert footage: the video for 'Didn't We Almost Have It All' (1987) was a live performance filmed during a New York stop on Houston's Moment of Truth World Tour of 1987–8. In contrast, the concert sequences for 'Greatest Love of All', 'So Emotional' (1987), and 'I Wanna Dance with Somebody (Who Loves Me)' were all simulated. 'Greatest Love of All' presents a fictional narrative, filmed at the Apollo Theater in Harlem, New York, which features flashbacks to a child Houston at an audition, before shifting to the present and showing her give an elegant concert performance accompanied by an orchestra. Similarly, the 'live' performance of 'So Emotional', while presented as raw concert footage, was in fact filmed over four hours with 2,500 extras during a break in Houston's touring schedule (Look 1987: B3); while 'I Wanna Dance with Somebody (Who Loves Me)' begins with a short black-and-white sequence that shows Houston taking a final bow and then leaving the concert stage as fans clamour to touch her before the song itself starts. The scene has no relevance to the rest of the video, which is a collection of colourful, energetic scenes that do not cohere to form a storyline. At the video's end, a short black-and-white sequence shows Houston arriving at her hotel after the concert, to see a group of friends entering a bar down the street. Houston hesitates, before smiling and running towards them – suggesting that she is finally cutting loose from her work schedule and further signalling the labour behind her star brand.

In addition to visualizations of her performing – and, by extension, working – on the concert stage, Houston further insisted on her status as a creative professional through the recurring settings of the recording studio and rehearsal space. Whether rehearsing with backing singers ('You Give Good Love' of 1985), recording in the studio ('Saving All My Love for You' of 1985, 'Where Do Broken Hearts Go' of 1988), leading a choir for 'How Will I Know', or performing onstage, Houston's presence on MTV in the 1980s repeatedly showed her explicitly working. Given that the stage, recording studio and rehearsal space are a performer's working environments, their frequent representations in Houston's videos place an accent on Houston's labour as a creative professional.

Houston's repeated stagings of her rehearsals and recording invite parallels with Michael Jackson, whose self-conscious displays of creative labour have also been considered by scholars. For example, Judith Hamera discusses the ways in which Jackson's descriptions of his labour-intensive choreography and rehearsal sessions in his 1988 memoir *Moonwalk* interrupted 'romantic constructions of virtuosity [that] obscure the mechanics of creative production', which, instead of acknowledging the sheer hard work that goes into every performance, position virtuosic performers as simply 'angel' or 'magician' (2012: 755). In particular, Hamera considers Jackson's descriptions of his gruelling rehearsals to '[disrupt] conventional visual equations of economy of input yielding spectacular output' (2012: 755), by explicitly drawing attention to the work behind his star brand. In the same way, Houston also drew attention to the labour behind her star brand via footage of her in rehearsal rooms, recording studios and performance spaces – showing not only the spectacular results via concert performance but also the work that led up to them.

Houston's music videos further drew attention to her creative labour through her singing. Frequent close-ups of Houston's face as she sings emphasize the role of her voice in her metanarrative of stardom, which scholars have previously analysed (Kooijman 2014). While artists' lip-syncing to pre-recorded tracks is a common, if not expected, element of music videos, Houston's distinctive lip quiver at several points in her videos suggests that she is singing live. Indeed, Brian Grant, director of 'How Will I Know' and 'I Wanna Dance with Somebody (Who Loves Me)', revealed in a 2012 interview that this was a deliberate choice: 'We used to do a thing called a master close-up, where we would put Whitney in front of the camera [. . .] And the rule was she had to sing it, you couldn't just mime' (Savage 2012). At certain points, Houston's live performance interrupts the recorded track: for example, in the video for 'I Wanna Dance with Somebody (Who Loves Me)', Houston's lips do not match the track at multiple points (including just before the first verse, where she adds a 'don't' at the beginning of 'you want to dance', and at the beginning of the second verse, where she appears to add an adlibbed 'and' that does not feature in the recorded vocal), drawing the viewer's attention to the disjointedness of Houston's live performance on camera and the commodified studio recording. The insistence on Houston's live performance of complex vocalizations – even if they were then dubbed over with the studio recording – thus explicitly drew attention to her creative labour, providing an immediate visual representation of the work involved in performing these technically demanding vocals. Scholars have previously identified a similar phenomenon in the work of Beyoncé. For example, Emily J. Lordi draws on Daphne Brooks to comment on Beyoncé's musical directions via verbal cues, and the ways in which they draw attention to Beyoncé's creative labour: '"Déjà Vu" registers Black women's emotional and technical labour by establishing Beyoncé's control over this production and by foregrounding the vocal work [the] song demands [. . .] Beyoncé at once announces her control of her music and performs its excessive demands' (2017: 135). Houston, too, draws explicit attention to the sheer work her complex vocalizations demand, by performing them 'live' for the viewer within the space of her music videos.

More than simply imbuing her metanarrative of stardom with notions of hard work and professionalism, the recurring trope of creative labour in Houston's music videos takes on particular salience when read in the context of Reagan-era United States. Indeed, as star studies scholars such as Richard Dyer remind us, stars 'need to be situated in the specificities of the ideological configurations to which [they] belong' (1988: 31), in order to fully understand the salience of their star texts. For example, previous scholarly considerations of Black stars' spectacular performance of creative labour in post-Civil Rights cultural texts have located them within their particular discursive moment in persuasive ways. A particularly pertinent example is *Mahogany* (Berry Gordy, 1975), which features spectacular creative labour as a central element. The film stars Diana Ross as Tracy Chambers, an aspiring fashion designer who finds fame in Europe as a model. Reading the film in the context of contemporary US sociopolitical dynamics – including the Moynihan Report of 1965, which famously located Black Americans' structural disadvantages in supposed familial dysfunction – Miriam Thaggert notes that while Tracy does go on to find success as a designer, the film 'ultimately weakens [her] by pathologizing her success as unnatural and abnormal' (2012: 733).[6] *Mahogany* asserts an 'intertwined racial, familial, and, more subtly, national paradigm' (Thaggert 2012: 733–4), whereby Tracy abandons her career to instead reconcile a romantic relationship with Brian (Billy Dee Williams), and aids him in his aspirations of holding political office. Thaggert concludes that *Mahogany* contradicts such American myths as meritocracy, to instead reassert a 'post-civil rights national and racial narrative of the family like that posited by Moynihan, [whereby Black women] must either disavow [their ambition and creativity,] or use [them] to improve a male partner' (2012: 723).

The repeated trope of Houston's virtuosic creative labour resonates with, but also supersedes, the closed ideological imperatives mapped by Thaggert. Indeed, Houston's spectacular performance represented a key way in which her brand engaged and disrupted contemporary gender discourses. As Thaggert reads Ross's creative labour in *Mahogany* in the discursive context of the Moynihan Report, so must we situate Houston in her contemporary context. As I will explore later, Houston's embodiment of the Reagan-era working girl archetype in her music videos served to partly challenge the constraints of strongly patriarchal gendered currents of the charged discursive moment, which had particular racial contours. Unlike Diana Ross's star vehicle heroine in *Mahogany*, however, Houston is not punished for her professionalism. Instead, her music videos' narratives reward her with popularity and prestige.

Reagan-era gender discourses and the working girl

Since a comprehensive discussion of the charged intersectional discourses of the 1980s is outside the scope of this chapter, I offer only a very brief summary here. The Reagan era was a polarizing moment in gendered terms, comprising an interplay of both feminist and antifeminist sentiments: at the same time that vibrant feminist, Black feminist and womanist movements, as well as new models of women's professionalism and empowerment occurred, American women found themselves subjected to a sophisticated antifeminist backlash, perpetuated by various forms of media, as well as insurgent New Right calls for a renewal of heteronormative gender roles (see Eisenstein 1982; Ryan and Kellner 1988; Faludi 1991; Collins 2000). In addition, Black American women faced particularly racialized discursive assaults from the New Right, not least through the figure of the 'welfare queen' – a conservative, anti-welfare discourse that functioned in Reagan-era political discourse as a racialized permutation of contemporary debates surrounding women's labour and non-/domesticity. This framing sought to pathologize Black women and families by coding poor and/or Black welfare recipients as lazy and dishonest, in order to shift blame for structural inequalities to the realm of the personal (Reeves and Campbell 1994; Hancock 2004). A more in-depth discussion of Houston's emergence would explore how she navigated each of these ambivalent affects at once – including the ways she, at times, capitulated to Reagan-era 'family values' discourse, through her performance of conventional signifiers of feminine passivity and vulnerability – with her glamorous reconciliation of these seemingly incompatible affects giving rise to the charismatic iconicity of her star-text.

For the purposes of this discussion, however, I focus mainly on the ideological implications of Houston's music-televisual performances of creative labour, and the ways in which they fed into her developing star brand. First, as seen earlier, Houston's repeated foregrounding of her labour arguably combated contemporary controlling images of Black women, imbuing her star brand with notions of hard work, discipline and technical proficiency at a charged sociopolitical moment. In this way, Houston's music videos can be read as Black feminist spaces – using an insistence on her professionalism as a counterpunch to white supremacist discourses of the day. Moreover, Houston's spectacular creative labour also allowed her to participate in emerging models of empowered femininity that began to find cultural purchase in the 1980s. Reading Houston's early music videos in the context of incipient postfeminist discourses – more specifically, the archetype of the working girl – allows us to think about how Houston's frequent, self-conscious staging of her creative labour served as rejoinders to antifeminist discourses of the 1980s and, instead, formed part of new patterns of female empowerment.

Within the realm of mainstream popular culture, the 1980s saw an 'entanglement of both feminist and antifeminist themes' (Gill 2007: 148–9) through the emergence of postfeminism, whose inception has been dated by scholars as emerging somewhere between the early 1980s and 1990s. Most relevant to this discussion is the emergence of new kinds of empowered femininity, albeit curtailed, within these incipient postfeminist discourses. A prominent example is the figure of the working girl, which appeared over several 1980s Hollywood texts, which captured competing gendered discourses of professionalism and a return to domesticity – speaking to the contradictory gendered contours of the Reagan era, which Houston would spectacularly embody. While Angela McRobbie uses the figure of the working girl as an example of the 'new sexual contract' (2009: 35) for women that emerged in the early 1990s, the name comes from the 1988 movie *Working Girl* (Mike Nichols), which suggests that this model had already begun to find cultural purchase around the time of Houston's emergence.

According to McRobbie, under the new sexual contract, women occupied more visible roles of agency within education, the workplace and consumer culture, as well as attempting to balance work and home lives, in exchange for an abandonment of critique of patriarchy (2009: 73). Rather than focusing on what women 'ought not to do', emphasis shifted within the realm of public debate, including popular culture, towards a series of 'incitements and enticements to engage in a range of specified practices which are understood to be both progressive but also consummately and reassuringly feminine' (McRobbie 2009: 54). McRobbie argues that the figure of the working girl is one of four 'luminosities' that work to sustain and revitalize the heterosexual matrix, as well as reinstating norms of racial hierarchy and class divisions (2009: 55). While taking its name from a specific movie, the trope appears across a range of Hollywood narratives, whereby the working girl character 'takes up her place in the labour market [and] enjoys her status as a working girl without going too far' – that is, continuing to perform conventional feminine vulnerability and avoiding critiques of masculine hegemony, while nevertheless embodying feminine empowerment through her professional status (McRobbie 2009: 72). Charlotte Brunsdon offers similar observations regarding the movie *Working Girl*, by identifying its engagement of both feminist and backlash themes. According to Brunsdon, the movie offers a 'splitting or dispersal of 'independent woman' characteristics' over the characters of Tess (Melanie Griffith) and Katharine (Sigourney Weaver), whereby the former's 'postfeminist girly' stands in contrast to the latter's 'monster-career woman' (1997: 102). The movie's narrative rewards Tess's 'ambition made cute', by positioning her as 'a new kind of girly heroine [that] disavows' 1970s feminism (Brunsdon 1997: 102). For Brunsdon, *Working Girl* demonstrates the ways in which women characters in Hollywood narratives are permitted career ambitions, but can also be pathologized as 'monstrous' if they attain too much power in the workplace (1997: 88–94).

McRobbie (2009), Brunsdon (1997) and Amelia Jones (1991) have all noted the overwhelming whiteness of the characters of these cultural texts, thus implicitly foregrounding whiteness in their analyses. This encapsulates a trend in postfeminist studies: as Kimberly Springer notes, 'To date, studies of postfeminism have studiously noted that many of its icons are white and cited the absence of women of color, but the analysis seems to stop there' (2007: 249). Scholars such as Springer and Jess Butler (2013: 48–9) have called for considerations of the presence of women of colour, and specifically Black women, within postfeminist media.

I suggest that Houston is an example of a Black woman star who could fit into these analyses. As seen earlier, Houston arguably coheres with the identified tropes of the working girl archetype across her music-televisual texts – appearing assertively in the workplace and enjoying her professional status, while still performing conventional femininity. As in the aforementioned Hollywood narratives, her videos' narratives reward her with success: indeed, Houston is presented as an immensely popular performer who possesses wide appeal across different audiences and genres – whether at a glamorous, sit-down performance backed by an orchestra, as in 'Greatest Love of All', or in the somewhat more rambunctious pop concert setting of 'So Emotional'.[7]

Conclusion

What, then, are the ramifications of Whitney Houston's spectacular and repeated performances of creative labour on MTV? On one level, by showing Houston before large crowds of enthusiastic fans, her music videos simply constructed her as a dynamic performer who enjoyed immense fame and popularity. On another, music videos allowed Houston to draw further attention to her voice as a key aspect of her star brand, by providing a direct visualization of her vocal abilities. More broadly, however, Houston's music videos repeatedly valorized her hard work as a Black woman creative professional – whether rehearsing, recording or performing. In so doing, she cohered with emerging cultural depictions of working girls, which allowed women new kinds of agency within popular culture and spoke to the contradictory ideological contours of the Reagan era. My analysis suggests that rather than reading the working girl archetype as 'invariably' white, we must also consider the ways in which Black women were forging new models of post-Civil Rights middle-class identity formation within the realm of mainstream popular culture in the 1980s – as well as the ways in which Black women should feature in analyses of postfeminism. In addition, Houston's very ascension to the upper echelons of MTV, given its problematic early racial politics, invites readings of the ways in which she implicitly struck a blow to contemporary white supremacist scripts of Black dysfunction – not least, the towering discursive figure of the welfare queen, which stood as a racialized counterproposal to the Black working girl archetype that Houston embodied. As a result, Houston's music videos can be read as Black feminist spaces – interrupting contemporary devaluation and denigration of Black women's labour through their presentation of empowered Black female professionalism.

Other aspects of Houston's videos invite detailed exploration. For example, the blurring of heteronormative gender roles, as well as images of queerness and androgyny, merit consideration for their implications on Houston's metanarrative of stardom. In addition, the productive tension between Houston's, at times, lovelorn and passive lyrical persona with the self-assuredness of her music-televisual image invite a deeper examination of Houston's comforting resolution of the contradictory contours of the 1980s, which gave rise to her complex and multilayered star brand. Overall, the opportunity that MTV offered for new modes of star-text construction, as well as her engagement with the contemporary discursive moment – where she engaged with and resolved ideological tensions 'complexly [and] variously' (Dyer 1986: 8) – arguably allowed Whitney Houston to become one of the most iconic stars of the 1980s – and beyond.

Notes

1 Houston's reference is to 'Video Killed the Radio Star' by the Buggles (1979), which was the very first video broadcast by MTV in the United States.
2 Throughout this chapter, data on music videos' performance on MTV are taken from its weekly Hit Clip lists, published in *Billboard* magazine. These charts do not always appear to be the most reliable: for example, 'Saving All My Love For You', released three months earlier than 'How Will I Know', did not appear in the Hit Clip list, while Houston specifically remembered in 2001 that it 'hit so hard and exploded so heavy that [MTV] had no choice but to play it' (MTV News 2001).
3 For in-depth discussions of MTV's process of racial incorporation, see Harper (1989), Goodwin (1992), and Dwyer (2015).
4 Examples of Black women artists who pre-dated Houston on MTV include Donna Summer, whose 'She Works Hard for the Money' moved between MTV's light, medium and heavy rotation playlists between June and September 1983; the Pointer Sisters, whose 'Jump (For My Love)' was in heavy rotation between June and August 1984; and La Toya Jackson, whose 'Heart Don't Lie' was in light rotation for two weeks in June 1984. In addition, Tina Turner's 'What's Love Got to Do with It' was awarded Best Female Video at the 1985 MTV Video Music Awards, held some four months before Houston's first appearance on the station.
5 For the full list, see: https://www.imdb.com/list/ls022380614/.
6 This report, *The Negro Family: The Case for National Action*, was authored by Daniel Patrick Moynihan for the US Department of Labour.
7 Elsewhere, Houston's fame is signalled in other ways. For example, 'Where Do Broken Hearts Go' does not show Houston onstage, but rather backstage. Her dressing room door reads 'WHITNEY', suggesting her fame is so established that she needs no surname – a move that both recalls and preempts other powerhouse divas.

Reference

Billboard (1990), 'Top Music Videocassettes', *Billboard*, 6 January, V26.
Brunsdon, C. (1997), *Screen Tastes: Soap Opera to Satellite Dishes*, London: Routledge.

Butler, J. (2013), 'For White Girls Only?: Postfeminism and the Politics of Inclusion', *Feminist Formations*, 25 (1): 35–58.

Collins, P. H. (2000), *Black Feminist Thought: Knowledge, Consciousness, and the Politics of Empowerment*, 2nd edn, New York: Routledge.

Dwyer, M. D. (2015), *Back to the Fifties: Nostalgia, Hollywood Film, and Popular Music of the Seventies and Eighties*, New York: Oxford University Press.

Dyer, R. (1986), *Heavenly Bodies: Film Stars and Society*, London: Macmillan.

Dyer, R. (1998), *Stars*, New edn, London: British Film Institute.

Eisenstein, Z. R. (1982), 'The Sexual Politics of the New Right: Understanding the "Crisis of Liberalism" for the 1980s', *Signs*, 7 (3): 567–88.

Faludi, S. (1991), *Backlash: The Undeclared War against American Women*, New York City: Crown Publishing Group.

Gill, R. (2007), 'Postfeminist Media Culture: Elements of a Sensibility', *European Journal of Cultural Studies*, 10 (2): 147–66.

Goodwin, A. (1992), *Dancing in the Distraction Factory: Music, Television and Popular Culture*, Minneapolis: University of Minnesota Press.

Hamera, J. (2012), 'The Labors of Michael Jackson: Virtuosity, Deindustrialization, and Dancing Work', *PMLA*, 127 (4): 751–65.

Hancock, A.-M. (2004), *The Politics of Disgust: The Public Identity of the Welfare Queen*, New York: New York University Press.

Harper, P. B. (1989), 'Synesthesia, "Crossover," and Blacks in Popular Music', *Social Text*, 23: 102–21.

Holden, S. (1985), 'Whitney Houston in Concert', *New York Times*, 28 October, section C: 13.

Jones, A. (1991), '"She Was Bad News": Male Paranoia and the Contemporary New Woman', *Camera Obscura: Feminism, Culture, and Media Studies*, 9.1–2 (25–26): 296–320.

King, J. (1999), 'Form and Function: Superstardom and Aesthetics in the Music Videos of Michael and Janet Jackson', *The Velvet Light Trap – A Critical Journal of Film and Television*, 44 (Fall): 80–96.

Kooijman, J. (2014), 'The True Voice of Whitney Houston: Commodification, Authenticity, and African American Superstardom', *Celebrity Studies*, 5 (3): 305–20.

Look, L. (1987), 'Whitney Houston Films Music Video at Stabler Arena', *The Morning Call*, 22 October, B3.

Lordi, E. J. (2017), 'Surviving the Hustle: Beyoncé's Performance of Work', *Black Camera*, 9 (1): 131–45.

McRobbie, A. (2009), *The Aftermath of Feminism: Gender, Culture and Social Change*, London: SAGE Publications.

MTV News (2001), 'Whitney Houston Reminisces about 80's Music on MTV (2001)'. Available online: https://www.youtube.com/watch?v=IzZgor4981M (accessed 6 November 2022).

Reeves, J. L. and R. Campbell (1994), *Cracked Coverage: Television News, the Anti-Cocaine Crusade, and the Reagan Legacy*, Durham: Duke University Press.

Ryan, M. and D. Kellner (1988), *Camera Politica: The Politics and Ideology of Contemporary Hollywood Film*, Bloomington: Indiana University Press.

Sanjek, R. (1988), *American Popular Music and Its Business: The First Four Hundred Years Volume III: From 1900 to 1984*, Oxford: Oxford University Press.

Savage, M. (2012), 'Whitney Houston "Was Very Shy", Says Director Brian Grant', *BBC News*, 12 February. Available online: http://www.bbc.co.uk/news/entertainment-arts-17005547 (accessed 31 August 2020).

Seideman, T. (1984), 'Changes in MTV Playlist: Expansion to Seven Categories', *Billboard*, 3 November, 42, 44.

Springer, K. (2007), 'Divas, Evil Black Bitches, and Bitter Black Women: African American Women in Postfeminist and Post-Civil-Rights Popular Culture', in Yvonne Tasker and Diane Negra (eds), *Interrogating Postfeminism: Gender and the Politics of Popular Culture*, 249–76, Durham: Duke University Press.

Thaggert, M. (2012), 'Marriage, Moynihan, Mahogany: Success and the Post-Civil Rights Black Female Professional in Film', *American Quarterly*, 64 (4): 715–40.

Thomas, K. L. (1986a), 'Video Music: Starship Crash Lands with Woeful "Sara" Clip', *Atlanta Journal-Constitution*, 30 March.

Thomas, K. L. (1986b), 'The High Cost of Making Music Come to Life', *Atlanta Journal-Constitution*, 4 May.

3

A girl of many colours

Dolly Parton's image evolution: 1967–2022

James Reeves

A girl of many colours

Few entertainers have successfully reinvented themselves the same way as Dolly Parton has. As with her song 'Coat of Many Colours' (1971), Dolly could be said to be a patchwork of different identities, personalities and talents – and all carefully constructed by her so as not only to adapt to each generation but also to appeal to a diverse legion of fans and admirers. Dolly has constructed her image and personality not only to stand out but as an ongoing artistic project: it is an evolving image that has been decades in the making. Each stage of her career is oriented around a new Dolly image. And yet every image was still distinctly Dolly. Every image in each stage of her career represented both a professional and physical metamorphosis.

Unlike other artists who construct different images in their careers in, order to reinvent themselves, sometimes expediently, sometimes embarrassingly, Dolly's evolving image reflected a metamorphosis *from within*. Each of Dolly's images reflects not a reinvention as such, but rather an adaption to each decade and stage of her career. So Dolly's evolving image represents, and indexes, her evolution as a singer, songwriter and (entwined with these two aspects), an individual. While each image is distinct and different, each remains a part of Dolly's growth as an artist and person: they are consistent while ever-changing, and a continuum of the performer and presence of Dolly Parton.

This chapter surveys these stages and offers a periodization. My primary source is Schmidt's collection of interviews (2017), but I draw too on Edwards (2018) and Hamessley (2020) for elements of Parton's career.

Dolly: A fairy godmother to us all

Growing up in the South, Dolly Parton was an intrinsical part of our cultural fabric. But also, as a young gay male growing up in a rural, conservative area of the States, Dolly was almost a fairy godmother to me. She represents everything that gay men are naturally drawn to, including glamour, sequins and a larger-than-life personality. Like those other blonde bombshell gay icons – Madonna, Mae West and Marilyn Monroe – Dolly was a caricature of glamour and sex appeal. But Dolly is distinct in that beneath her blonde bombshell and garish image is something that gay men also gravitate towards: something maternal and accepting. Dolly embraces her diverse fan base with open arms and an open spirit. Gays, conservatives, liberals, drag queens, working folk, young and old, she is the accepting and loving fairy godmother to us all. She gives us something that we often don't find in society or even in our own families: she gives us faith, love, acceptance and down-home wisdom with the absence of judgement. Few if any popular artists have been able to appeal to a diverse fan base and accept and love them for exactly who they are. She's a diva in the sense that she wears glamorous costumes, towering wigs, diamonds and rhinestones, but what makes Dolly different from other divas is that she is without superficiality or a sense of entitlement. Dolly considers her career and artistry as a form of mission work: always glorifying God, and never herself; always working for positivity and her responsibility to help others, not self-service. More than a diva, Dolly is a disciple. A disciple of God, humanity, faith, acceptance and kindness.

Backwoods Barbie: 1946–63

Dolly Rebecca Parton was born on 19 January 1946 in Sevierville County, Tennessee, the fourth of twelve children. Dolly was raised in extreme poverty in the foothills of the Smoky Mountains. Because she and her siblings were raised without the conveniences other families may have enjoyed, individuality and personal identity were of little concern to such 'mountain people', as basic survival was at the forefront of their minds. And yet the resultant lack of focus on personal identity and individualism spurred Dolly on to be as original as she could be, even though she and her family lacked the finances and the luxury to be able to encourage and nurture one's own emerging personal identity. But Dolly seems to have been born with an impeccable talent for songwriting and wisdom beyond her years, and with this set out to gain all her heart desired.

A quest to be noticed, loved and appreciated would drive Dolly from poor Appalachia to stardom, where every facet of her image and personality was carefully constructed so that the Smoky Mountain girl of humble beginnings would come to be loved and appreciated worldwide.

At the beginning of her career, Dolly's image could be said to reflect a country girl's idea of glamour. This Backwoods Barbie image was rebellious in nature; young Dolly was on her own, forging her own career and appearing the way she wanted. An over-exaggerated femininity was Dolly's outer representation of a concept of a country girl rising out of Smoky Mountain's very masculine world and setting her own path. Dolly's early look earned her the title of the 'Blonde bombshell of the Smokies' by reviewers (Jack Hurst, cited in Schmidt 2017: 22) who initially saw her as a beautiful, blonde hillbilly, but once they began to interview her, and to listen to her songs, they began to realize that she was 'much more than her beauty' (Hurst, cited in Schmidt 2017: 10). This Backwoods Barbie image served Dolly two purposes: it allowed her to look the way a poor country girl always imagined, and also allowed herself to be distinct from the crowded pool of female country singers. Instead of constructing her early image to fit into the mould of what female country singers were supposed to look like, Dolly constructed her own distinct image. In this way, Dolly's first image speaks of a certain imagining of localized glamour, and homemade divadom, that relates quite specifically to a time and a place not favoured with a sense of cultures of privileged divadom. First fans of Dolly were able to appreciate an authentic articulation, 'errors' and all, of the image of the nascent singing star – and one that radically broke with previous models of glamour (as associated with Hollywood of the 1920s and 1930s, or the pin-up girl model remembered fondly by American servicemen serving overseas).

Dumb Blonde: 1964–73

As Dolly began her early career, she began to extend the Backwoods Barbie image for which she had become known. Specifically: because Dolly had grown up without 'luxuries' such as makeup, eye shadow, perfume or wigs, she had to construct her image based on whatever items she was able to make, or obtain from others. To her, exaggerated beauty, femininity and sexuality were her ways of resisting the arguably diminishing experience of her poor upbringing where beauty and femininity were not encouraged, nor appreciated. To Dolly, image matters then were no gimmick.

Soon after moving to Nashville, Tennessee, Dolly began to find jobs as a songwriter for various record companies before releasing her first album of songs penned completely by her. The album *Hello I'm Dolly* (1967) was a manifesto of sorts, in that it challenged men's views of women, Appalachia's treatment of women and Southern culture's representation of women. Songs such as 'Dumb Blonde' called out the men who judged her exclusively on her outer appearance and assumed she was a naive blonde, lacking in depth or intelligence. This tendency has remained something Dolly has consistently challenged in her career ever since. 'Dumb Blonde' then was Dolly's particular way of announcing to her audience, and to those in the music business, that she was not as naive or unintelligent as her exterior portrayed her to be. Soon after the release of *Hello, I'm Dolly*, Dolly was invited to be the new 'girl singer' on the widely popular *Porter Wagoner Show* (1960–81). Dolly's acceptance on the show was not a given, as she had just replaced an extremely popular costar to Wagoner, Norma Jean. And yet Dolly began to gain or earn that acceptance as her costumes became gaudier, her wigs bigger, her makeup extravagant and her jewellery more flashy. Dolly seemed to know that by crafting an original, over-the-top outer image, audiences would be drawn in and captivated. Of her image in this period, Dolly stated, 'I don't know if I could ever look normal. It's like Groucho [Marx] without his cigar, or [Adolf] Hitler without his mustache. People take me more seriously now' (Cited in Schmidt 2017: 78). This quote shows that Dolly understood that to be truly captivating to an audience, she would have to create a persona that would be instantly recognizable and beloved. She knew she had to use her natural and exaggerated assets to her advantage, and this tactic worked: Dolly began to eclipse Wagoner as the true star of the programme, to his annoyance and jealousy (Schmidt 2017: 46). Dolly continued to sing her songs of women's rights and treatment, life in poor Appalachia and songs about the human condition. Wagoner insisted she stop singing 'sad ass songs' (as Dolly described his understanding of them; cited in Abumrad and Oliaee 2019), which he felt did not match her outer exterior of glam, glitz and sex appeal. Despite Dolly's dismay at the prospect, she agreed to sing love song duets with Porter. But she knew that this was only a temporary arrangement, as she was building a devoted fan base and had plans to expand that base to include a more diverse audience.

As her stardom rose, Dolly duly eclipsed Porter in popularity. Her image in this period seemed to reflect that desire of hers to be her own individual: towering wigs, brightly sequined clothes and heavy makeup, so standing out from Porter, and gaining the attention of audiences. Dolly stated that in this period that she would like to be the 'female Elvis', a singer who had 'great magnetism, and that great mysterious thing, that great love, that charisma and magic to draw people to her, that can help people in many ways just through her music' (Cited in Schmidt 2017: 118).

Dolly's glitzy and glamorous image now helped her to stand out from her female country music peers, and also gain the same kinds of recognition and admiration as other glitzy and glamorous singers – such as Presley. Dolly's glamorous image in this period also arguably served another purpose; not only to stand out from Porter, as noted, but to preemptively erode any potential ways in which others would come to seek to control every aspect of her career and talent.

In these respects, the image that evolved was more than just an appearance: it was the locus of self-determination, a degree of autonomy, but within the confines of expectations of the appearance of a country singer. Essentially, this image was power. And this strategy occurred during parallel thought associated with second wave feminism – albeit, in Dolly's case, with no resort or embrace of second wave feminism. In terms of framing an understanding of that power, the concept of the diva, then, becomes fundamental.

Light of a clear blue morning: 1974–5

In 1974, Dolly Parton decided to leave *The Porter Wagoner Show* for a solo career. Porter, along with country music journalists, called the move a nail in the coffin of her career: these primarily male commentators felt that Dolly could not make it on her own, without her male duet partner and boss (Cited in Schmidt 2017: 46). Dolly refused to be deterred by their doubts or negativity. During her tenure on *The Porter Wagoner Show*, Dolly was evolving into a fully realized star: she did not tone down her image, though executives and Porter himself told her to, and her songwriting flourished. By now, Dolly had cemented herself in a country music consciousness as not only a glamorous Dixie diva but a talented and prolific storyteller/songwriter. Porter refused to let Dolly out of her contract, saying that she 'owed' him her success and, without him, her career would be non-existent. Instead of stooping to the levels of threats and manipulation, Dolly decided that the best way to get through to Porter was to use her gift of songwriting. Thus Dolly composed her classic song 'I Will Always Love You' (1973) as both a farewell and plea to Porter, begging him to understand that though she was thankful for all that he had given her, it was time for her to have her own career as a solo artist. Porter finally relented and released Dolly from her contract.

Now Dolly was free to craft her own career and moves towards stardom without the help of or reliance on any male executive. In an interview with *The Tennessean* during this period, Dolly stated: 'I've always pretty well done things my own way as far as my personality is concerned, but now I want to do things more my way than I have in the past. I was proud to be a part of Porter and his show, but now I have a chance to carry on and do things my own way', (Cited in Schmidt 2017: 48). This interview highlighted Dolly's excitement at her new-found independence, and also her acknowledgement that she was now free to be exactly the kind of songwriter and star that she wanted to be.

Shortly after leaving Porter Wagoner and his show, Dolly adopted a Gypsy style and butterfly logo which, according to her, represented that new-found freedom. The Gypsy image was furthered by her band, now named the Gypsy Fever Band. Both Gypsy iconography and butterfly represented her freedom from male bosses and superiors and her demeaning or limiting label as a 'girl singer'. Dolly, these moves announced, was now free to find her own style, voice and independence. Dolly toned down her towering wigs and glittering costumes and donned Gypsy, and even hippie, apparel, as resonant of such freedoms. (One could note in passing the dramatic art of Mervyn LeRoy's tale of a singer breaking free from her domineering mother, in the 1962 film *Gypsy*, or even Jimi Hendrix's 1970 live album, *Band of Gypsys* – a sense of travelling musicians, unencumbered by contractual obligations to major record companies, joining Hendrix once he had left the UK.) But this Gypsy image of Dolly would be a short experiment, even if it was necessary for Dolly's personal and professional growth. As she learned to be on her own, and embraced independence, she came to crave further stardom: she would, then, merge her past Backwoods Barbie image with one that was even more glamorous and over-the-top. Thus both diva reinvention and consistency.

Star of the show: 1976–9

After Dolly left Porter's show, and after her short-lived Gypsy period, Dolly began to hunger for wider acclaim and a more diverse audience, hearkening back to her goal of becoming the 'female Elvis'. Dolly set out to achieve a crossover from the small and targeted country music fan base to a broader audience. She began to tour, created her own variety show (1976–7), and began to record the kinds of music that Porter would not allow. In this, Dolly had begun to construct the career she always envisioned, without the help of her male superior or male record executives who sought to control her image and songwriting. During this period, Dolly's fan base grew from country music fans to women who were attracted to, and applauded, her bravery in donning such an over-the-top and glamorous image, and to children who saw her as an almost fairytale-like character, who embodied magic and all things fantastical, and to men who saw her as a sex symbol. In her careful calculations, she was able to be all three of these things. Male country music reviewers began to focus on her sex appeal, and in interviews in *Playboy*, *Playgirl* and *Rolling Stone*, her image and sexuality were usually at the forefront of these male interviewers' minds.

Undeterred or offended by this focus on her sexuality, Dolly playfully and brilliantly toed the line between her Mae West-type vixen image and one of an estimable songwriter and astute businesswoman. She stated in an interview:

> People have thought I'd be a lot farther along in this business if I dressed more stylish and didn't wear all this gaudy getup. Record companies have tried to change me. I just refused. If I am going to look like this, I must have a reason. It's this: If I can't make it on my talent, then I don't want to do it. I *have* to look the way I choose to look and this is what I've chose. It makes me different a little bit and isn't that what we all want to do: to be a little different?
>
> (Cited in Schmidt 2017: 86)

If considered in respect to the aspiration to be the 'female Elvis Presley' – at this time unmatched in celebrity or financial status – then it would seem that Dolly was refusing to be limited because of her gender, so seeing herself as a comparable and potentially worthy equal to a very male, and supremely successful, superstar. This period saw Dolly reinvent herself for a broader audience through a transition from making traditional country music to a more pop-oriented and contemporary sound. The 'refusal' noted earlier was seemingly now no block to this: the image had attained its own autonomy, with the diva figure – anticipating more contemporary icons in pop – free to switch from one genre of music to another.

Working girl: 1980–9

At the start of a new decade, Dolly began a further crossover journey: from a moderately well-known country singer to a full-fledged movie star. While such a crossing over was criticized by Wagoner and some male country music reviewers as selling out, her transition to contemporary pop music was welcomed by most of her fans and the music industry, (Cited in Schmidt 2017: 127). With pop-oriented hits like 'Here You Come Again' (1977), Dolly emerged as a new and rising sensation in the pop universe. Dolly had intuited that financially and professionally, country music could only offer so much success and notoriety. So, in order to transcend the small, targeted country music domain of fandom, she would have to embrace and record pop- and disco-style records. In response to the criticism that followed, Dolly stated

> I want to take my music into new areas that I have never taken it before. I have had a large following in the contemporary field for a number of years, but I'd just never really gone on their territory. But that doesn't mean that I won't still be doing country, because I will. I love the public, but I have no fear of them. I don't want to offend country fans because I love them most of all. I'm doing this because I enjoy it. I'm not gonna stand still for nobody.
> (Cited in Schmidt 2017: 57)

This interview highlights another key dive facet: resilience, finessing desires to cross over to other music idioms, and the attendant criticism of as much.

During this period, Dolly's image became still flashier and more over-the-top: Dolly was emulating the glitz and glam of 1980s fashions but adapted to fit her own distinct Dolly image. The wigs were bigger, the makeup still more exaggerated, and the clothing more sparkly. This showcased the way in which Dolly was able to take on trends in fashion without losing or diminishing her distinct personality and, by now, 'brand' image. While it could seem as if Dolly was simply adapting to ever-changing fashion and trends, in this transition she could more accurately be said to effectively be critiquing them, and re-designing or re-tooling them to fit her own style. In this way, the free-ranging diva effectively advances the evolution of fashions and looks of the time too.

Workin' 9 to 5: Dolly's transition to Hollywood

Further to this reinvented image, of the late 1970s and early 1980s, Dolly found herself cast in a lead role in the self-consciously feminist and 'Women's Lib' Hollywood comedy *9 to 5* (Colin Higgins, 1980) alongside two equally strong and (by now) stars, albeit of different routes into the public imagination: actress/

activist Jane Fonda and comedian Lily Tomlin. The theme song to the film, written by Dolly, perfectly complimented the film's message of women's rights, of fighting against patriarchal oppression, and of female empowerment – indeed, elements already present in her early songs. The film was a critical and financial success, with Dolly praised as being a natural-born actress. Further films such as *The Best Little Whorehouse in Texas* (Colin Higgins, 1982), *Rhinestone* (Bob Clark, 1982) and *Steel Magnolias* (Herbert Ross, 1989), solidified Dolly in the Hollywood firmament as a serious popstar and actress. In this, Dolly achieved what she had set out to accomplish, which was to bring her name and image to a large, diverse fanbase. Film was an ideal medium: Dolly could be herself while playing fictional characters.

As Dolly Parton transitioned into a film career, her image shifted again to represent a multi-faceted entertainer. Although she did not lose her glamorous and over-the-top image of the late 1970s, Dolly decided to introduce, and reintroduce, herself to the general public in such a new and yet familiar way. Dolly had been offered film roles in the late 1970s, but she stated that she did not want to play a character that was separate from herself. Instead, Dolly advised that she would only take film roles in which she could play herself. Her roles in *9 to 5*, *The Best Little Whorehouse in Texas* and *Rhinestone* are, indeed, in essence, Dolly playing herself. These performances highlight how Dolly wishes to maintain her individuality and well-constructed image, even while playing fictional characters. This represents a characterization complexity familiar from Star Studies academic disciplines: performing oneself performing a role. That is: a kind of double presence on the screen from the star – and so the basis of a star performance. From a diva perspective, this is also quite familiar, particularly with respect to opera divas – the sense of an irreducible star presence, shining through the particulars of the performance of fictional characters.

Hollywood to Dollywood: Dolly builds an empire

During the late 1980s, Dolly shifted her focus from music and her film career to focus on becoming an entrepreneur. This entrepreneurship started with the creation of the theme-park Dollywood, which opened in 1986 in Pigeon Forge, Tennessee. Opening Dollywood meant that not only was Dolly able to showcase her Smoky Mountain heritage, but also give something back to the place that formed her. Dolly evolved from a country music star to a fully-fledged businesswoman – a further verification of what in which she must not be considered to be a product of anyone but herself: no dumb blonde, as per this demeaning term, but an astute businesswoman and entertainment mogul. Dolly spent the greater half of the late 1980s and early 1990s concentrating on Dollywood and its growth.

This represented something of an acknowledgement that her popularity and airplay on country music radio stations were dwindling, and so diversification of a Dolly portfolio was needed. Besides Dollywood, Dolly branched out to open the dinner theatre spectacular *The Dixie Stampede* (first produced in 1988): a Civil War-inspired dinner theatre that proved to be an instant success. Dolly's image in this period transformed once again: from country singer and artist across a variety of media outlets into a businesswoman. But, again, the formative experiences determined this course: from the lessons of her solo career to the ways in which male superiors had treated her. While country music politics and its shift into commercialism left Dolly behind musically, she thrived in her business ventures which cemented her as a brilliant and lasting artist and icon. As with the film performances, Dolly adopted, chameleon-like, a new role – but one that was uniquely her.

Hungry again: 1990–2000

The 1990s saw Dolly shift from an icon to a staple of American culture. Dolly eclipsed and transcended any one category of performer – achieving something which has eluded her template aspiration: Elvis Presley. Dolly began to focus on the type of music and projects that she felt would best complement her personal style and would also help her achieve musical prestige. During the 1990s, country music had become fully, industrially commercial, with young country artists typically manufactured by record companies instead of organically grown. Dolly now had to compete with the 'new country' of this culture: one that focused on overtly sexual cowboy figures, drinking hymns and women who embraced their sexual prowess. And, now over forty, Dolly would have seemingly been deemed 'too old for radio'. Though Dolly's country albums were critically praised, country radio had shifted to only play the new and young country artists such as Garth Brooks, Reba McEntire and Shania Twain. Even though her business empire thrived, her film roles were plenty and her star power was still unmatched, the ever-changing landscape of the music industry and its move towards manufactured artists left Dolly hungry for a return to the type of music that she had written and recorded in her earlier career. These were the songs that dealt with the real trials and lives of Southern women and Appalachian people. In stark contrast to the manufactured country music of the 1990s, and finding a closer alignment to the emotional 'authenticity' that underpinned grunge during the early years of this decade, Dolly's songwriting dealt with the reality of the human condition and the struggles of human existence.

During the late 1990s to early 2000s, Dolly's dream of four decades before, of becoming a country star, then superstar (and then mogul) had come true. Her image had evolved in each decade of her career, so that she was now a patchwork of different images and styles, melded in a way that were all still distinctly her. Even with the yearning for a return to her simple roots and earlier music, Dolly's glamour and style still remained intact. But the image deepened earlier characteristics, harking back to her beginnings as an Appalachian girl whose voice and storytelling transcended genres. Her image and sound during this era took on a more organic feel and sonic patina, as Dolly strove to reconnect with the heartbeat of the Smoky Mountains and her own origins.

Little sparrow: 2001–7

During the early 2000s, and in the context of the culture of manufactured and younger country music artists, the unimaginable happened: Dolly was dropped by her record label. Unlike some contemporaries who, without a record deal, simply retired, Dolly aimed to take her power and her creative control back. Dolly created her own record label and began to produce her albums so that she could write, produce and release the type of music that she desired without interference.

Dolly's return to her musical roots saw experimentation with bluegrass and traditional mountain music. Dolly's new albums were filled with stories about heartbreak, redemption, life in Appalachia, women's role in society and spiritual evolution these albums included the critically admired *The Grass is Blue* (1999), *Little Sparrow* (2001) and *Halos and Horns* (2002). Dolly used this period, and her new-found freedom, to reveal a part of herself that had been overshadowed in previous decades by her meteoric rise to fame and over-the-top image. Beneath the glitz and the glam, Dolly revealed, again, that formative part of herself that was present in her early years as a singer. Though commercially unsuccessful, her new, experimental albums were praised by the critics who saw Dolly reconnect with the raw, truer parts of herself – no longer encumbered by the image of Dolly that had evolved. Dolly spent this part of her career considering or developing her own perception of herself as a genuine songwriter and storyteller, rather than on the public or music industry's perception of her. This period, for some, renewed enthusiasm for Dolly, both professionally and personally.

During this time, Dolly's over-exaggerated costumes, glitz and glamour were toned down, representing Dolly's yearning to reconnect with her simple, organic roots. Dolly was able to let her public focus on what truly was her talent: her songwriting and voice.

Iron butterfly: 2008–22

Unlike many of her predecessors and contemporaries, Dolly refused to become a relic of the past or let herself be confined to popular lore. Instead, Dolly began to reinvent herself, once again, as a phenomenon. After spending the previous decade working on experimental albums, Dolly was clearly ready to evolve once again. And, as if emerging from a cocoon, Dolly set out to reintroduce herself to her fans, and the public, as a determined and inspired songwriter, and living icon, who was again ready to rise to the top. This reemergence – renaissance, even – also allowed Dolly to connect to a new generation of fans who were unversed in her journey and backstory. Dolly utilized the rise of social media to market herself in a way that no other country artist had ever done: not only to advertise her projects but also to cement herself, once again, in the popular imagination. From memes to tweets, Dolly began to promote her brand and image in a way that was accessible and appealing to a mass and diverse audience.

Dolly now ventured to Broadway, composing more music for the musical adaption of *9 to 5*, starred in and produced films, released new albums which were followed by sold-out stadium tours, and expanded her empire to include merchandise, food, novels and her perfume 'Scent from Above'. To the media, Dolly was having a comeback, and riding the crest of a wave of new forms of mass communication. But to Dolly, she was simply re-introducing herself. Dolly's image for the present incarnation of her career remains a patchwork of her previous image styles: both the glamorous and over-the-top image of the late

1970s and 1980s, the business savvy mogul and her earlier Backwoods Barbie incarnation. Which other living entertainers are able to create a caricature of themselves without becoming totally enveloped by it? Dolly's artistry now appears to be the way in which she fashions images for both her personal and professional use and evolution.

Light of a clear blue morning: The Dolly renaissance

While other icons have lost themselves to the public and the media's expectations of who they should be, sometimes with fatal consequences, Dolly Parton has never compromised herself in order to gain acceptance. Instead, she has taken on many different facets of her personality in order to attract a diverse and loyal fan base. To some, she remains a glamorous icon worth emulating. To others, she is a sex symbol. And many see her as a talented songwriter who can access the depth of human experience of her times. Like the colours of her famous childhood 'Coat of Many Colours', Dolly is a collection of many distinct parts, that come together to make a beautiful and brilliant whole. Despite her many transformations and evolutions, Dolly has retained her image as someone who dares to be different and reinvents herself continually to adapt to or for each generation. Dolly's career is currently in the stages of a renaissance due to a mixture of her devoted fans, a new social media following and the ever-growing desire for nostalgia in popular culture. If anything, Dolly's consistency with her image and public persona has grounded her in the popular imagination as a familiar and reliable presence and figure. In uncertain times, Dolly Parton and her image have proven to be a beacon of consistency.

Few if any celebrities have undergone the physical and artistic metamorphosis that Dolly has. And yet every image Dolly has acquired or created has been distinctly her. The ability to adapt to each decade without losing oneself is a gift and an artistic project in itself. In this, Dolly's evolution across nearly half a century comes to illustrate an essential aspect of the diva: the constant star presence, irrespective of context. And, despite each period of her career having its own distinct 'brand' and style, they all were essentially Dolly: from Backwoods Barbie to glitzy and glamorous star, to torch song songbird hearkening back to her roots, to a global icon . . . all have been Dolly expressing her inner self and aspirations in a physical and professional manner, to a global audience.

Reference

Abumrad, J. and S. Oliaee (2019), 'Sad Assed Songs', *Dolly Parton's America* podcast, 15 October. WNYCStudio. Available online: https://www.wnycstudios.org/podcasts/dolly-partons-america/episodes/sad-ass-songs (accessed 1 November 2022).

Edwards, Leigh H. (2018), *Dolly Parton, Gender, and Country Music*, Indiana: Indiana University Press.

Hamessley, L. (2020), *Unlikely Angel: The Songs of Dolly Parton*, Urbana: University of Illinois Press.

Schmidt, R. L. (2017), *Dolly on Dolly: Interviews and Encounters with Dolly Parton*, London: Omnibus, 2017.

4

A fondness for shock

The celebrated outburst of Grace Jones

Mark Duffett

In 2006, to mark the launch of its nostalgic programme, *Wogan: Now and Then*, the UK TV network channel, Gold, ran a poll in Britain among 2,000 viewers to find the 'most shocking' moments in international chat show history (BBC 2006). Grace Jones's November 1980 appearance on *The Russell Harty Show* topped the listing, beating moments such as the Sex Pistols' famous expletive-laden 1976 Bill Grundy interview (which came sixth) and Tom Cruise's infamous 2005 appearance on *Oprah* (ninth), during which he hyperactively enacted his feelings about being in love. In other words, if dedicated fans loved Grace for her videos and concerts, the wider public had a TV appearance from twenty-five years earlier foremost in this mind. Gold's head James Newton expressed the complexity of the show's reception when he added, in a BBC news story, that such moments were ones 'which people throughout the country talked about at the time and still remember with great fondness' ('Jones Slap . . . ' 2006). The 'shock' was not simply an occasion for moral outrage, but either always had been, or had gradually become, recouped as something seen with 'fondness'. What is interesting here is why was there such 'fondness'? For many people, some perhaps now of an older generation, Grace Jones is the epitome of divahood. Anthony Haden-Guest ended his 1997 'biography' of the New York discotheque Studio 54 with a 'cast list' that recorded the occupations of its habitués: writers, photographers, publicists, paparazzi and so on. Next to Grace, he simply wrote, 'diva' (389). Reviewing one of her 2008 shows, *Times* journalist David Sinclair called her a 'Headstrong Diva . . . at her Exotic Best' (13). Rather than a moment of mere 'slap' or 'fisticuffs', her *Russell Harty Show* appearance was a performance that had complex cultural resonances. My argument about Jones's diva moment is that it emerged as a sign of the times: both an economic symptom and artistic strategy, as well as an inscription of identity.

To begin, it is worth considering Robin James's (2008) discussion of 'Robo-diva R&B'. Drawing on the innovative work of Kudwo Eschun (1998), James argues that 1980s Black robotic electro and breakbeat acts reversed the 'classic '60s [rock] myth' (404) in which White male musicians equated pre-industrial Black male blues performance with an authentic expression of heterosexual swagger. This cross-racial reading, which Eschun suggested, seems apt, albeit one that ignores the complexity of geographically separated, cross-*class* dynamics involved the cross-racial patronage of the British invasion era. On the basis of the claim that Black female sexuality has been positioned as a doubly compounded threat to the social order, James further extends this usurpation of organic 1960s thinking, to say that the adoption of cyborg technology by women is itself threatening and feminine and that Black female robotic performers only emphasize the threat:

> Thus, to adopt the aesthetic of the robo-diva is to throw in White patriarchy's face what it most fears – black women and Black femininity . . . as competent, empowered agents of their own destiny, whose very existence challenges the political and aesthetic norms of White patriarchy.
> (James 2008: 417)

In recent decades the notion of 'divahood' has been reclaimed and applied by those of Black and queer identities: in other words individuals who face multiple forms of oppression in the light of how their identities are socially perceived. The era of identity politics has reinforced this to the extent that discussion of divahood is almost always about empowerment. Specifically, in relation to Grace Jones, however – who is a kind of prototype figure in this debate – James cites Eschun, saying, 'Jones, as both a Black woman – implicitly farther from embodying White beauty norms – and as a model – who is expected to embody the ideal perfectly – requires a greater-than-average degree of [technological] alteration' (2008: 408). This is a complex argument. To begin to address it, Grace Jones's emergence as a diva needs more social context. Rather than simply dismissing Grace on *The Russell Harty Show* as committing an act of personal vengeance, or worst still as 'mad' or intoxicated, it might be better to locate her action in relation to the social changes and discussion going on around popular music and pop in particular in the era.

If we are to consider Grace Jones in her time (and not just in our own), we should explore the kaleidoscopic social changes that occurred between the late 1960s and late 1980s: a time of 'creative destruction' (Harvey 2007: 3) in which computer tech usurped industry in Western nations as engines of profit. This was associated with a series of momentous changes summarized in the exemplary debate from forum contributors to *The Journal of Modern European History* geographic: social dislocation, postcolonialism and the rising social status of marginalized people such as gay men, women and people of colour. While one might imagine that their comments only apply to a European context, different parts of the world had long been interlinked in various ways. Despite a range of viewpoints, a broad summary of the changes is as follows: left-wing paternalism and welfare were reversed in a complex phase which saw the rise of militant right-wing liberalism, privatization and market deregulation. The Keynesian consensus of the post-war economic boom crumbled. Industrial society's gradual collapse was reflected by the rise and fall of Marxism, both in terms of academic discussion and labour organization, 'before the new norm of high inflation, rising unemployment and low growth . . . [in which] welfare states also passed into crisis' (Wirsching et al. 2011: 13). As part of this change, 'What we now call globalization deprived social democrats of their ability to manage national capitalisms in the interests of their working class supporters' (15).

What matters here is that historians rightly describe the turbulent shifts *as the opposite of a smooth transition*: as a 'turning point' in European history (Wirsching et al. 2011: 8), 'the end of industrial society' (10), where 'circumstances changed very rapidly' (12), 'welfare states passed into crisis' (13), 'profound ruptures occurred with the past . . . during the turbulence of 1967–74' (14), where we saw 'the violent denouement of European decolonization' (16).

This moment of 'creative destruction' was associated with significant social and political transformations. The women's liberation movements and changes to the family happened alongside the shift towards a post-industrial economy. New technologies both created a demand for skilled labour and increased wage inequalities (Woods 1998). Rather than creating communal unity, the emerging era was alienating and fragmenting.

Postmodern pop

I don't believe personally that rock'n'roll is meant to endure through the ages as great art. That's what makes it so great – it's 'now'; it's me, right now. Use it, dispose it, throw it away. Forget it. But then there was like this sense of defeat

[in the early 1970s], of defeatist music, and now it's totally into an escapist thing: Elton John, and disco, and [all] this. People want slick, shallow music. Superficial: here today and gone tomorrow.
(Lester Bangs on *Whatever Gets You Through The Night*, 1977)

Social shifts were registered in the mass adoption of 'pop art' sensibilities (which merged art and advertising) and 'the rise of postmodernism in the arts and human sciences' (Wirsching et al. 2011: 19). It is interesting, for instance, to consider the way in which genres emerging in the 1970s and 1980s began to herald a significant reformulation of pop.

Glam rock had been an early response, embracing postmodern forces which mixed rock and pop, art and business. Tony Palmer's seminal music documentary series *All You Need Is Love* aired an episode on 'glitter rock' in May 1977 in which the famous critic Lester Bangs opined:

> In Roxy Music what you see is the triumph of artifice, because what they're about is that they're not about anything. Musically, they are an incredible synthesis of a lot of things, but I think their longevity and vitality will be quite limited due to the fact that the leader of this group is a fellow named Bryan Ferry who is possibly the most vacuous excuse for a superstar that has yet been presented to us ... He doesn't care about rock'n'roll at all. The ascendance of these people is an indication of the level to which rock has sunk. It's appearance and artifice. There's nothing, I believe, truly committed, about either a Bryan Ferry or a David Bowie. It's much more a using of rock for their own ego aggrandizement rather than a belief in the music they're working with.
> (*Whatever Gets You Through The Night*, 1977)

Bang's thinking painted the late 1960s as a watershed where the leading rock musicians appeared to be deeply committed to music, politics and art, and the time since then as a retreat in which rock had been drained of its most noble qualities, leaving nothing except music as commodity (vacuity, artifice, *pop*).

As if replying to Bangs, Palmer edited in footage of Bryan Ferry explaining:

> Presenting your music in a kind of fun way helps to attract a wider audience. It is very much a 24 hour business. You have to be totally dedicated to your work, like an actor on a stage, I suppose, when you're doing a tour. Instead of throwing yourself into one part, you have to throw yourself into lots of different parts. I try to write lots of different types of songs with different kinds of mood ... There isn't much time to stop and think, 'What am I doing it for?'
> (*Whatever Gets You Through The Night*, 1977)

In Ferry's thinking, pop is first and foremost a commodity or business. Creating a spectacle is central to it. 'Glitter' is not mere gloss, however, but a medium through which art can be created. The metaphor of the 'actor on a stage' is interesting here as it implies both artifice *and* art.

Glam rock subverted the rock aesthetic of 'honesty' and self-consciously located rock as a pop commodity. Since glam's 'unholy' combination of business, artifice and art proved so popular, for some musicians the next artistic and political step was to create a critique, either in the form of punk, which protested, or new wave music, which subverted glam from within.

As the times got economically, socially and politically turbulent, culturally up-ended, and geographically fragmented, groups with a sense of self-awareness and social conscience began to produce musical commentary that itself negotiated between appalled opposition and subversive participation (see, e.g. Hackett 2019). I am going to suggest this was played out across at least two fields: gender and technology. Bryan Ferry's discussion of the place of gender in his glittering art-commodity spectacle defined the glam aesthetic:

> As well as the stage presentation, you use everything – the packaging of your work, which in the business is called 'product'. Things like album covers, and posters, and souvenir programmes, which you can either totally ignore or take an interest in and try and raise the standard of.
>
> There's a great tradition in advertising of using glamour girls for selling cars through to Coca-Cola. The first album cover we did [for the 1972 *Roxy Music* LP], I sort of had a pin-up girl on the cover, because I thought that was a lethal way of selling any kind of product. That worked incredibly well. Business can be artistic as well.
>
> (*Whatever Gets You Through The Night*, 1977)

In the form of the 'pin-up girl' – the models or supermodels who regularly graced Roxy Music's album covers – female beauty was used to affirm a certain taste, based on a shared sense of the aesthetic, which was one that added the gloss of glamour. Yet it was also window dressing: an ingredient which marketed and propagated the product.

Post-punk and new wave groups critiqued such stances. Sometimes they linked this to the uncritical adoption of technology. A good example was Devo, a male group from Ohio, who began in the art world of Kent State University and went on to become a cult act in the new wave. Like Bangs, their approach was McLuhanesque: society was *devolving* as deindustrialization was deepening material inequality, but distracting with the lure of new consumerism. Technology was at the centre of this: deskilling the workplace, yet also offering new opportunities. The crisis of manufacturing had already taught Western workers that making adjustments to new technology would not bring lasting material benefits. That crisis associated adjusting to technology with false promise.

As a raft of new musical instruments appeared, such as synthesizers and sequencers, they seemed to reflect the pervasive nature of this technological change. For the artists of the new wave, however, technology was not abandoned. Instead it was to be controlled or redirected:

> We always had a healthy interest in technology. We loved new technology when we saw things, but we were also fairly sceptical. So, to me, there were artists that I thought their artwork looked like they worshipped technology – and they were, you know, especially in the entertainment industry. I just see it as something to use or to misuse, and make it more interesting than it was intended to be.
> (*Oral History of Mark Mothersbaugh*, 2017)

With its mechanistic beats, objectifying aesthetic and association with hedonistic consumerism (the party or club night), the 'synthetic music' of disco symbolized the coming of a post-industrial age. The genre became a contested terrain; its emancipating ethos liable to be interpreted as false promise, culture without protest, advertising without product.

In 2017, Devo founder member Mark Mothersbaugh explained:

> There were riots at a number of campuses, but in America, when it got too real for everybody, they all kind of like put their heads in the sand. And everybody went to sleep, and there were no Bob Dylans in 1971.
>
> Instead, what you got was disco, and you got, erm, basically, corporate rock. You got like White rock, like guys on stage that were singing, 'I'm White. I'm a misogynist, and I'm proud of it, and I'm a conspicuous consumer.' I remember describing disco as, 'A woman with a beautiful body but no brain.' So we decided we wanted to do something different.
> (*Oral History of Mark Mothersbaugh*, 2017)

Mothersbaugh's 'beautiful body but no brain' comment could be used to suggest a critique of the *uncritical adoption* of new technology, epitomized in popular music by sequencers which, critics argued, were often used to produce pleasant beats devoid of any political messages. To some ears, the 'woman with a beautiful body but no brain' metaphor might be construed as deeply misogynist – or, perhaps, given that the disco genre famously had its roots in New York's marginalized gay and Black club cultures, something even more resentful or unjust. Mothersbaugh's disavowal of the misogyny of straight White 'corporate rock' suggests that new wave discourse was complex. Perhaps he *wanted* music made by women with brains, *audible in some critical form.*

Grace Jones looms large in such a debate, partly because she began as a modestly successful disco covers artist. Her disco music was not always appreciated because of the materialism it was thought to signify. Consider this 1983 review, for example, from Iman Lababedi (1983), parodying the attitude understood to be embodied in Jones's music in *Creem*: 'Her music? Yuck – jet-setting, hedonistic, cocaine-freaked, blanked-out – double yuck – disco.' Dramatic changes were being played out in the fields of technology, geography, gender and race, and could be critiqued by making music that adopted a pop art approach. Devo symbolized the shifting techno-social-gender dynamics of the era in their video for 'Whip It' which was set on a 'dude ranch' and featured a statuesque diva having her clothes whipped off her by a band member who seemed both nerdish and aggressive:

> You have all the imagery being messed around with that is familiar imagery to people: the ranch, you know; the cowboy mythology of America, down home, with the ranch; the family; mom baking the pie. But then you have this woman that looks like she's Grace Jones, as if she's a refugee from the Alamo here, being *whipped – being whipped!*
>
> (Gerald Casale: *Oral History of Devo*, 2015)

In other words, for Casale, the video for 'Whip It' offered a strange and disturbing pop art take on the complexities of the changing era. It located Grace Jones as a certain iconic 'type': the disco diva as a 'woman with a beautiful [Black] body but no brain'. By the time 'Whip It' was released in August 1980, however, Jones's own trajectory had complicated this interpretation. She was embracing an enlarged, dislocated, post-soul, post-disco, post-punk musical territory.

The miracle of creolization

In a recent discussion with Paul Gilroy, Thomas Hylland Eriksen drew on Richard Price's (2001) term 'the miracle of creolization' and described it as 'the fact that so much inexplicable suffering and misery has led to this wonderful cultural creativity which continues to reverberate throughout the world . . . I mean all the rhythmic music we have mainly comes from that historical experience' (*The Holberg Laureate* . . ., 2019). Later in the discussion, Gilroy explained the dynamics of this process in relation to Civil Rights from the 1960s onwards:

> And then, you know, you get James Brown and Nina Simone and all of these cultural people coming to West Africa and playing in FESTAC [1977 Nigerian cultural festival]. And it's there on film, so you see B. B. King and the voices of East Harlem playing with Fela [Kuti] and playing with African musicians.
>
> That Creole conversation is really something that's being rendered attractive not just to African Americans, not just to Africans, *but also to the people who are consuming these new, emergent, popular forms of Black music as a kind of adjunct to rock music as well.*
>
> (*The Holberg Laureate* . . . 2019; emphasis mine)

What interests me here is *the way in which* the 'miracle of creolization' was entering into popular music in the late 1960s, 1970s and early 1980s, as a way to enhance musical commodities for the White audiences who dominate the mainstream music marketplace 'people who are consuming . . . Black music as a kind of adjunct to rock music'. The tensions of this process can be seen around the Whitening of rock, the ambivalent acceptance of disco, the rejection and eventual embrace of Michael Jackson on MTV, the racial complexity of post-punk and the new pop (where, broadly, punk, funk and glam fused in art music made by White musicians who challenged gender norms), and the complex emergence of World Music.

To put this another way, the 1970s and 1980s were not only a period where there was a cultural trajectory in Western popular and high arts, including music, from modernity (which notionally opposed high art to commerce) to postmodernity (which used art concepts to market mass commodities). Those decades were also an extended moment where the 'miracle of [cultural] creolization' – which stemmed from the diasporic, displaced, postcolonial, aspirational predicament of many of the world's population – provided the creative engine for that process to happen.

Western cultural traditions began to embrace postcolonial, multicultural hybridity. Here, 'the space of the "in-between" becomes re-thought as a place of immense creativity and possibility' (McLeod 2000: 215). The creative industries of the 1970s and 1980s – fashion, art, music, literature – thrived on this new sense of cosmopolitanism, which celebrated racial diversity as an indicator of human liberation, even as economic inequalities were exacerbated. In that sense, I would further return to James's (2008) work, and agree with her invocation of Sandra Bartky's notion of the 'fashion-beauty complex'. This idea pinpoints the high-gloss creative industries that were invigorated by the social shift towards postmodernity, as epitomized in both pop and pop art. However, I disagree with the conclusion that Jones's Black body, in that context, required 'a greater than average' degree of alteration. Instead, I would argue that the 'fashion-beauty complex' thrived on a touch of perceived primitivism that Jones artfully performed.

Grace was not simply, however, the queen of glam. There was something else going on. To understand what that means, I wish to invoke the earlier conversation with Paul Gilroy, where he distinguishes '1% cosmopolitanism' from 'cosmopolitanism from below' (*The 2019 Holberg Conversation . . .* 2019). In other words, the 'miracle of creolization' in the arts draws its very authenticity from the *juxtaposition of or trafficking between* the fraught realities of postcolonial displacement (with its difficult racial encounters and moments of economic exploitation) and the Studio 54 fantasy of globe-trotting, jet-setting cosmopolitanism, where the injustices of racial oppression were supposedly soothed by embracing the dictates of capital and enjoying an overabundance of money.

Rather than an 'immigrant', Jones was a 'nomad': raised by a wealthy Jamaican family and traversing world cities: New York, Paris and London. One could go further, however, by saying that in the fragmented, creolized, global hybrid pop created by Grace Jones, forms of identity arguably lost their folk moorings. It is prescient here to remember Stuart Hall's thoughts from 1992:

> Where would we be, as bell hooks once remarked, without a touch of essentialism? . . . This moment essentializes difference . . . And it is therefore unable to grasp the dialogic strategies and hybrid forms essential to the diaspora aesthetic . . . You can be Black and British . . . The essentializing moment is weak because it naturalizes and dehistoricizes difference . . . [and] we valorize, by inversion, the very ground of the racism we are trying to deconstruct.
> (Hall [1992] 2003: 295)

On the next page, he summed up, 'it is to the diversity, not the homogeneity of Black experience that we must now give our undivided creative attention' (296). Both Hall and Jones were born in Jamaica and rose to prominence in other places.

Both began their lives in countries where, from one perspective, generations with African ancestry lived in colonial exile and were shaped by European colonizers. Such a complex geographic experience helped them understand how race relations and racial oppression operated differently in these diverse and changing locales. For Hall, this consisted in part of being privileged for his relative White skin tone in the Caribbean but pronounced Black and conflated with a range of other people in Britain. Jones's Jamaican family life was shaped by Christian authoritarianism. Her international trajectory was self-defined as a rebellion against, or onstage reworking, of it. Each different location where she lived left its mark. Her accent changed audibly. Her displaced, globalized, fragmented existence was an effervescent source of creativity in her art. In it, her agency was necessarily a kind of oceanic construct – visibly coming and going as she switched careers, artistic styles and collaborators. Like the divas who came in her wake, Jones's agency would necessarily 'vibrate queerly out of range' (Burton 2017: 10) even though, here perhaps by compromise and there perhaps by adjustment, she maintained control the whole time.

If Grace's disco days partly consisted of reworking chansons, her new 1980s period became more experimental. Her Warhol-fostered journey from supermodel to pop star was thus one of enfranchisement: she became *both* the author and the story of the pop commodity, and yet this process was discussed through, and fraught with, the limited possibilities of the glam aesthetic held at the time. Paul Morley's (1981) profile was especially instructive, and written quite soon after *The Russell Harty Show* incident:

> Grace Jones is a purposeless system. Grace Jones is a random event meticulously controlled. Grace Jones is no more than a surrealist object with the shock removed . . . She is nothing in herself. She is only the roles – that is the contradictory roles – she enacts for others.

It is instructive here that Morley both articulated Jones's predicament in relation to the questions of the glam aesthetic, as postmodern 'art into pop', but that he also later became her biographer, in effect collaboratively reasserting the 'nothing-there-ness' (though certainly not 'vacuity') of her celebrity image. Morley comments, for instance, about her being 'a purposeless system' are negated in the same review by claiming that he is not saying she is of no value. There is a sense there of art for art's sake as pop. This approach, however, went further, when Jones *creolized* the new wave. Such blending was elaborated by Alistair Dougall:

Island Records' boss Chris Blackwell had decided to involve himself in shaping his singer's future, calling in the crack reggae rhythm section of drummer Sly Dunbar and bassist Robbie Shakespeare. Whereas her previous records had featured comatose camp standards like 'Send in the Clowns,' 'La Vie En Rose' and 'Autumn Leaves,' *Warm Leatherette* [1980] contained funk/reggae interpretations of songs by adventurous modern songwriters such as Bryan Ferry ('Love Is the Drug') and the Pretenders' Chrissie Hynde ('Private Life').

(Dougall 1984: 2300)

Emblematic of such change was Jones's dub cover of Joy Division's 'She's Lost Control'. Mark Fisher (2006) argued it reworked Ian Curtis's alienation as an objectifying entry into the world of the machine. Post-punk was mainly made by White musicians but adopted elements of dub and other Black music to help express hybridity and alienation. Grace covered glam and post-punk music, not necessarily to return it 'home' to Jamaica, but to express her race as a case of refracted identity. To Russell Harty, when asked 'Do you understand what I'm saying to you?', with a pointed stare she replied, 'No – your accent is a bit foreign', raising laughter from the audience. When he asked if she had been photographed recently, she said, 'No, no, not recently. I think I'm homesick, maybe, right?' Such phrases were provocations, asking political questions about what was to be expected or seen as appropriate in a multicultural society.

Unruly: Grace Jones as (Post-Punk) Rock star

I think Devo's final contingent [message] about the path of rock'n'roll, whatever that is, was that it had gone as far as it could, and I don't care if you bring in world beat music and influence it that way, or bring in reggae and influence it that way, use samples or don't use samples – whatever you want to do, it doesn't have the same power anymore, just as paintings don't have the same power, because, as we race at a faster and faster pace towards bigger and bigger problems of survival, it's inadequate. It's merely relegated to, you know, a runway show.

It's a fashion show. That's all it is.

(*Gerald Casale: Oral History of Devo*, 2015)

For many commentators, the shift from an industrial to a post-industrial society marked a catastrophic political and artistic descent. Grace Jones, however, found a larger audience when she embraced the pop art traditions of glam and the new wave. The idea that 'robo-divahood' threateningly inverted the 'classic '60s [rock] myth' is open to question. Ironically, while new technologies threatened male industrial employment and the masculinity associated with it in the 1970s, Black women had no more claim on embodying such changes than anyone else. The positing of a pre-industrial Black aesthetic among White rock musicians may have held true in the 1960s but, by the 1980s, the situation was more complicated due to the technological shifts. Rock audiences started using figures like Bruce Springsteen to locate an 'authentic' performance of *industrial*-era masculinity. The new technologies of pop often floated new *male* maestros of all races who had different masculinities. There were plenty of male rock and pop bands who thrived on adjusting to the new technological conditions and hybridizing their musical styles, just as there were mixed and female bands who did the same. The tradition of the rebel was ironically reworked too.

In the span of the twentieth century, Black music was often associated with a kind of personal and sometimes sensual freedom. As epitomized by the idea of the juke joint as an illicit space, this association was older than rock'n'roll, and arguably emerged from the highly regimented cultures of manual labour to which many Black folks were subjected during slavery and much of the Jim Crow era (see Murray 1976). Here, Saturday night notionally formed a liberal space of release from the rigours of each working week, and both sides of the equation were, in mythology as much as in actuality, intensified in relation to Black culture as Southern working-class US culture. This notion filtered through the popular arts, particularly jazz and, even before it was embraced in rock'n'roll and articulated to what came later, appealed to a growing minority of White bohemians – such as the jazz player Mezz Mezzrow and the Beats.

In the 1960s, the modelling of 'pre-industrial' Black masculinity by White R&B and then rock musicians gave them their permissive swagger. Rock stars were taken to exemplify such swagger, as referenced in President Jimmy Carter's eulogy for a freshly dead Elvis Presley in 1977: 'He was unique and irreplaceable . . . he was a symbol to people the world over, of the vitality, rebelliousness, and good humor of his country (Carter 1977).' In other words, the project of post-war popular music was indelibly associated with what I would call a 'project of personal freedom,' epitomized by the persona of the White male rock star, whether Bob Dylan, Jim Morrison, Mick Jagger or Axl Rose. According to Leerom Medovoi (1995), individuals with rebellious stances in pop culture became useful to post-war America because, in contrast to the conformity demanded by communist or religious authoritarian regimes, they advertised the benefits of being part of the capitalist 'free world' to postcolonial trading partners. The approach celebrated exceptionalism epitomized in youthful rebellion. Moreover, this exceptionalism's value was *consistent* between the breakout of 1950s rock'n'roll, the communal idealism of the 1960s, and the me-first entrepreneurism of the 1980s.

Grace Jones's 'fit' with such notions of individualism is interesting. Reviewing one comeback show, a *Times* journalist noted: 'Her performance began half an hour late – what else would you expect?' (Sinclair 2008: 13). Such 'fashionable lateness' was also a hallmark of White male rock stars. Such stars had often been described as individualists rather than divas. As Fulgani Sheth (2009) has argued, Orientalism in perceptions of race itself defines racial differences through notions of 'unruly' Otherness. All this raises the question of what being a 'disruptive diva' might mean, and to whom. Grace's rebellion is perhaps easier for people to locate: not as something rocking – though it definitely is punk rocking – but, rather, as a kind of revenge of the social and geographic periphery, an appropriation of music stardom as a rightful assertion of incivility.

It is interesting to compare the Sex Pistols interview with Bill Grundy to Grace Jones's *Russell Harty Show* interview. In Grundy's hands, the taunts came in such forms as asking his guests whether they liked classical composers. When Johnny Rotten said, 'That's just their tough shit', Grundy seized his chance: 'No, no, what was the rude word? . . . Was it really? Good heavens – you frighten me to death!' When Steve Jones piled on further swearing, the host's response was, 'Go on, keep going . . . Say something outrageous . . . What a clever boy.' In other words, Grundy's aim was to expose the distance between the Pistols and 'polite' society, then use that distance to put them down. Now compare some of Russell Harty's lines: 'Have you calmed yourself down, in clothes over the years?' When Grace mentioned eating Thanksgiving turkey, Harty added, 'Or the stuffing, even . . . If you relax her any more, she'll slip off the chair and fall away.' These could be construed as references to sexual availability and stereotypical assumptions about 'looseness' (or in music, 'loose-jointedness') associated with a Black Other. When Jones began to get playfully aggressive, Harty referenced monstrosity: 'It's coming to life! It's coming to life!' Then, when Harty asked Jones if she was wearing perfume, she decides to play for the low position. He asked, 'Are you wearing perfume at all?' She replied, 'No, I've got my body odour perfume.' He came in, pushing his hand downwards, with the stiff upper lip style retort: 'Let's try and keep it on a slightly higher level, if we may?' It was at that moment that Jones's complaints about being ignored escalated. She started to slap him. Ironically, in her memoir (2015), Jones reversed the hierarchy: for treating her with such ill-mannered contempt, for literally turning his back on her, it was Harty who was being uncivilized.

In both the cases of the Grundy and *Harty* shows, relatively haughty, White male interviewers attempted to use the longstanding cultural hierarchy to dismiss their guests. Grundy was goading, swaggering, heterosexual and chauvinist, whereas Harty was more gentle: a gay presenter from a Northern, grammar school background whose affable, empathetic approach regularly won guests and audiences over. Both Grundy and Harty found themselves deposed from the control of the conversation, with guests behaving unconventionally. In their conversational pattern, despite their differences as presenters, their approach was the same. A modified stiff upper lip modus operandi, offered their guests – as hypothesized representatives of a subaltern Other – further space to assume the licence associated with their position and to display its vulgarity, which could then provide precisely the excuse needed to put them in their place for not adhering to a 'correct' standard of civility. It was a ruse: their errant guests would be enticed and ambushed, or so they thought. On *The Russell Harty Show*, Grace Jones opposed the traditional, respectful, but bland turn-taking of the chat show format. She boldly fought back. Perhaps the moment has been remembered so 'fondly' because it epitomized what the cultural conservative Roger Scruton (2007) called a 'world besieged'.

An art of failure?

Watching Harty's show again one is reminded of the Christmas 2007 episode of Ricky Gervais's comedy show *Extras* ('The Extra Special Series Finale'), where the protagonist attempts to move up in the movie industry following his initial role as an extra. After much struggle and success, he finds himself in a much more prominent position only to end up under surveillance as part of the house in the TV series *Celebrity Big Brother*. Apart from the veteran tap dancer and choreographer Lionel Blair, Andy (Gervais) fails to recognize any of the other contestants, which include an *X-Factor* finalist, a member of manufactured pop group, a mother whose son was murdered and a woman who leaked a sex tape of herself on the internet. Through this experience, he realizes that not only have people traded their dignity for fame, but a boundless process of commodification has erased meaningful distinctions between different types of talent, and relocated an unfathomably diverse range of people through one blunt measure: whether they can increase the show's popularity rating. The episode was, of course, metaphorical of the business culture, which disrespects depth, specialization or social care, and instead prioritizes competition organized through universal, levelling metrics which make all workers interchangeable. On *The Russell Harty Show*, the other guests that week were highly diverse: Patrick Litchfield, the glamour photographer whose other claim to fame was that he was the Queen's cousin, the eccentric landscape photographer Walter Poucher and roller-skating clothing designer Tom Gilbey.

We might liken this scenario to a daily ritual in the traditional casual manual work environments of dock workers depicted in *On The Waterfront* (Elia Kazan, 1954), where jobs 'were filled by selecting workmen from a milling crowd seeking employment at the morning "shape-up" or "call"' (Donovan 1999: 68). In these 'shape-up' scenarios, workers would, 'jockey against each other for a job for the day' (*Longshore Workers and Their Unions*, 2012). They were in a ritual in which the cold eye of the marketplace judged mercilessly between competing labour. The entertainment industry and celebrities within it are constantly subjected to such pressures via metrics of competition, whether in the shape of audience ratings, advertising revenue, movie test screenings, catwalk review pieces, music chart positions, streaming counts, Twitter trends, TikTok engagement rates or YouTube hits. In this attention economy, to be ignored is to suffer a death of sorts.

Looking at *The Russell Harty Show* in this way, we can see that the questions the host asked were designed to relegate Grace as a cultural worker who failed to fulfil her role in the freshly reformulated, competitive society of the spectacle. Consider dialogue from the show:

> RH: I thought your costume would be more lavish than that which you appear to be wearing?
> GJ: I'm over-estimated. [Shoots interviewer a glance.]
> RH: By the world at large, or by your public?
> GJ: By everybody I think, yes.
> RH: How do you think you've received this over-estimation? Why's your estimation inflated?
> GJ: That's just a lyric from a song!
> RH: Oh, I do beg your pardon. I thought that was a judgement you were making.
> GJ: No.
> RH: Have you calmed yourself down in clothes over the years?

GJ: Try me!
RH: Are you hearing what I say to you?
GJ: Umm-hmm . . .
RH: Did you have a late night last night?
GJ: I haven't slept in three days.
RH: That explains it. Do you understand what I'm saying to you?
GJ: No – your accent is a bit foreign.
RH: [Hides head in hands.] How shall I go around the back of this, I wonder. Have you been photographed recently?
GJ: Just now, on television?
RH: Have you been photographed as a model recently?

(*Grace Jones – The Russell Harty Show interview + Love is the Drug*, 2017)

It is instructive here that Grace was not exactly competing against traditional, straight White masculinity on the show. Harty's formulation was already somewhat queer. Not only did he describe his struggle to talk to her as being a case of 'have you ever tried to climb the north face of the Eiger in high heeled shoes?' but his other guest that day, Walter Pouter, was an 88-year-old mountaineer and photographer who wore gloves, perfume and make-up especially for his host, in a display of rebellion against traditional, middle-class British masculine norms.

It was almost as if Poucher's departure from the stiff upper lip put him in direct competition with Jones, making Harty forced to choose on behalf of his audience between the equally titillating TV spectacles of a seemingly masculine Black female supermodel and a queer, old White British male. In this context, we can perhaps understand Grace Jones as an agent who inevitably struggled to maintain control in a working environment that was highly unstable.

In the *Times*, Sophie Heawood reported in 2009:

> I had been told by everybody, ever, that Grace Jones would be intimidating. And drunk, and stoned, and a demanding diva, and might not make much sense, and would quite possibly make a pass at me. But the most intimidating thing about her is how unintimidating she is.
>
> (11)

In the same article, the Irish milliner Philip Treacy explained, 'This is the thing, people think she's going to be a monster! And she's not. But she is a trip' (11). He then clarified the 'trip' aspect by explaining how 'everything has to be right' when you work with her. At one point on *The Russell Harty Show* when the host was reading the autocue, introducing the clothes designer Tom Gilbey, Grace explained the fashion business:

> RH: Women can get away with what they like. It's as if they wear a uniform for men.
> GJ: You know why?
> RH: Nevertheless, there are pioneers – Are you going to tell me why?
> GJ: Because men always make the fashion for women, that's why. It's their fantasies.
>
> (*Grace Jones – The Russell Harty Show interview + Love is the Drug*, 2017)

Much of the research on Grace Jones has attempted to affirm her creative agency as a Black female genius working in an idiom where women's contributions are often unrecognized or forgotten. That is a worthwhile project, but it forgets another side of the equation. The idea of the shape-up (with its connotation of getting 'in shape') resonates throughout depictions of key moments in Grace's career. She described Studio 54, for example, as a series of 'minor celebrities fighting among minor celebrities to avoid losing their fame, demented role-playing . . . [and] doing whatever it took to get some attention' (Jones 2015: 159). What seemed to be a high-gloss career was itself distinctly precarious and unstable. Grace moved between the fashion, music and Hollywood film industry, but not with the Machiavellian prowess of, say, David Bowie in his early 1970s heyday – though, certainly, she was a successful model. The earliest part of Grace's career, in modelling, for instance, has been described like this:

> 'I'd never thought about it, honestly! But we took some pictures and next thing, I was off to New York.'
>
> But not before Grace had done a stint as 'a nudist in Philadelphia. Which was good because it helped me to accept myself, accept my body – I used to think I had horrible legs – and accept people, the world.'
>
> In New York, in 1971, Grace immediately began contacting various modelling agencies and although she had some success, she encountered considerable frustrations.
>
> (Nathan 1977)

Similarly, her Hollywood career has been rather erratic. Her entrée into the world of film-making was described thus:

> Finally, she landed a part in *Gordon's War* [Ossie Davis, 1973], after she was asked to act as though she was angry.

'Believe me, that was no problem because by then, I really was fed up with not getting accepted for parts so it came real easy! And I got the part.' This was 1973 and Grace notes: 'There were other parts offered but they had such little depth. Most of the good parts were going to men,' she concludes.

(Nathan 1977)

Such depictions locate Grace's anger not as a 'dotty' personal quirk, but more as an empowered response to the systematic objectification and associated competitive rejection of women in the 'fashion-beauty complex' of the culture industries. Although she has worked as a film and TV actor since 1973 (and consistently since 1978), her acting career has been characterized by a series of minor parts. She has been best known for playing the Amazonian, Zula in *Conan the Destroyer* (Richard Fleischer, 1984), the high-kicking Bond girl, Mayday, in *A View to a Kill* (John Glen, 1985), and the off-edge Strangé in Eddie Murphy's comedy vehicle *Boomerang* (Reginald Hudlin, 1992). None of these roles offered more than a parody of her existing celebrity image. To return to Bryan Ferry's words: 'Instead of throwing yourself into one part, you have to throw yourself into lots of different parts . . . There isn't much time to stop and think, "What am I doing it for?"'

One of the means Jones could use to portray her struggle for control at work was by drawing on assumptions about Black female sexuality, sexual availability and its ambivalent association with high-gloss beauty imposed upon her. To put this another way, and drawing on the work of Audre Lorde (1998) in a world where 'cosmopolitanism from below' leaves some Black women the only option of trading on the associations of their beauty – as sexual objects, as singers – the Black female body has marked a territory upon which a struggle for empowerment and dignity in the face of rapacious commodification takes place. It is, however, also the sovereign territory of the individual woman, who can dramatize her (lack of) choice by acting up to the stereotype.

Jones's playful evocations of sexual availability did not begin or end, of course, with *The Russell Harty Show*. When her partner Jean-Paul Goude was quizzed about his Afrophiliac fetishism and objectification of her, he explained:

When I portrayed Grace Jones naked in a cage chewing on a piece of raw meat, I was attacked for being racist, which is unfair if you consider that Grace always took great pride in behaving like a wild animal. I only dramatized the image she was promoting.

(Hedley 2006: 113)

There is, at least, *something* in this claim: Grace was adept at using her illusion and, gradually, the world became more understanding. As she explained, 'I wasn't born this way. One creates oneself' (quoted in Goude 2016: 61). Like Andy Warhol, she came from a migrant background and relocated the expectations associated with it to shape her art. What she had to sell, visually, in part, were things imposed upon her from the outside: intimations of sexual availability, conceptions of high-gloss female beauty. In the context of left-right politics, this was perhaps a betrayal of sorts: artful irony substituting for direct protest. In the context of gender and the representation of the 'miracle of creolization', however, it was a moment where multiple oppressions could be artistically broached and explored.

Here, being a diva means not simply demanding perfection, but causing a commotion which commodifies by generating publicity. Seen in this way, divahood is not only a shared Black female response to structural racism or, worse still, a uniquely female personal quirk but is instead a mode of economic empowerment in the celebrity economy. Causing a commotion can be located in this context as a strategy of self-assertion (Burns and LaFrance 2002) coded as feminine and perhaps feminist: in music, a way of marketing yourself and having your creativity acknowledged in an environment that might otherwise relegate you to window dressing.

Conclusion

Hannah Yelin has argued that Grace Jones's self-portrayal as an informed pop art or performance art practitioner 'could be argued to be something of a betrayal of other female pop stars as she seeks to escape the cultural field of female pop stardom, with its associated [commercialist] denigrations' (2019: 8). While emphasizing Jones's agency, this claim, I think, misunderstands her postmodern context, something which was *already* drawing art into the service of pop commerce and 'denigrating' *all* artists. Grace Jones's work was a response to that. What she had to sell as a pop singer was a performance and a recording, commodities that could be framed as art. 'Grace Jones' was the result: that much was clear when she appeared in a gold catsuit on another chat show, the *Wogan* show, interviewed by David Frost in 1990 (*Grace Jones – Interview Wogan Show 26.03.90*, 2019):

> DF: Welcome, under-dressed as ever?
> GJ: I said, Mr T [avuncular character actor known from the popular *The A-Team* television series], eat your heart out!

DF: Terrific outfit. How would you describe it for people listening to us on radio?
GJ: I think if I came on stage crawling – and going, 'Meow, meow!' – I think they would get an idea. I'd say, I'm on all fours, and this is the sound. It's a bit sleek, cat-like.
DF: Very much the story of your life, yes! You're touring the country at the moment, on your tour. When did you decide to be this exotic figure Grace Jones: this androgynous, macho, attractive – when did you decide to be larger than life?
GJ: When did I decide to be myself, really? I think that's what you are saying.

Jones's chart heyday was in the early 1980s, a period after second wave feminism, when a Black performer could no longer be Josephine Baker – thrillingly exotic, a bit knowing, but also catering to straight White male desire – yet one could not quite be Beyoncé: entrepreneurial, empowered, and iconic for that and ready to explore one's own oppression and personal vulnerability from a position of supreme strength. As a musical diva, she became the queen of a new economic terrain based on celebrity culture, shrewdly exploring a moment of fragmentation and turbulence in which the power balances of class, race and gender were significantly shifting. Gradually, Grace found her place and reflected the shifts.

Her ascent to musical divahood was distinctly pop (art): in quotes, compared to, say, the doyens of classical Hollywood. Even her 'dancing on the table' days of being discovered in the world of disco were not quite what they seemed: Haden-Guest (1997: 24) reported that in the early years a party promoter 'filled two school buses with celebs and ferried them out to the nightery. And that Grace Jones performed for free'. In tipping the tables in favour of herself, she was part of something contemporary, reflecting an era in which, not only, after glam, was art a part of commercial pop, but also, after punk, *resistance was part of commercial pop marketing.*

The performance continued. In 2006, for instance, after she left a London staging of the musical *Guys and Dolls* in Piccadilly, Hugo Rifkind reported, 'Some stars attack their paparazzi tormentors. Shortly after this picture was taken, Jones kissed hers with such vigour that an excited young photographer was later seen wiping his face dry' (2006: 11). Reporting on a live show three years later, Lisa Verrico (2009: 2) described Grace's performance, saying that, 'In 'La Vie en Rose' she flung her legs round a fan and rode him up an aisle.' Grace continued, periodically, in this vein, arriving late and flashing her breasts at book signings for her autobiography, *I'll Never Write my Memoires*, at the age of sixty-seven in 2015, when such an act might be considered, by some at least, to be déclassé. She has also had her inheritors.

To close, I want to consider another contemporary Black female act in the context of Grace's approach: Janelle Monáe. As the editors of *The International Journal of Screendance* recently explained:

> As we write these opening remarks to our guest edited issue on screendance and race, Janelle Monáe has recently released *Dirty Computer – An Emotion Picture* [Various directors, 2018]. Its tagline states it is a narrative film with an accompanying music album. But Monáe's persistent jabs at the vectors of oppression she navigates as black, femme, and pansexual successfully come together in this Afrofuturist utopian screen fantasy she helms. *Dirty Computer* celebrates love, Black excellence, sex-positivity, Otherness and queerness. While couched within the neoliberal discourses of empowerment and celebrations of selfhood, that Monáe wields creative control attests to the extensive contributions Black women make to global popular culture.
>
> (Borelli and Monroe 2018: 2)

Here the emergent state of us, as post-human-droids, is that we are fused with a make-work machine. By its standards, we are 'dirty computers' since we are hybridized and not efficient enough. This fallen condition is allegorized by stereotypes of Black femininity as sexually available: creolized, loose, 'dirty'. As humans, though, we know it is also a lie. We see this post-industrial technology – with its (wet) dream of fusion – as 'dirtying' us all: offering entertainment in place of remuneration or welfare; locking us down into panoptic grids of surveillance; making burdensome demands on our attention, our time, our effort, our physical and mental health. Perhaps any fondness of the shock of divahood is therefore that it can reveal the lie of this 'dirtiness' and redeem it through a discourse of empowerment. The 'diva' has come to stand for almost any female performer of colour, and the message of divahood is unapologetically uplifting.

Reference

BBC (2006), 'Jones Slap Tops TV Chat Show Poll', *BBC News Channel*, 22 January. Available online: http://news.bbc.co.uk/1/hi/in_pictures/4637648.stm (accessed 3 November 2022).

Borelli, M. and R. Monroe (2018), 'Editorial: Screening the Skin: Issues of Race and Nation in Screendance', *The International Journal of Screendance*, 9: 1–6.

Burns, L. and M. LaFrance (2002), *Disruptive Divas: Feminism, Identity and Popular Music*, Abingdon: Routledge.

Burton, J. (2017), *Posthuman Rap*, Oxford: Oxford University Press.

Carter, J. (1977), 'Statement by the President on the Death of Elvis Presley', 17 August. Available online: https://www.presidency.ucsb.edu/documents/statement-the-president-the-death-elvis-presley (accessed 3 November 2022).

Donovan, A. (1999), 'Longshoremen and Mechanization', *Journal for Maritime Research*, 1 (1): 66–75.

Dougall, A. (1984), 'Living My Life', *The History of Rock*, 10 (115): 2298–300.

Eschun, K. (1998), *More Brilliant That The Sun: Adventures in Sonic Fiction*, London: Quartet Books.

Fisher, M. (2006), 'I, The Object', K-Punk blog, 4 December. Available online: http://k-punk.abstractdynamics.org/archives/008729.html (accessed 3 November 2022).

Gerald Casale: Oral History of Devo (2015), YouTube video posted by Edward Kunz. Available online: https://www.youtube.com/watch?v=Mqtfx5_zD9Q (accessed 3 November 2022).

Goude, J. P. (2016), 'Jean-Paul Goude + Grace Jones', *Fashion + Music*. Available online: https://www.jeanpaulgoude.com/images/presse/2016_Fashionmusic.pdf (accessed 3 November 2022).

Grace Jones – Interview Wogan Show 26.03.90 (2019), YouTube video posted by TravisBickle1963. Available online: https://www.youtube.com/watch?v=BAPRppkZlg8 (accessed 3 November 2022).

Grace Jones – The Russell Harty Show interview + Love is the Drug (2017), YouTube video posted by Fiona Apple Rocks. Available online: https://www.youtube.com/watch?v=XLLtS50UCBQ (accessed 3 November 2022).

Hackett, J. (2019), 'Productive Boredom and Unproductive Labour: Cabaret Voltaire in the People's Republic of South Yorkshire', in L. Brooks, M. Donnelly and R. Mills (eds), *Mad Dogs and Englishness: Popular Music and English Identities*, 106–24, London: Bloomsbury.

Haden-Guest, A. (1997), *The Last Party: Studio 54, Disco and the Culture of the Night*, New York: William Morrow.

Hall, S. ([1992] 2003), 'What is this "Black" in Black Popular Culture?', in J. Gaiger and P. Wood (eds), *Art of the Twentieth Century: A Reader*, 290–6, London: Yale University Press.

Harvey, D. (2007), *A Brief History of Neoliberalism*, Oxford: Oxford University Press.

Heawood, S. (2009), 'Amazing Grace', *The Times*, 23 January, 11.

Hedley, T. (2006), 'The Politics of Jean-Paul Goude', *Dutch*, 110–15.

James, R. (2008), '"Robo-Diva R&B": Aesthetics, Politics, and Black Female Robots in Contemporary Popular Music', *Journal of Popular Music Studies*, 20 (4): 402–23.

Jones, G. (2015), *I'll Never Write My Memoirs*, London: Simon & Schuster.
Lababedi, I. (1983), 'Grace Jones: Are You Ready for a Brand New (Disco) Beat?', *Creem*, April. Available online: https://www.rocksbackpages.com/Library/Article/grace-jones-are-you-ready-for-a-brand-new-disco-beat (accessed 4 November 2022).
Longshore Workers and Their Unions (2012), 'Waterfront Workers History Project, University of Washington', website. Available online: http://depts.washington.edu/dock/longshore_intro.shtml (accessed 4 November 2022).
Lorde, A. (1988), *A Burst of Light: Essays*, New York: Firebrand Books.
McLeod, J. (2000), *Beginning Postcolonialism*, Manchester: Manchester University Press.
Medovoi, L. (1995), *Rebels: Youth and the Cold War Origins of Identity*, Durham: Duke University Press.
Morley, P. (1981), 'Grace Jones: Theatre Royal, Drury Lane, London', *New Musical Express*, 17 October. Available online: https://www.rocksbackpages.com/Library/Article/grace-jones-theatre-royal-drury-lane-london (accessed 4 November 2022).
Murray, A. (1976), *Stomping the Blues*, New York: McGraw Hill.
Nathan, D. (1977), 'Grace Jones: The New Dahling of the Disco Set', *Blues & Soul*, November. Available online: https://www.rocksbackpages.com/Library/Article/grace-jones-the-new-dahling-of-the-disco-set (accessed 4 November 2022).
Oral History of Mark Mothersbaugh (2017), YouTube video posted by Computer History Museum. Available online: https://www.youtube.com/watch?v=YfeLBV3J6NI (accessed 4 November 2022).
Price, R. (2001), 'The Miracle of Creolization: A Retrospective', *NWIG: New West Indian Guide*, 75 (1): 35–64.
Rifkind, H. (2006), 'People', *The Times*, 9 August, 11.
Scruton, R. (2007), *Culture Counts: Faith and Feeling in a World Besieged*, New York: Encounter Books.
Sheth, F. (2009), *Toward a Philosophy of Race*, Albany: SUNY Press.
Sinclair, D. (2008), 'Headstrong Diva is at her Exotic Best in this Sensational Display', *The Times*, 21 June, 13.
The 2019 Holberg Conversation with Paul Gilroy (2019), YouTube video posted by Holberg Prize. Available online: https://www.youtube.com/watch?v=PBntPdPcQes (accessed 4 November 2022).
The Holberg Laureate LIVE: Prof. Paul Gilroy in conversation with Prof. Thomas Hylland Eriksen (2019), YouTube video posted by Holberg Prize. Available online: https://www.youtube.com/watch?v=bEK1g_EJqas (accessed 4 November 2022).
Verrico, L. (2009), 'Pop', *The Times*, 24 January, 2.
Wirsching, A. ed., with G. Therborn, G. Eley, H. Kaelble and P. Chassaigne (2011), 'The 1970s and 1980s as a Turning Point in European History?', *Journal of Modern European History*, 9 (1): 8–26.

Wood, A. (1998), 'Globalization and the Rise in Labour Market Inequalities', *The Economic Journal*, 108 (450): 1463–82.

Yellin, H. (2019), '"I am the Centre of Fame": Doing Celebrity, Performing Fame and Navigating Cultural Hierarchies in Grace Jones' "I'll Never Write My Memoirs"', *Celebrity Studies*, 10: 1–13.

Section two

The diva and our times

5

Aaliyah's voice and after

Benjamin Halligan

A difficult task presents itself: to write about Aaliyah, as encountered in and through her debut album, *Age Ain't Nothing But A Number* (1994), in the light of subsequent, destabilizing knowledge about its creation. Pogus Caesar's mostly unseen, semi-cinéma-vérité *Aaliyah Live in Amsterdam*, shot in 1995, allows for an access to this generative moment. The documentary captures the energy and sass (and slight chaos, and laughter) of the developing live show, interviews with a subject who is canny and savvy, and disarmingly confident, but not quite sufficiently armoured against the media, and a sense of glee, even disbelief, that the music and show are touring 'the world' (or, at least, outside North America, and albeit with some family in tow, making it all a bit of a summer holiday too). The argument of this chapter was to be that a certain dynamic can be tracked across the brief career of Aaliyah Dana Haughton (born 1979) – a dynamic that could be said to represent, in microcosm, the ascendency of the diva figure: clear phases of the evolving hip-hop diva persona, from intimate to global, from singing about individualized experiences to universalizing experiences respectively, from teen Aaliyah alone to adult Aaliyah as superstar. This dynamic would show how a time had come, around the end of the 1990s, for hip-hop to gain its belated place in the mainstream of a wider popular music culture – and position Aaliyah as a catalyst in this traction, with her music suitably bridging the old school and the new school, and so with Aaliyah as a key consideration for this edited collection on divas. The Crunk Feminist Collective (CFC), in 'Hip Hop Generation Feminism: A Manifesto', identify this

> linguistically and rhetorically rich cultural milieu and transformation that was the 1990s, the decade of the woman, but also the decade of the female emcee: Queen Latifah, MC Lyte, Da Brat, Left Eye (and TLC), Foxy Brown, Lil' Kim, and Lauryn Hill. We not only jammed to new jack swing, we reveled in the beats

of new jill swing too, because we understood what Queen [Latifah] meant when she sang, 'In a nineties kind of world, I'm glad I got my girls.'[1]

(Cooper, Morris and Boylorn 2017: xix–xx)

Such a story of renewal in popular music is a familiar one, which David Sanjek identified as a 'Manichean Narrative': 'a battle for supremacy between opposing elements' that structures how we write, think, talk about and feel music cultures (Sanjek et al. 2019: xix).

But those senses of nascent diva intimacy of the early years, which enrich *Age Ain't*, and that I wanted to translate into a sense of Aaliyah and her music's co-created 'vibe', have been perhaps irretrievably sullied. In short – and in drawing on the excoriating information of Iandoli's biography of Aaliyah (2021), the documentary *Surviving R. Kelly* (Lifetime, 2019–20) and coverage of R. Kelly's trial and guilty verdict (of 'run[ning] a scheme to sexually abuse women and children over two decades', as well as standard elements of financial criminality; BBC News 2021) – *Age Ain't*, written and produced by Kelly, now comes to seem to be an artefact of, or even the very process of, the sexually exploitational grooming of an underaged Aaliyah.[2] Even the album's title seems to defiantly proclaim as much. And that predatory, honing-in ambience of sexual suggestiveness – rhetorical stratagems, finessed by 'naughtiness', as offering experience in the name of gaining street cred – seems present, sequentially, in the song titles:

(Track Number/Title)
5. 'Down with the Clique';
6. 'At Your Best (You Are Love)';
7. 'No One Knows How To Love Me Quite Like You Do';
8. 'I'm So Into You';
9. 'Street Thing';
10. 'Young Nation';
11. 'Old School';
12. 'I'm Down'.

Any victim would recognize the talk, and the progression, and establishing and enforcing that circle of abuse and personal reliance in this sequence (as per Loring 1994, and Stark 2007, or even Nan Goldin's 1986 collection *The Ballad of Sexual Dependency*). Subtextually, then –

5. as a part of our group;
6, 7, 8. and yet now individuated as special, and so removed from that group, by the suitor.

9, 10, 11. Then a validation of the suitor's and object's joint interactions against or as part of a wider culture, identified as –
   9: the street (evolving urban cultures)
   10: the new collective (with the object as understanding themselves as at its centre)
   11: the shared history of the old school (i.e. a shared, empathetic cultural appreciation);
12. And a coda of being in need, and so returning to the individual interactions of 6, 7 and 8.

One is used, now, to slinging (or, at least, not spinning) albums by questionable figures. So something like Michael Jackson's *Off the Wall* (1979, a favourite of Aaliyah's – and released in the year of her birth) goes from constantly to rarely or never played. And this 'by questionable figures' is balanced by a whole subgenre of albums 'by victims', which are understood to resonate, typically intimately, with their distress. So personal crisis or psychosis becomes understood as audible in the music of Nirvana, Daniel Johnson, Wild Man Fischer or Judee Sill, or with music read as having effectively masked distress, as per Smit on Britney Spears (2011), McKay's discussion of Karen Carpenter's anorexia (2018) or, more generally, Whiteley's study of young female pop stars (2005). But to have the victim *and* her victimizer, together, on the same album, in the same grooves and indeed with the album as the way in which the victimizer brought the victim into his orbit . . . how can one find a way to enjoy or appreciate such music? 'Down with the Clique' even notes and includes this coupling, as if bluntly pre-emptive of criticism of the same, with Aaliyah ventriloquizing 'R. Kelly's on the track/and it's a good thing'. Furthermore, Kelly is seen on the cover of *Age Ain't* too, out of focus, seemingly looking on at Aaliyah, who is positioned in the foreground. She stands next to her name, and he is placed beneath the album's title, as if the title is a mantra, or an excuse as if he is whispering the boast into the mobile phone he seems to be cradling. Above this title is a phonetic guide of '(ah – lee – yah)', rendering Aaliyah's name into semi-orgasmic gasps and fetishizing it, Nabokov-like; *Lolita* opens thus: 'Lolita, light of my life, fire of my loins. My sin, my soul. Lo-lee-ta: the tip of the tongue taking a trip of three steps down the palate to tap, at three, on the teeth. Lo. Lee. Ta.' (Nabokov 1960: 11). The opportunity has gone in terms of asking Aaliyah, who died in 2001 at twenty-two, whether that 'good thing' was a fair comment regarding her future former husband, Robert Kelly. (Their marriage and ambiguities around its date in terms of Haughton's age, and indeed whether the marriage had happened at all, had been a matter of gossip and speculation for decades, and reappeared during the Kelly trial.) Aaliyah's early death seemed, but for criminality and expediency, entirely avoidable – and remains a matter of speculation still on a number of fronts; '[t]here really is no adequate settlement to this case', Iandoli concludes in her biography (2021: 188)

The track 'Age Ain't Nothing But A Number', written by Kelly, as with all other *Age Ain't* tracks (bar an Isley Brothers cover, 'At Your Best You Are Love') delivers the unpalatable, abusive imbalance in all its opportunism, and articulates its very operationalization.[3] The track opens with mutterings over a soulful piano; Aaliyah talks to herself as she reads or writes her diary (pages rustle): 'May 5th, 1993 . . . Aaliyah's diary'. The words that follow then, one should assume, are a diary entry, as written when she was fourteen (the album was released in May 1994, when she was fifteen). The object of her affection is invited, by her, for a sexual encounter: his 'eyes' call her to his 'heart', so 'all you got to do is knock [and] I'll let you in', whereupon they will both 'feel the passion that flows within' – clarified, later, to 'true ecstasy', and 'tonight we're going to go all the way'. The shifts into the chorus contain some grace-note exhalations, as attaching 'my' to 'age ain't nothing but a number'. To be clear, in terms of this kind of projection: Kelly is imagining a sexual desire, for him, by the fourteen-year-old – and having her sing this back to him. (The generic video is moody and meaningless, but splits the object of affection across a number of affable-looking male suitors.) So Aaliyah here is cast as siren and temptress, repeatedly asserting autonomy over proactive sexual advances attributed to her, as if dispelling any ambiguities as to what she would like, and warding away any scruples in the object of her affection and desire, concerning her age. That vocal assertion is breathy, and reassuring, pointedly come-hither in its insistence, and at times maturely deep and almost throaty. Towards the end, the words are said – 'come here!', with what then sounds like a kiss. All this now seems like little more than a future-proofing defence, as the writer/producer of the track casts his victim or victim-to-be as the initiator, or assembles the grounds on which any complaint from the victim can be later undermined by the accused, as being made in bad faith.

Nonetheless, the process of seeing or finding in cultural artefacts evidence of abuse, associated with the #MeToo movement (see Boyle 2019), which exploded across social media in 2017, cannot be one of wholly purging tainted material since this would also remove, and so erase, in this instance, the victim too. Aaliyah's voice was seemingly already silenced in the two decades after her death: associates unwilling or unable to talk, the music only very belatedly available via digital streaming, a dearth of archival materials made available, and crucial documentation, such as *Aaliyah Live in Amsterdam*, remaining out of reach.[4] So this chapter will attempt some kind of negotiation with the difficult task, so as to consider the ways in which Aaliyah, who broke with Kelly, came to divadom. And, for this, the chapter seeks to consider the sonic construction of the diva in Aaliyah's music, offered as an exemplar for as much in the hip-hop and r 'n' b that came in Aaliyah's wake.

To consider how Aaliyah then expressed herself beyond *Age Ain't*, in working with Timbaland, Missy Elliott, Static Major and Damon Dash, I want to turn to the four best-remembered singles, associated with the next two albums released during her lifetime.[5] These are: from *One in a Million* (1996), 'One in a Million' (1996) and '4 Page Letter' (1997) and, from *Aaliyah* (2001), 'More than a Woman' and 'Rock the Boat' (both 2001). At first there seems a depressing paucity of artistic worth or interest. The songs' lyrics are hackneyed and inconsequential, the videos dull, cliched and technologically dated (with fuzzy greenscreen technology rendering them more the work of a sophomoric computer programmer than a capturing of performance or presence), and with the video for '4 Page Letter' overloaded with storylines to the point of incomprehensibility. And, while the choreography and outfits are always arresting, these elements are the work of others. In all this, the sense of an operation around Aaliyah – sporadically interested in her, sporadically disinterested in her – seems at work: the promotion and management of the diva too young to exert a strong steer on this project, including the music and lyrics.[6] The emergence of Alicia Keys can be read in a particular light, in this context, in terms of presenting a sense of authenticity: the continual foregrounding of her actual piano-playing, with the 2001 debut album connecting the music with the person, *Songs in A Minor*.[7]

Despite this crowd of collaborators, there is a sense of Aaliyah's omnipresence in these four singles, solely via her voice, and the use of her voice across these songs – her voice, that is, quite specifically, rather than her vocalization (in the sense of the delivery of lyrical content). The concern of '4 Page Letter' seems merely to be one of nerves in declaring affection to 'this one particular guy', further to parental advice on the matter of courtship. So a letter, 'enclose[d] . . . with a kiss', is deemed to be a more palatable way of dealing with the matter, in the hope that when a meeting does finally occur, he won't 'diss me'. Such content does not even seem to be Aaliyah-specific: these are more the dilemmas of someone younger than eighteen, in 1997. (The song is credited to Missy Elliott and Timbaland, as Tim Moseley – although at this point both were seemingly focused on presenting

Aaliyah rather than presenting themselves in the mix.) But the post-*Age Ain't* voice, of 1996–2001, seems to exert control over the music. '4 Page Letter' opens with spoken words: an insistent, repeated instruction from Aaliyah, as if emceeing at a spontaneous warehouse party, and that the mixer duly obeys: 'Yo – turn my music up ... Up some more ... Up – some more ... Up a little bit more.' But what is turned up is a steady beat and one that then achieves amplification and space for Aaliyah to move into and occupy unimpeded. At this point, the voice barely ceases in terms of sonic constancy. This is part voice delivery and part voice overdubs. The mixing splits the voice into multiples, layered into and away from each other: calls and answers, questions and answers, harmonization and guide vocals (offset by backing singers). In the upper register, lyric-less: sighs, scales, wails. This is strikingly different to a run of music, from Michael Jackson's *Off the Wall* (1979) to the soul of Sade or Des'ree: here the vocal is often clean, singular (i.e. seemingly not multi-tracked), and mixed as apart or even 'above' the music in terms of sonic spacing. This effect is one of imagining the sole singer, in her spot, as or at the centre of a group, and as the central attractor of attention.

The affect is one of feeling encircled: the listener is placed in a removed sonic space, surrounded by Aaliyah's voices. One reaches for parallels: the reverberating overlaps of Gregorian chant, where the stone hollows of monastic architecture mix voices into echoes; Othello (in Act 1, Scene 3) describing loving Desdemona as finding 'a world of sighs'; the #Occupy activist technique of completely filling up, and refusing to be shifted from (and too dense and too numerous to be shifted from), public spaces; the density and psychedelia of some Western encounters with 'world' music, as with the Master Musicians of Joujouka in Brian Jones's field recordings or Archie Shepp at the Pan-African Festival; the enveloping experience of some Bill Viola video installations, such as the *Nantes Triptych* (1992), with crying, bubbling (of water) and breathing from, respectively (and as seen in three monolithic video screens), birth, immersion and death.[8] A bass drum beat, reduced to operating as a click track, marks the rudimentary forward progression of '4 Page Letter', and even seems at times to attempt to hold the multiplicity of voices back. Finally, Aaliyah seems to step back from the microphone and a disconcertingly slinky, retro synth sound suddenly cuts in, at minute four and a half (in the unabridged, album version of the song), for an outro solo – as distinctive, and sudden, as Aaliyah's voice in and across the intro. It is as if Aaliyah's voice, now spent, gives way and melds into the instrument. 'One in a Million' functions in the same manner: maximal vocalization, the slight lyrical content soon forgotten: an ambience, a vibe, the trajectories of yearning – and then the voice stops again, with a twangy guitar sound picking up the outro. When the voice ceases well before the ending of 'More Than a Woman', Aaliyah's last single, released at the time of her death, this exit would seem to anticipate something else altogether: that the music will or must continue, even after the singer has taken her leave. Nevertheless, as with this end moment, her leave has been taken: the music is suddenly bereft of her omnipresence – and the silent spaces between the beats disconcertingly empty. Tellingly, Timbaland describes the experience of the loss of Aaliyah's voice in metaphysical terms, in his autobiography – as engendering a breakdown and profound crisis of a theological, and then existential, nature.

> 'Tim, if you want to be happy, you have to do the thing that makes you happy,' [my mother] would say: 'Make some music.'
> It was like she didn't get it. When God silenced Aaliyah's voice, he had silenced me too.
> 'I don't want to make music, Ma.' I said.
> Then she took a sterner tone. 'Killing yourself won't bring her back, baby.'
> I didn't answer. Didn't want to say how often that very thought – killing myself – had crossed my mind.
> (Timbaland and Chambers 2016: 149)

The voice, then, seems the sole vector for this music: the channelling inwards of the thought and skill and work (the artistry, the people involved), into this voice, and then that voice projected outwards, as expressing and interpreting, to and for a universal audience. In these respects, the Aaliyah model of divadom is that of the opera diva (rather than a Sill- or Keys-like singer-songwriter): the interpreter rather than creator – but, in that interpretation, the culmination and, with this, the mutual enhancement, of all other inputs. In this sense, the experience – as rendered in the sonic patina of these songs – is one of bombast.

When this bombast was encountered, with a first hearing of 'Rock the Boat' in 2001, the resultant music seems almost absurdly, even comically, crude. 'Rock the Boat', through a clunking metaphor (where boat = vagina), delivers a series of explicit sexual instructions. One could argue, in the context of third wave feminism, that the song articulates a pro-sex, counter-patriarchal reversal of gendered norms – in that it is now the female who instructs, and instructs for herself alone (in that litany of 'me's): 'you make me float', 'you get me high', 'you serve me', 'change positions on me', 'stroke it for me' and so on. The male presence (demoted to 'boy', 'baby', 'babe') is almost entirely absent, or reduced to a biological anonymity. Likewise, in the context of third wave feminism, one could argue that the use of the catamaran as a floating performance space, in the music video, reclaims the repurposing of the yacht as a method of male kidnap or seduction of the female which, as I have argued elsewhere (in relation to British New Romantic music), is a MTV-calibrated heteronormative standard of 1980s 'yacht pop'; see Halligan (2017: 97–108).[9] But the disorientation arising from the song seems aligned to the way in which pop performers associated with third wave feminism are more typically understood to be defiant in public, on social – even consumer – issues (a general position explored in Heywood and Drake 1997, and Gillis, Howie and Munford 2007), rather than on the details of matters of intimacy. The latter more typically seem almost entirely confessional and tend to result in the female being placed alone while thinking/singing longingly about the absent male (often via the visual metaphor of solo dancing, as with Cassie's 'Me & U' of 2005), or spearheading a defiant posse of friends into a nightclub to publicly decry, and dismiss or belittle, sexual boasts ('I'm not into it/ . . . /[despite the way that] You claim that you're so hot/And you say you got skills in the bedroom' of Cassie's 'Long Way 2 Go' of 2006, or 'Don't Cha' by the Pussycat Dolls of 2005 too). To vocalize and blast sexual instructions across (and, via underwater sequences, even into) the placid waters of the Bahamas that serenely cradle the catamaran seems scandalous – a spelling-out of the unsaid, an unspoken rule-flouting misstep. But this too is the experience of the diva and, in particular, the diva live, where the bombast, and maximalism, are not a matter of studio mic'ing and mixing, but an audio experience of presence. To return again to the matter of first encounters or first listens: the diva's voice, live, can beggar belief that such volume can emanate from the body. This makes better sense of the cliched connection between God and voice: not that the voice is angelic, or heavenly, or uniquely beautiful (a kind of Botticelli imagining of homogenized aesthetic beauty) – but that the voice, as with the vengeful God of the Old Testament, seems sonically bigger and wider than life: the voice of command, echoing across the plains, rolling down mountains, coming from all-points, everywhere, without break, defying corporeal logic and saying the unsayable. The volume of mezzo-soprano Magdalena Kožená's voice in a live performance of Martinů's *Juliette (The Key to Dreams)*, at the London Barbican in 2009, conducted by Jiří Bělohlávek, shocked and disoriented in just such a way.

In this context, the voice itself – irrespective of the lack of clear authorial creativity on the part of the diva – becomes the only matter of consideration.

Indeed, the removal of authorial creativity allows the diva to interpret freely, rather than being beholden to the communication of a certain meaning intended by the singer in the song that they wrote and now deliver. It is not that the diva supplies the voice to the score, but that the score allows the diva to become the diva – an animation, a creating of their very presence. That is: Sirmon identifies 'the diva archetype' in a meshing together of both 'detached distance and embodiment with abandon' in the one diva performer (2021). Specifically, writing about the experimental actress Magdelena Montezuma's work with Werner Schroeter, Sirmon identifies Montezuma's 'knack for both frenzy and detachment' which 'delivered a nuanced vision of the diva as sexual persona who defies but is also constrained by patriarchal norms'. And (albeit in relation to camp appropriation of divas and diva-isms, and the gay appeal of divas): 'The diva turns her suffering into triumph, her flaws and freakishness into exceptional talent and dazzling divinity. In assuming her glamorous form, the diva becomes her true self.' Schroeter, in his obituary of preeminent opera diva Maria Callas, identifies the meaning of this art – as, as it were, chafing against the materialist and cognitive parameters of life itself by momentarily arresting life's flow: 'Those moments of artistic expression driven to excess . . . demonstrate nothing other than the need to halt the march of time. That is, to ignore the finiteness of human needs . . .' (cited in Siegel 2018: 68).

Many of Aaliyah's millennial contemporaries seem to have mostly vanished from the public eye, in tandem with a capriciousness that seems even more unsympathetic in the world of hip-hop and r 'n' b than other (and whiter) genres of popular music. The beginnings of the elevation of a smaller group of post-millennial diva figures could be discerned at this point: the journey towards the adult mainstream of Alicia Keys, and the superstardom of Beyoncé, outside of Destiny's Child (for whom Aaliyah had choreographed 'Get on the Bus', 1998; Iandoli 2021: 118), across the next two decades. But this shift occurred at the point of the fragmentation of the standard channels of music dissemination, away from the commercial releases of physical formats of music, in favour of touring and a myriad of online outlets through the utilization of social media. And, in this post-millennial, digital space, a place still seems to remain for divas once in the public eye. (Following this line of development is aligned to the CFC's advice to 'wield technology', and 'how the technological universe affects hip hop culture and feminist studies'; Cooper et al. 2017: 173). Ashanti veered towards in-person appearances, shorter sets at events, emceeing in clubs (as did Amerie) or providing selfie opportunities – akin to the ways in which celebrity

Figure 5.1–5.3 From a live Instagram stream: Ashanti emcees with a small club crowd and DJs with a laptop; December 2021. (Screengrabs from Instagram).

or influencer figures would be welcomed into the social media feeds (such as streaming via Instagram) of nightclubs, as with the advert 'Announcing Fyre Festival' and social media endorsements from models of the projected Bahamian Fyre Festival of 2017; see Davis (2019) (Figures 5.1–5.3).

This repositioning, when considered in respect to the cultural cache of the figure of the diva, seems more than just a lower-level option for making a living after the spotlight has swung elsewhere. Just as a sense of a Top Forty or Hit Parade, as the central structuring or evergreening of popular music, has faded, the figure of the r 'n' b or hip-hop diva has seemingly been returned to their place of origin. I am thinking in particular of a synchronicity of a certain aesthetic arrangement, both in music videos and live performances. This is a circular moving lattice, via a digital display screen, from which shifting halos of light are projected onto and around the diva, positioned (and performing) in front. Or the lattice criss-cross of a cage, with actual stage or spotlights behind, shining through the bars (as per any factory/warehouse party of decades before: the space occupied by revellers, the performance area make-shift, the industrial or factory detritus of the space still visible). This is not a matter of a backdrop, as with 'Get on the Bus', with screen imagery illustrative of bits of lyrics, or the space for a face of the guest rapper. Rather, this is a direct interaction: beholding a performance of blended light and movement. This does not result in a flattened or depthless plain to be surveyed. This is, instead, a directing of light outwards – which then invariably periodically plunges the performer into silhouette – at the watcher, creating for them a kind of tunnel effect. Moments of this occurred in the video of Amerie's 'I'm Coming Out' (2003, a cover of the 1980 Diana Ross song): the cage or metal fence, the rotating lights

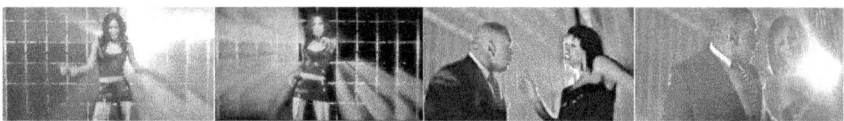

Figure 5.4–5.7 Return to the industrial setting, with cage, fence and lattice designs and light bleeding across the image. Screengrabs from the videos for Amerie's 'I'm Coming Out' (2002) and Timbaland's 'The Way I Are' (2007).

behind, periodically engulfing vision altogether – as if in a nightclub, looking up, and spying a dancer on a ledge or raised platform, in close proximity to the full lighting rig, and so bathed in the intense illumination (Figures 5.4–5.7).[10] Similar arrangements are found in Jennifer Lopez's 1999 'Waiting for Tonight' (green lasers, rave in a 'tropical' forest) or the wooden caged tunnel, white light seeping through its cracks, of Britney Spears's 2003 'Me Against the Music' (a design lifted from Orson Welles's *The Trial*, 1962), or just a straight tunnel, cage, lights in Timbaland's 2007 'The Way I Are'. This removal of the performer seems to globalize them: no longer locked into a specific locale, and a Top Forty-generating urban centre – but as if transported, and still doing their thing, to 2010s and 2020s glamorous nightclubs the (first) world over (and where travelling to the nightclub is part of the glamour): a Dubai-ization. It is the diva, and the diva's presence, that is transported.

In all these respects, the identified aesthetic model – or affective aesthetic turn, in this tendency – is somewhat akin to the aesthetics and functioning of the religious icon. The plaster-covered lime or cypress wood board, depicting the figure for devotion, is now replaced by the digital display screen or the tunnel of light. And the dazzle, and goldenness or silveriness, and embedded beads or jewellery and emanating halo, remain the same. (so that, in this comparison, the flattened plain of the music video seems more like an altar piece, with its vignettes of visual narratives.) This parallel then encapsulates the sense of the meaning of the actual presence of the diva. Icons have historically been understood not just to be the focus of devotion, but the very means of devotion: not a visualization of the divine so much but a portal to the actual presence of the divine. For Brajovic and Erdeljan:

> As *eikones*, i.e. matter imbued with divine *pneuma* [roughly: spirit or soul or essence], releasing *charis* [grace], icons were intended to be physically experienced through the ritual act of *proskynesis* [devotional practice] which implied touching, kissing and an all-encompassing 'seeing' of an icon of which touch, smell, taste and sound were an integral and defining part.
>
> (2015: 57)

and where the precious stones and gold and silver repussé were intended to enhance the icon via candle or oil lamp illumination, so that '[t]his tactile visuality or the haptic and visual experience of the holy thus produced a feeling of true communion with the divine . . .' (2015: 57) So in this respect, in the presence of the haloed diva, communion (the possibility of devotion, and a haptic encounter with the possessor of the voice) becomes a very possible matter.

The live rendition of all this, drawing on a performance by Amerie (at the Milton Club in Manchester, 15 April 2017, only a few miles from the location of the video shoot for 'The Way I Are') however, remains, unsurprisingly, redolent of the lower-level option of diva work (Figures 5.8–5.10). In some senses, the diva merely delivers a live PA over familiar pre-recorded tracks shorn of vocals, against a predesigned video sequence (both via a laptop, plugged into the DJ booth). Yet, in this combination, those light/cage shots of 'I'm Coming Out' occur in-person: a live icon-ization, with mobile phone screen lights, and photo flashes, replacing the candle or oil lamp illumination. The voice cuts through the hubbub, the notes are held – and have to be blasted out: how else do clubbers know that the diva is actually present in the room, other than the positioning of this voice in the upper echelon of amplification? The diva is haptically (i.e. touch-ably) present too, against the illuminated background: call and response, holding the hands of those present while singing, high-fiving, within the midst of attendees (i.e. without the distance typical of formal concerts), singing directly to them, at them, for them, with them. The social media adverts – promising an opportunity to 'party with' Amerie, hold then an element of truth.

My initial approach to Aaliyah, as tracking an ascendency to the year 2000 of the diva figure, and a redefining of the diva figure through her work, which was then waylaid by trying to understand or recover the distinctive present-ness of Aaliyah – her voice – in her own music, terminates, in 2017, in an unexpected place: the Milton Club. But the grace and sense of shared moments of Amerie live connects back to the millennial Aaliyah template, as starting out with *Age Ain't*. Debuts, as with *Age Ain't*, tend to need to be foundations of the coming diva ascendency: the nascent or embryonic diva, but here encountered at an early stage or start of the journey, where any glamour or diva deficit is made good by the force of personality, and the freshness of the encounter, and their (to use a term that is a constant in hip-hop) realness. All this remains, after the glamour phase has been and gone, with the same diva, and voice, now haloed through the icon-like presentation, and with their realness delivered through their haptic presence.

Figure 5.8–5.10 Amerie performing and emceeing live at the Milton Club in 2017. (Photos by Benjamin Halligan).

Notes

1 This identification by the CFC also verifies my observation with respect to the cultural importance of this decade – a necessary verification as I write from the position of a white and British heterosexual male, but one immersed in these music scenes since his teens; the Collective also requests a declaration of positionality for those writing about hip-hop too, (Cooper et al. 2017: 172).
2 Journalistic books on Aaliyah prior to Iandoli's all speculate that something seems to have been potentially problematic in terms of Kelly and Aaliyah, as discussed around the ambiguities regarding their possible marriage: Farley (2001), Footman (2003), and Timbaland and Chambers (2016). In Farley's case – but this is true of all the books, and Iandoli's – there is a sense of only being able to comment on the story from afar, and an omertà in operation around those who knew Aaliyah.
3 From the 1976 Isley Brother's album *Harvest for the World*.
4 On #MeToo, see Boyle (2019); on the streaming availability matter, see Sisario (2021). The Caesar documentary has been extremely infrequently shown: in Birmingham (see Young 2011) and in the University of Wolverhampton, at the conference convened by myself, Diva, on 17 July 2019, with Caesar as a keynote speaker, talking vividly about his strong impressions of Aaliyah in those days, and her confidence in interview and in performance – remembered a quarter of a century later.
5 Timbaland (born 1972), producer, singer and song writer. Debut album, *Tim's Bio: Life from da Basement*, released in 1998.
6 On this process: Timbaland notes first meeting Aaliyah with a completed track (including vocals, 'so Aaliyah could hear how it should sound'): 'Missy [Elliot] and I had brought a track [*If Your Girl Only Knew*] with us. Something we thought she might like . . . "We wrote you a song . . . "' (Timbaland and Chambers 2016: 113), which Aaliyah then effectively rerecorded (114–15). Through such a process, Elliott

and Timbaland were effectively 'audition[ing]' to work with Aaliyah', Iandoli 2021: 79), at Aaliyah's invitation to them (75).
7 The pun is not quite as terrible as it first seems: 'a minor' as a minor scale key, and the young Keys herself. Stevie Wonder's 1976 *Songs in the Key of Life* may have been in mind.
8 Timbaland mentions Gregorian chant, in terms of the wideness of his mental sonic palette and eclecticism of styles and genres (which he owes, he notes, to the influence of the music of Prince and Rick James, the latter via his father). The Gregorian chant is in relation to his work on Justin Timberlake's 'Cry Me A River' (2002) and, as a second example of such eclecticism, Timbaland then mentions a 'psychedelic trancelike beat, the kind you find in acid house, in Aaliyah's "Try Again" [2000].' (Timbaland and Chambers 2016: 15–16) The connection of psychedelia seems apt, as with the LPs mentioned here, which are: *Brian Jones Presents the Pipes of Pan at Joujouka* (1971), and Archie Shepp's *Live at the Panafrican Festival* (1969), recorded in Algiers and Morocco respectively. Mariah Carey's multi-tracked vocals sometimes work in this way, but seem to use her vocalizations to fill out the spaces that would otherwise be occupied by separate instruments – as with 'Dreamlover' (from the 1993 album *Music Box*), 'The Roof (Back in Time)' (from 1997's *Butterfly*) or 'Heartbreaker' (from 1999's *Rainbow*), where she will sing the riff, harmonize with herself, whisperingly repeat or echo her own vocals, scat across her own vocals, and so forth.

On #Occupy and crowds, see Ossewarde (2013).
9 On the shooting of this music video, see Iandoli (2021: 161–4).
10 Amerie (born 1980); debut album, *All I Have*, released in 2002.

Reference

BBC News (2021), 'R. Kelly Found Guilty in Sex Trafficking Trial', *BBC News*, 28 September. Available online: https://www.bbc.co.uk/news/entertainment-arts-58714203 (accessed 14 August 2022).

Boyle, K. (2019), *#MeToo, Weinstein and Feminism*, London: Palgrave-Macmillan.

Brajovic, S. and J. Erdeljan (2015), 'Praying with the Senses: Examples of Icon Devotion and the Sensory Experience in Medieval and Early Modern Balkans', *Zograf*, 39: 57–63. Available online: https://www.degruyter.com/database/BYZ/entry/byz.5cf5b46c-ce06-4ec8-91d0-5d240bb56bbc/html (accessed 1 August 2022).

Cooper, B. C., A. Durham, S. M. Morris and R. Raimist (2017), 'Ten Crunk Commandments for Reinvigorating Hip Hop Feminist Studies', in B. C. Cooper,

S. M. Morris and R. M. Boylorn (eds), *The Crunk Feminist Collection*, 172–4, New York: Feminist Press at the City University of New York.

Cooper, B. C., S. M. Morris and R. M. Boylorn (2017), *The Crunk Feminist Collection*, New York: Feminist Press at the City University of New York.

Davis, J. (2019), 'Kendall Jenner and Emily Ratajkoski Are being Sued over Fyre Festival', *Harper's Bazaar*, 2 September Available online: https://www.harpersbazaar.com/uk/celebrities/news//kendall-jenner-and-emily-ratajkowksi-fyre-festival/ (accessed 3 August 2022).

Farley, C. J. (2001), *Aaliyah: More Than A Woman*, London: Pocket Books.

Footman, T. (2003), *Aaliyah*, London: Plexus.

Gillis, S., G. Howie and R. Munford (2007 [2004]), *Third Wave Feminism: A Critical Exploration*, expanded second edn, London: Palgrave-Macmillan.

Goldin, N. (1986), *The Ballad of Sexual Dependency*, New York: Aperture Foundation.

Halligan, B. (2017), 'Liquidities for the Essex Man: The Monetarist Eroticism of British Yacht Pop', in G. Arnold, D. Cookney, K. Fairclough and M. Goddard (eds), *Music/Video: Histories, Aesthetics, Media*, 97–108, London: Bloomsbury.

Heywood, L. and J. Drake, eds (1997), *Third Wave Agenda: Being Feminist, Doing Feminism*, Minneapolis and London: University of Minnesota Press.

Iandoli, K. (2021), *Baby Girl: Better Known as Aaliyah*, New York and London: Atria Books.

Loring, M. T. (1994), *Emotional Abuse*, New York: Lexington Books.

McKay, G. (2018), 'Skinny Blues: Karen Carpenter, Anorexia Nervosa and Popular Music', *Popular Music*, 37 (1): 1–21.

Nabokov, V. (1960), *Lolita*, third edn, London: Weidenfeld and Nicholson.

Ossewarde, M. (2013), 'The Crowd in the Occupy Movement', *Distinktion: Journal of Social Theory*, 14 (2): 134–50.

Sanjek, D., with T. Attah, M. Duffett and B. Halligan, eds (2019), *Stories We Could Tell: Putting Words to American Popular Music*, London: Routledge.

Siegel, M. (2018), 'Longing Is Your Own Affair (I Always Remained Underground)', in R. Grundmann (ed.), *Werner Schroeter*, 66–77, Vienna: Synema Publikationen.

Sirmons, J. (2021), 'For Magdalena Montezuma', *Another Gaze*, 28 July. Available online: https://www.anothergaze.com/for-magdalena-montezuma/ (accessed 25 August 2022).

Sisario, B. (2021), 'Aaliyah's Music Will Finally Be Streaming: What Took So Long?', *New York Times*, 5 August. Available at: https://www.nytimes.com/2021/08/05/arts/music/aaliyah-catalog-streaming.html (accessed 9 August 2022).

Smit, C. R. (2011), *The Exile of Britney Spears: A Tale of 21st Century Consumption*, Bristol: Intellect.

Stark, E. (2007), *Coercive Control: How Men Entrap Women in Personal Life*, Oxford: Oxford University Press.

Timbaland, with V. Chambers (2016), *The Emperor of Sound*, New York: Amistad, HarperCollins.

Whiteley, S. (2005), *Too Much Too Young: Popular Music and Gender*, London: Routledge.

Young, G. (2011), 'Pogus Caesar Premieres His Aaliyah Movie in Birmingham', *Business Live*, 22 July. Available online: https://www.business-live.co.uk/retail-consumer/pogus-caesar-premieres-aaliyah-movie-3919688 (accessed 18 August 2022).

6

'Suck On My Balls, Bitch!'
#MeToo and Beyoncé – A paradigm shift

Hannah M. Strong

Beyoncé.
Bey.
Queen Bey.
Mrs. Carter.

. . . regardless of the moniker you prefer, she dominates. Or, rather, in Bey terminology (from 2016's 'Formation', from *Lemonade*): she 'slays'. Arguably, Beyoncé is the most successful artist of her generation, has been awarded (at the time of writing) more Grammys than any other woman and has launched her own fashion line. Unlike contemporaries Lizzo, Cardi B, and Nicki Minaj, Beyoncé as a performer presents a very different persona to that of Beyoncé the public figure. Her music normally features explicit representations of her sexuality and promotes feminist ideals, while off-stage Beyoncé is surprisingly absent from social media (only posting occasionally on Instagram and without any caption or description), and absent from the public eye in general. When she does appear, Beyoncé's image is highly polished, presented in high fashion and the image itself does the talking as Beyoncé is predominately silent. And this public personality largely toes the line of respectability politics. These aspects of her personality all peacefully co-exist, with each playing its role in creating and reaffirming the success of Beyoncé, the brand.

During her 14 April 2018 Coachella performance, however, Beyoncé broke with this trend, during a rendition of 'Sorry' (2016), via a step routine that was crude, lewd and insulting – chanting 'suck on my balls, bitch!' This moment is an outlier for Beyoncé: it pandered to no extant audience. This chapter will contextualize this song with respect to her most recent albums, specifically focusing on the dichotomous relationship of Beyoncé the feminist and Beyoncé the sex symbol, situated against the backdrop of her highly respectable off-stage persona. In this discussion of sexuality, feminism and respectability politics, I conclude that the #MeToo movement created a general culture shift that indirectly inspired Beyoncé to step away from the pillars of her brand, with the Coachella performance. This chapter will first analyse examples from *Beyoncé* (2013) and *Lemonade* (2016), with added context from Brittney Cooper, Audre Lorde and Valerie Chepp, and ultimately conclude that Beyoncé's turn away from respectability politics, in favour of irreverence and ratchet feminism, can be attributed to the #MeToo movement and its culture.

Beyoncé's 2013 self-titled album offered her fans a glimpse into her personal life, as she bounced back from her first pregnancy. In an interview with *Good Morning America*, Beyoncé recognized that she now wanted to show off her body: 'I worked crazily trying to get my body back [. . .] I wanted to show my body. [. . . It was about] getting back to my sensuality.' (Good Morning America 2013) While the album indeed displays Beyoncé's post-pregnancy body, and a sensual relationship with her husband, it also offers a close-up of the artist's competing interests: many of the songs are explicitly sexual while other songs unapologetically promote feminism. This chapter turns to 'Partition' and 'Drunk in Love', which are hypersexual in nature, while 'Flawless' and 'Pretty Hurts' (all 2013) promote feminist ideals. This seeming contradiction could be read as an attempt to win over two different audiences: heterosexual male audiences, or those understood as identified by the phrase 'sex sells', and an audience that identifies with feminist lyrics. Despite these messages arguably confounding each other, the self-titled album was wildly popular.

Three songs on *Beyoncé* stand out for their semi-pornographic lyrics, 'Partition', 'Drunk in Love' and 'Blow' (2013). The first two are objectifying, mainly focusing on descriptions of her partner's sexual pleasure. 'Partition' and its music video summon a scene of Beyoncé and Jay-Z having sex in the back of a limousine: 'He bucked all my buttons and he ripped my blouse. He Monica Lewinsky'd all on my gown.' This description of fellatio and ejaculation are surprisingly explicit, and with her pleasure and desires taking a back seat to her husband's. Invoking Monica Lewinsky in this way puts further distance between Beyoncé and feminism, by reducing Lewinsky the person to the now infamous moment that then-President Bill Clinton reputedly ejaculated on her dress.[1]

'Drunk in Love' is equally sexually explicit. However, it offers a slightly different view of Beyoncé's sex life: instead of raunchy sex in a limousine, Bey and Jay describe having sex 'all night' in their foyer and bathtub. Beyoncé spares few details of her favourite sex position – the surfboard – and how it is executed, while Jay-Z raps about being unable to wait: '[s]lid the panties to the side/ain't got time to take drawers off in sight'. This scene celebrates continued passion in their marriage, but the unrestrained details of slipping panties to the side, and Beyoncé grinding on her husband's 'wood', come across as *overly* intimate and pornographic. That is: while 'Drunk in Love' and 'Partition' glorify Bey's post-pregnancy body and her relationship with her husband, the lyrics feel objectifying, and focus intently on heteronormative, male-centred sex.

'Blow' offers an opposing glimpse at Beyoncé's sex life; this time *she* receives oral sex. The song celebrates cunnilingus and the lyrics range from describing the encounter, compare performing this sex act to eating Skittles candy and instructing her partner as to exactly what is needed in order to make her climax. The song gives way to an even more explicit description, invoking the oft-used 'cherry' metaphor for a woman's genitalia – 'I want you to turn the cherry out' – and then commands her partner: 'give me that daddy-long stroke'. These commands, and the scene that they paint, are very different from 'Partition' and 'Drunk in Love'. They depict Beyoncé advocating for her own pleasure – a behavioural trope which Roxanne Gay associated with being a good feminist (2014: 316). Whether or not the type of sex described by 'Blow' is feminist or not, it is unapologetically sex-positive and centred on Beyoncé's pleasure in a way that feels less objectifying than the descriptions of 'Partition' and 'Drunk in Love'.

What is seemingly confusing in these three songs is just *how* Beyoncé uses sex. In 'Blow' we are gifted with a glimpse at sex-positive feminism. Feminista Jones, in *Reclaiming Our Space*, advocates for sex-positive feminism, as that which 'offers a sanctuary for those who believe sexual liberation is key to women's liberation and that sex and sexuality have been weaponized against women as a method of controlling women's bodies' (2019: 69). In this context, 'Blow' and Beyoncé's impetus to show her reclaimed, post-pregnancy sensuality are validated, and such identification supports Beyoncé's identification as a feminist, instead of detracting from it. However, the sex described in 'Partition' and 'Drunk in Love' offer countervailing examples of self-objectification and reliance on the male gaze. In what she terms 'resilience discourse', Robin James analyses Beyoncé's earlier works, noting a similar reliance on men and the male gaze. Thus, as Beyoncé objectifies herself, she increases profitability through resilience discourse, which 'turns objectification (being looked at) into a means of subjectification (overcoming). It also makes *looking* even more efficient and profitable than simple objectification could ever be' (James 2015: 89). In this context, Beyoncé reveals her resilience in bouncing back from her pregnancy with an enviable body, and a steamy sex life, and fans are given permission to witness this resilience – so completing Beyoncé's objectification and subjectification.

The album offers further support to feminism with two songs that critique gender stereotypes and unrealistic beauty standards: 'Pretty Hurts' and 'Flawless'. The opening track on the album, 'Pretty Hurts', reveals Beyoncé's struggles as a child performer: her mother promoted the idea that Beyoncé's mind and personality were insignificant, and that her appearance was of the utmost importance. Beyoncé draws the summation: 'What's in your head/it doesn't matter.' But ultimately she concludes that '[p]erfection is the disease of a nation'. The music video shows Beyoncé in a plastic surgeon's office; lines from a blue pen are drawn on her face, to mark the coming cosmetic surgery. The lyrics and accompanying video critique this culture of perfectionism that emphasizes looks over intellect, contrasting sharply with other female hip-hop stars, such as Cardi B and Nicki Minaj, who flaunt their surgically-altered bodies. 'Flawless' also promotes feminist ideals, and even features a segment from Chimamanda Ngozi Adichie's TED talk, 'We Should All Be Feminists' (April 2013). Here, Adichie addresses the disjunction between raising boys and girls, and the harmful ways in which girls are taught to relate to each other. The excerpt ends with Adichie's definition of feminism, which matches the definition found in the *Encyclopedia Brittanica*: 'the belief of the social, economic, and political equality of the sexes' (Burkett 2021). She then describes the challenges that girls across the world face in making friends, pressures to marry and reproduce, and expectations of modestness. The remainder of the song contains lyrics that are so affirming that they border on braggadocious: 'I look so good tonight – Goddamn!' But the inclusion of Adichie's message grounds the song in a larger feminist discussion concerning societal pressures on women. The song proceeds with a positive message for women fans: 'We flawless, ladies, tell 'em!' Beyoncé's message in 'Flawless' is clear: she is a feminist, and in case her fans cannot understand feminism, a definition is included in the song too. Beyoncé affirms that all women are inherently flawless, from the moment they wake up in the morning. These positive messages echo Audre Lorde's call to build the 'love of black women for each other', to give 'more [love] to the brave bruised girlhood', and to 'quiet [the] frenzy toward perfection' (1984: 175). The lyrics echo Lorde's positions in an almost verbatim fashion, and in this solidify Beyoncé as a feminist.

The discrepancies between feminist leanings and a reliance on men continue. Though omitted from the previous quotation, Adichie's TED talk addresses the double standard in the pressure to marry: 'Because I am female, I am expected to aspire to marriage. I am expected to make my life choices, always keeping in mind that marriage is the most important. Now, marriage can be a source of joy and love and mutual support, but why do we teach girls to aspire to marriage and we don't teach boys the same?' (Adichie 2013). Although this is explicitly presented by Adichie in 'Flawless', Beyoncé's 2013–14 world tour, the *Mrs. Carter Show*, arguably delivered sent a very different message. Upon marrying Jay-Z in 2008, Beyoncé hyphenated her surname: Beyoncé Knowles-Carter. The tour began in April 2013, before *Beyoncé* was released in December of that year. Upon its release, the *Mrs. Carter Show* immediately focused on the new album – so it is plausible that the tour was named Mrs Carter before 'Flawless' was recorded. (I should acknowledge too that a 'Mrs. Knowles-Carter Show' does not sound as catchy as the 'Mrs. Carter Show'.) Nevertheless, the very title of the tour diminishes the weight of Beyoncé's feminist message. In addition, the stage-sized backdrop of the tour featured the word 'FEMINIST' – spelled out in twelve-foot tall lights, and on every television screen throughout the venue, which further obfuscated the theme of the tour. These aspects of the tour perfectly encapsulate the dichotomy of Beyoncé: flashy feminist messages flanked by heteronormative and male-centred imagery. And, while the message was not unified, or remained unsettled or paradoxical, Beyoncé, as a brand or commodity, profited from the spectacle.

On two occasions, Beyoncé discussed her self-identification as a feminist: once in an interview and once in a self-produced short film. This eleven-and-a-half-minute short, *Yours and Mine* (Beyoncé Knowles, 2014), commemorated the one-year anniversary of *Beyoncé*, and described the necessity of her identification as a feminist:

> I always consider myself a feminist, although I was always afraid of that word because people put so much on it. When, honestly – it's very simple. It's just a person who believes in equality for men and women.

In a 2016 interview with *Elle* magazine, Beyoncé echoed these sentiments:

> I put the definition of feminist in my song ['Flawless'] and on my tour, not for propaganda or to proclaim to the world that I'm a feminist, but to give clarity to the true meaning. I'm not really sure people know or understand what a feminist is, but it's very simple. It's someone who believes in equal rights for men

and women. I don't understand the negative connotation of the word [. . .] I'm exhausted by the labels and tired of being boxed in.

(Gottesman 2016)

Although she denies using the term 'feminist' as propaganda, or self-promotion, it is unclear why Beyoncé would use the term so overtly *just* to 'give clarity to the true meaning'. bell hooks famously took issue with Beyoncé, her album, and her identification as a feminist, calling her instead an 'antifeminist' and a 'terrorist' (hooks 2014). Despite the way in which the aforementioned quotations were intended to reveal Beyoncé's true intention, in identifying as a feminist, they only underscore that she is deeply concerned with fan reactions.

Given the raunchy lyrics, drive for success and importance of men, many prominent feminists, such as bell hooks, and celebrities Annie Lennox and Emma Watson, have questioned the validity of Beyoncé's identity as a feminist. Although Chimamanda Ngozi Adichie granted Beyoncé permission to use part of her TED talk in 'Flawless', Adichie struggled with Beyoncé's identification as a feminist as well. In a 2014 interview with *Urban Belle*, Adichie defended Beyoncé's feminism, while in a 2016 interview, she questions it deeply. Her initial defence of Beyoncé is centred on the identity of feminists:

> There's something very disturbing to me about the idea that a woman's sexuality somehow is not hers. So when certain feminists who will say, it's about the male gaze, it's for the man, there is this kind of self-censoring about that that's similar to what they're fighting . . . as long as women have a choice . . . why shouldn't women own their sexuality? Why shouldn't a woman who does whatever with her sexuality identify as a feminist? I've always found that very troubling. It's almost unfeminist to make that argument that if you shake your booty you're not a feminist.
>
> (Anderson-Niles 2014)

It is clear from this quotation that Adichie does not personally believe that being overtly sexual precludes anyone from being a feminist. And, furthermore, that it is un-feminist to deny someone's identification as a feminist because they are sexual. But in a later interview with Dutch magazine *De Volkskrant*, Adichie did not sound so certain of Beyoncé's feminism because of her relationship with men:

> Her style is not my style, but I do find it interesting that she takes a stand in political and social issues . . . Still, her type of feminism is not mine, as it is the kind that, at the same time, gives quite a lot of space to the necessity of men.

(Kiene 2016)

In this later interview, Adichie perfectly encapsulates the Beyoncé paradox: she is independent and socially conscious but relies on men to a great degree. Adichie is still hesitant to fully stand behind Beyoncé's brand of feminism. This is unrelated to her explicit sexuality and is solely based on the necessity of men in her work. There is a greater implication in these two interviews: that the *impetus* behind Beyoncé's booty-shaking causes the confusion. If her sexually explicit performances are a representation of her own sexuality, then that is a feminist endeavour. If the performances instead are sexually explicit to pander to male audiences, however, then that is not feminist and is, instead, self-objectification to the ends of commercial success.

Similar to *Beyoncé*, the album *Lemonade* (2016), though significantly more unified in its message, offers several conflicting representations of Beyoncé-as-feminist and Beyoncé-that-caters-to-the-male-gaze. The concept album chronicles the way in which Beyoncé coped with her husband's infidelity. Yet the songs all revolve around men, instead of self-love or self-care. In 'Hold Up' (2016) Beyoncé implies that her husband took her agency, and as a result she lost her self-esteem, acted up and even threatened to physically harm the 'other' woman: 'I don't wanna lose my pride/but I'mma fuck me up a bitch.' She questions her sanity and public appearance: 'What's worse/looking jealous or crazy?' The lyrics claim causation – Jay-Z, or men in general, can make women jealous, crazy or lose their pride – but all the while Beyoncé still pays her unfaithful husband compliments. She calls him royalty, heralds his success, and re-states her love for him. Though these examples and the songs on the album are emotionally typical responses to betrayal, and may simply factually depict how Beyoncé reacted and coped, they still revolve around men.

Other aspects of the album underscore the importance of men in Beyoncé's art, including her collaborations with other musicians. Four artists were featured in collaborations on the album – all men. Although the album boasts of her resilience, independence and agency, the presence of these male artists suggests otherwise. That is, even Beyoncé's grief over her philandering husband requires the assistance of men. Though the Weeknd, Kendrick Lamar, Jack White (reputedly a good friend of Jay-Z) and James Blake, all co-wrote songs with Beyoncé, echoing her message of strength and independence, the album lacks *any* collaboration with female artists. It is unclear whether these collaborators were chosen because of their talent, popularity or friendship with Beyoncé.

However, it *is* clear that Beyoncé fights against her pain by using the same yoke that binds her: relationships with men. She even alludes to personal struggles with unfaithful men in 'Daddy Lessons' in which her father warns her about men like him.[2] The collaborations with these men further demonstrate that although Beyoncé is a feminist, supports women's empowerment and pushes the boundaries of women popstars, she is seemingly unable to do so without men at the centre of her work.

While a raw sexuality is firmly at the core of Beyoncé's musical persona, her polished and classy public image appears highly sophisticated and respectable. She rarely wears revealing clothing, shields her young children from the spotlight, does not give interviews and controls the images of herself that are released to the media. She supports social movements, although seemingly only once other celebrities have first lent their support. Her Instagram mainly features non-contentious matters of fashion. Off-stage, she is seemingly neither sexual nor emotional: her public persona is no-nonsense and business-like. This persona is her brand; she is the commodity. It is clear that Beyoncé is not beyond the reach of respectability politics or the belief that 'Black people can overcome many of the everyday, acute impacts of racism by dressing properly and having education and social comportment' (Cooper 2018: 147). Robin James identifies the dichotomy of Beyoncé's public/stage personas as a 'feigned conformity' between 'respectability and ratchet' (2019: 77). The overtly sexual musical persona is the opposite of respectability – which is to say: ratchet. While her focus on men, as noted earlier, only aligns with respectability in its acquiescence to heteronormativity, a moment in her 2018 Coachella performance nonetheless would codify Beyoncé's use of respectability and retaliation against it.

#MeToo and Coachella

Beyoncé has not publicly spoken about the #MeToo moment at the time of writing, and her only gesture towards it was pulling her athleisure line, Ivy Park, from TopShop, due to allegations of sexual misconduct against its CEO (BBC News 2018). Although the #MeToo movement was officially founded in 2006 by Tarana Burke, to support women and girls of colour against sexual violence, it only gained significant traction in 2017, once Alyssa Milano tweeted #MeToo and asked women to respond in kind, if they also had been a victim of abuse. The movement quickly spread, across various industries, particularly the film industry and into politics – but it did not have a significant impact on hip-hop. The backlash against patriarchal power was notably strong, and women everywhere responded by claiming agency for themselves. *Lemonade* was released a year before the movement gained such global recognition, but the reclaiming of agency, as a strategy or benefit, is apparent in it. Beyoncé was initially slated to headline the Coachella music festival in 2017 but, due to her pregnancy, her participation was postponed until the following year. So, just months after the #MeToo movement fully occurred, Beyoncé finally took the stage. And the skit during the performance of 'Sorry' reflected the influence of the #MeToo movement.

'Sorry' is held to be one of the most popular songs on *Lemonade*, and offers a slightly different view of Beyoncé: one in which she is not sorry, *he* is sorry. Beyoncé repeats over and over that she does not concern herself with her partner, and adds to this declaration 'I don't give a fuck, chucking my deuces up/Suck on my balls, pause, I've had enough.' She continues with flippant disregard: 'Middle fingers up, put them hands high/Wave it in his face, tell him "boy bye."' These lyrics echo the control, detachment, and disdain that many rappers use to depict women as dispensable – commanding them in terms of when to perform sexual acts, and when to stop, without thinking twice. In 'Sorry', Beyoncé flips the script, showing that cheating men are dispensable. These lyrics alone are abnormal for Beyoncé, although the accompanying video is not. This depicts Beyoncé lounging on a throne while tennis star Serena Williams twerks next to her. In the video, the phrase 'suck on my balls, pause!' does not receive any special attention. But when Beyoncé took the stage at Coachella in 2018, the phrase literally stopped the show: the music cut out, Beyoncé reached out towards a video camera and shoved it back. A row of male backup dancers stood next to her, and she addressed them: 'Buggaboos, I need a good laugh! Make me laugh!' The men dance, but Beyoncé cues them to stop. She turns to her female backup dancers, who had been watching with their arms crossed over their chests. 'Did they make us laugh?' she asked. A resounding 'no!' follows. Beyoncé then turned to the crowd: 'ladies, are we smart? Are we strong? Have we had enough? Show 'em!' Flanked by her female dancers, Beyoncé began a step routine while yelling 'Suck on my balls!' The women stomp with their open hands pressed together, pointing downward, pointing repeatedly, that is, in a phallic representation. Then, after several repetitions, the male backup dancers join the skit and the crowd erupts in response. This moment of flippant disregard for men is entirely uncharacteristic

Figure 6.1 Beyoncé performs 'Sorry' at Coachella; screengrab from *Homecoming* (Beyoncé and Ed Burke, 2019).

of Beyoncé and her performances. Now *she* asks the men to entertain her, and when they fail, she and her female dancers take over, doing a step routine and taking a phrase associated with a misogynistic power and using it against men, entertaining herself. The reassociation of 'suck on my balls' in this instance does not remove agency from women by making them the object. Instead, it openly mocks men (Figure 6.1).

This moment did not go unnoticed. In every recording posted on *YouTube*, the audience goes wild. Many proclaimed that Beyoncé's Coachella performance 'broke' Twitter (i.e. overwhelmed it with responses), and the 'suck on my balls' skit was a significant part of that. Micah Peters, a writer for the pop culture website *The Ringer*, was taken aback to the extent that he sought and compiled reactions to the concert from his colleagues for an 'Exit Survey'. They selected their favourite 'Beychella' moment:

OBVIOUSLY THE STEP SEQUENCE TO THE 'SUCK ON MY BALLS' CHANT. ARE THERE OTHER ACCEPTABLE ANSWERS? NO – NO, THERE ARE NOT.

(The Ringer Staff 2018)

Roger Sherman, another staff writer, picked the same moment: 'I really think the phrase "suck on my balls" hasn't been given enough opportunity to shine as an insult available to all people, regardless of whether or not they have testicles. Beyoncé is finally shifting the paradigm.'

Yes indeed: shifting the paradigm. The Beyoncé paradigm, the misogynist paradigm . . . it is the first time that Beyoncé shifted the paradigm, and it is, I would argue, a part of the general culture shift of the #MeToo movement. This moment was not centred around making Beyoncé more likeable to men or even women. It is vulgar and, as Sherman states, insulting. Though her music does not often toe the line of respectability, apart from its conformity to heteronormativity, it does so with a specific audience in mind. This moment *mocks* heteronormativity. It is irreverent, insulting and ratchet.

Irreverence and ratchetness have long been used by Black women musicians as a different way of garnering respect. These do not follow the heteronormativity of respectability politics, and in many ways are an equal and opposing force – claiming the same outcome. Though irreverence and respect are often viewed as mutually exclusive and even direct opposites, Valerie Chepp argues that they are engaged in a 'recursive relationship, each continually shaping the meaning of the other' (2015: 208). Beyoncé's use of phallic imagery, such as dangling the microphone between her legs or gesturing with her hands pressed together, aligns perfectly with a politics of irreverence as a 'discursive adoption of the phallus to assert power over others'. (2015: 219) Chepp provides specific examples of Lil' Kim and Foxy Brown, rapping about fellatio and ejaculation (as if, as males, they were on the receiving end), and which, thematically, is not so far from 'suck on my balls'. The main result in such gestures, as Chepp identifies, is that they blur 'the boundaries between respectability and irreverence' and so intervene 'in patriarchal and racist discourses' (2015: 217) and which, as discussed in terms of respectability politics and feminism, are the two competing personas present in Beyoncé's music. Regina N. Bradley similarly replaces irreverence with ratchetness, as an 'intervention of sliding contemporary politics of respectability currently in place against women of color'. (2013) Beyoncé's sudden shift from respectability politics and heteronormativity to a politics of irreverence and ratchetness can only be seen as a response to changing patriarchial and racial modes, and a precise reflection or channelling of this moment of change too.

The major cultural and social difference, between the release of *Lemonade* in 2016 and Beyoncé's Coachella performance in 2018, was the advent and continuation of the #MeToo movement. As a self-identified feminist and an entrepreneur who severed business relations with a CEO accused of sexual misconduct, it is clear that Beyoncé was impacted by the social movement. In the context of her known propensity for remaining silent in public, Beyoncé's performances then are the best representations of her personal ideas. And, in one of the most significant performances of her life, Beyoncé took a decidedly different approach. Even considering her significant gestures towards historically Black colleges and universities, which were also worked into the performance, the moment of the show that garnered the greatest attention was the moment in which she told Coachella, and the world, to 'suck on [her] balls, bitch!' This moment was not inherently feminist – although I am sure many feminists lauded such a rejection of heteronormativity. And it did not embrace the male gaze: it rejected the male gaze. She insulted the audience and then finished the song – and singing too that she would not apologize. In this moment, Beyoncé broke with respectability politics, turning *instead* to ratchet feminism, and a politics of irreverence, to claim respect and dominance. She even went so far as to ignore male audience members in her affirmations, only telling the women fans that they were smart and strong. When she asked the women if they had had enough, she echoed another part of the general culture shift of the #MeToo movement – the 'Time's Up' movement. Although Beyoncé did not participate in the #MeToo movement by stating #MeToo or voicing allegations of sexual misconduct, she broke away from her brand of feminism and hypersexuality that had garnered such dedicated fans. And she told them to 'suck on [her] balls, bitch'. Beyoncé, in her supreme diva moment, had simply 'had enough'.

Notes

1 For Lewinsky on this lyric, see France (2022).
2 Mathew Knowles was notoriously unfaithful to Beyoncé and her sister, Solange's, mother, Tina Knowles-Lawson; he had purportedly led a double life, with a second/secret family. See Cox (2014).

Reference

Adichie, C. N. (2013), 'We Should All Be Feminists', *TED Talk*, April 2013. Available online: https://www.ted.com/talks/chimamanda_ngozi_adichie_we_should_all_be_feminists?language=en (accessed 10 November).

Anderson-Niles, A (2014), 'Highly Respected Feminist Chimamanda Ngozi Adichie Defends Beyoncé', *Urban Belle*, 24 March. Available online: https://urbanbellemag.com/2014/03/feministchimamanda-ngozi-adichie-defends-Beyoncé/ (accessed 10 November).

BBC News (2018), 'Beyoncé Buys Out Ivy Park Venture from Sir Philip Green', *BBC News*, 15 November. Available online: https://www.bbc.co.uk/news/business-46220057 (accessed 10 November 2022).

Bradley, R. N. (2013), 'I Been On (Ratchet): Conceptualizing a Sonic Ratchet Aesthetic in Beyoncé's "Bow Down"', *Red Clay Scholar*, 19 March. Available online: http://redclayscholar.blogspot.com/2013/03/i-been-on-ratchet-conceptualizing-sonic.html (accessed 10 November 2022).

Burkett, E. (2021), 'Feminism', *Britannica*, 27 August (date of last modification), 2021. Available online: https://www.britannica.com/topic/feminism

Chepp, V. (2015), 'Black Feminist Theory and the Politics of Irreverence: The Case of Womens Rap', *Feminist Theory*, 16 (2): 207–26.

Cooper, B. (2018), *Eloquent Rage: A Black Feminist Discovers Her Superpower*, New York: St. Martin's Press.

Cox, L. (2014), 'Matthew Knowles: DNA Test Confirms 2nd Love Child Is Beyoncé's Sibling', *Hollywood Life*, 18 September. Available online: https://hollywoodlife.com/2014/09/18/matthew-knowles-love-child-model-taqoya-branscomb-dna-test/ (accessed 10 November 2022).

France, L. R. (2022), 'Monica Lewinsky Wants Beyoncé To Remove Lyric About Her from "Partition"', *CNN*, 3 August. Available online: https://edition.cnn.com/2022/08/03/entertainment/monica-lewinsky-beyonce-lyric/index.html (accessed 10 November 2022).

Gay, R. (2014), *Bad Feminist*, New York: HarperCollins.

Good Morning America (2013), 'Beyoncé Reveals Secrets Behind the Making of Her Chart-Topping Album', *ABC News*, 30 December. Available online: https://abcnews.go.com/GMA/video/Beyoncé-interview-2013-singer-reveals-secrets-making-chart-21367273 (accessed 10 November 2022).

Gottesman, T. (2016), 'EXCLUSIVE: Beyoncé Wants to Change the Conversation', *Elle*, 4 April. Available online: https://www.elle.com/fashion/a35286/Beyoncé-elle-cover-photos/ (accessed 10 November 2022).

hooks, b. (2014), 'Are You Still A Slave? Liberating the Black Female Body', talk for *The New School*, 7 May. Available online: https://www.youtube.com/watch?v=rJk0hNROvzs (available online 10 November 2022).

James, R. (2015), *Resilience and Melancholy: Pop Music, Feminism, Neoliberalism*, Alresford: Zero Books, 2015.

James, R. (2019), *The Sonic Episteme: Accoustic Resonance, Neoliberalism, and Biopolitics*, Durham: Duke University Press.

Jones, F. (2019), *Reclaiming Our Space: How Black Feminists Are Changing The World From the Tweets to the Streets*, Boston: Beacon Press.

Kiene, A. (2016), 'Ngozi Adichie: Beyoncé's Feminism Isn't My Feminism', *De Volkskrant*, 7 October. Available online: https://www.volkskrant.nl/cultuur-media/ngozi-adichie-Beyoncé-s-feminism-isn-t-my-feminism~bd0661ea/? (accessed 10 November 2022).

Lorde, A. (1984), *Sister Outsider*, Berkeley: Crossing Press.

Ringer Staff, the (2018), 'The Beyoncé-at-Coachella Exit Survey', *The Ringer*, 16 August. Available online: https://www.theringer.com/music/2018/4/16/17242666/Beyoncé-coachella-exit-survey (accessed 10 November 2022).

7

Amuro Namie

Japan's diva in the postmodern era?

Dorothy Finan

Introduction: 'Diva of the Heisei era'

Artists as stars can make eras, in the same way that artists are shaped by the eras in which they come to stardom. The idea of the era, however, carries a specific cultural weight in Japan, which is the world's second-largest market for popular music (IFPI 2021). When a new emperor is enthroned, a new historical era is declared, carefully named and referred to on official documents, and used to frame discussions about the past, the present and the future, including those of popular music. When the most recent Heisei imperial era (1989 to 2019) ended, with the abdication of Emperor Akihito, media outlets scrambled to crown the era's ultimate diva ('utahime'), by polling members of the public. The star worthy of the title of 'Diva of the Heisei Era' (Excite News 2019) was declared to be Amuro Namie.[1] Amuro, a genre performer who made her debut at the age of fourteen, and had only recently retired after twenty-five years in the music industry, had been active during a time when many charismatic women achieved widespread success and visibility in Japanese popular music. So, what made Amuro deserving of the 'diva' title, in the eyes of the Japanese public? In this chapter, I argue that Amuro's status as a 'legend' – in the words of one individual polled by a magazine (Nikkan Spa 2019) – comes from her embodiment of Heisei as the era of the postmodern, and of a new Japanese ideal: a Japan primed for economic and cultural exchange, able to hold its own on the world stage, and elevating women and girls to arbiters of both cultural trends and their own lives.

As other contributors to this volume show, although divas' legacies may seem timeless, the concepts surrounding the diva change across time and place. An example of this would be the 'utahime' (diva) – the Japanese term used to describe Amuro as a diva – which was historically applied to a woman who could be said to be beautiful, cultured and with artistic talent. However, in the late twentieth century, utahime became a self-declaration for women who had a proven legacy in the popular music industry – a way of taking their place in the canon of music in an industry dominated by men. For example, singer Nakamori Akina released a greatest hits album in 1994 that was simply titled *Utahime (Diva)*. In this way, the idea of the diva in Japan embodies not only the image of a woman in popular music but her very right to a legacy. Amuro is, and always has been, an expert at asserting both. Similar chapters could also be written on Amuro's contemporaries, such as Utada Hikaru, who wrote and released their own music bilingually from the very outset of her career, and Hamasaki Ayumi, who was a fashion icon in her own right and sold many more records than Amuro (Oricon 2019). However, as I will argue in this chapter, Amuro's significance lies in her personal ambition, as a young working woman taking control of her artistic destiny during a time of personal upheaval, publicly documented, mirroring the struggle to make sense of the nation's story during the socioeconomic upheaval of Japan's recessionary Heisei era. That is, in the language of Christine Yano (2018: 96) her 'star text enacted . . . Japan's supra-text'. These words, however, do not directly apply to Amuro, but to an earlier diva who had a similar era-spanning impact without whom it is impossible to understand Amuro's discovery and eventual elevation to 'diva of the Heisei Era'.

The discovery of a diva

The Japanese diva can be traced back to Misora Hibari, a diva of Japan's Shōwa era (1926–89).[2] Debuting as a child star in the 1940s, Hibari was active throughout the Second World War, the United States occupation of Japan (from 1945 to 1952), and Japan's period of rapid economic growth, from the 1960s to the 1980s. A successful recording artist and movie star, and who grew up in tandem with screen stars during what was a golden age for Japanese cinema, Misora Hibari's 'clear, strong, working class, and female' (Yano 2017: 128) persona meant that she could embody the possibilities of the modern age, and the 'exhilarating' (Yano 2017: 132) potential of world music to opened up other cultures. For example, she was known for her fondness for jazz and r'n'b (Yano 2018: 103). As Jennifer Coates has noted, the women film stars of the post-war period in Japan – those young women who were considered to be icons – allowed audiences to 're-imagine' national identities in a rapidly changing Japan, and a rapidly changing world (Coates 2014: 24). Misora Hibari passed away in the same year as Emperor Hirohito, just as the Shōwa era came to a close. The timing of her passing only added to what Christine Yano describes as Hibari's 'diva status as a morality tale that Japan may tell of itself, to itself' (2017: 113); Misora Hibari had somehow merged into people's imaginings of an entire modern era.

As Japan moved into the Heisei era and the 1990s, the economic bubble burst and a resultant sense of social instability set in. All this, in the wider global context of new political and social paradigms emerging after the ending of the Cold War, led to Japan experiencing something of a 'crisis of modernity' (Iida 2000) – in other words: the Heisei era had a distinctive *post*-modern flavour. While many industries in Japan declined and even collapsed, people simply kept on buying CDs, with sales peaking in 1998 (Mōri 2016: 168). It was also around this time that the genre and term 'J-pop' (short for Japanese pop) was established. A radio station coined the term J-pop in 1988, and used it as a way of distinguishing its playlists as neither the Japanese folk music (enka) of Misora Hibari, nor the bubble-gum pop of hyper-manufactured idols (Miyairi 2015: 127). In this landscape of economic and popular music upheaval, Amuro's birthplace of Okinawa became known as a reliable source of new performing talent. A group of tropical islands, located in the far south of Japan and previously part of the independent Ryukyu Kingdom, the Okinawa region was annexed by Japan after years of 'colonial-type' rule in 1879 (Bhowmik and Rabson 2016: 3). Okinawa, home to the majority of US military bases in Japan, was distinguished by the performance and production of popular music on the principle of 'cultural mixing', so as to 'meld and maintain distinctions' between different identities (Roberson 2001: 234).[3]

This popular musical mixture had been perfected and branded by the Okinawa Actors School, founded in 1983, into which Amuro was scouted. Summing up the particular appeal of the school's graduates, Stevens (2008: 26) notes that they bring 'an "authentic" representation of American-inspired popular music with the regional image of a sun-kissed, leisurely resort-dominated lifestyle'. Famous contemporaries included the girl band SPEED, and the r'n'b boyband Da Pump. For Amuro, the Okinawa Actors School was a chance to get ahead and prove herself as a performer. Raised for most of her life by a single mother working two jobs to support her four children, Amuro would later recall how her late mother's

Figure 7.1 Screengrab of Amuro Namie in the music video for 'a walk in the park' (1996).

work ethic and dedication to her children was an inspiration and gifted her a 'positive' attitude to her own work (Lewis 2005).⁴ Amuro was placed in a dance pop girl band called Super Monkey's, which debuted in 1992, as Amuro was on the verge of turning fifteen years old. As the lead singer of the group, Amuro was becoming popular in her own right, so that in 1994 the girl group was renamed *Amuro Namie with Super Monkey's*, releasing their first major chart hit 'Try Me (Watashi o Shinjite)' ('Try me (Believe in Me)') in December of that year. Amuro soon moved to a new record label and achieved her first solo number one in 1995, with 'Chase the Chance'. This replicated the Eurodance sound of 'Try Me', and was the high point of her association with the celebrity DJ, dance pop producer and an all-round auteur figure, Komuro Tetsuya (Figure 7.1).

By the late 1990s, Amuro was considered to be a cultural phenomenon. She had her own iconic look: short skirts and knee-high boots, paired with highlights in long, glossy, dyed hair, thinly styled eyebrows and pale eyeshadow. Amuro's fashion at the time was copied by her young women fans, who were better known as 'amurā' ('Amur-ers'), and who frequented new centres of youth fashion such as Shibuya in Tokyo. Her signature style is evident in her music videos, such as 1996's 'a walk in the park'. Aoyagi argues that the fashion of Amuro and her followers represented a move towards a new type of 'adolescent femaleness' and 'a self-affirmative style of sexualized performance' (2005: 120), but this style only served to mask the more submissive 'cute' performance that Amuro still took part in. One could equally argue that Amuro's display of different types of femininity represented a public contestation of what it meant to be a young woman in Japan in the 1990s, where school-aged girls and their rebellious fashions were simultaneously condemned and objectified by the male-dominated media as a 'new social force' (Kinsella 2014: 185).[5] Amuro has spoken of her wish to express both the strength and vulnerability of women in her music during this time, a drive that came from her personal admiration of Janet Jackson (Josei Jishin 2018). And her engagement with African American popular music styles (both hip-hop and r'n'b) and creators (such as choreographer Shawnette Heard, who had worked with Michael and Janet Jackson, as well as Madonna and Beyoncé), in a bid to remake herself as a new type of pop star, demonstrates how incorporations of other types of music could be said to walk a thin line between informed appreciation and outright misappropriation.

'Queen of Hip-Pop'

By February 1997, Amuro was at the peak of her popularity, having released her bestselling single 'Can You Celebrate'. The song became the top-selling Japanese single by a solo artist in Japan (Okwodu 2017) and won the grand prize at the Japan Record Awards, Japan's answer to the Grammys. As a young woman in pop, she was already confounding expectations, and her mythology, as a headstrong icon for women in (post)modern Japan, started to form. Later that year in October, aged just twenty, she surprised the Japanese public by announcing her marriage to Sam, a member of dance pop group and label-mates TRF, as well as her pregnancy. At a time when women were still typically expected to leave work upon marriage or pregnancy (Hendry 1993: 131), Amuro's announcement would have left supportive fans wondering if they would ever see her on stage again – especially after she appeared in a Japanese government campaign, with her husband and newborn son, 'encouraging young Japanese to settle down and have children' (Lewis 2005). But after a year away from the music industry, she made an emotional return to live performance, at the close of 1998. Amuro has said that because she was so young at the time that a year's hiatus 'felt like an eternity' (Uchida 2018), and that she was forced to think about why her maternity leave made her so anxious. She concluded that part of the anxiety stemmed from worries concerning whether she would reach her full potential as a performer, and this prompted her to move to gain more creative control over her career.

Amuro stepped away from the spotlight again in March 1999, after her mother's death, but was back to her project of self-determination later that year, with a fan recalling on the occasion of Amuro's retirement how she was 'so cool to seek her own way ... even when things were tough for her' (Mainichi 2018).

Her change in musical direction saw her moving away from dance pop and more towards r'n'b (Mainichi 2018). This was evident in her r'n'b comeback album, *Genius 2000* (2000), a collaboration between Komuro Tetsuya and famed US r'n'b producer Dallas Austin. 'SOMETHING 'BOUT THE KISS' (1999), the first Austin-produced single from the album, featured English backing vocals that resembled the vocals of TLC, for whom Austin had worked, for their debut album.[6] The single's b-side featured a duet with US r'n'b boyband Imajin, further showing how committed Amuro and her label were to this new sound.

Amuro's working relationship with Dallas Austin and other US r'n'b producers of the late 1990s and early 2000s was so longstanding that on an anniversary edition of the TLC hit 'Waterfalls' (first released in 1994), released exclusively in Japan in 2013, Amuro took the place of the late Lisa 'Left-Eye' Lopes, so as to circumvent copyright issues around the re-use of Left-Eye's vocals. However, as noted in the previous section, there have been some occasions when Amuro's engagement with Black musical talent has appeared somewhat shallow. For example, in the music video to 'Don't Wanna Cry' (1996), Black actors perform as singing service staff, moonlighting as backup singers at an upscale bar – an uncomfortable metaphor for the way they are 'servicing' Amuro's trendy pop image. In this way, Amuro's empowered divahood for Japanese women cannot be studied without understanding how that empowerment was mediated through the cultures of Black American popular music, especially the idea of the Black woman as an independent diva. Kimberly Springer (2007: 255) has argued that the image of the diva as a Black woman who is 'powerful and entertaining, if pushy and bitchy' is strongly linked to the stereotype of the angry Black woman, whose voicing of her struggles is not necessarily heard or taken seriously (Springer 2007: 258). Still, these problematic mediations do not negate the significance for Japanese listeners of hearing Amuro's own voice through her music, and after a second album with Austin's involvement within the space of the year (*Break the Rules* of 2000), Amuro penned her first lyrics in her 2001 single 'Say the Word'. Amuro was now the voice of the agency of young Japanese women, and when Okinawa was one of the Japanese prefectures selected to host the twenty-sixth G8 summit of world leaders in the year 2000, Amuro was chosen as the 'Okinawa-born' representative to perform the theme song 'Never End' – a song that represented 'a vision of harmony and interaction in the world in the twenty-first century' (Ministry of Foreign Affairs of Japan 2000).

The early 2000s saw Amuro continue to construct her own r'n'b sound; for example, Amuro was one of the key voices of the Suite Chic project, an initiative by a collective of Japanese producers and musicians to bring hip-hop and r'n'b styles, as performed by Japanese artists, into the popular music mainstream. After moving away from the more exclusive production influences of both Komuro Tetsuya and Dallas Austin (and divorcing, in 2002), Amuro began to direct her own concerts and live performances, and became increasingly confident in presenting a more sexualized, postfeminist version of herself in her lyrics and through her stage persona. She speaks of having regularly listened to 'hundreds' of demo songs, and selecting only those with an 'immediate hook' that she could picture accompanying her grand entrance onto a concert stage with her backing dancers (Zamami 2019). In her live performances, Amuro inhabited extravagant sets that recalled the shapeshifting aesthetics of her music videos (including a car maintenance garage in 'Put Em' Up' of 2003, and a jet engine in 'the SPEED STAR' of 2004), and sporting a mixture of streetwear and bright miniskirts. Aided by her long-time female collaborator and songwriter Michico, the hip-hop and r'n'b-style singles from the album *Queen of Hip-Pop* (2005) covered topics from friendship and solidarity between women ('Girls Talk') to the importance of practising safe sex ('Want Me, Want Me'). As a high-profile divorced celebrity mother, not shying away from her ownership of her sexuality, and now declaring herself the 'Queen' of one of Japan's hottest popular music scenes, Amuro was once again pushing the boundaries of what it meant to be a successful woman in public in postmodern Japan, after newspapers had once criticized her for the 'abandonment of her child' (Lewis 2005). In another sense, Amuro's trajectory is one of the conventional 'lifecycle' of the woman as pop star, where the 'good girl' becomes a 'temptress' (Lieb 2018). This transition was undoubtedly aided by something akin to what Gaunt (2015: 255) describes as American pop's appropriation of 'black cultural phenomena' to assist in the casting off of one's 'commercial identity', showing again how Japanese popular music's engagement with Black American popular music styles has not always properly attributed or understood.

Amuro Namie's legacy

To become a woman who was open about her own ownership of her artistry and of her destiny – that is: Amuro as postfeminist, and as the Heisei-era icon – Amuro had to, arguably, first shed both the high-profile men she collaborated with, and her teen star persona. In respect to this, it is important to note that Amuro's legacy is not only meaningful for fans within Japan; she was part of the first wave of J-pop stars to gain popularity in East and Southeast Asia (Ng 2002). This was the result of a concerted effort by producers like Komuro to market Japanese popular music and stars as 'fashionable' and 'Asian' (Iwabuchi 2002: 117), and of that which Iwabuchi describes as Japan's economic and cultural 'return to Asia' (1995: 94), as a countermove to the history of the country's colonialism. If we take Amuro to represent a postmodern Japan, then part of her appeal in, for example, Hong Kong and Taiwan, lay in her embodiment of Japan as a fashionable Asian future – albeit an embodiment not without its 'othering' aspects for those outside of Japan (Taylor-Jones 2017: 130). Nonetheless, on her farewell tour of 2018, Amuro was greeted warmly by East Asian fans at venues in Hong Kong, Shenzen and Taipei. Moreover, Amuro featured on Taiwanese pop star Jolin Tsai's track 'I'm Not Yours' (2015) for a story of Asian women working together to combat sexism. In the video, Amuro and Tsai play mythical fox-spirits, which is a shared aspect of East Asian folklore that evokes the unknowable power of women as 'femme fatale' (Balmain 2017), singing 'boys are stupid/let them fall'.

Collaboration has helped to cement Amuro's postfeminist legacy in Japan, too. *Checkmate* (2011) was an album that brought together Amuro's musical collaborations with the likes of the K-pop girl group After School, and J-pop singers AI and Anna Tsuchiya. These collaborations may also have their roots in Amuro's admiration of the Black female hip-hop and r'n'b musicians, and how collaborations between artists such as Missy Elliot and Lil' Kim show 'the collective power of Black women to help each other be self-sufficient and not dependent on men' (Emerson 2002: 127). By 2016, Amuro would prove once again that not only was she a heroine for the women who looked up to her, but was also a figure considered worthy of representing Japan: she was chosen to sing 'Hero' (2016), the theme song to national broadcaster NHK's coverage of the Olympics. In the music video she is dressed in an ethereal white gown, surrounded by falling petals in a grand CGI landscape. The imagery resonated with the idea that Amuro was indeed the Queen of J-pop. The announcement of Amuro's retirement in 2017 preceded the release of a compilation album in November, *Finally* (2017), which even featured a track penned by her old producer Komuro. As Emperor Akihito's planned abdication was announced in December 2017, Amuro's retirement announcement must have felt like the end of a (musical) era. Mobile phone operator Docomo even released an advert

Figure 7.2 Screengrab of Amuro Namie in the music video for 'Hero' (2016).

looking back at the mobile phones and fashions of the past few decades, with Amuro seen clutching a brick-like phone while showing off her famous 1990s thigh-high boots. No doubt many of these promotions were carefully timed to usher Amuro into the role of 'Diva of the Heisei era' (Figure 7.2).

Even so, Amuro's legacy is more than a simple promotional stunt. Her influence can be heard and observed in many different aspects of Japanese popular music. As Japanese pop singer May'n (eleven years Amuro's junior) explained, 'before I even knew what a singer was, my first ever dream was to be like Amuro Namie . . . without Amuro Namie, there would be no me'. (2017) Thus, in respect of her versatility in genre and fashion, Amuro helped women in Japanese pop, like May'n, to break away from the dichotomy of the 'real' singer and the manufactured pop idol. Okwodu (2017) notes that Amuro's continued fame as a 'performer over the age of 30 who fearlessly sport(ed) sexier styles' made her stand out within a youth-obsessed Japanese popular music industry. Contemporary Japanese artists, ranging from Okinawa-based rapper Awich to virally successful r'n'b singer RiRi, and dance-focused girl group Happiness, are all indebted in some way to Amuro's style and story. Though that story is entirely Amuro's own, its trajectory of sisterhood, empowerment and the means for telling it, is in turn indebted to African American musical creators and performers. Amuro's final transformation has been into a transcendental star of an era.

Conclusion

A successful pop diva needs epochal charisma – and nowhere more so than in Japan, where the notion of 'era' is central to national storytelling. However, as

Yano writes in her work on Japan's modern diva Misora Hibari, to acknowledge the significance of a star to a whole group of people need not mean adding to that star's 'hagiographic narrative' (2017: 113). In this chapter, I have attempted to account for Amuro's publicly lauded status as a diva of Japan's postmodern era without unnecessarily elevating her above the many talented women in Japanese pop who were also icons of the Heisei era. As I have argued, it is the way Amuro's career spans the Heisei era so neatly, and how her personal and musical journeys connect to discourses around new postmodern femininities and ideas of what it means to be Japanese in the twenty-first century that entitle her to such an accolade. Though this chapter cannot hope to address the full scope of Amuro's story and career, I have attempted to lay out what are arguably the more significant moments in her road to divahood.

Writing about divas of national significance inevitably obscures some of the people who do not feel able to identify with dominant notions of Japanese-ness, or indeed of femininity. Those in Amuro's hometown are still coming up against an educational system that tries to fit the diverse identities of the Ryukyu islands into a 'Japanese' identity, or into simple East–West dichotomies (Taira 2019: 122). For those in the Japanese government, the maintenance of Japan's post-Cold War status quo has meant supporting the running and construction of US military bases on the islands – a 'longstanding source of tension' (Inagaki and Lewis 2020). Moreover, as Dayna Chatman (2015) argues in relation to Beyoncé, elevating divas who appear to have it all can risk using 'discourses about women as autonomous empowered citizens to ignore the conditions that continue to systematically oppress women' (2015: 927). In a country that continues to occupy a low ranking in the World Economic Forum's Gender Gap Index as a result of wage gaps and 'male-dominated management' (Yamaguchi 2019: 22), Amuro Namie's story is striking. Her rising above the restrictions of her own industry and of society to become the type of woman that she herself once admired is as much a story of the diva as the symbol of past eras, as it is a story of the diva as communicating or embodying hope for better things to come.

Notes

1 Emperor Emeritus Akihito's abdication in favour of his son, Emperor Naruhito, was so unprecedented in modern times that it required a change in legislation

to accommodate it. Naruhito's reign, and the current Reiwa era, began on 1 May 2019.

In this chapter, Japanese names (Amuro Namie, Misora Hibari) are written in the Japanese order (family name first, given name last). They may appear in the reverse order in other English language contexts.

2   The Shōwa era ended with the passing of the then Emperor Hirohito on the 7 January 1989. He is now posthumously referred to as 'Emperor Shōwa', after the imperial era over which he presided.
3   The United States retained control of islands, which were a strategic battleground during the Second World War, 'as a precondition for ending US-led Occupation' of Japan, in 1952 (Kapur 2018: 12). Despite being nominally returned to Japan in 1972, US military bases have remained in Okinawa – part of Japan's ongoing post-war security agreement with the United States. As of 2015, 80 per cent of people polled in Okinawa expressed their opposition to the expansion of military bases (Wingfield-Hayes 2015).
4   Taira Emiko, Amuro's mother, passed away in 1999.
5   Although girls were at the forefront of 1990s popular music and culture in Japan, economic power lay squarely with star producers such as Amuro's mentor Komuro Tetsuya, who 'took [commercial] advantage of young women's rising interest in music . . . and provided this sector of the audience with artists who corresponded to their ideals and aspirations' (Stevens 2008: 56).
6   His other production credits include work with Grace Jones, Monica, Blu Cantrell and Janet Jackson.

Reference

Aoyagi, H. (2005), *Island of Eight Million Smiles: Idol Performance and Symbolic Production in Contemporary Japan*, London: Harvard University Press.

Balmain, C. (2017), 'East Asian Gothic: A Definition', *Palgrave Communications*, 3 (1): 1–10.

Bhowmik, D. L. and S. Rabson (2016), 'Introduction', in D. L. Bhowmik and S. Rabson (eds), *Islands of Protest: Japanese Literature from Okinawa*, 1–20, Honolulu: University of Hawai'i Press.

Chatman, D. (2015), 'Pregnancy, then it's "back to business": Beyoncé, Black Femininity, and the Politics of a Post-Feminist Gender Regime', *Feminist Media Studies*, 15 (6): 1–16.

Coates, J. (2014), 'The Shape-Shifting Diva: Yamaguchi Yoshiko and the National Body', *Journal of Japanese and Korean Cinema*, 6 (1): 23–38.

Emerson, R. (2002), '"Where My Girls At?": Negotiating Black Womanhood in Music Videos', *Gender & Society*, 16 (1): 115–35.

Excite News (2019), '"Heisei no utahime" to ittara dare?' [Who was the 'Diva of the Heisei era'?], 31 May. Available online: https://www.excite.co.jp/news/article/Sirabee_20162057772/ (accessed 11 June 2020).

Gaunt, K. D. (2015), 'YouTube, Twerking & You: Context Collapse and the Handheld Co-presence of Black Girls and Miley Cyrus', *Journal of Popular Music Studies*, 27 (3): 244–73.

Hendry, J. (1993), 'The Role of the Professional Housewife', in J. Hunter (ed.), *Japanese Women Working*, 223–40, New York: Routledge.

IFPI (2021), 'Global Music Report', *International Federation of the Phonographic Industry*, 23 March. Available online: https://gmr2021.ifpi.org/assets/GMR2021_State%20of%20the%20Industry.pdf (accessed 30 April 2021).

Iida, Y. (2000), 'Between the Technique of Living an Endless Routine and the Madness of Absolute Degree Zero: Japanese Identity and the Crisis of Modernity in the 1990s', *positions*, 8 (2): 423–64.

Inagaki, K. and L. Lewis (2020), 'Okinawa's Anger over US Military Bases Stoked by Coronavirus Surge', *Financial Times*, 21 August. Available online: https://www.ft.com/content/c04caf13-654c-441a-8ef9-d940339bde88 (accessed 1 September 2020).

Iwabuchi, K. (1995), 'Return to Asia? Japan in the Global Audio-Visual Market', *Media International Australia*, 77 (1): 94–106.

Iwabuchi, K. (2002), *Recentering Globalization: Popular Culture and Japanese Transnationalism*, London: Duke University Press.

Josei, J. (2018), 'Amuro Namie intai kōen chokuzen ni katatta Janetto Jakuson ai', [Amuro Namie takes time out before her final concert to discuss her admiration of Janet Jackson], 22 February. Available online: https://news.livedoor.com/article/detail/14339575/. (accessed 25 August 2020).

Kapur, N. (2018), *Japan at the Crossroads: Conflict and Compromise after Anpo*, Cambridge, MA: Harvard University Press.

Kinsella, S. (2014), *Schoolgirls, Money and Rebellion in Japan*, London: Routledge.

Lewis, L. (2005), 'Comeback Queen of J-Pop', *The Times*, 26 January. Available online: https://www.thetimes.co.uk/article/comeback-queen-of-j-pop-ksth79qb9nz (accessed 30 April 2021).

Lieb, K. J. (2018), *Gender, Branding, and the Modern Music Industry: The Social Construction of Female Popular Music Stars*, New York: Routledge.

Mainichi, The (2018), '"I Did It My Way": Icon Namie Amuro Retires after Unique 3-Decade Career', *The Mainichi*, 17 September. Available online: https://mainichi.jp/english/articles/20180917/p2a/00m/0et/017000c (accessed 3 May 2021).

May'n (2017), '"Kashu" nante kotoba o shiru mae . . . ' [Before I even knew what a singer was . . .], *Twitter*, 20 September. Available online: https://twitter.com/mayn_tw/status/910500066816753664 (accessed 1 September 2020).

Ministry of Foreign Affairs of Japan (2000), 'Kyushu-Okinawa Summit 2000 Reference Materials', *Ministry of Foreign Affairs of Japan*. Available online: https://www.mofa.go.jp/policy/economy/summit/2000/outline/eng/pdfs/reception.pdf (accessed 29 August 2020).

Miyairi, K. (2015), *Jēpoppu bunkaron* [A Thesis for J-pop], Tokyo: Sairyusha.

Mori, Y. (2016), *Popyūrā ongaku to shihonshugi* [Popular music and Capitalism], Tokyo: Serika Shobō.

Ng, B. (2002), 'Japanese Popular Music in Singapore and the Hybridization of Asian Music', *Asian Music*, 34 (1): 1–18.

Nikkan, S. (2019), 'Heisei no utahime to ieba dare?' o tōhyō [We asked: 'Who was the Diva of the Heisei era?'), 27 February. Available online: https://nikkan-spa.jp/1552747 (accessed 11 June 2020).

Okwodu, J. (2017), 'Namie Amuro, "The Madonna of Japan," Is Retiring, But Her Style Influence Lives on', *Vogue*, 20 October. Available online: https://www.vogue.com/article/namie-amuro-tokyo-fashion-week-muse (accessed 30 April 2021).

Oricon Music (2019), 'Orikon heisei sēruzu rankingu' [The Oricon Chart of the Heisei Era's Best-Selling Artists], *Oricon Music*, 11 April. Available online: https://www.oricon.co.jp/confidence/special/52827/2/ (accessed 13 January 2022).

Roberson, J. E. (2001), 'Uchinaa Pop: Place and Identity in Contemporary Okinawan Popular Music', *Critical Asian Studies*, 33 (2): 211–42.

Springer, K. (2007), 'Divas, Evil Black Bitches, and Bitter Black Women: African American Women in Postfeminist and Post-Civil Rights Popular Culture', in D. Negra and Y. Tasker (eds), *Interrogating Postfeminism*, 249–76, Durham: Duke University Press.

Stevens, C. S. (2008), *Japanese Popular Music: Culture, Authenticity and Power*, Abingdon: Routledge.

Taira, K. (2019), 'A Systematic Form of Japanization in Okinawa: Japanese Identity Construction through a Japanization Discourse in Textbooks and a Textbook Guide', *International Studies in Sociology of Education*, 28 (2): 110–26.

Taylor-Jones, K. E. (2017), *Divine Work: Japanese Colonial Cinema and its Legacy*, New York: Bloomsbury Academic.

Uchida, R. (2018), 'J-Pop Icon Namie Amuro Speaks to NHK before Retirement', *NHK World*, 17 September. Available online: https://www3.nhk.or.jp/nhkworld/en/news/backstories/241/ (accessed 28 August 2020).

Wingfield-Hayes, R. (2015), 'Okinawa Residents Protest Over New US Military Base', *BBC News*, 27 April. Available online: https://www.bbc.co.uk/news/av/world-asia-pacific-32485485 (accessed 3 May 2021).

Yamaguchi, K. (2019), 'Japan's Gender Gap', *Finance & Development*, 56 (1): 26–9.

Yano, C. R. (2017), 'Diva Misora Hibari as Spectacle of Postwar Japan's Modernity', in A. N. Weintraub and B. Barendreght (eds), *Vamping the Stage: Female Voices of Asian Modernities*, 127–43, Honolulu: University of Hawai'i Press.

Yano, C. R. (2018), 'From Child Star to Diva: Misora Hibari', in L. Miller and R. Copeland (eds), *Diva Nation: Female Icons from Japanese Cultural History*, 95–114, Oakland: University of California Press.

Zamami, K. (2019), '"Yarikitta. Chanto kui naku": Amuro Namie-san ga watashi no mae de katatta "hikigiwa" no bigaku' ['I've done it all. I have no regrets': Amuro Namie Discusses the Art of 'Knowing When to Bow Out'], *Bunshun Online*, 21 February. Available online: https://bunshun.jp/articles/-/10787 (accessed 30 April 2021).

8

Reconstructing the American Dream
Janelle Monáe's Afrofuturist performances

Timmia Hearn DeRoy

A blue door slides open, revealing a white industrial-looking hallway, and a slim figure in a white body suit and a gold and black gas mask enters, arms hiding something behind her back. Two similarly white-clad people, one lying on a hard surface and the other sitting, look up at her. As the first chords of 'Americans', the final song on Janelle Monáe's 2018 album *Dirty Computer* sound, the figure at the door takes off her mask, revealing that she is Zen (played by Tessa Thompson), a young woman designated as a 'dirty computer' by the unnamed authoritarian regime under which she lives. Zen flings two matching masks to Jane (Janelle Monáe) and Che (Jayson Aaron), her lovers and fellow 'dirty computers'. The three make their way down the hallway, heading towards a door and presumably freedom from the centre where 'dirty computers' like them are collected by the authorities, and 'cleaned' and 're-programmed' through having their memories wiped, and a brain-washing program. As Monáe's face fades into the whiteness around them, her voice sings out a wish to be loved 'for who I am'. Her lyrics demand space for herself and those like her, calling America her country and stating 'I will defend my land'. She concludes the verse with a proclamation: 'I'm not crazy, baby; naw – I'm American'.

The aforementioned, as described, follows the credits of *Dirty Computer*, the 'Emotion Picture' which was released alongside the same-named album.[1] *Dirty Computer* is a stunning visual story, drawing on the struggle between Monáe's version of what it means to be American, and an authoritarian regime which seeks to control its citizenry. While the imagery of *Dirty Computer* is futuristic – complete with hovering cars and advanced mind-wiping computer technology – the lyrics of the album's fourteen songs are grounded in contemporary conversations which tackle, head-on, the ideologies and mythologies of the 'American Dream'.[2]

Ever since Kansas City-born Monáe released her 2003 demo album, *The Audition*, her performances have utilized futurist iconography and Afrofuturistic discourse to perform a reconstruction of the American Dream mythology, centring Black, working class and queer people. Monáe's performances include the characters that she plays in her music, her ever-developing public persona as displayed through interviews and the characters she has played on the silver screen. She first came to public prominence, and my own awareness, when her breakout EP *Metropolis: The Chase Suite I* (alternatively called *Metropolis: Suite I (The Chase)*), was released in 2007 by Bad Boy Records. Growing up a few years behind Monáe myself, in Kansas, as a Queer mixed-race woman, I found that songs like 'Sincerely, Jane' (2010) and 'Many Moons' (2010) captivated me by centring stories of those othered by society, and by their giving voice and visual prominence to young, Black, gender-non-conforming women. Even in these early songs, Monáe was using a visual landscape and setting for her stories of Afrofuturism, while lyrically addressing inequality in America.

Much of the scholarship on Monáe's work focuses on its science fiction and Afrofuturist elements, as with Hassler-Forest (2022), either placing her in conversation with white sci-fi creators like Fritz Lang, Isaac Asimov and the Wachowskis (Jones 2018; Miller 2015; Palmer 2020; Piper 2001; Ramsey 2017), or focusing on her sonic, visual and stylistic position within Afrofuturist discourses, with influences including James Brown, Sun Ra, George Clinton and Prince (Aghoro 2018; Brown 2018; Gipson 2016; Murchison 2018; Valnes 2017). The former focuses on Monáe's cyborg characters and the dystopian worlds that her work creates, but rarely considers her lyrical content. Monáe herself has listed *Metropolis* (Fritz Lang, 1927) and *The Matrix* (The Wachowskis, 1999) as inspirations, but a close analysis of her lyrics and visual landscape reveals that while she is also using science fiction to question capitalism and those in power, the social situations that her work deconstructs speak to realities that Lang, the Wachowskis and other white science fictions, tends to completely ignore.

The branch of scholarship that positions Monáe within Afrofuturism takes a deeper look at the political messages in her work. This scholarship understands that she is investigating the place the 'other' has been relegated to American life, and exploring the echoes of the past in the present, while looking towards a future where escape, reconstruction and thriving are possible for these 'others', or, in Monáe's term, 'cyborgs'. The cyborgs in Monáe's work are often mistaken for cyborgs as described in Donna J. Haraway's 'A Cyborg Manifesto' (1991: 149–81) as St. Felix (2018) notes. However, while Haraway, in her writing, positions the cyborg as crossing the boundaries between human and machine, as an aspirational direction for people to move towards, beyond the harm of '"Western" science and politics – the tradition of racist, male-dominant capitalism' (1991: 150), Monáe's cyborg characters are actually explorations: not of what could be in the future, but of the roles that Black bodies have been forced to occupy in the past, and into the contemporary moment. Black and other marginalized people within American history have been relegated to the position of machines, often revered and admired as extremely capable physically, or talented musically, but never given the full humanity of their white counterparts. Monáe tells the stories of slave actions, slave hunts and the erasing of (cultural) memory in an imagined future in her work.[3] She makes the past legible to a contemporary audience through metaphoric cyborgs – looking at what happens when humans are considered to be or as machines, and when those 'machines' are regulated, controlled and/or owned by someone else.

The British-Ghanian writer, theorist and film-maker, Kodwo Eshun, argues that the entire genre of science fiction may be read as not actually focused on the future but, rather, as a way of looking towards the future with emphasis, consideration and exploration of the past and present. He provocatively states: 'Black existence and science fiction are one and the same' (Eshun 2003: 298). And he argues that science fiction sets up an alienated subject who must face and contend with power structures, usually supported by advanced technology, that seek (or have already achieved) control of the alienated subject and her/his/their people. This, Eshun points out, has been the reality Black people have faced since the start of the Maafa (commonly known as the transatlantic slave trade), which continues today in the forms of systematic racism and disenfranchisement, neocolonialism and the policing of Black bodies, communities, labour and families.[4] Eshun frames Afrofuturism as studying 'the appeals that black artists, musicians, critics, and writers have made to the future, in moments where any future was made difficult for them to imagine' (2003: 294). It is exactly into this place that Monáe's work fits. She samples the past through her work, exhaling the power of dance, song, and storytelling within African American tradition, and making visible histories of trauma, while simultaneously providing agency, strength, skill and hope to her various characters, personas and selves.

Monáe ascended to superstardom with the release of her first studio album, *The ArchAndroid* (2010), produced at her newly-founded studio Wondaland Art

Society, and by Bad Boy Records. Hits from the album – 'Tightrope', 'Dance or Die' and 'Cold War' – solidified Monáe's status as a musical icon (Hoard 2010), and her life became the subject of speculation. Holding tightly onto her public image, Monáe performed her cyborg persona both in her music and during her public appearances, claiming to 'attend an Android community church in Metropolis' (quoted in Hoard 2010) when asked about her religion, and routinely stating that she only 'dates androids' (Hoard 2010). I would argue that more than simply constructing Afrofuturistic worlds, Monáe's work performs what Soyica Colbert has described as 'reconstruction': 'an act of creation that results from reparative reading' (Colbert 2019: 505). Such creation aims

> to reimagine black people's relationship to slavery as a historical institution that prescribes forms of embodiment rooted only in subjection. The result is reconstructive forms of intimacy and touch we rarely associate with slavery and its fleshy repercussions.
>
> (Colbert 2019: 505)

Monáe's cyborg protagonists, who later in her work can be seen in other iterations as 'dirty computers' (in *Dirty Computer*), actually enslaved people (in *Antebellum* of 2020) and Black people in contemporary America fighting for their rights ('Turntables' 2020), rebel against oppression through song and dance, but also through their desires. Cindi Mayweather, Monác's first and best known character, was on the run from those who would destroy her for falling in love with a human: Anthony Greendown. Reconstructive work is, at its heart, 'the reconfiguration of material legacies and the (re-)enactment of sustaining repertoires of embodiment, intimacy, and touch' (Colbert 2019: 515). For Monáe's characters, love and rebellion go hand-in-hand. The very existence of the Black gender non-conforming body is a rebellion. As Monáe moved into *The Electric Lady* (2013) she starts revealing that her cyborg characters are, in fact, metaphors for Black lives – a revelation which she makes ever more clear in her subsequent work.

Landscapes of Monáe

Monáe's visual, sonic and textual landscapes are most noticeable on 'Many Moons', 'Americans' (2018) and 'Turntables' (2020), as well as sample versions of these terrains in other works, including 'Crazy, Classic Life' (2018), 'Violet

Stars, Happy Hunting!!!' (2010), 'Sincerely, Jane' (2010), 'Mr. President' (2007), 'Django Jane' (2018), 'Q.U.E.E.N.' and the film *Antebellum* (Gerard Bush and Christopher Renz, 2020), in which she stars. Monáe's work performs reconstructions of the American Dream mythology by inserting Black and disruptive cyborg characters that are non-binary and who challenge the ideologies that normalize whiteness and heteronormativity as oppressive world constructs. The New American Dream that Monáe reconstructs through her work reveals what her version of America might be – and how this America, as she constructs it, has images of selfhood, empowerment and a sense of being, afforded to Black, brown and mixed Queer, working class and gender-non-conforming Americans.

The American Dream: A false promise

Jennifer L. Hochschild, in *Facing Up to the American Dream: Race, Class, and the Soul of the Nation*, identifies the American Dream as 'an impressive ideology' which

> has for centuries lured people to America and moved them around within it, and it has kept them striving in horrible conditions against impossible odds. Most Americans celebrate it unthinkingly, along with apple pie and motherhood.
> (Hochschild 1995: 25)

Monáe belongs to a distinctly different group than Hochschild's '[m]ost Americans' as she examines the cultural roots and the violence of the American Dream narrative, pointing out its misogyny, violence and its mythological nature, and utilizes clashes between lyrical and visual content to emphasize the different populations that have access to, and are excluded from, this reading of American Dream. In her song 'Americans', her lyrics emphasize the way in which the American Dream is designed to empower and uphold a specific kind of man: one who teaches his 'childhood superstitions', keeps 'my two guns on my blue nightstand' and embraces traditional gender roles, such as women 'in the kitchen' who can 'wash my clothes' but will 'never ever wear my pants'. Monáe distorts this imagery by inserting same-sex, loving non-binary, non-white subjects into the story, who also have guns and occupy domestic stereotypes, in order to evacuate these conceptions or behavioural tropes (of guns and domesticity) of their power and meaning.

Monáe's critiques of American social systems start as early as *Metropolis (The Chase Suite)*. Like Lang's *Metropolis*, Monáe uses an individual's story (her own) through which to criticize inequality. While Monáe credits Lang as one of her formative influences, the analysis her work performs is a departure from, or perhaps a development on, Lang's. The only music video Monáe released for a song on her first EP was for 'Many Moons' and (while she was not yet using the term) this early 'emotion picture' contains layers of cultural critique and analysis which, combined with the lyrics, are a ringing attack on American histories of enslavement and ongoing systematic racism, and a look at the ways in which the dreams of Black Americans, far from being realized, are crushed by the same structures that uphold the American Dream narrative for others.

The 'Many Moons' emotion picture starts by letting the viewer know that we are in the Metropolis city, at the 'Annual Android Auction'. An announcer, with a British accent, is heard – saying, before the song actually begins, that in Metropolis 'we offer you the finest fashions and androids'. The announcer then introduces different androids for sale, many of them played by Monáe herself in different costumes. As she names the different droids for sale, we see Monáe also performs in the video as Lady Maestra, the Master of the Show Droids, in a red military jacket and hat, atop a white horse, and 'the prototype of the line, the toast of the town: Cindi Mayweather'. Mayweather initially appears in this video with chalk-white skin and then, after pressing a button on her head, turns to Monáe's natural brown flesh colour. Mayweather runs on stage to a wildly cheering crowd and begins to sing and dance.

Dancing free

Monáe, as Cindi Mayweather, flings her body around – feet shuffling fast, and rhythmically, to the hype beat of the music. A chorus of droids, also played by Monáe, sing the intro 'voo-voos', and the Mayweather version of Monáe performs her lively dance for the audience. Mayweather's facial expressions and the tension in her body indicate that she does not want to be there, nor does she wish to perform. She goes on to say that although the androids can dance 'free' they are, in fact, 'stuck here underground', where 'all we ever wanted to say' was silenced, and they 'live in a daze'. Here the cyborg Mayweather is a metaphor for the enslaved person, and her dance references the ways in which those who enslaved others used to force those enslaved persons to dance, sing, laugh and jump about to entertain them, even after long days of labour in the field (Thompson 2014: 69–70). 'Many Moons', more than offering a simple analogy to enslavement, tracks forward through American history, referencing the Civil War, as well as marching and the Civil Rights movement. When Monáe calls on those listening, saying 'You gotta ooo-ah-ah like a panther' – this then seems to be a reference to the Black Panther Party.

Monáe's music video, directed by Alan Ferguson, mixes visuals of contemporary fashion shows and rock concerts with a slave auction. As Mayweather continues her wild dance, Monáe, as different other versions of the Alpha Platinum 9000 robot, walks up and down the catwalk, while spectators dance to Mayweather's music and bid on the androids. All the while, Monáe's lyrics continue to reference Black America's ongoing struggles for freedom. In Monáe's Metropolis, the rich live lavish lives while the android sub-class exists to serve their every need, and are hunted down for sport when they transgress the boundaries of what is expected of them. As Monáe reaches the bridge of the song, the mood changes briefly from an upbeat dance number to privileging her voice, over relative stillness, before the beat comes back in. She speaks over the beat, her words and the accompanying visuals tell of the American Dream – an American nightmare, which flashes behind the images of Mayweather and her fellow androids performing, as the humans of Metropolis dance and bid. The words tell of systemic inequity, including welfare, lack of food and job opportunities, illness as well as often racialized class-based slurs like 'hood rat' and 'crack whore', and white supremacist beauty standards that call Black hair 'bad', and the frequent result of this Nightmare: one of a 'lost hope'. The images on the screen behind these words include Civil Rights protests and police violence, extreme poverty, soldiers fighting in wars and an atomic bomb exploding.

Monáe's re-enactments of histories of enslavement, portrayed through Afrofuturist aesthetics, effectively perform a reconstruction of narratives of enslavement. The enslaved body here is described as an android – a creature that is sub-human and disposable: a machine. Monáe illustrates how justifications of enslavement worked: by positioning the Black body just as sub-human and akin therefore to a machine. Her androids may be presented as machines, but they are also fully human in important ways: they long for freedom, they have dreams and hopes and they fall in love. In fact, the lyric right before the bridge is: '[a]re you brave enough to reach for love?' Within the context of this complex song about freedom, such a question stands out. What does love mean, in this instance? We know that Mayweather is persecuted and hunted down for falling in love with a human, from 'March of the Wolfmasters' and 'Violet Stars, Happy Hunting!!!', the first two tracks from *Metropolis*. But Mayweather's love of Greendown is more than the story of star-crossed lovers; it is an illustration of the fundamental relationship Monáe draws between love and protest. Throughout her work, people (and androids) who love boldly and bravely – that is, who follow their hearts and exercise their agency – are targeted by power structures. Despite Monáe's performance then as an android, she nevertheless grounds these characters in their desires for touch, affection and intimacy. In her performances and shedding light on systems of inequality and legacies of human ownership of each other, Monáe affirms 'her agency under the circumstance of unequal power relations' (Aghoro 2018: 330). Through desire, and the way in which the braver 'reach for love', Monáe centres the android (i.e. enslaved human's) agency, positioning the Black body not as a victim, but as an agent of change – a hero struggling against forces of great powers.

The 'Many Moons' music video ends with Mayweather rising upwards, into the air, transported by an unknown power, and surprising and even scaring all the humans in the room, while the androids join together to support her. And Lady Maestra: Master of the Show Droids rides in on her white horse, surrounded by billowing white smoke, reminiscent of images of the Haitian revolutionary leader Toussaint Louverture. By this point Mayweather's body is back on the ground and, accompanying Maestra, are three barefoot women in white, with bridal veils over their faces, and their eyes glowing with an eerie electric green. They all walk around Mayweather's fallen body, in a circle, until her eyes open, now with the same green light. Monáe as Maestra sings the words: 'And when the world just treats you wrong/Just come with us and we'll take you home.' As the screen fades to darkness words are written across it: '"I imagined many moons in the sky, lighting the way to freedom" – Cindi Mayweather.' The video ends with women who visually reference an Orisha spirit (of several African religions) or Santeria priestesses. And Mayweather's words suggest an allusion to the Underground Railroad (the clandestine routes and safe houses for endangered African Americans, of the mid-1800s). This heightens the emphasis on that which Soyica Colbert describes as the way in which reconstructive performances can reveal how 'the history of black embodiment cannot be mapped onto linear chronologies organized around legal distinctions between slavery and freedom' and, in or through Monáe's performance, 'the ways in which that history [of enslavement] compels black people', in order to, and as especially in the analogy with androids, 'contend time and again with the fundamental alienation at the heart of slavery' (2019: 503). It is in the context of just such alienation that the question 'are you brave enough to reach for love?' resonates: love is not only romantic love but also self-love and community love – love, in short, as an act of defiance and protest.

Monáe's performances reject the narrative that all Americans have access to the same opportunities, and that hard work is all that is needed to succeed – as aligned to the idea of the 'American Dream' (and as a particularly potent promise for outsiders and immigrants). Instead, Monáe consistently inverts this narrative, looking to the counterbalance of an 'American Nightmare'. In this inversion, hunting looms large: 'Violet Stars, Happy Hunting!!!' offers a direct analogy to slave hunts, recalling the offence of falling in love on the part of the enslaved person. And this is true of Mayweather too, in her love for a human, which is presented as an act of transgressive love that is punishable by death. And the stories of Monáe's characters reference both queer love and interracial love – illegal for most of American history – and so emphasize the ways in which the activity of hunting, humiliating and killing is a part of, and indeed was a social activity of, American history. Its grim legacy resonates in Monáe's counternarrative.

The messaging becomes more explicit for the final song on the initial release of *Metropolis*, 'Sincerely, Jane'. Here Monáe talks about life in the communities passed over by the American Dream. In this nightmare scenario, she talks about young people dropping out of schools, selling drugs, 'babies with babies' and street shootings. She asks: 'Are we really living or just walking dead now?' and responds, to herself, that she is 'terrified' by the 'tragedy' of '[t]he way we live/the way we die'.

Still because of slavery

The Monáe performance that is the most explicit in its embodiment of the effects slavery still has on American culture is found in her first starring role in the feature film *Antebellum*. Despite negative critical reception, the story it tells is nonetheless arresting: a reconstruction and exploration of ways in which the past remains present. The film sets up a contemporary analogy for the stealing and enslaving of people during the period of legal enslavement – a successful academic is kidnapped and enslaved by a white supremacist group – and seeks to explore the hold that white supremacy continues to have on the country.

Monáe's performance throughout the film visually references, and could even be said to remix, her performances as Mayweather – through similar facial expressions and physical movements.

But two key songs that critique American life most straightforwardly, without resorting to analogy or metaphor, are 'Mr. President' (2007, on the special edition of *Metropolis*) and, over a decade later, 'Turntables' (2020). Though largely overlooked in commentary on Monáe, 'Mr. President' evidences that she has always been fully present in her music, and not hiding behind or simply becoming Mayweather. Rather, this persona is used temporarily and strategically: to reach the truth of her political inheritance. In 'Mr. President' – released during President George Bush's second term in office – Monáe sings to the president to 'quit slowin' me down'. She references high costs of fuel and rent, so holding up a mirror to then-contemporary America, hinting at its daily struggles, while creating a space for the marginalized to see themselves as actors with agency, as heroes, as leaders – defined by movement and purpose. Over a decade, superstardom and indeed two presidents later, Monáe released 'Turntables'. This was during a period of her most forthright activism, in the lead-up to the 2020 election – and indeed the song was released as part of the soundtrack for documentary *All In: The Fight for Democracy* (Liz Garbus and Lisa Cortés, 2020). Monáe also issued a stunning emotion picture for the song.

'Turntables' proclaims: 'America, you a lie'. Thereafter, Monáe's repetitive lyrical structure and repeated intonation of 'the table's about to turn' is seemingly a reference to Tracy Chapman's song 'Talking About a Revolution' (1989). Like Chapman, Monáe calls on the disenfranchised to finally rise up, and take their rightful place.

Monáe's reconstructed American Dream – 'America, You a Lie'

'Turntables' continues Monáe's questioning and probing of the American Dream. As she sings the opening lines of the song, in the emotion picture, she walks through the affluent-looking house of what appears to be a Black nuclear family: father, mother, son and daughter. This is the perfect American family . . . but something is wrong. The mother joins Monáe for the line, 'America, you a lie'. And, while the other three eat at the table, the daughter is watching Monáe's video on a virtual reality headset. The contrast between this family's seeming calm and the rage contained within them (and all the time while, on the streets, protests rage and around the world war is raging, both depicted in the emotion picture) brings to the foreground the sense of the 'lie' with which America in its totality is identified. In her call for a new world order, and a new American reality, Monáe mixes lyrical references to enslavement ('burning down plantations') with imagery of the violent anti-police protest of the summer of 2020, underscoring the continued legacy of slavery, as effectively upheld by contemporary policing. Monáe's work then is a part of wider conversations being held, from the streets to the academy, by Black activists, scholars and artists. And, indeed, this is a conversation that has stretched back for centuries.

Paradoxically, while Monáe's work consistently criticizes America, she also states her sense of pride in being American. And, as noted, paints her own (revised) version of the American Dream through her work. This is a version grounded in working-class politics, in Blackness, in Queerness and in sisterhood and women's empowerment. In a 2018 interview with *NCPR* (North Country Public Radio) at the time of *Dirty Computer*, Monáe stated that the album is about

> my love and hate relationship with this country. I love being American, I love being born here and having roots here. But there are some really evil things that have happened and continue to happen. And it speaks to being afraid of forgiving. I think of being hurt again, or being manipulated, or not fully standing my ground. And forgiving myself, also – you know, it's two parts. It's about being able to love yourself through it all, being able to love where you are right now, and to give yourself permission to forgive yourself when you make mistakes, when you let other people down.
>
> (Chang, Lonsdorf and Cala 2018)

But instead of junking the whole of the American Dream, Monáe states in 'Turntables' that she '[g]ot a new agenda with a new dream'. She sings that the 'old regime' must go, and instead make way for '[l]iberation, elevation, education'. It is in this new dream that we find the ways in which Monáe's reconstructive work provides agency for herself and those like her.

Monáe refuses to give in to the violence of the American Dream. Her performances reject the idea that this white supremacist American Dream is all that remains available. In 'Americans' she brings in the voice of the Los Angeles-based real-life Reverend Sean McMillan, who says that saying: 'Until women can get equal pay for equal work/This is not my America.' The same reprise is then given to matters around 'same gender loving people', 'Black people com[ing] home from a police shot/without being shot in the head', and around disenfranchised white members of the working class, and criminalized Latinos and Latinas. But the critique is clear: 'it's goin' be my America before it's all over'.

This song, looking to different Americas, was released during the presidency of Donald Trump. And this sense of different Americans had, during this presidency, become suddenly apparent to mainstream white media – which now engaged with concerns long familiar from Black American discourse. It was just this turn in mainstream public conversations, I believe, which prompted or allowed Monáe to shed her more metaphoric personas, and then focus on saying exactly what she meant, and had always meant. While Monáe's work certainly advances progressive cultures, in creating narratives which centre Black, working-class women and Queer folks, she also moves cautiously – articulating what she means when useful and possible, and using metaphor and analogy to communicate her meanings when not. And this precise political moment of 2018 also allowed Monáe to come out as pansexual – to call for freedom not for cyborgs, but for the people they always represented, and to come right out and express just the kind of future she is working to construct.

In 'Crazy, Classic Life' (2018) Monáe paints a picture of her 'new dream' for the 'young, Black, wild and free', beyond the kicking out of the old regime. She sings of free sexual expression ('naked in a limousine . . ./I just wanna party hard/sex in the swimming pool'), as disaggregated from materialist gain ('I don't need a lot of cash'), in favour of reconnecting with nature ('I love it when I smell the trees') and a natural inclination to freedom or self-expression ('I just want to break the rules').

For Monáe's characters, like Lauren Olamina in Octavia E. Butler's science fiction novels *Parable of the Sower* (1993) and *Parable of the Talents* (1998), position the concept of change, as freedom, at the centre of struggles. There is no single futuristic utopia that Monáe presents, and her Afrofuturist worlds, as encountered, overflow with oppressions, suppressions and struggles. And yet they are also full of love, celebration and protest. While Monáe's messages seem to get clearer over time, they remain consistent. Just as Mayweather resists Metropolis through her love of Greendown, Jane in *Dirty Computer* resists an unnamed totalitarian regime through partying with like-minded people, freely loving her two partners, Zen and Che Achibe and living her life to the fullest.

Monáe's American Dream rejects marriage and/or capitalist consumption ('I don't want a diamond ring'), rejects police brutality, and ties contemporary prisons to enslavement. This backdrop to the American Nightmare occurs in

Monáe's contemporary or even futuristic aesthetics with flying cars, droids and other advanced technologies, while visually remaining within contemporary and historic Black aesthetics – from Monáe's own punk-rock style black leather studded jacket to her bantu knot hairstyle. In this (Afro)future, Black, brown, indigenous and even white young people are rebelling against an authoritarian state through song and dance, pansexual loving and personal style choices. Monáe depicts a kind of freedom which she situates as deeply American, while simultaneously acknowledging or interrogating the ways in which the structures surrounding her and her fellow rebels seek to control, even to the point of their very thoughts. The mind-wiping that we see enacted throughout the *Dirty Computer* emotion picture reads as a reconstruction of the cultural erasure enacted upon enslaved Africans through the suppression of spiritual practices, changing of names, destruction of the ability of families to track their lineage, and blocking and disconnecting peoples from their languages. The fact that most African Americans today do not know where their ancestors came from, or what their names or cultures were before enslavement, speaks to the success of North America's own mind-wiping technology: the brutalities of enslavement as in themselves hidden and its evidence and histories atomized.

Monáe continues to tie her work to a rich archive of Black scholarship, art and thought that came before her. She launches her 'Turntables' emotion picture with the voice of James Baldwin, famously stating:

> I can't be a pessimist because I am alive. To be a pessimist means that you have agreed that human life is an academic matter. So, I am forced to be an optimist. I am forced to believe that we can survive, whatever we must survive.

In aligning herself with the work of Baldwin, Monáe positions herself within a Black Queer radical space – though not always in so many works. 'Turntables' expands this vision beyond performance to 'testifying' against the actually existing American Military Industrial Complex and historic colonial practices. She now situates the protest she depicts in her earlier work explicitly within contemporary Black Lives Matter and Water Protector (see LeQuesne 2018) protests: visuals are not analogies or of Afrofuturist worlds, but of the world of today. She visually ties the Civil Rights protests of the 1960s to contemporary protests, advocating for voting and education about environmental degradation. This short emotion picture ends with Monáe pulling a new Statue of Liberty up out of the ocean: a statue of an Indigenous woman who represents both the past and the future – a vision of what freedom can mean.

I'm American: Monáe as young Harriet Tubman

In a country where proudly claiming to be American has historically, legally and institutionally only been permitted to white Americans, Monáe's deconstruction of what this has meant for Black and Brown, working class and queer Americans, and the construction of her own version of the American Dream, loads the words 'I'm American' with new meaning. Thus Monáe's warning 'don't try to take my country, I will defend my land' (from 'Americans') directly overturns his sentiment as expressed, historically, for the benefit of generations of white Americans. The defence of 'American' land against the non-white 'other' stretches back to the first colonial invaders, and continued as colonists spread West, and was then revitalized during the Civil War and then the failure of the period of reconstruction. The notion of defending one's land and heritage was used as a reason for lynchings (Michaels 1995: 62), for racist immigration laws, including the Chinese Exclusion Act of 1882, for Japanese internment and, into the contemporary moment, for former President Trump's Muslim Ban (see Maltz 2018), and a zero-tolerance policy at the US–Mexican border. Monáe reconstructs this bleak continuum but now positions America as 'her' land – as the land of the Black, brown, working class, Queer, of (to use a term she frequently employs in interviews and conversations) 'free-ass motherfuckers'. Monáe walks a line of being a proud American, and of being self- and nation-critical, as demanding and calling for accountability, and testifying for and working for the elevation of Black, brown, Queer and working-class peoples. Monáe's American Dream is built through Afrofuturist reconstruction, which pulls in the past to reveal the present, and calls on her listeners to stand up, and 'preach', as per the ending of 'Q.U.E.E.N.'.

At the start of the music video for 'Q.U.E.E.N.' another British voice positions Monáe, this time as herself (and not Mayweather, or any other android), as a 'legendary rebel' and 'notorious leader' of Wondaland, organizing the launch of 'freedom movements' disguised as songs, emotion pictures and works of art. Though still emanating from the phase in which Monáe deployed analogy to communicate her messages, 'Q.U.E.E.N.' may be seen as a turning point for Monáe: it is the first song she released that hints that she may, in fact, be queer. She had previously refused to acknowledge, or deny, speculation as to her sexual orientation. It was in a 2018 interview with *Rolling Stone* that Monáe first declared that she is queer, and noted that the original title of 'Q.U.E.E.N.' was 'Q.U.E.E.R.' (Spanos 2018). Despite replacing the intended 'R' with an eventual

'N', Monáe still created what many have referred to as a 'queer anthem' (Opie 2018; Jackman 2019), despite its lack of outright clarity, as well as a 'feminist anthem' (Thomas 2014). Monáe herself said at the time that the song is 'meant to make you JAM. DANCE. FUNK OUT. And dialogue later . . . ' (Wickman 2013).

The song holds particular importance for the reconstructive work that Monáe is doing in relation to the way in which it positions 'freedom movements'. The aforementioned voice-over at the outset goes on to explain that Monáe and 'her dangerous accomplice Badula Oblongata [Erykah Badu]' have been 'frozen in time' by the 'Time Council'. This Time Counsel is never explained but, like the oppressor state of *Dirty Computer*, it is suggested as a non-specific future oppressor, most likely a development of current forms of oppression, and against which Monáe situates her own work as an ongoing movement of resistance, more than simply music. She positions herself, and her characters, as freedom fighters and situates her creations as weapons through which to gain freedom. Then, in the closing rap of the song, Monáe states that no matter the oppression she and those like her face, she will 'keep leading like a young Harriet Tubman'. Thereafter, the rap scopes historic strategies around liberation: she is 'tired of Marvin asking me, "What's Going On?"' (in a reference to Marvin Gaye's seminal 1971 album *What's Going On*), of categorization ('I defy every label'), of cultures of crime overwhelming revolutionary potentials ('you're selling dope, [but] we're gonna keep selling hope'), and references two 1968 cultural artefacts: Philip K. Dick's future dystopia of *Do Androids Dream of Electric Sheep?* and the Jimi Hendrix Experience's *Electric Ladyland*. When she ends with the question '[e]lectric ladies – will you sleep? Or will you preach?', this electricity now seems to denote both the future oppression apparatus of the android, and the electrification of music (and emotions, and audiences) exemplified by Hendrix's guitar soloing.

By situating herself as 'a young Harriet Tubman' (the abolitionist and social activist) Monáe again underscores the ongoing or living legacies of enslavement in our lives. In the video, 'young Harriet Tubman' is presented as a sexy, sexually free, rebellious woman, who will 'love who I am' even if it 'makes others uncomfortable'. Thus Monáe takes Tubman out of the past, as imagined as a motherly figure, and recalibrates her as a woman who has desires and needs, and for whom love is part of the wider fight. Monáe also (re-)places her own hometown of Kansas City firmly on the map, as right next to Egypt: 'My crown too heavy like the Queen Nefertiti/ Gimme back my pyramid, I'm trying to free Kansas City'. Such a reference to colonial legacies, and the stealing of people from Africa, situates Monáe's creative interventions within international Black dialogues. When she asks 'are we a lost generation of our people?' the reference seems to be the 'lost generation' of those who lost their lives during the First World War. But in this Monáe implies that the ongoing attacks on Black communities are tantamount to a (literal) war and that her generation is as lost (and bereft) as white America was, after 1918.

In concluding her anthem with the line, 'or will you preach?' – while looking directly at the audience in her emotion picture – she makes us all accountable: who we are serving, and who we are going to stand for? In this, and in the inclusive reconstruction of the concept of the American Dream in her work, Monáe can be identified within the long legacy of Black American performers who used their art simultaneously as activism and entertainment, and progressively shifting conversations, even as their audiences sing, and dance along.

Notes

1. 'Emotion Picture' is the term Monáe uses to describe visual stories/collages that accompany her music, as a cross between a music video and a film (Palmer 2020: 215). Monáe first used the term 'emotion picture' in the lyrics of her song 'Q.U.E.E.N.' (2013), in which a voice-over refers to 'a musical weapons program in the twenty-first century disguised as songs, dances, and emotion pictures'. The forty-four minute video project, released alongside the *Dirty Computer* album, however, contained the first time that Monáe referred to her video creation itself as an 'emotion picture'. The *Dirty Computer* emotion picture was first aired on MTV and BET networks, and then released on YouTube and Vimeo for viewing (Palmer 2020: 215).

2. On the American Dream, I draw on Hochschild (1995), but see too: Calder (1999), Samuel (2012), and Wolak and Peterson (2020).

3. 'Many Moons' from *Metropolis: The Chase Suite* (2007) is a cyborg slave auction. 'March of the Wolfmasters' from *Metropolis* launches both the EP and the story of Cindi Mayweather and her transgression of falling in love with a human. Critically, it is the cyborgs and bounty hunters (who may or may not overlap) who are tasked with hunting Mayweather down and destroying her. Also, notably, the character of Anthony Greendown (the human in question), is not hunted.

    The entire *Dirty Computer* emotion picture can be read as a meditation on the erasing of cultural memory, told through the metaphor of literal memory erasure in a futuristic world.

4   While I here use the term 'transatlantic slave trade' for the sake of legibility, I find Sandra L. Richards argument for the use of the alternative term 'maafa', to describe this particular history, more persuasive. Maafa means 'great disaster' in Kiswahili, and was first suggested as a more appropriate term to refer to this period by Afrocentric scholar Marimba Ani (Richards 2007: 171).

Reference

Aghoro, N. (2018), 'Agency in the Afrofuturist Ontologies of Erykah Badu and Janelle Monáe', *Open Cultural Studies*, 2 (1): 330–40.

Brown, A. (2018), 'New Formation: Janelle Monáe's Radical Emotion Pictures', *Los Angeles Review of Books*, 28 May. Available online: https://lareviewofbooks.org/article/new-formation-janelle-Monáes-radical-emotion-pictures/ (accessed 3 November 2022).

Calder, L. (1999), *Financing the American Dream: A Cultural History of Consumer Credit*, Princeton: Princeton University Press.

Chang, A., K. Lonsdorf and C. Cala (2018), 'Janelle Monáe On Her Dirty, World-Dominating Year', *NCPR*, 21 December. Available online: https://www.northcountrypublicradio.org/news/npr/678450755/janelle-mon-e-on-her-dirty-world-dominating-year (accessed 2 November 2022).

Colbert, S. (2019), 'Reconstruction, Fugitive Intimacy, and Holding History', *Modern Drama*, 62 (4): 502–16.

Eshun, K. (2003), 'Further Considerations of Afrofuturism', *CR: The New Centennial Review*, 3 (2): 287–302.

Gipson, G. D. (2016), 'Afrofuturism's Musical Princess Janelle Monáe', in R. Anderson and C. E. Jones (eds), *Afrofuturism 2.0: The Rise of Astro-Blackness*, 91–107. Lanham: Lexington Books.

Haraway, D. J. (1991), *Simians, Cyborgs, and Women: The Reinvention of Nature*, New York: Routledge.

Hassler-Forest, D. (2022), *Janelle Monáe's Queer Afrofuturism: Defying Every Label*, New Brunswick: Rutgers University Press.

Hoard, C. (2010), 'Artist of the Week: Janelle Monáe', *Rolling Stone*, 30 June. Available online: www.rollingstone.com/music/music-news/artist-of-the-week-janelle-Monáe-186564/ (accessed 2 November 2022).

Hochschild, J. L. (1995), *Facing Up to the American Dream: Race, Class, and the Soul of the Nation*, Princeton: Princeton University Press.

Jackman, J. (2019), 'Janelle Monáe Released a Queer Anthem in 2013 and No-One Noticed', *PinkNews*, 26 June. Available online: www.pinknews.co.uk/2018/04/28/janelle-Monáe-dirty-computer-queer-anthem-in-2013-and-no-one-noticed/ (accessed 2 November 2022).

Jones, C. L. (2018), '"Tryna Free Kansas City": The Revolutions of Janelle Monáe as Digital Griot', *Frontiers: A Journal of Women Studies*, 39 (1): 42–72.

LeQuesne, T. (2018), 'Petro-hegemony and the Matrix of Resistance: What Can Standing Rock's Water Protectors Teach us about Organizing for Climate Justice in the United States?', *Environmental Sociology*, 5 (2): 188–206.

Matlz, E. M. (2018), 'The Constitution and the Trump Travel Ban', *Lewis and Clark Law Review*, 22 (2): 391–412.

Michaels, W. B. (1995), *Our America: Nativism, Modernism, and Pluralism*. Durham: Duke University Press.

Miller, M. L. (2015), 'All Hail the QUEEN: Janelle Monáe and a Tale of the Tux', *Journal of Contemporary African Art*, 37: 62–9.

Murchison, G. (2018), 'Let's Flip It! Quare Emancipations: Black Queer Traditions, Afrofuturisms, Janelle Monáe to Labelle', *Women and Music: A Journal of Gender and Culture*, 22: 79–90.

Opie, D. (2018), 'Five Queer Janelle Monáe Songs You Might Have Missed', *INTO*, 29 May. Available online: www.intomore.com/culture/five-queer-janelle-Monáe-songs-you-might-have-missed/ (accessed 2 November 2022).

Palmer, L. (2020), *Rock Star/Movie Star: Power and Performance in Cinematic Rock Stardom*, Oxford: Oxford University Press.

Piper, K. (2001), 'Notes on The Mechanoid's Bloodline: Looking at Robots, Androids, and Cyborgs', *Art Journal*, 60 (3): 96–8.

Ramsey, W. (2017), *Let All the Children Boogie: Occult Presences Through the Musical Performances of Sun Ra, David Bowie, Magma, and Janelle Monáe*, University of Colorado: Unpublished Masters thesis.

Richards, S. L. (2007), 'Remembering the Maafa', *Assaph: Studies in Theatre*, 21: 171–95.

Samuel, L. R. (2012), *The American Dream: A Cultural History*, New York: Syracuse University Press.

Spanos, B. (2018), 'Janelle Monáe Frees Herself', *Rolling Stone*, 26 April. Available online: www.rollingstone.com/music/music-features/janelle-Monáe-frees-herself-629204/ (accessed 2 November 2022).

St. Felix, D. (2018), 'The Otherworldly Concept Albums of Janelle Monáe', *The New Yorker*, 1 March. Available online: www.newyorker.com/culture/culture-desk/the-otherworldly-concept-albums-of-janelle-Monáe (accessed 2 November 2022).

Thomas, S. (2014), 'Janelle Monáe's Q.U.E.E.N, A Feminist Anthem?', *Media Diversified*, 4 September. Available online: mediadiversified.org/2013/09/04/q-u-e-e-n-a-feminist-anthem/ (accessed 2 November 2022).

Thompson, K. D. (2014), *Ring Shout, Wheel About: The Racial Politics of Music and Dance in North American Slavery*, Urbana: University of Illinois Press.

Valnes, M. (2017), 'Janelle Monáe and Afro-Sonic Feminist Funk', *Journal of Popular Music Studies*, 29 (3): e12224.

Wickman, F. (2013), 'Does Janelle Monáe's New Song Address Her Sexuality?', *Slate Magazine*, 23 April. Available online: www.slate.com/blogs/browbeat/2013/04/23/janelle_mon_e_new_single_q_u_e_e_n_singer_aims_to_defy_every_label_sexual.html (accessed 2 November 2022).

Wolak, J. and David A. M. Peterson (2020), 'The Dynamic American Dream', *American Journal of Political Science*, 64 (4): 968–81.

9

'WAP'

Erotic revolutionary hip-hop by Cardi B and Megan Thee Stallion

Shawna Shipley-Gates

Black women and femmes face sexual oppression daily. At work, at home or in spaces of entertainment, they must navigate the public scrutiny and vilification of their bodies as targets of sexual injury rather than sources of pleasure. If their bodies are viewed as sexual pleasure sites then these bodies are only used as objects of desire or violence, and that renders the physical bodies as landscapes used for capital creation or consumption. Eroticism, described as the desire for pleasure, has been utilized as a form of resistance against sexual oppression in many forms of cultural production, including hip-hop music and culture. Hip-hop divas Cardi B and Megan Thee Stallion's 2020 track hit record 'WAP' utilizes sexually explicit musical and visual content as an unapologetic erotic expression while, as Shayne Lee describes it, 'dismantling politics of silence, deconstructing gendered double standards on sexuality and demolishing sexual expectations that deny women a full range of sexual expressivities' (2010: 130). By using Black sexual politics and a hip-hop feminist lens, 'WAP' comes to exemplify erotic revolutionary hip-hop. The track subverts a hip-hop hegemony consisting of traditional gender roles, toxic masculinity and misogynoir; it employs erotic metaphysics and illicit eroticism; it rejects respectability politics and culture of dissemblance; and it redefines sexually oppressive controlling images of Black women and femmes.[1]

'We Know We Can Aspire'

Shayne Lee, author of *Erotic Revolutionaries: Black Women, Sexuality, and Popular Culture*, writes that 'without picking up a textbook, we can experience subversive sexual politics by watching pop cultural divas deconstruct conventional borders of female sexuality' and that – as erotic revolutionaries – hip-hop divas 'effectively wage war against the politics of respectability and challenge traditional scripts that offer men greater space to indulge in a fuller range of sexual expressivities' (Lee 2010: xiv). Cardi B and Megan Thee Stallion's 'WAP' roots itself in Black feminist standpoints in order to challenge the objectifying and violent gaze of toxic masculinity, traditional gender roles and misogynoir that assault the Black woman and femme in popular culture without apology, explanation or justification. The singers' strategic use of sexual promiscuity and agency serves as a tactic to promote illicit eroticism as they fight against respectability politics and a culture of dissemblance in attempts to redefine pervasive and controlling images of Black women and femmes' bodies. 'WAP' is a hip-hop diva cultural production that centres Black feminist sexual politics and quests for erotic freedom that liberates the Black female body from male-centred hip-hop culture.

As a self-declared 'Black, lesbian, mother, warrior, poet', Audre Lorde described the erotic as 'an internal sense of satisfaction to which, once we have experienced it, we know we can aspire' (Lorde 1984: 54). From a sexual standpoint, Black feminist critic Jennifer Nash views eroticism as a 'tender space of sanctuary, self-imagination, intimacy and creative play, [and] a vibrant space of collective world-making that takes the violence of the ordinary and turns it on its head, mobilizing it to unleash sexual pleasures, erotic longings and disrespectable desires' (Nash 2018: 3). Black feminist writer and activist bell hooks argues 'when black women relate to our bodies, our sexuality, in ways to place erotic recognition, desire, pleasure and fulfillment at the center of our efforts to create radical black female subjectivity, we can make new and different representations of ourselves as sexual subjects' (hooks 2015a: 76). Black feminist scholar Patricia Hill Collins introduced the idea of eroticism as resistance when she argued that

> when self-defined by Black women ourselves, Black women's sexualities can become an important place for resistance. Just as harnessing the power of the erotic is important for domination, reclaiming and self-defining that same eroticism may constitute one path toward Black women's empowerment.
> (Collins 2000: 138)

In other words, Black women and femmes need to prioritize their eroticism as a form of resistance against sexual oppression in order to rewrite their own sexual narratives. Black female hip-hop has a strong erotic revolutionary history that encourages fans to focus on pleasure and unite against sexual oppression that harms Black female sexuality.

LADIES FIRST – Erotic revolutionary hip-hop divas

Legendary erotic revolutionary hip-hop divas, including Queen Latifah, Salt-N-Pepa, Lil' Kim and Foxy Brown, introduced the utilization of eroticism for reclaiming and self-defining the sexual narratives of Black women. Queen Latifah set the erotic revolutionary tone with the epic track 'Ladies First', from her 1989 debut album *All Hail the Queen*, which unapologetically declared that 'when it's time for loving it's the woman that gets some'. Provocative hip-hop trio Salt-N-Pepa's 1990 track 'Let's Talk About Sex', and the 1993 track 'None of Your Business', challenged the toxic masculinity within hip-hop, encouraged sexual health dialogue and discouraged sexual shaming, because 'the [only] difference between a hooker and a ho ain't nothin' but a fee . . . [so] really it's none of your business'. On 12 November 1996, Lil' Kim debuted her first album, *Hard Core*, which was presented as an anthem for Black women who loved to musically and fashionably express their eroticism. Known for her iconic lavender ensemble, complete with a matching wig, jumpsuit and nipple pastie, Lil' Kim is credited for shifting the hip-hop game towards hardcore sex-positivity. During her 1997 *Paper Magazine* interview with bell hooks, Lil' Kim shared her position that male hip-hop artists are not ridiculed for their use of sexually explicit language

> but all of a sudden, we have a female who happens to be a rapper, like me, and my doin' it is so wrong. And 'cause I like doin' it, it's even more wrong because we've fought for years as women to do the same things that men are doing.
>
> (hooks 2018)

Exactly a week after Lil' Kim's release of *Hard Core*, Foxy Brown's track 'Big Bad Mama', from her debut album *Ill Na* (1997) – slang for good pussy – demonstrated how to unabashedly use sexual assertiveness, through sexually explicit lyrics: she informed sexual partners to ' . . . use your tongue. Find my g-spot, get me hot . . . '

All of these iconic women confirmed the fact that erotic revolutionary hip-hop is a legitimate genre of music and one that was led by brazen and Black hip-hop divas.

'A Feminism Brave Enough to Fuck With the Grays'

Hip-hop scholar Gwendolyn Pough made it abundantly clear that most Black female hip-hop artists are not

> checking for the F word ... This is not to say that there are no feminist women rappers. However, the fact remains that as much as we champion and claim certain women rappers for their lyrics, their outreach activities, their 'positive' messages, or their 'pro-woman' messages, very few women rappers will go on record saying that they are feminist.
>
> (Pough 2007: 88)

In spite of this tension, a new form of Black feminism arose as an intellectual way to continue hip-hop's revolutionary mission. For Joan Morgan, hip-hop feminist and author of *When Chickenheads Come Home to Roost: A Hip-hop Feminist Breaks It Down*, hip-hop feminism is a feminism that is 'brave enough to fuck with the grays ... we need a feminism committed to "keeping it real" ... where truth is no longer black and white but subtle, intriguing shades of gray' (Morgan 1999: 59–62). Hip-hop feminism then performs a complicated manoeuvre: it critiques the hip-hop industry for its sexism, existing hegemony and hypocrisy while celebrating its potential as an artistic representation of feminism for Black women and femmes of the hip-hop generation. In connecting Black feminism and hip-hop, hip-hop feminism comes to represent the 'perfect antidote to the sexist morass that has become hip-hop and young black women's antifeminist resistance' (Sharpley-Whiting 2007: 152). Patricia Hill Collins defines Black feminism as 'a process of self-conscious struggle that empowers women and men to actualize a humanist vision of community' (1997, cited in Garner 2004: 30). Hip-hop, typically held to be 'the cultural movement that attained widespread popularity in the 1980s and 1990s' (Light and Tate, no date), incorporated elements of deejaying or turntabling, rapping (also known as MCing or rhyming), graffiti painting, breakdancing or b-boying, street fashion and language and that most important element, for Black feminism, which is the knowledge of self and consciousness. Crunk Feminist Collective members Aisha Durham, Brittney C. Cooper and Susana M. Morris define hip-hop feminism as

> a cultural, intellectual, and political movement grounded in the situated knowledge of women of color from the post-civil rights or hip-hop generation

who recognize culture as a pivotal site for political intervention to challenge, resist, and mobilize collectives to dismantle systems of exploitation'.[2]

(Durham, Cooper and Morris 2013: 721)

Pough explains that

> while we cannot in good conscience place the label of 'feminist' – hip-hop, third-wave, black feminist, or womanist – on most contemporary women rappers, we can – as feminist scholars and activists – use the music they produce and the issues they raise to begin to enact change.

(Pough 2007: 88)

Morgan conceived of hip-hop feminism as containing the sexually subversive cultural, intellectual and political contributions of these erotic revolutionary hip-hop divas in the 1980s and 1990s, while paving the way for the contemporary work of Black female hip-hop artists in the twenty-first century – particularly Cardi B and Megan Thee Stallion.

New school hip-hop divas: The house that hip-hop feminism built

Following in the footsteps of their predecessors, new school hip-hop divas continue the erotic revolutionary tradition, both in their respective solo careers and in collaborations with each other. This new generation of hip-hop divas is identified as 'strong, smart, edgy, ambitious, socially-conscious, independent women who implicitly and explicitly encourage new generations toward sexual agency, exploration, and empowerment' (Lee 2010: xiv). Nicki Minaj, Saweetie, City Girls, Rapsody, Azealia Banks and Young M.A. are just a few of the Black women and femmes who have utilized hip-hop to express their eroticism. But among all of the current hip-hop divas, at the time of writing, there are two in particular who have had a significant influence on Black female sexuality: Cardi B and Megan Thee Stallion. In their own right, Cardi B and Megan Thee Stallion represent the next generation of hip-hop royalty and will further that generation's erotic revolutionary mission.

Cardi B (Belcalis Marlenis Almánzar) is an Afro-Latinx and Afro-Caribbean self-proclaimed hip-hop diva from the Bronx, New York. Cardi B started out as a stripper turned social media celebrity on Vine and Instagram. From 2015 to

2017, Cardi B was a cast member on the VH1 reality television show *Love & Hip Hop: New York*, which revealed her unapologetic rawness. Cardi's 'open and free' personality is expressed by candid discussions of sexual acts, shameless admissions of personal flaws and desires for money, sex and fame and an unabashed sharing of her sexual desires, fetishes and expectations. After two seasons on the show, she left to pursue her passions in the music industry. She signed with Atlantic Records in 2017 and released her triple-platinum debut album, *Invasion of Privacy*, in 2018. With this, Cardi B became the first solo female artist to win a Grammy Award for Best Rap Album in 2019, since the category was established in 1995. Via her signature song, 'Bodak Yellow', Cardi B sent a clear message to all of her enemies: although she credits her introduction to sexual assertiveness and financial freedom to her history of stripping, she let her audience know that she 'don't dance now' because she makes 'money moves'. In this way, Cardi B supports the normalization of sex work by openly discussing her own personal experience. As with Lil' Kim and Foxy Brown, Cardi B boldly flaunted her sexuality and body positivity, proclaiming that 'my pussy feel like a lake/he wanna swim with his face'. Lyrically, then, she celebrates her vagina's ability to lure sexual partners with its excessively lubricating abilities. Besides such erotically revolutionary lyrics, Cardi B also promotes eroticism as a form of resistance by endorsing sex technology. For example, she partnered with sex toy company Bellesa to showcase some of her favourite pleasure devices through fan giveaways and cameos in her music video 'Up' (2021). This self-identified feminist is committed to a sense of female empowerment that pushes against a male-centred hip-hop industry that insists on exploiting her sexual aesthetic, by taking back control and authoring and expressing her own erotic narrative, on her terms.

Similarly, Megan Thee Stallion (Megan Jovon Ruth Pete) reclaimed a stereotypical Southern term that oversexualizes Black women and femmes by celebrating her tall height and thick body structure. Raised in Texas by her mother, who rapped under the name Hollywood, Megan gained attention from her freestyling videos on YouTube and Instagram and released some mixtapes and EPs, including *Make It Hot* in 2017, and *Fever* in 2019. Unlike contemporary female rappers, those earlier erotic revolutionary hip-hop divas, including Lil' Kim and Foxy Brown, did not have social media platforms to share their music and erotic selves, and so were often essentially controlled by record labels who constructed and edited their images. That process included the removal (and so rejection) of traces of hip-hop feminism. While many female hip-hop artists did not claim feminism per se as their mindset, and a feminist critique of such hypersexualized artists is certainly easy to imagine, hip-hop feminism allows for and accommodates such paradoxes or contradictions. So hip-hop feminism is the appropriate lens with which to unpack the personas and performances of a Black feminist sexuality – even in digital realms since, for new school hip-hop divas like Megan Thee Stallion, 'digital and social media offer "new" mediums in which hip-hop feminists can bring wreck' (Lindsey 2015: 7).

In January 2019, Megan released the career-changing single 'Big Ole Freak', from her *Tina Snow* EP. During an interview with *Mic* (a popular media company for millennials), Megan shared how she is not afraid to talk about Black female sexuality, "nor does she feel boxed in to either the "intelligent" or "freak" dichotomy' the interview observed (Whaley 2018). Indeed, when the single 'Hot Girl Summer', featuring Nicki Minaj, was released in August 2019, Megan effectively provided a summer anthem that encouraged her female audience to dismiss respectability politics and toxic masculinity, and embrace their inner 'hot girl' in order to enjoy uninhibited sexual exploration – even if only for one season. 'Savage', from the 2020 EP *Suga*, featuring fellow Texan and superstar, Beyoncé on a remix, was Megan's follow-up. A 'Savage' dance challenge, created by TikTok performer Keara Wilson, subsequently went viral, with more than 15 million views on the social media platform at the time of writing. In addition, 'Savage' became Megan's first chart-topper in the United States, as number one on Billboard's Hot 100 (Trust 2020). Most importantly, however, the 'Savage' lyrics reminded Black women and femmes that we have a right to be 'savage, classy, bougie [aspiring to attain a higher social class], ratchet, sassy, moody, [and] nasty' without the patriarchal gaze. As a college student at Texas Southern University, a respected lyricist and a well-endowed lover of crop tops and body-hugging outfits, Megan Thee Stallion has consistently stated that 'it's not just about being sexy, it's about being confident and me being confident in my sexuality' (Kameir 2019).

Wet and gushy divas

On 7 August 2020, Cardi B and Megan Thee Stallion came together, in solidarity, to exemplify what it means for Black women and femmes to be sexually confident with the erotic revolutionary music video 'WAP' (an acronym for 'Wet Ass Pussy', or the censored title 'Wet and Gushy'). In the words of Audre Lorde, Cardi B and Megan Thee Stallion are using the erotic as 'an assertion of the lifeforce of women; of that creative energy empowered, the knowledge and use of which we are now reclaiming in our language, our history, our dancing, our loving, our work, our lives' (Lorde 1984: 55). Not only did this song debut at number one on Billboard's Hot 100 list, and come to be certified as six times platinum, but it also spent multiple weeks at number one in Australia, Canada, Greece, Ireland, Lithuania, New Zealand and the UK, proving its global influence. 'WAP' featured up-and-coming hip-hop divas Latto, Rubi Rose and Sukihana, all of whom were scantily clad in latex outfits, while dancing confidently and in sexually suggestive ways.[3] From constant imagery of excessive water to a plethora of provocative bodysuits and flamboyant hairstyles, to sensual movements including caressing, gyrating, twerking and strutting down the hallway, Cardi B and Megan Thee Stallion prioritize body positivity and natural lubrication as a way to claim their capacity to arouse and control sexual outcomes without acts of sex. Their ability is contained in their 'WAPs', and they are not afraid to draw attention to their comfortable relationships with their vaginas, as a site of erotic power. In fact, Cardi B and Megan Thee Stallion suggest, in 'WAP', that sexual partners should 'bring a bucket and a mop for this wet ass pussy'. The 'WAP' music video serves as a sex-positive, intersectional and pleasurable contribution to an evolving erotic revolution for Black women and femmes by confronting a hip-hop hegemony that consists of traditional gender roles, toxic masculinity and misogynoir. 'WAP' utilizes erotic metaphysics (discussed later), and illicit eroticism, negating respectability politics and culture of dissemblance and redefining controlling images.

Hip-hop hegemony versus punanny politics

Cardi B and Megan Thee Stallion use erotic revolutionary lyrics – for example, '[i]f he fuck me and ask, 'Whose is it?' when I ride the dick, I'ma spell my name' – to defy so-called 'traditional' gender roles, toxic masculinity and misogynoir in hip-hop. This is done by not only centring the bodies of Black women and femmes but also challenging the notions of the phallus and heteronormative sex acts as the only pathway to sexual satisfaction, pleasure and desire. Traditionally, hypermasculine and heteronormative gender roles allow male hip-hop artists to gatekeep sexual assertiveness in terms of who owns the rights to erotic expression. Such toxic masculinity is perpetuated by cultural norms that are harmful to men and society as a whole.

In her book *Pimps Up, Ho's Down: Hip Hop's Hold on Young Black Women*, feminist writer T. Denean Sharpley-Whiting discusses how hip-hop's perpetuation of 'sexual violence, sexism, "beat-downs," sexual dishonesty, anti-lesbianism, and the legacy of color prejudice all hammer away at [the] self-esteem' of Black women and femmes (2007: 12). 'WAP' responds to traditional gender roles, toxic masculinity and misogynoir by providing an anthem that exudes love, pleasure and autonomy as erotic revolutionary tactics for their Black female audience and any ally that wants to reclaim their sexuality through Black feminist political strategies of resistance. Though the hip-hop divas engage the idea of 'dicks', they do not dictate who has the right to have or control one. There are no male artists, models or celebrities present in the music video – implying that hip-hop or sex does not always require masculine presence or representation. Additionally, the visuals of the two rappers physically celebrating each other's bodies signify an erotic revolutionary act that Audre Lorde would refer to as 'women loving women' – that is, women who are unbothered by heteronormativity. Cardi B and Megan Thee Stallion literally revised Black female sexuality in hip-hop by sampling DJ Frank Ski's 1993 single 'Whores in This House' in order to 'disrupt routines of sexual stratification by providing counter-narratives against societal prescriptions that relegate proactive displays of sexuality to the male domain' (Lee 2010: 128). Using hip-hop feminism, Cardi B and Megan Thee Stallion raised their voices, like their music – 'that samples and layers many voices, injects its sensibilities into the old and flips it into something new, provocative, and powerful' (Morgan 1999: 62).

Unsurprisingly, therefore, some male hip-hop artists vocalized their disdain with Cardi B and Megan Thee Stallion's 'flipping the sexual script'. In his interview for *Central Ave* (a hip-hop culture weekly magazine) Snoop Dogg, the famous West Coast hip-hop artist and marijuana aficionado, offered a masculine critique of 'WAP' that suggested a preference for having some privacy, and 'some intimacy where he [the male] wants to find out as opposed to you telling him' (Jokic 2020). Dogg continues by sharing the sentiment that he wants to avoid the trend whereby young Black girls 'feel like they can express themselves like that without knowing that this is a jewel that they hold on to until the right person comes around' (cited in Jokic 2020). So, prioritizing the sexist gaze, Dogg is suggesting that women should not celebrate their body, as a healthy endeavour, but, rather, leave that body to the imagination and ownership of male sexual partners. These hypocritical statements conflict with decades' worth of sexually explicit lyrics from Dogg, at times concerning his own genitals, including 'lick on these nuts and suck on this dick' (from his verse in hip-hop mogul Dr Dre's 'Bitches Ain't Shit' of 1992). Cardi B and Megan Thee Stallion effectively say 'f this' to Dogg, and other male rappers, and assert themselves as hip-hop divas who challenge the hypocrisy and toxic masculinity of the Black men who keep the hip-hop hegemony in place.

More specifically on this strategy: that male hip-hop hegemony and its hypocrisies are undermined by hip-hop divas' use of punanny politics. Since punanny is the one thing that Black women and femmes can control, and men have an uncontrollable urge for, female rappers effectively practice a 'punanny politics' while standing up against traditional gender roles, toxic masculinity and misogynoir in hip-hop. T. Denean Sharpley-Whiting introduced a politics of the punanny (a slang term for the vagina) that posits the Black female body as a place of agency rather than oppression. Cardi B and Megan Thee Stallion's 'WAP' embodies punanny politics in or through lyrics such as '[m]y head game is fire, punani Dasani. It's going in dry and it's coming out soggy. I ride on that thang like the cops is behind me. I spit on his mic and now he tryna sign me'. This can be read as demanding female sexual gratification, which includes pleasure reciprocation towards male sexual partners, on their own terms.

'Give Me Everything You've Got'

According to Black feminist scholar bell hooks, some Black women and femmes are estranged from their erotic power:

> Their estrangement is just as intense as that of black females who have learned from childhood on that they can protect themselves from objectification, from commodification by repressing erotic energy, by denying any sensual or sexual dimension in themselves.
>
> (hooks 2015b: 87)

hooks delves into the different reasons for Black women's and femmes' erotic estrangement, including being used as 'breeding machines, as receptacles for pornographic desires, [and] as "hot pussies" to be bought and sold' (87). As a response to such erotic estrangement, hooks introduces the concept of erotic metaphysics. This 'evokes a vision of life that links our sense of self with communion and community . . . we become more fully who we are in the act of loving', in order to fight against a white supremacist capitalist patriarchal culture (87). Cardi B and Megan Thee Stallion's lyrical and visual profession of self-love and erotic desires is a revolutionary act of erotic metaphysics, therefore, and that posits them both outside of, and within, the male-centred hip-hop hegemony, while also retaining or gaining the ability to control what takes place within the industry. Instead of enslaved 'hot pussies', Cardi B and Megan Thee Stallion employ illicit eroticism as another response to erotic estrangement by demanding of their sexual admirers that they pay for cars, college tuition or just 'give me everything you got for this wet-ass-pussy'. 'Illicit eroticism' was coined by Black feminist Mireille Miller-Young, as referring to the recovery and deployment of formerly negative stereotypes, such as those associated with a woman's hypersexuality, in order to achieve mobility, erotic autonomy and self-care (Miller-Young 2014). Hip-Hop feminist icon Queen Latifah applauds hip-hop divas who work their erotic power 'to the best of their ability – instead of letting somebody else pimp that power' (cited in Morgan 1999: 218). Cardi B and Megan Thee Stallion's use of erotic metaphysics and illicit eroticism reject an erotic estrangement and allow for a regained control of Black female sexuality despite, or in the face of, existing sexual oppressions. These hip-hop divas demand payment for the right to experience their beauty, intelligence and talent, galvanize erotic autonomy to disrupt sexual hierarchies and utilize their WAPs as sites of the erotic power that they regulate and control.

Sexuality, righteousness and discontent

'WAP' also exemplifies erotic revolutionary hip-hop by dismantling two additional sexually oppressive strategies: respectability politics and the culture of dissemblance. In her book *Righteous Discontent: The Women's Movement in the Black Baptist Church: 1880–1920*, Evelyn Brooks Higginbotham introduced the concept of respectability politics as a way for Black women and femmes to suppress their erotic expression in an attempt to prevent the perpetuation of negative sexual images and stereotypes against all Black Americans. Black women and femmes were understood to be on a quest for 'societal propriety [that] leads many to assume a particular kind of sexual saintliness' (Lee 2010: viii). Similarly, the culture of dissemblance – coined by African American author and professor Darlene Clark Hines in her article 'Rape and the Inner Lives of Black Women in the Middle West: Preliminary Thoughts on Culture of Dissemblance' – is understood as a theoretical prism through which Black female identity is read. This vantage point identifies the acts of protection that are used to protect Black women and femmes who hide their eroticism by presenting a false, asexual image. Quite simply, respectability politics and the culture of dissemblance are two sexually oppressive strategies that are understood to have historically influenced Black women and femmes to 'accept sexual chastity for the greater good of social responsibility' (Lee 2010: ix).

On the other hand, Cardi B and Megan Thee Stallion's 'WAP' challenges respectability politics and culture of dissemblance by 'bringing wreck': that is, using pleasure politics and disrespectability as strategies of resistance, to undermine historical binaries of Black female sexuality as at once asexual and hypersexual, as pious and ratchet. Gwendolyn Pough introduced 'bringing wreck' as an important theoretical intervention of hip-hop feminism, as one that allows Black people to reshape 'the public gaze in such a way to be recognized as human beings – as functioning and worthwhile members of society – and not to be shut out of or pushed away from the public sphere' (Pough 2004: 17). Cardi B and Megan Thee Stallion empower fans who may want to privately use 'handcuffs, leashes [and] switch my wig, make him feel like he cheating' or 'make it cream, make me scream, out in public, make a scene'. In this case, 'WAP', as sonic dissonance and visual culture of redemption, forces mainstream society to respect Black women and femmes as sexual human beings by promoting pleasure politics and disrespectability.

Pleasure politics – coined by Joan Morgan – is a framework that not only respects Black women and femmes as sexual human beings but also embraces erotic agency and challenges sexual stereotypes outside a 'singular heteropatriarchal lens[,] while also looking at the nexus of hierarchical structures that shape our sexual selves' (Durham, Cooper and Morris 2013: 721). Morgan explains that 'as black feminist theorists, we've made a commitment to reframe the existing narrative about black female sexuality by positioning desire, agency and black women's engagements with pleasure as a viable theoretical paradigm' (Morgan 2015: 36). Cardi B and Megan Thee Stallion practice the disownment of respectable standards – known as disrespectability – which allows Black women and femmes to focus on a theoretical shift towards pleasure politics. This means that Black women and femmes can choose to exercise erotic autonomy, free of judgement and shame. By 'bringing wreck', Cardi B and Megan Thee Stallion continue the fight against respectability politics and culture of dissemblance within and outside of the hip-hop industry, by incorporating pleasure politics and disrespectability into their sexually empowering lyrics and visual representations.

From jezebels to hip-hop divas

Historically, the jezebel, as a concept or image with the potential to exert control, is characterized as a Black woman who is uncontrollably promiscuous, aggressive, an uncaring sexual deviant and who uses her sexuality for manipulation and deception. Patricia Hill Collins introduced the concept of controlling images as a part of an ideology of domination, as 'designed to make racism, sexism, poverty, and other forms of social injustice appear to be natural, normal and inevitable parts of everyday life' (Collins 2000: 69). Cardi B and Megan Thee Stallion's 'WAP' normalizes a Black female sexuality that opposes the controlling images of modern hip-hop versions of jezebels – video vixens and chickenheads (hip-hop vernacular for women given over to performing oral sex) – who are typically sexually objectified and commodified by male hip-hop artists for profit and street cred. Black feminist and hip-hop scholar Treva Lindsey and her colleagues argued that

> although a gyrating, pulsing, and percussive Black female body may be legible as a more recent invocation of a Jezebel . . . incorporating a hip-hop feminist lens onto those moving bodies allows for differing close readings rooted in somatic herstories of ecstatic, playful, and inventive Black female bodies.
> (Lindsey and Petchauer 2015: 60)

Cardi B and Megan Thee Stallion renounce these controlling images by cultivating sex-positive lyrics and performances that encourage Black women to self-define their own sexual images as, as per 'WAP': 'certified freaks seven days a week'. 'WAP' encourages the rejection of the jezebel-adjacent video vixen and chickenhead controlling images that tarnish the sexual narratives of Black women by channelling one's inner hip-hop diva, and so replacing these images with visions of erotic power, agency and liberation.

In conclusion, Cardi B and Megan Thee Stallion are two hip-hop divas who collaborated on a musical masterpiece that 'carve[s] spaces for eroticism and sexual freedom' (Lee 2010: 128) by defying traditional gender roles, toxic masculinity and misogynoir, promoting erotic metaphysics and illicit eroticism, fighting against respectability politics and the culture of dissemblance, and redefining controlling images. Punanny, pleasure and disrespectability politics are just a few powerful weapons to dismantle sexually oppressive strategies that have been put in place to suffocate Black female sexuality. Furthermore, Cardi B and Megan Thee Stallion's 'WAP' uses visually arousing imagery and titillating lyrics as embodiments of a Black feminist theoretical framework that is focused on Black sexual politics and hip-hop feminism to continue the legacy of erotic revolutionary hip-hop as a form of resistance against sexual oppression among Black women and femmes.

Notes

1. Misogynoir – a term coined by Black feminist scholar Moya Bailey (2021) – describes the hatred towards Black women that the male-centric hip-hop industry has historically possessed, as expressed through continuous harmful behaviours including sexual exploitation, commodification and abuse of Black women.
2. According to these hip-hop generation feminists of colour, 'the term "Crunk" was initially coined from a contraction of "crazy" or "chronic" (weed) and "drunk" and was used to describe a state of *uber*-intoxication, where a person is "crazy drunk, out of their right mind, and under the influence. But where merely getting crunk signalled that you were out of your mind, a crunk feminist mode of resistance will help you *get your mind right*, as they say in the South"' (Crunk Feminist Collective, no date).
3. Latto or Big Latto (formerly known as Miss Mulatto) is a Southern hip-hop artist who changed her moniker in May 2021 due to the sexually oppressive and controlling image of biracial women known as 'tragic mulatto'. She won the first season of the reality television show *The Rap Game* in 2016 and went mainstream with her 2019 single, 'Bitch from da Souf'.

   Rubi Rose started as a model in hip-hop trio Migos's music videos, including 'Bad and Boujee' (2016), and became popular with her 2019 single 'Big Mouth'.

   Sukihana started as a reality television star on the VH1 show *Love & Hip Hop: Miami* (2018–present), and released her 2020 debut mixtape *Wolf Pussy*; profile information sourced from Williams (2020).

Reference

Bailey, M. (2021), *Misogynoir Transformed: Black Women's Digital Resistance*, New York: New York University Press.

Collins, P. H. (2000), *Black Feminist Thought: Knowledge, Consciousness, and the Politics of Empowerment*, New York: Routledge.
Crunk Feminist Collective (no date), 'Mission Statement'. Available online: https://www.crunkfeministcollective.com/ (accessed 3 June 2022).
Durham, A., B. C. Cooper and S. M. Morris (2013), 'The Stage Hip-Hop Feminism Built: A New Directions Essay', *Signs*, 38, no. 3 (March): 721–37.
Garner, R. (2004), *Contesting the Terrain of the Ivory Tower: Spiritual Leadership of African-American Women in the Academy*, New York: Routledge.
hooks, b. (2015a), *Black Looks: Race and Representation*, New York: Routledge.
hooks, b. (2015b), *Sisters of the Yam: Black Women and Self-Recovery*, New York: Routledge.
hooks, b. (2018), 'Hardcore Honey: bell hooks Goes on the Down Low with Lil' Kim', Paper, 1 July. Available online: https://www.papermag.com/lil-kim-bell-hooks-cover-1427357106.html (accessed 5 November 2022).
Jokic, N. (2020), 'Snoop Dogg Made a Bunch of Sexist Comments About "WAP," and Offset Responded', *Buzzfeed*, 13 December. Available online: https://www.buzzfeed.com/natashajokic1/snoop-dogg-wap-controversy (accessed 28 February 2022).
Kameir, R. (2019), 'The Thrill of Megan Thee Stallion's Real-Time Rise', *Pitchfork*, 28 March. Available online: https://pitchfork.com/thepitch/the-thrill-of-megan-thee-stallions-real-time-rise/ (accessed 5 November 2022).
Lee, S. (2010), *Erotic Revolutionaries: Black Women, Sexuality, and Popular Culture*, Lanham: Hamilton Books.
Light, A. and G. Tate (no date), 'Hip-Hop', *Encyclopedia Britannica* website. Available online: https://www.britannica.com/art/hip-hop (accessed 6 November 2022).
Lindsey, T. B. and E. Petchauer (2015), 'Let Me Blow Your Mind: Hip Hop Feminist Futures in Theory and Praxis', *Urban Education*, 50, no. 1 (January): 52–77.
Lorde, A. (1984), *Sister Outsider*, Berkeley: Crossing Press.
Miller-Young, M. (2014), *A Taste of Brown Sugar: Black Women in Pornography*, Durham: Duke University Press.
Morgan, J. (1999), *When Chickenheads Come Home To Roost: A Hip-Hop Feminist Breaks It Down*, New York: Simon and Schuster.
Morgan, J. (2015), 'Why We Get Off: Moving Toward a Black Feminist Politics of Pleasure', *The Black Scholar*, 45 (4): 36–46.
Nash, J. (2018), 'Black Sexualities', *Feminist Theory*, 19 (1): 3–5.
Pough, G. D. (2004), *Check It While I Wreck It: Black Womanhood, Hip-Hop Culture, and the Public Sphere*, Boston: Northeast University Press.
Pough, G. D. (2007), 'What It Do, Shorty?: Women, Hip-Hop, and a Feminist Agenda', *Black Women, Gender and Families*, 1, no. 2 (Fall): 78–99.
Sharpley-Whiting, T. D. (2007), *Pimps Up, Ho's Down: Hip Hop's Hold on Young Black Women*, New York: New York University Press.

Trust, G. (2020), 'Megan Thee Stallion & Beyonce's "Savage" Surges to No. 1 on Billboard Hot 100', *Billboard*, 26 May. Available online: https://www.billboard.com/pro/megan-thee-stallion-beyonce-savage-number-one-hot-100/ (accessed 6 November 2022).

Whaley, N. (2018), 'These Female Rappers Don't Want to Be Defined by Industry Sexism, They're Setting Their Own Rules', *Mic*, 17 November. Available online: https://www.mic.com/articles/191485/female-rappers-industry-sexism-interviews-oshun-megan-thee-stallion-latasha (accessed 4 November 2022).

Williams, A. (2020), 'Meet the Next Wave of Female Rap Stars, Courtesy of Cardi B's "WAP" Video', *Uproxx*, 11 August. Available online: https://uproxx.com/music/cardi-b-wap-video-mulatto-rubi-rose-sukihana/ (accessed 1 November 2022).

Putting divas back in their place

Controversy and backlash at the 2020 Super Bowl Halftime Show

Gina Sandí Díaz

Introduction: Latinx Women take the 2020 Super Bowl Halftime Show

On 2 February 2020, J.Lo and Shakira took to the stage for the Super Bowl Halftime Show, making history as the first-ever halftime show led by Latinx women.[1] The fifteen-minute performance was viewed by approximately 103 million people, which was roughly 4 per cent more than Maroon 5's Halftime Show of the year before (Adgate 2021; Thorne 2020). The performance was a culturally affirming, women-centred spectacle and a celebration of both artists' mixed heritages.

Although the show received critical praise, controversy followed too – with most of it targeting the two Latinx identifying bodies on stage.[2] The stars were first criticized for accepting an invitation to perform for the National Football League (NFL) amid the controversy that had started four years earlier when then 49ers quarterback Colin Kaepernick protested against police brutality and systemic racism against Black and Brown communities by kneeling – refusing to stand – for the National Anthem.[3] In 2019, artists such as Rihanna and Jay-Z publicly spoke out on their passing up of the offer to perform at the Super Bowl stage, in support of Kaepernick's activism.[4] As the Black Lives Matter (BLM) movement, and accompanying social media hashtags such as #TakeAKnee and #BlackLivesMatter, gained momentum on social media and on the streets, pressure over the question of who would headline the show that year intensified.[5] In such a wider context, it comes as no surprise that J.Lo and Shakira should find themselves subject to criticism for accepting the job; after all, both of them identify as women of colour – and so, one would assume, would have sympathy for anti-racism activism. Their agreement to step foot on the NFL stage was perceived as a betrayal to some in Black and Brown communities.

A second wave of criticism occurred after the performance on social media and via news outlets. This time, the backlash and criticism focused on the performance and the performers: as women of colour, J.Lo and Shakira were both criticized for their wardrobe choices and physical appearance, for their song and choreography choices, for using the platform to make political statements, for adding a pole-dancing number and for including foreign cultural markers in the performance. Much of the criticism referred to the show as un-American because of the inclusion of cultural markers from the artists' heritage.

As a performance scholar, what interests me most about this backlash is the sexist and racist undertones of that criticism. In particular, I wish to interrogate what is it about the intersectionality of Latinx identifiers and womanhood that motivates such criticism. Three perspectives will help guide my analysis of this. First, fourth wave feminism's emphasis on women's empowerment in an age of social media prompts me to consider the nature of these online conversations. Second, the understanding of 'contact zones' aligned to Transnational Studies, as places where cultures meet and negotiate cultural exchange, will help to unpack the backlash, with regard to North America's 'official' narratives of citizenship and belonging. These, along with – third – intersectionality, as an analytical tool for the study of identity in relation to power structures, will help excavate the pervasive ways in which racism, sexism and ageism are manifest in public responses to the performance.

'Get off that pole – you are getting too loud!'

On 2 February 2020, conservative media journalist Monica Matthews tweeted: 'As a woman, all I can say about the Halftime Show . . . disappointing.'[6] Her reaction is one of the many placed on Twitter, with hashtags like #Fleshshow, #Sorrykids and #Stripperbowl2020 to express censorious disapproval. In opposition to these reactions, the Latinx community deployed the hashtags #MiGente and #VivaLatinos, so as to express support and appreciation for the performance. Although, at first glance, these two opposing responses merely seem to be fueled by ideological affiliations, a deeper analysis will reveal how these responses are rooted in colonial structures of power centred on heteronormative maleness and whiteness.

Fourth wave feminism defines itself in opposition to previous waves by its movement towards intersectional analysis: a model that allows for the study of identity in relation to power structures. The term intersectionality was first coined by Kimberlé Crenshaw, a critical race theorist, who used it to explain the multiple layers of oppression that are at play in wider society, particularly through a justice system which, she observed, overwhelmingly incarcerates Black women (Crenshaw 2012: 1427). In a patriarchal white order, women of colour are doubly oppressed by racism and sexism and which, coupled with the systematic political and social disenfranchisement that Black communities experience, creates a vicious cycle of mass incarceration for Black women.

Today, intersectionality is widely used to analyse the complex overlap of identifiers that make up a person's identity across gender, class, race, religion affiliation, (dis)ability, ethnicity and the like. As Crenshaw notes, intersectionality '... points to the relationship between established hierarchies that structure the relative vulnerability of subjects to the public and private exercises of social power' (1426). In other words, intersectionality accounts for the ways in which a subject views their own sense of belonging to a state and, more importantly, how the state in turn views the subject. Intersectionality thus allows us to see the gaps, and the incongruencies, in these two sets of perceptions.

The 2020 Super Bowl Halftime Show included J.Lo and Shakira's most popular hits, merged with dance numbers that included the Latinx and Afro-Latinx influences of salsa, merengue, reggaeton, R&B, and more. The show also included guest appearances of rappers Bad Bunny and J Balvin. But, more significantly, most of the artists' backup dancers and musicians were women, thus centring womanhood in a heavily male-dominated space such as the NFL. More generally, the whole show was filled with positive messages of women and empowerment. Shakira displayed her versatility as a musician, showing off her skills with the guitar and the drums, and so inspiring young women in audiences around the world. Meanwhile, J.Lo's physical versatility and agility, as displayed during the performance, must really be considered to be a contemporary indicator of the notion of women's strength. She started her segment with 'Jenny from the Block' (2002), as she climbed down a model of the Empire State Building while dressed in a black leather biker suit – a tribute to her native New York. 'I wanted it to be like women are on top of the world, [as] we're on top of the world right now', Lopez told Jimmy Fallon during an interview for *The Tonight Show*, on 8 February 2020.[7]

Towards the end of the live performance, Lopez's daughter, Emme Muñiz, joined her mother and Shakira on stage to Lopez's 'Let's Get Loud' (1999), so making a final statement on women's empowerment. They were accompanied by a chorus of girls, dressed in white, bursting out of cages. This staging suggested a strong political commentary: directly engaging, through a performed visual critique, with then-President Donald Trump's policies on migrant family separation at North American borders – something which had very directly impacted on Mexican and Central American families. Yet despite this intervention into a wider (indeed global) concern in relation to the horrors of this abrogation of human rights, the general atmosphere of the performance remained positive and uplifting; the chorus of girls, and the stars, moved to a rendition of Bruce Springsteen's 'Born in the U.S.A.' (1984), claiming this space and their voices as American citizens.

So – here we have two Latina, iconic figures, sharing one of the biggest stages of the world in terms of audience reach. They identify as women, Latinas and they are middle-aged. One should not separate out any of these identifiers from the others, as they are all intersected, and meaningful, to the understanding of the backlash. That is: these images of two successful Latinas taking up space on one of the most profitable stages in the world are not congruent with the American image of success as reserved for white and heteronormative men. Critical race theorists call attention to the multiple ways in which factors such as skin colour, socioeconomic status, gender and sexuality, among many others, work to exclude and systematically discriminate against Black women; see (Crenshaw et al. 1995; Delgado and Stefancic 2017). American Scholar Koritha Mitchell coined the term 'know your place aggression' to refer to the violence that marginalized groups often experience when they are perceived as successful. In the light of histories of colonialism and enslavement in the United States, Mitchell posits out that the goal of violence is straightforward: to function as 'an organizing mechanism that enforces society's existing hierarchies' (2015: 229). In other words, violence emerges when someone crosses (or is perceived by the oppressor to have transgressed) a boundary. At a macro level, this notion refers to the boundaries of citizenship, and the use of violence to mark, bluntly, who is and who is not a citizen.

Although today's citizenship extends beyond white straight men with property, this does not erase or mitigate the history of colonialism, patriarchy and slavery, that founded North America and denied citizenship to a vast global majority. As Mitchell boldly points out, violence functions as 'a performance of the denial of citizenship' (2015: 229). The weight of the history of oppressive exclusion can still be felt in daily interactions in which marginalized people are made to feel like guests in their own country as if they can never fully gain a sense of belonging. And those that dare to feel that they belong are punished, and 'put back in their place'. So it is not surprising that in the context of North America, and systems accustomed to rewarding and upholding the success of straight white men, two non-white women, seen to be dominating the Super Bowl's stage and taking up that privileged space, were met with commentator aggression. After all – the motivation for violence usually stems from a victim's success rather than criminal behaviour.[8]

To return to Mitchell's reading of violence as a social marker of citizenship: women have been the target of know-your-place aggression since time immemorial. Across decades, feminist thought and activism have identified a wide spectrum of aggressions: from unwelcome comments about appearances to legislation around, or detrimental to, reproductive rights. And the internalization of as much as a norm allows such aggressions to pass without question.

The very definition of the word 'diva', as a term reserved for women in showbusiness who are perceived to be difficult or high maintenance, points to the marginalization of women as subjects worthy of success and admiration. The fact that 'diva' has no male form equivalent also points to the ubiquitous ways in which women are dismissed from powerful positions and kept at the margins of success. While society values the success of white heteronormative men, women in the same positions are often subject to questioning. And this becomes particularly apparent if the successful woman is not white. Black pop icons in general are labelled as divas – from Aretha Franklin to Whitney Houston and Rihanna to Beyoncé, pretty much every successful pop artist identifying as a Black woman has seen the term 'diva' tagged onto her name.

The mass of criticism that erupted after the halftime show, targeting J.Lo and Shakira, can reasonably be read then as articulating the intention of putting them back in their place. CNN reported the Federal Communications Commission (FCC) received over 1,300 complaints from parents deeming the show not appropriate for families and children. The complaints identified the outfits worn by the artists, and the inclusion of a pole dance number, which some social media critics called 'a porno show' (Elassar 2020). A quick survey of negative Tweets (collated for a piece boosting the outrage, from the British tabloid *The Daily Mail*) begins to indicate something of the tone of the condemnations: moralistic, outraged, stern and repulsed:

Jennifer Lopez's performance at the Super Bowl halftime show was extremely explicit and completely unacceptable.

(Cited in Elassar 2020)

I was not prepared to explain to my 11 y[ear] o[ld] daughter why Jennifer Lopez was dressed so scantily or why she kept grabbing her crotch. (Cited in Elassar 2020)

It's all too much for kids. Fine for a show in Vegas, but definitely not family fare!!! Very poor taste NFL! Didn't need to be like that at all.

It was NO example to young kids anywhere and a disgrace to have this Burlesque show come into all our living rooms! So pathetic and disgusting at the SUPERBOWL! The NFL have idiots running the Show!! Glad I'm not alone!

It was crass. Over-sexed. Pole dancing, really? Glad I don't have young kids anymore . . . JLo trying too hard as usual. Loved the Spanish. Love Shakira (minus the snake-tongue thing). Didn't love all the cracks, and ass in face thing . . . When did we forget that Less is More?

Answer: Lewd. Crude. Disgusting. Nasty. Vulgar. Crossed the line. Gloried porn. Crass. Inappropriate. Gross. Untalented. Sickening.

Question: What was the halftime show?

That was completely an immoral, classless soft porn pole dancing performance! How dare you allow something so provocative knowing children were watching. Then having children perform around these TRAMPS.

People: JLo and Shakira's halftime performance was totally inappropriate. They were naked on stage. Bumping and grinding on stage.[9]

(Cited in Edmonds and Edwards 2020)

As Mitchell points out: the success of marginalized peoples is 'more often "the offense" that will make them a target' (229). In this case, J.Lo and Shakira 'dared' to take to one of the most profitable stages in the world, and created a show to claim and validate their identities as multicultural, middle-aged women, mothers, business entrepreneurs, social activists and pop icons. But such accusations of vulgarity point to another area of rhetorical response too, which I now want to turn to.

Jennifer Lopez was fifty years old when she performed at the Super Bowl. Just the year prior, she had performed the role of Ramona Vega in the film *Hustlers* (Lorene Scafaria 2019), in which she played an experienced pole dancer/girl-gang leader masterminding a massive extortion operation. She prepared both physically and mentally for the role, training for extensive hours for the pole-dancing routines. Thus, in the Super Bowl show, she displayed the fruits of her success, by sharing her new dance moves, and the control she had gained over her body – a total 'power move', to demonstrate women empowerment in the twenty-first century. (When it was announced that J.Lo had not been nominated for an Oscar for *Hustlers*, people took it to social media to express support of her, citing racism and misogyny as possible causes.) In reaction to criticism over J.Lo's Super Bowl performance, some viewers jumped to her defence by claiming it was a sexist double standard: just the year before, the Maroon 5 frontman had performed shirtless:

> So Adam Levine is allowed for [*sic*] perform shirtless during the Halftime Show and sexually dance across the stage ... but as soon as two confident Latina women do it, with just as much coverage, of [*sic*] not more, it's deemed 'inappropriate'?
> (Victoria 2020)

The perception of the over-sexualization of J.Lo's performance is also rooted in colonial ideas that have historically exoticized brown bodies. After all, North American culture has exploited the image of the 'overly' sexual Latina/o through the 'widely circulated narratives of sexual availability, proficiency and desirability' (Guzmán and Valdivia 2014). In particular, J.Lo's booty has been the subject of much scrutiny since her rise to success in the mid-to-late 1990s. Guzmán and Valdivia further point out that

> Lopez is simultaneously celebrated and denigrated for her physical, bodily and financial excess. Whenever she appears in the popular press, whether it is a newspaper, a news magazine, or *People*, Lopez's gorgeous stereotypical Latina butt is glamorized and sexually fetishized. Indeed, she is often photographed in profile or from the back looking over her shoulders – her buttocks becoming the focus of the image, the part of her body that marks Lopez as sexy but different from Anglo female bodies.
> (Guzmán and Valdivia 2014: 212)

Aside from gender and age dismissal, criticism of J.Lo also resonates with perceptions of the roots of her heritage; her Puerto Rican heritage marks her, in the eyes of her detractors, as less of an American than other white-identifying artists, adding an extra layer of 'otherness' which fuels the backlash. Perhaps Shakira's proximity to whiteness, her younger age and the audience's perception of her as a Colombian artist that crossed over to the American market, as opposed to a non-white American reaching for success, protected Shakira from the type of attacks directed at J.Lo.

Countering Narrative – Who is this for?

Intersectionality is also crucial in respect to understanding how privilege operates in proximity to whiteness. Since the 1990s, scholars have been concerned with contesting the definition of Latinidad as a monolithic representation of a very diverse community, and with the commodification and consumption of Latina/o bodies in media and its influence on American culture (Guzmán and Valdivia 2014). Although Latino identity is multidimensional, and differs greatly by region, it is certainly not defined by race per se; Latin America is culturally and racially diverse. In the United States, however, Latinos are marginalized by markers other than skin colour, such as economic status, linguistic accent and for their cultural practices. Rosaura Sanchez calls this phenomena cultural racialization, referring to the dynamics by which Mexican Americans in the United States are categorized as non-white, but with this identification pivoting on factors such as accent, language and cultural practices rather than appearance. In respect to the discrimination and marginalization of Mexican Americans in the United States, she argues that 'the racism suffered has always been intersected by ethnocentrism, classism, linguistic oppression, and judicial prejudice' (1995: 285). These considerations are then of a heightened significance, 'given the equation of whiteness and citizenship and all its attending rights in the United States' (Beltran 2009: 8). This is evident in the success and appeal that white Latino actors have, versus Indigenous or Afro-Latino actors.[10] It is here that we can call on an intersectional critical apparatus to unpack the complexities of know-your-place aggression, and the overlap of oppressive forces that prevent marginalized women of colour from success.

As suggested earlier, an unquantified but (social media-) amplified perception of J.Lo and Shakira's citizenship status is also noteworthy because it can go some way to explain why J.Lo was the subject of scrutiny, and not Shakira. In her book, *Latina/o Stars in US Eyes*, Mary Beltran explores the reception of Latina/o stars across different time periods in North American history. She points out that actress Dolores Del Rio was perceived as an upper-class foreigner, and so contributing to American culture from that partially excluded vantage point, but which nonetheless granted her a privileged status among critics and audiences that other artists of colour could not enjoy or access, since they were primarily perceived as non-white American citizens (2009). This observation is one that can be parlayed into the reading of the backlash towards the halftime show. Both J.Lo and Shakira are US citizens, but some segments of the American public hold different perceptions of their backgrounds and citizenship, which may impact the perception of their work or their particular contributions to American culture. Shakira is a US citizen born in Colombia, and with Lebanese roots, while J.Lo is a US citizen of Puerto Rican descent. Both artists also identify as mothers, social activists and businesswomen with personal interests of their own. The halftime show seemed to intentionally highlight the multiple facets of womanhood, and of the artists' cultural identities, not least in the way in which both imprint the mark of their cultural heritages onto their performances. The result can be read as a defiant celebration of womanhood, and of the multiple cultures that come to make up contemporary America – a unique quality for a halftime show. In an interview with *Faze* magazine, verifying an awareness of her identity as intersected, fluid and constantly morphing, Shakira stated: 'I am a fusion. That's my persona. I'm a fusion between black and white, between pop and rock, between cultures – between my Lebanese father and my mother's Spanish blood, the Colombian folklore and Arab dance I love and American music.' (Ma 2002) Likewise, in an interview with Christian Acosta for *Somos Radio* in October 2020, Lopez spoke of her awareness at being giving an opportunity to address a global audience via the Super Bowl stage: 'For me at the Super Bowl this year it was such a big deal to kind of make some statement because I knew I was representing women, I knew I was representing Latinos, and I knew that I was representing that I was American as well' (White 2020).

Mary Louise Pratt coined the term 'contact zones' to refer to places where 'cultures meet, crash, and grapple with each other, often in highly asymmetrical relations of power' (1991: 34). In a society dominated by Western models of patriarchal heteronormativity, this contact potential translates into everyday interactions in which marginalized subjects are constantly negotiating their existence and value in white-dominated spaces, and are forced to strategize survival mechanisms to simply exist within a system that seeks to oppress and even dehumanize them. Cultural performances of marginalized cultures usually function as contact zones because they must traverse the gaze of the dominant culture in order to reach their target audiences. As artists with intersected identities stemming from varied cultures, and thus looking to a diverse audience, J.Lo and Shakira's Super Bowl Halftime Show can also be read as a site of collision between the 'official' narrative of America and the version of America displayed on stage by two Latina-identifying artists. Their American audience was seemingly disappointed that the show moved away from traditional performances of patriotism and viewed the multicultural elements of the performance as un-American. Much of this criticism of the performance came from a place of not understanding the cultural markers displayed in the show. However, I would argue that the artists effectively expanded the very notion of 'America' by speaking to a global majority audience in the United States and, crucially, abroad. In this regard, the show became a kind of megaphone to the world, where two Latinas (literally) got loud and unapologetically so.

The show consisted of three segments, with Shakira leading the first, J.Lo in the middle segment and the two artists sharing the stage for the final one. Shakira's opening segment was carefully crafted to represent her intersected sense of identity: it purposely presented cultural elements of her native Colombia, and her Lebanese roots, including a musical dance number of Champeta (an Afro-Colombian musical style, stemming from the Caribbean coast of the country but then popularized throughout the nation, especially in urban settings) and Middle Eastern belly dancing. Many elements of her performance were a homage to her Lebanese roots – this included a rope dance, as traditionally Lebanese. Tellingly, and depressingly, this segment was used by media outlets to call-out Shakira – she 'dances like an Arab' (Mason 2020) – so linguistically marking her as a non-Arab. And perhaps the most talked about moment of the night was Shakira's tongue-swirling sting, called a zaghrouta: an Arab gesture that signifies joy and celebration. American audiences, without the context to understand this reference, interpreted the gesture as overly sexualized and even vulgar. A multiplicity of memes circulated in social media, associating the gesture with sexual matters. In addition, Shakira's tribute to Colombian culture paid credit where credit was due: the Colombian influences in the show all stemmed from Afro-Caribbean roots and proudly represented these roots in the performance, moving away from traditional Eurocentric representational practices of Latinidad (that prioritize Latinx connections to Spain as the motherland). For the Champeta number, Shakira was joined on stage by a group of mostly Afro-Latina dancers, dressed in gold: an image resembling Colombia's Indigenous ancestry, prior to Western exploitation.

Similarly, J.Lo's performance included markers to entice Puerto Rican audiences and other Latinx communities that call the United States their home. The most impactful such moment was when she came out wrapped in the US flag that once opened (as she sang to the tunes of 'Let's Get Loud' and 'Born in the U.S.A.') revealed the Puerto Rico flag – a straightforward message that Latinx communities in the United States are here to stay. A few months after the performance, J.Lo revealed that she had kept the Puerto Rico flag a secret from everyone in the production as she feared censorship: '. . . I didn't even show it to anybody until the last minute, because I didn't want anybody telling me I couldn't do it. So, it was kind of a secret.' (White 2020). This revelation is important as it demonstrates that even when occupying powerful positions, women of colour are still wary and cautious of the censorship they might encounter or incur if they speak their truth.

Conclusion: Divas of intersectionality

The 2020 Super Bowl Halftime Show contested America's official narrative of citizenship by addressing a global majority of non-white Americans and, in turn, validating their existence and amplifying their voices as American citizens. The show also promoted a modern understanding of womanhood by showcasing the many hats that artists wear as creatives, mothers and entrepreneurs. The artists paid homage to their multicultural heritage with the performance, effectively using the stage as a contact zone where American audiences had to confront their definitions of citizenship, womanhood and Latinidad. The efficacy of this cultural moment was founded on both intersectionality and divadom. In reviewing the historical contextualization of responses – in respect to patriarchy, colonialism and slavery – it becomes apparent just how rooted these oppressive forces are, and how they continue to permeate social understandings, and everyday conversations, around the idea of 'belonging' in America.

Notes

1 Jennifer Lopez (1969–present) and Shakira Rippoll (1977–present). In keeping with their persona names, I have used J.Lo, or Jennifer Lopez, and Shakira, across this essay.
2 The *New York Times* called it '[a] Spanish flavored halftime, full of sparkle and spectacle' (Hoffman 2020) and *US Today* 'one of the best, most empowering and flat-out fun Super Bowl halftimes of the past decade' (Ryan 2020).
3 In an interview with NFL.com, Kaepernick explained: 'I am not going to stand up to show pride in a flag for a country that oppresses black people and people of color', and added '[i]f they take football away, my endorsements from me [. . .] I know that I stood up for what is right' (Boren 2020). The controversy attracted comment from the highest office; in 2017, the then-President of the United States,

Donald Trump, posted the following comment to his since-cancelled Twitter account: 'If a player wants the privilege of making millions of dollars in the NFL, or other leagues, he or she should not be allowed to disrespect our Great American Flag (or Country) and should stand for the National Anthem. If not, YOU'RE FIRED. Find something else to do!'

4 In 2019, the NFL and Jay-Z's company, Roc Nation, had signed a partnership agreement, giving Roc Nation a voice and a vote on the NFL's biggest music events, including the halftime show. The agreement also allowed Jay-Z's company to collaborate on education and economic initiatives for communities at risk, including justice reform. This partnership sparked criticism and backlash towards the star who, two years prior, had also voiced support for Kaepernick. In response to this criticism, Roc Nation executives noted that: 'the higher purpose is to get inside the establishment to bring representation of color and try to foster a nationwide cultural dialogue' (Rosman 2020). Shakira is a client of Roc Nation.

5 Pop-rock band Maroon 5 ended up headlining the show in 2019. The band ignored calls to back down in support of Kaepernick; in an interview for Entertainment Tonight, front man Adam Levine said that he expected controversy over the band's decision to perform, but said the band would 'keep doing what we're doing, hopefully without becoming politicians' (Frazier 2019).

6 See: https://twitter.com/monicaonairtalk/status/1224141950766534660

7 See: https://www.youtube.com/watch?v=UGFz2B-7DBc

8 Mitchell urges us to study violence with keen awareness of its purpose: '[t]t is not simply an injustice inflicted on human beings; it is an organizing mechanism that enforces society's existing hierarchies' (2015: 229). Such a conception promotes a different conversation around violence – a conversation centred on inclusion and exclusion, rather than criminality.

9 The *Daily Mail* article also presents Tweets critical of the outrage, but as a secondary concern (and in a secondary position) in an article with 'parents slam' in its headline.

10 An example is Karla Souza (*How To Get Away With Murder*), an upper-class white Mexican born actor who has experienced relative success in the United States versus Yalitza Aparicio (*Roma*), an Indigenous Mexican actor who played the main role in Alfonso Cuarón's 2018 film *Roma* and was the subject of many critiques.

Reference

Adgate, B. (2021), 'Facts About Super Bowl LVI: Advertising, Ratings, Halftime Show and Tom Brady', *Forbes Magazine*. Available online: https://www.forbes.com/sites

/bradadgate/2021/02/01/facts-about-super-bowl-lv-advertising-ratings-halftime-show-and-tom-brady/?sh=2bce949b7da7 (accessed 1 November 2022).

Beltran, M. C. (2009), *Latina/o Stars in U.S. Eyes*, Chicago: University of Illinois Press.

Boren, C. (2020), 'A Timeline of Colin Kaepernick's Protest against Police Brutality, Four Years after they Began', *The Washington Post*, 26 August. Available online: https://www.washingtonpost.com/sports/2020/06/01/colin-kaepernick-kneeling-history/ (accessed 1 November 2022).

Crenshaw, K., N. Gotanda, G. Peller and K. Thomas, eds (1995), *Critical Race Theory. The Key Writings that formed the Movement*, New York: The New Press.

Crenshaw, K. W. (2012), 'From Private Violence to Mass Incarceration: Thinking Intersectionally About Women, Race, and Social Control', *UCLA Law Review*, 6 (59): 1418–72.

Delgado, R. and J. Stefancic, eds (2017), *Critical Race Theory: An Introduction*, third edn, New York: New York University Press.

Edmonds, L. and V. Edwards (2020), 'Too Sexy for the Super Bowl! Parent slam J-Lo's Pole-Dancing and Shakira's Tongue-Wagging Half-Time Performances Blasting that they were Inappropriate for Kids', *The Daily Mail*, 4 February Available online: https://www.dailymail.co.uk/news/article-7964217/Parents-slam-J-Los-Shakiras-halftime-performances-inappropriate-kids.html (accessed 1 November 2022).

Elassar, A. (2020), 'Over 1,300 Complaints were Sent to the FCC about Shakira and J.Lo's Super Bowl Show', *CNN*, 26 February. Available online: https://www.cnn.com/2020/02/25/us/shakira-jlo-super-bowl-halftime-show-fcc-complaints-trnd/index.html (accessed 1 November 2022).

Frazier, K. (2019), 'Adam Levine Talks Super Bowl LIII Halftime Show', YouTube video. Available online: https://www.youtube.com/watch?v=uznUl3yoJrA (accessed 1 November 2022).

Guzmán, I. M. and A. N. Valdivia (2014), 'Brain, Brow, and Booty: Latina Iconicity in U.S. Popular Culture', *The Communication Review*, 7: 205–21.

Hoffman, B. (2020), 'How the Chiefs Beat the 49ers to Win the Super Bowl', *The New York Times*, 2 February. Available online: https://www.nytimes.com/2020/02/02/sports/football/chiefs-49ers-super-bowl.html (accessed 1 November 2022).

Ma, S. (2002), 'Shakira Cover Story: Cultural Fusion', *Faze*. Available online: https://faze.ca/shakira-cover-story-cultural-fusion/ (accessed 1 November 2022).

Mason, J. (2020), 'Shakira Dancing Like an Arab at the Super Bowl', *Arab America*, 29 January. Available online: https://www.arabamerica.com/shakira-dancing-like-an-arab-at-the-super-bowl-hips-dont-lie/ (accessed 1 November 2022).

Mitchel, K. (2015), 'Keep Claiming Space!', *CLA Journal*, 58 (3/4): 229–44.

Pratt, M. L. (1991), 'Arts of the Contact Zone', *Profession* 1 (1): 33–40.

Rosman, K. (2020), 'Jay-Z Takes on the Super Bowl', *The New York Times*, 1 February 2020. Available online: https://www.nytimes.com/2020/02/01/style/jay-z-super-bowl-roc-nation.html (accessed 1 November 2022).

Ryan, P. (2020), 'Jennifer Lopez and Shakira Dazzle in One of the Best Super Bowl Halftime Shows in Memory', *USA Today*, 2 February. Available online: https://www.usatoday.com/story/entertainment/music/2020/02/02/super-bowl-halftime-show-2020-jennifer-lopez-and-shakira-dazzle-one-best-super-bowl-halftime-shows-m/4642154002/ (accessed 1 November 2022).

Sanchez, R. (1995), *Telling Identities: The Californio Testimonios*. Minneapolis: University of Minnesota Press.

Thorne, W. (2020), 'Jennifer Lopez and Shakira Provide Super Bowl Halftime Show Ratings Boost', *Variety*, 3 February. Available online: https://variety.com/2020/tv/news/jennifer-lopez-shakira-super-bowl-halftime-show-ratings-boost-1203491139/ (accessed 1 November 2022).

Victoria, Z. (2020), 'Criticism of J-Lo and Shakira's Halftime Show Reveals a Sexist Double Standard', *SBC*, 4 February. Available online: https://www.sbs.com.au/topics/voices/culture/article/2020/02/04/criticism-j-lo-and-shakiras-halftime-show-reveals-sexist-double-standard (accessed 1 November 2022).

White, A. (2020), 'Jennifer Lopez Reveals Why She Featured Dual American-Puerto Rican Flag Cape, Kids in Cages During Super Bowl Halftime Show', *The Hollywood Reporter*, 15 October. Available online: https://www.hollywoodreporter.com/news/general-news/jennifer-lopez-reveals-why-she-featured-dual-american-puerto-rican-flag-cape-kids-in-cages-during-super-bowl-halftime-show-4077253/ (accessed 1 November 2022).

Simultaneously Black

Drake and Nicki Minaj and the performance of hip-hop cosmopolitanisms

Nicole Hodges Persley

1. Simultaneously Black: Drake and Nicki Minaj remixing hip-hop cosmopolitanisms of Blackness

The diversity of Black cultural, ethnic, class and national histories that exist simultaneously under the signifier African American are complex and always already transnational. However, discussion of African American identity is rarely discussed in transnational contexts in the media and is most often conflated with rags-to-riches stories that rarely consider the complexity of Black experience within one family unit, let alone a whole community. The wide range of voluntary African migrants to the United States, after the forced migrations of US slavery, coupled with the African cultural retentions that remain in African American cultural practices as a result of slavery, are all connected by shared histories of subjugation that persist in the twenty-first century. Revisiting the work of Transnational American Studies scholar Shelley Fisher Fishkin's assertion in the early 2000s that to forge a truly transnational approach to American Studies requires that we must 'pay as much attention to how ideas, people, culture, and capital have circulated and continue to circulate, physically, and virtually, throughout the world, both in ways we might expect, and unpredictably; it requires that we view America, as David Palumbo-Liu put it, as a place "always in process itself"' (2005: 21). Drake and Minaj's choices to work in the United States as artists invested in Black cultural representation and, ultimately (to use Bourdieu's term) 'cultural capital', are a part of the circulation of 'ideas, people, culture and capital' that challenge how we view American identity. These artists push definitions of Blackness to include connected experiences of transnational Black belonging across ethnic, class, gender and national lines. The capacity of these artists to engage multiple national positions, simultaneously, suggests a lesser-explored aspect of diva tropes which is the cosmopolitan aesthetic, associated with hip-hop superstardom. The rise of hip-hop as a cosmopolitan genre of music, aesthetic and performance created and performed by artists all over the world, in several languages and cultural cadences, challenges the default perceptions of the music and culture's decidedly African American 'hood' tropes (which I deal with later). The work that Drake and Minaj do in their performance work strategically unsettles lazy entertainment industry projections that greatly impacts the making of Blackness as a deliberate subversive act of world-making creativity and that seeks to expand the legibility and possibility of what hip-hop music and culture has permission to be on the world stage (Kondo 2021: 30) The global positions these artists occupy as international stars, suggests hood-cosmopolitan binaries are intrinsically false and that resisting and subverting them is more than inextricably tied to quests for citizenship, equal opportunity and parity by Black artists. In the twenty-first century, Fishkin's prescription for deeper, more complex and messy investigations of American identity still rings true as the identities of Drake and Minaj operate in comfortable contradiction to any fixed trope of Blackness. They, like the personas they create and perform, are always in process, thus challenging elitist notions of transnational subjectivity and cosmopolitanism that suggest elitist acts of alienation. But they more arguably use their art to forge a grey space that embraces the ghettoization of urban culture of the late 1990s and early 2000s aesthetic of hip-hop culture to rethink new concepts of cosmopolitanism that are relevant to our current scholarly discussion of anti-Blackness and transnational popular culture of the 2020s. These artists offer their personal theorizations of Black migration, citizenship and kinship that are excluded from mainstream academic discourse, yet offer fresh new imaginings that redefine the contours of cosmopolitanism and level the set of who can make claims to diva culture. Diva culture has its own particular tropes and assumptions, tethered to its recognition and performance. I want to complicate the ways that Drake and Nicki Minaj render 'hood' tropes within hip-hop that redraw gender, race and national boundaries to suggest that cosmopolitanism within hip-hop is malleable and simultaneous, as it moves from time zone to time zone, and from aesthetic practice to making the world through acts of creative audacity that constantly remake the world anew. A diva is a transformative performer who makes demands on the world to conform to their ideas of originality, creativity and craft. Both Drake and Minaj have forever changed the sonic, aesthetic and cultural expectations of what hip-hop can imagine itself to be. And this is exactly what a diva culture demands.

Canadian-born rapper and actor Drake, and Trinidadian-born rapper and actress Nicki Minaj, use the performance mediums of hip-hop music, television and film to shift the borders of Black popular culture by using their bodies and voices to play African Americans in transnational contexts. By analysing how their biographies shape their work, this chapter works to connect the simultaneity of Black identities that exist between social spaces and dominant and marginal tropes of Blackness within hip-hop cultures' engagement with notions of being a diva. In hip-hop, the term diva, used as a noun to describe a person, is most often associated with women identified as artists. However, in hip-hop, the term has been used as an adjective to describe the behaviour and expectation of highly successful artists: 'diva' behaviour that has a high expectation of excellence. To be a diva is to expect to have authority and dominion over creativity, space, body and place without apology. And it is for this reason that Drake comes within the scope of my discussion.

Internationally recognized performers, Drake and Minaj move across multiple national contexts to perform culturally and country specificities of Blackness that complicate binaries forged between dominant US-based narratives of the hood and aspirational tropes of upper-middle Black cosmopolitanism. These artists connect the complex class representations of Black life that occur within African American cultural practices and their connection to other African and African diasporic experiences through the mediums of hip-hop, television and film performance. Moving literally and figuratively across public spaces, their biographies, coupled with their artistic choices, create unexpected linkages between Black cultural expressions that reimagine a critical Black cosmopolitanism in twenty-first-century popular culture that is simultaneously Black, multi-ethnic and transnational. Together, these artists forge prescriptive narratives of citizenship and belonging that redefine how we understand cosmopolitanism, hip-hop's global reach and the implications of diva culture in the twenty-first century.

Scholars of Black Performance Studies have initiated and continued conversations over the past decade about the embodied, cultural and material moving of Blackness across national borders as a contingent and dynamic construct (Elam and Jackson 2005: 406). The exploration of the transnational qualities of African American expressions of Blackness globally, as a social construct that is dynamic and always in process, has been the subject of anthologies by Heike Raphael-Hernandez (2003) and Thomas DeFrantz and Anita Gonzalez (2014). This chapter works to expand these conversations by imagining Blackness from an always already transnational and cosmopolitan perspective and one that sees Blackness in performance as a process of theorization that produces new sonic, visual and textual vernaculars of Black identity through the artist's lived experiences, and that are used to develop the art that they create. By exploring representations of Blackness across national, class and ethnic lines, this chapter attempts to address the transnational qualities of so-called 'hood' and 'cosmopolitan' identities of Blackness that occur through implicit and explicit performance that finds synergy with notions of diva culture in the entertainment industry. (On the concept of the 'hood', in both American and British contexts, see Gilroy 2004: 89–92.) My goal is to interrogate how Black artists themselves theorize cosmopolitanism through acts of performance on their terms, often completely outside of the theorizations of Black performance in academe, and that produce some of the cadences of diva culture most often racialized as white, and gendered as cis-gendered female.

David Featherstone argues that historically forms of cosmopolitanism that foreground white Eurocentrism place other, seemingly 'subaltern', cosmopolitanisms on the margins (2008: 23). I argue that the artists whose biographies and performances I explore here unsettle false dichotomies of cosmopolitanism that reference 'the Eurocentricity of older unitary cosmopolitanisms that assume universals' (Featherstone 2008: 21). These artists provide a critical cosmopolitanism that forges connections between 'the simplified hood', which is used as a global Black trope across ethnic lines, and cosmopolitan life experiences, that are marked by education, wealth, and a distinct disavowal of low-to-moderate income Black life experiences (i.e. hood, ghetto, experiences). Drake and Minaj's public personas and performed roles in their music, film and television remind us of the collective denial of Black citizenship across class and national lines of Black difference while theorizing new critical Black cosmopolitanisms that demand more diverse representations of Black life experiences which consider the complexity of class, ethnicity and nationality. The sophisticated social, cultural and contextual demands these artists make by playing across national spheres of influence challenge audiences to read their artistic work within simultaneous national contexts of Blackness, which can be read as collective acts of divadom.

2. Whose cosmopolitanism is it anyway?

Drake and Minaj complicate tropes of African American identity in the United States – often conflated with the hood within various modes of entertainment – by forging personal, cultural, and artistic cosmopolitan connections across African diasporic spaces that suggest that 'the hood is everywhere'. I theorize their simultaneous Black identifications in a twofold manner. First, simultaneous Blackness recognizes that Black people from diverse ethnic and national backgrounds can occupy more than one nation-specific context of Blackness through lived or projected meanings of belonging. For example, Drake fills two identifications of African diasporic subjectivity; African American (father) and African Canadian Jewish (mother). He identifies as racially Black in two or more national and ethnic contexts. Second, simultaneous Black subjects can also derive from a single national location, yet be incorporated by another through social acts of belonging and self-identification. For example, former US President Barack Obama is Kenyan and Irish American, yet identifies as African American in a US context and Kenyan in an African context. These figures refuse to privilege one unique Black identity over another and, instead, make simultaneous claims to shared Black experiences to theorize a critical cosmopolitanism that is not dependent upon assumed ethnicity, class and nationality but is, more specifically, at work in connecting Black experiences globally. Diverse Black communities worldwide suggest that 'have and have-nots' collectively constitute Black intellectual, political and creative histories that shape modernity.

A 2010s argument regarding the flexible boundaries of Black masculinity, written by US-based Black Studies scholar and pop culture critic Mark Anthony Neal, offers a lens through which we might see simultaneous claims that connect class and nationality differences in Black life. In his article 'A Man Without a Country: The Boundaries of Legibility, Social Capital, and Cosmopolitan Masculinity', Neal gestures towards the simultaneity of Black identities in performance by drawing our attention to how Black British actor Idris Elba's performance of the African American character Stringer Bell, in the HBO series *The Wire* (2002–8), effectively expanded Western perceptions of Blackness and Black masculinity beyond stereotypes of the 'hood'. Neal suggests Elba's portrayal of Bell complicates stereotypes of Black masculinity by performing a cosmopolitan world view – that is, one that positions Black men as 'citizens of the world'. Neal's focus on the translatability of diverse Black masculinities (in this case Elba's Black experiences in Britain), and the variances of social currency that Black masculinities afford to American popular culture, opens opportunities for further considerations of transnational perspectives of Blackness. And these transnational perspectives potentially challenge easy binaries of Black identity, as constructed by the American entertainment industry, that polarize localized Black American 'hood' experiences through constructions of cosmopolitanism that privilege the Black experiences of performers from African diasporic spaces outside the United States. Speaking of the challenging views of Black identity presented in *The Wire*, a show that chronicled Black life in a poor community in Baltimore, Maryland, in the early 2000s, Neal asserts:

> Indeed, part of the appeal of *The Wire* is that it privileges the worldview of the block, though, in the absence of experiences beyond the confines of Baltimore's so-called inner city, the block becomes a nation – something that must be policed and defended at all cost for far too many of its characters. To speak of concerns beyond the block – something perhaps akin to a cosmopolitan worldview in which one is seen as a citizen of the world – is to risk censure from tightly knit hood (i.e., neighborhood) relations and to raise suspicions about even more tightly held convictions of what constitutes legitimate hood masculinities.
>
> (Neal 2010: 403)

Though Neal is specifically addressing hood-cosmopolitan binaries, implied through Elba's performance of Bell, as a cosmopolitan Black actor from Britain, I am expanding on Neal's assertions to broaden the discussion to include the binary oppositions suggested by these subject positions, and how the mainstream media values their respective representations, and locations, in Black performance in hip-hop, television and film, throughout the African diaspora.

Neal's assertion here speaks to the limited world view that notions of the commodified 'hood (i.e., neighborhood)' imposes on the life chances of real and fictional Black people in the United States and other diasporic locations. Speaking to how the 'boundaries of the block' (or seemingly localized Black expressions – in this case African American male identities) limit the perceived world view of African American men to tropes of the hood in global popular culture, Neal gestures towards the lost experiences that happen 'beyond the block' and that are overshadowed by one-dimensional stereotypes of Black men that never go deeper than their surface portrayals of criminalization. Neal offers a representative example of the type of contradictions that Black cosmopolitan views as he describes the character Bell's Black male cosmopolitanism in *The Wire*:

> Central to that worldview are the conflicts and contradictions that animate his efforts to move beyond the block, yet remain wedded to it because it is where his Black masculinity is so firmly inscribed and vital. Bell may no longer be of the block, but the block still matters to him, else he would be content with just being another Black businessman. No, Bell thrives on his mobility but has little language at his disposal to sing the praises of that mobility in ways that resonate on the block.
>
> (Neal 2010: 399)

The assertions that I make about Black cosmopolitanism here expand on Neal's astute observations of the simultaneity of Black masculinity, to further develop his idea of a localized hood defined through African American cultural practices as a dialogical space that speaks to global experiences of Blackness, in order to imagine what Gerard Delanty calls a more complex cultural cosmopolitanism. In building on Neal's observation of the process of translation that occurs as Black actors (and I expand the parameters of his discussion of masculinity to include female performances by Nicki Minaj here), from one ethnicity and national context performing Blackness in other ethnonational contexts, my revised definition of Black cosmopolitanism now allows for the consideration of how performances of localized African American expressions of Blackness, by the Black artist from other African diasporic spaces, help us rethink notions of that which Neal calls 'the block'. This 'block' then is understood as not so much of a nation that must 'be policed and defended' but as a transnational point of departure, from which real and fictionalized stereotypes and tropes of the hood work to shape a cosmopolitan imagination that is always connected to the block, and what it means to Black communities in and outside US contexts. Gerard Delanty argues that the 'Cosmopolitan Imagination' occurs

> when and wherever new relations between self, other, and world develop in moments of openness. [The idea of cosmopolitanism] is an approach that shifts the emphasis to internal developmental processes within the social world rather than seeing globalization as the primary mechanism and is also not reducible to the fact of pluralism.
>
> (2006: 27)

Delanty's definition of a cosmopolitan imagination usefully works to supplement Neal's seemingly subconscious valuing of Elba as more cosmopolitan than the character he portrays, simply because he is a Black British male. Delanty asks for an unsettling of normative universals of cosmopolitanism that are dependent upon European ideals of modernity, derived from Kantian ideals that share 'a vision of a world political community extending beyond the community into which one is born or lives', and yet then 'became linked with the universalism of modern western though and with political designs aimed at world governance' (2006: 27). This alternative theorization of cosmopolitan imagination suggests that we see cosmopolitanism less as 'a particular or singular condition that either exists or does not, a state or goal to be realized' and more as 'a cultural medium of societal transformation that is based on the principle of world openness, which is associated with the notion of global publics' (2006: 27).

My understanding of Black cosmopolitanism incorporates the work of Black performers such as Drake and Minaj, to suggest performance as a cultural model of cosmopolitan mediation by the ways that Black artists use creative acts of openness that occur through performance, to connect transnational encounters. They thus contribute to defining a Black cosmopolitanism that sees shared experiences of oppression and success as mutually constitutive to the state of being Black. Black cosmopolitanism, writes Ifeoma Nwankwo, is not a replacement for Blackness, but more an understanding that

> a person of African descent's citizenship in his or specific nation of residence has been denied, negated, and generally troubled. Positioning national identity and cosmopolitanism as opposites presume that national identity is available to all individuals. Our understanding of cosmopolitanism must consider that for some (people of African descent in this case) national identity may be desired but inaccessible, and consequently, that cosmopolitanism, while not necessarily the object of desire, may be conceptualized as a means to the end of gaining access to national identity.
>
> (2014: 12)

While Nwankwo is speaking specifically about nineteenth-century Black expressions of cosmopolitanism, as articulated by people of African descent from Cuba, the United States and the British West Indies, her discussion of the complexity of Black cosmopolitanism and the nation-state still applies to twenty-first-century expressions and interrogations of cosmopolitanism. These often move through an expansive culture, rooted in Black urban environments, as chronicled through the theatrical and sonic practices of Drake and Minaj.

The select work and public personas of the artists explored here connect local and global representations of Blackness using the mediums of hip-hop music, television and film. As simultaneous citizens of the world, they expand upon that which Neal identifies as 'tightly held convictions': what constitutes so-called legitimate and/or authentic Black identities in performance. By using performance to act out the various cultural rights they can assume in different national contexts, these artists create what Delanty calls critical cosmopolitanism by building spaces of openness for coalition-building that occurs through their embodiments of overlapping, and thus, simultaneous Black identities. Their performances further our understanding of Nwankwo's observation that people of African descent fight for legibility as fully recognized national subjects, and yet must employ alternate means to gain accessibility as a collective state through cosmopolitan acts that shape perceptions of divadom in new contexts, defined by the artists on their terms.

My theorization of simultaneous Blackness draws attention to the labour of Black performers who use performance to identify connections and allegiances across Black communities. Turkish-American cultural theorist Seyla Benhabib strengthens this assertion in her theorization of the more complex cosmopolitanism needed for twenty-first-century identity negotiations (i.e. that exceed previous historic understandings of race, nation, and citizenship) by highlighting the simultaneity of cultures. Thus 'cultures themselves, as well as societies, are not holistic but polyvocal, multilayered, decentered, and fractured systems of action and signification' (2002: 25–6). While this position supports my point about simultaneity and selective allegiances, I wish to add to her observation: Benhabib's polyvocal standpoint must be considered further, into the multiple ways that people live that which Stuart Hall has called the modality of race and class; see Hall (1980) and Benhabib (2008).

For Benhabib, collective human interaction is always already cosmopolitan, and must show 'concern for the world as if it were one's polis', with cosmopolitanism, 'furthered by such multiple, overlapping allegiances [as] sustained across communities of language, ethnicity, religion, and nationality' (Benhabib 2004: 174–5). Such cosmopolitanism inspires multivalent and polyvocal expressions of Black identity. For Benhabib, collective critiques of European-derived universal norms of citizenship directly challenge ideologies that render Black contributions across classes and spaces to modernity as exceptions to, instead of integral components of, human history. Drake and Minaj are using their performances and public commentary to contribute to conversations about cosmopolitanism by forging a dialogue between the local and the global that resists the polarization of Blacks based on class and nation.

3. Drake and Nicki Minaj: Performing the intersecting boundaries of Black cosmopolitanism

Many know Drake as an African American artist who began his rise to superstardom in the early 2000s, with the circulation of his famed mixtapes to radio stations around the United States. His unique sound and emotionally vulnerable content caught the ear of African American rapper Lil Wayne, who adopted Drake into the Young Money conglomerate of rappers, of which Nicki Minaj is also a member. Few US fans were aware that Drake was born Aubrey 'Drake' Graham (in 1986) and was raised in Toronto, Ontario, by a Jewish-Canadian mother and an African American father, who migrated to Canada. Toronto is often referred to as one of the world's most cosmopolitan cities because of its diverse racial and ethnic makeup, with a multivalent and polycultural composition among the most diverse in the world. Drake's biography maps multiple cultural and racial backgrounds that connect him to a wide range of Black and non-Black fans, around the world, that identify with the simultaneity of his identities. He is read as simultaneously African Canadian Jewish and African American, with both Canadian and American identities contributing to his international fan base. As a rapper and actor, fans around the world read his work as both local and global, and his body in simultaneous national, racial and ethnic contexts.

Drake's performing began as an actor, in the Canadian television series *Degrassi: The Next Generation* (2001–15), a teen television drama in which he portrayed the Black Canadian character Jimmy Brooks – a basketball athlete who becomes wheelchair-bound after being wounded in a school shooting. The show catapulted Drake from a teen in Canada (who went to a predominantly white high school, and lived with his Jewish mother after his parents divorced when he was five) to a Canadian superstar and heartthrob. But Drake eyed a bigger prize: becoming an internationally recognized rapper and film star.

Historically, the route to success for rappers in the hip-hop community is through the United States: the home of hip-hop music and culture. Saeed Saeed, a pop culture writer for the website *The National*, addresses Drake's cosmopolitan status and the ways he used his platform, as a Canadian actor in Canada, as a springboard to something bigger:

> He could have easily cashed in on his fame and landed a record deal. Instead, particularly in the later years, he kept it low-key and almost lived an artistic double life: during the day he would shoot episodes of the series, while at night

he would make unannounced visits to quiet Toronto music spots and perform spoken-word poetry over instrumentals. (2015)

Drake's dedication to the craft of rapping via spoken-word performance connects him to African American spoken-word traditions, which were in turn embedded into the art of rapping and hip-hop, particularly with respect to social commentary, from the early 1970s (most notably with Gil Scott-Heron and the Last Poets).

Three years before Drake left *Degrassi* in 2006, he released a mixtape entitled *Room for Improvement*, which launched him into the sonic landscape of US-based hip-hop. In 2007, his mixtape *Comeback Season*, also self-released, earned him a spot on the African American television show *106 & Park*. With 'Replacement Girl', he was the first Black Canadian rapper to have a video on the network, while an unsigned artist. This appearance situated Drake as a simultaneous citizen, as he was presented (and read) as both African American and African Canadian.

In 2008, Lil Wayne heard Drake's mixtape and invited Drake to tour with him: an internationally recognized rapper, then, introducing Drake as an unsigned member of the Young Money family. Young Money is owned by Lil Wayne and his partner Mike Maine and includes artists such as Drake, Nicki Minaj, Cory Gunz, Tyga and R&B singer Christina Milian as part of the team.[1] Drake, who had remained independent for several years, would eventually sign with Young Money in 2009. And Drake's endorsement from Lil Wayne helped to introduce him and his music to the US-based rap scene, as both an African American and an African Canadian artist.

At the same time that Drake began to infiltrate American hip-hop in 2007, his fan base of teens began to grow in the United States because American audiences, across racial lines, began to make connections between his work as an emerging rapper in the United States and his previous work as a Black Canadian actor, in Canada, on *Degrassi*. Transnational connections were made between US and Canadian fans when the television drama began to find a cult following in the United States once back episodes of *Degrassi* began to air on The N (formerly Noggin), a late-night Nickelodeon channel geared towards American teen audiences. Drake's critical work as a simultaneous Black subject is evident here: a capacity to play a complex Black Canadian character, Jimmy Brooks, who hailed from a suburban background and yet still faced racism and gun violence (something which unsettles tropes of the hood as an African

American-specific location). That is: he connects seemingly disparate class and location dynamics of Blackness (hood vs. suburbs, United States vs. Canada) to do cosmopolitan work. Through his identity as Drake (an African American rapper) and his identity as Aubrey Graham (an African Canadian actor), Drake connects experiences of Black life across national, class and ethnic lines.

Before Aubrey Graham became known uniquely as Drake, his performance work as a Black Canadian actor playing African American characters also did critical cosmopolitan work. Since 2001, Drake (as Aubrey Graham) had minor guest-starring roles in American television shows such as the acclaimed African American drama *Soul Food* (2002) and Canada-produced films about African American life, such as *Conviction* (Kevin Rodney Sullivan, 2002), a biopic about a convicted felon turned activist Carl Upchurch. And then Drake's shift to hip-hop stardom was facilitated by and through his openness to remixing Black identities in acts that make strategic connections between African Americans/African Canadians. His Billboard chart-topping debut album *Thank Me Later* (2010) marks Drake's status as the most successful African Canadian rapper yet and, simultaneously, as one of the most successful African American rap artists of the twenty-first century.

In an interview with *Paper* magazine in 2010, Drake commented that while he feels that he is a versatile performer, most of the roles he is offered perpetuate stereotypes of African American men, such as basketball players and rappers. He argues that his goal is to not occupy such limited stereotypes of Black men, as pushed by mainstream American and Canadian entertainment industries. Rather, an aspiration could be to play Obama – half Kenyan and European American of Irish descent, but read in a US context as African American, and not uniquely Kenyan or Irish American. US registers of Blackness default to African American specificity and incorporate all people of African descent, no matter what their known country of origin or ethnicity, to African American (i.e. Black). Drake, then, identifies both with Obama's 'mixedness' and his self-identification as a Black subject, despite or even because of the media's early construction of Obama as 'differently' Black than most African Americans, and tendencies to exoticize his Kenyan ethnicity as essentially different from African American Blacks, whose cultural history links them directly to slavery:

> I hope somebody makes a movie about Obama's life soon because I could play him. That's the goal. [Laughs] I watch all the addresses. Anytime I see him on TV, I don't change the channel – I definitely pay attention and listen to the inflections

of his voice. If you ask anyone who knows me, I'm pretty good at impressions. Nobody's called me about anything, but I just pay attention so when the day comes I'm not scrambling to learn how to speak like him. I want to be involved in great film projects. I don't want to do the basketball movie that everyone does. I don't want to do the typical Black film that everyone expects. I think that I have enough experience to actually be involved in a real meaty project full of substance.

(Cummings 2010)

Here, 'great film projects' are more than stereotypical representations of Black men in the hood, that remain so integral to Hollywood film formulas. Drake uses 'basketball movies' to stand in for formulaic rags-to-riches narratives of African American rappers and athletes, which are often devoid of depth and complexity. Using Obama's life story as a representative example of the types of cosmopolitan roles he would like to play, Drake's interview response critiques Hollywood assumptions about cosmopolitanism's opposition to the hood and posits seemingly more sophisticated world views. Drake positions himself among Black men, such as Obama, who are viewed by the mainstream media as global subjects and capable of anything.

Drake does not disavow his connection to stereotypical hood narratives. He is cognizant of the fact that rappers in the United States are almost always assumed to have some connection to these tired tropes. And yet he gestures here towards Obama as a complex Black citizen, and as connected to both hood and cosmopolite identities: African American and Black 'other', and one who lives in the space between both life trajectories. In an interview with *Rolling Stone*, Drake positions himself as a representative of his community – the Black community, utilizing the assumed power to 'speak for' African Americans: 'I've been reading scripts for a while . . . I want to do something great. I want to do something for my culture: the younger people who are still in tune with everything going on. I'm actually writing with my friends right now' (Rolling Stone 2012). In diva fashion, Drake's confidence in his skill sets and desire to be viewed as an iconic artist in his field was shared with *Rolling Stone*: information that he is writing stories that complicate notions of Black subjectivity, and that consider the complexity of class, ethnicity and nationality, is an important correction to the mass media. Drake's work and commentary are emblematic of a new wave of Black artists, boldly challenging simplistic and overtly negative associations of the hood, and connecting such experiences with the overlapping borders of Blackness that cross national and class lines that they witness and experience in everyday life.

In 2014, Drake, very comfortable in his capacity to cross borders of race, nation, class and ethnicity, played himself as the host of the long-running sketch and music programme *Saturday Night Live*. Drake asked the producers if he could write and perform a rap that played on his identity: a Black Bar Mitzvah. The lyrics, in part, ran: 'Please don't forget I'm Black, please don't forget I'm Jewish/I play ball like Lebron and I know what a W-2 is.' Singer Lenny Kravitz is then referred to as a 'mensch', there is a mention of Kosher food, and a promise that at his live shows, a recitation of a Jewish prayer could occur. Drake's performance, entitled 'Bar Mitzvah 1999' (the date of his symbolic passage to Jewish manhood), connects him to other Black Americans who share his Jewish heritage such as Kravitz, shows a fluency in Yiddish vernacular, and mentions a 'purple drink' – a reference both to Manischewitz Kosher wine and to an African American 'hood' trope of using American Robitussin cough syrup as a stimulant. This then is the theorization of Black cosmopolitan identity across racial, class, ethnic and nation divides.

Another artist who builds connections between her cultural biography and her performances of Blackness is Nicki Minaj. Minaj, as Onika Tanya Maraj, was born in 1982, in Saint James, Port of Spain, in Trinidad and Tobago. She moved with her family to Queens, New York (one of the original birthplaces of hip-hop) when she was five years old. Minaj's father is Afro-Trinidadian and South Asian and her mother is Afro-Trinidadian. Minaj claims both Trinidadian and South Asian heritage, and also identifies as African American, as per Drake and Obama's simultaneous Black identifications.

Minaj's career as a performer began with her acceptance at the renowned Laguardia School of Music and Art in New York City, where she studied acting. Her capacity to channel alter-ego characters into her rap narratives, ranging from a blonde, presumably white British male sociopath named Roman Zolanski, to a pop fantasy doll named Harajuku Barbie, marked Minaj as a shapeshifter; the *New York Times*, identifying straightaway work in a tradition of critical self-transformation, dubbed her 'the Cindy Sherman of rap' (McGarry 2009). Minaj was discovered via the MySpace website by Dirty Money CEO Big Fendi, bringing her to Lil Wayne's attention, who signed her to his Young Money label in 2009, launching her career and global brand.

Minaj's family origins are important because of the multiple cultural and ethnic border crossings that they map, and that signal the exchanges of openness identified by Delanty and Nwonko in terms of reimagining new constructions of critical cosmopolitanisms, around the complex experiences of minoritized people negotiating national identity. Minaj is a person who symbolizes the work of Trinidadian Americans, other African immigrants to the United States, and African Americans that negotiate the multiple facets of their Blackness daily. Minaj, a savvy businesswoman, plays characters in almost every aspect of her hip-hop career and does not shy away from using costumes, accents and dialects to perform her constructions of an intersectional Black identity, challenging Black racial and gender stereotypes. Like Drake, Minaj positions her body and voice to transcend the paradigms of imposed boundaries of national identity – laying claims to an American-ness as much as she does to other national identities in true diva fashion.

All this is apparent in Minaj's albums: her 2010 debut, *Pink Friday*, the 2012 *Pink Friday: Roman Reloaded* and 2014 *The Pink Print*. The latter two album titles riff on the name of controversial film-maker Roman Polanski (a Pole who worked in the United Kingdom and United States, before being exiled to Europe, where he sometimes shoots films set in United States), and rapper Jay-Z's acclaimed hip-hop album *The Blueprint* (1999). This riffing points to the progeny of her work as a female artist, preempting the ways in which her work will be invariably compared to male artists. The use of theatrical performance on each album creates a hybrid between theatre, rap, television and film; Minaj not only creates characters that recur from album to album but also performs using different alter egos, a variety of accents and evolves episodic content, coalescing her work into one master narrative. (Her acting roles, on the other hand, have held less consistency.)

Minaj deftly negotiates, and profits, from the simultaneous identities she occupies as a Black woman. She is unafraid to forge connections between the stories of everyday Black women from low-to-moderate income communities (i.e. the hood) with those who live lavish, upper-middle-class lifestyles, aka divas. The narratives in her songs, such as 'Hood Story' (2007), reflect on the value she places on street credibility, while songs such as 'Fuck Da Bullshit' (2009, with Drake, Lil Wayne and Gudda Gudda) are vehicles for her to brag about her extreme wealth and high-end fashion addiction. Minaj plays at the intersectional space between hood and cosmopolitan positions, refusing to value Eurocentric ideals of cosmopolitan lifestyles rooted in ethical dictates and high intellectualism in favour of questioning urban depictions of Black subjectivity that challenge the fallacy of the racial binary. Minaj complicates notions of African American identity by drawing attention to the complexity of transnational African migration stories that are often lost within generic construction of Blackness, as projected on to all-Black artists (both in the United

States and abroad) which neglect to consider the unique cultural experiences that exist simultaneously within expressions of Black identity.

Minaj's subject position as a Black woman who is read as both African American and Trinidadian American in the United States and other national contexts is flexible. And yet, like Drake, this subject position places her within geopolitical spheres of cultural imperialism with which many African American artists have engaged, via hip-hop. In exploring US-based hood narratives that establish her street credibility through notions of 'rachetness' (or seemingly overtly sexual displays of sexuality), Minaj works to counter mainstream media narratives of Black female hypersexuality, objectification and criminalization by drawing attention to (and also critiquing) commodified stereotypes of Blackness in hip-hop culture. For example, through her platinum hit 'Anaconda' (2014) Minaj effectively critiques what Nicole Fleetwood calls the 'excess flesh' (2010) of Black women's bodies in hip-hop videos, in the way in which Minaj's feminist practices are fluid. That is: racial and gendered expectations, on the part of the assumed viewers, are very much forefronted in the video; in these senses, the video could be read as 'just another' such video. But, simultaneously, the presence of Minaj, performing both to expectations and yet performing as a Trinidadian American and African American, globally expands a sense of Black female solidarity. This then is not just a 'generic' US Black performer, working in the context of a white ruling class industry that still conflates Black behaviour, culture, ideologies and experiences into one sole set of assumptions, and with little exploration or consideration for the complex social and diverse cultural histories that connect Black that live in the United States. Thus Minaj embraces, and even performs, the contradictions of divadom that Black women entertainers must face, working to redefine themselves against a white male patriarchy that is invested in exploiting Black female labour, imagery and sexuality for cultural capital. The 'surplus' of Black women with bodies that do not fit Eurocentric beauty standards, and performing overtly sexual dance moves in 'Anaconda' begins to overwhelm expectations on the part of the assumed viewers. Minaj problematizes the hypervisibility of Black women, presented as objects of fetish in American visual culture, by both maximally delivering this hypervisibility and thereby reclaiming the sexual power of Black women to have agency over how and when their bodies will be used to fuel the American pop culture machine.

Minaj's biography is a hybrid of the African immigrant and American Dream narratives, and the poverty narratives of African Americans who grew up in the so-called hood. In an interview describing her upbringing, Minaj relays the fantastical images of the United States she encountered when living in Trinidad and Tobago:

> A lot of times when you're from the Islands, your parents leave and then send for you because it's easier when they have established themselves; when they have a place to stay; when they have a job. I thought it was going to be for a few days, [but] it turned into two years without my mother . . . [When I went to New York] I thought it was gonna be like a castle. Like the white picket fence, like a fairytale. I got off the plane and it was cold. I remember the smell. I could always remember the smell when I got out of the airport of the snow, and I had never seen snow. I remember the house. I remember that the furniture wasn't put down. It was, like, piled up on each other, and I didn't understand why, 'cause I thought it was gonna look like a big castle.
>
> (Welteroth 2010: 96)

Minaj understands the power in the overlapping spaces that occur between African American hood tropes and the stories of Trinidadian immigrants and positions her biography there. She creates cosmopolitan kinships between Black 'have-nots' who share racial positions as African diasporic subjects (here African American US-born Blacks, and Trinidadian American immigrants). And this sensibility functions with little regard for the details of the cultural and/or ethnic differences that shape the specificities of Black cultural practices within and outside the United States. Minaj remixes the visual and sonic vernaculars of African American and Trinidadian beauty and cultural practices in order to highlight the commodification of racial, gender and sexual 'norms' in American popular culture, reflecting them back into the mainstream media in a Technicolour excess, as overblown indicators of Black female subjectivity. In just this way, Janell Hobson addresses the vexed position of Black female artists in hip-hop whose works circulate both liberating and oppressive imagery of Black female subjectivity in transnational contexts: 'within these geopolitical spheres of cultural imperialism and cultural exchange, the African American artist is precariously positioned in ways that perpetuate racial essentialism while simultaneously suggesting transnational solidarity' (Hobson 2014).

4. Black like me: Conclusion

We must recognize how Black cultural production around the world circulates in spaces of vulnerability and simultaneity. No matter how abstract, seemingly original or unoriginal, not Black enough or too Black, the cultural products and the people that create them are always read against a shared global archive of Black stereotypes created by and through acts of racism that attempt to relegate all-Black subjects to ghettoized notions of a mythical Black hood. The 'hood', as described by the white mainstream media, continues to perpetuate (and profit from) stereotypes of poor, hopeless Black men, women and children, as 'inferior' people without education, access to capital and who have limited life aspirations. When these tropes are subverted, they are often depicted as 'revelatory' anomalies that seemingly have to be compared to European texts, past or present.

For Black audiences of Canada, Trinidad and England that enjoy the work of Drake and Minaj, the performers are Black like them. And, as seen in their national and ethnic contexts, they are made comprehensible to other audiences through their successful performances of Blackness in other cultural contexts. To Black audiences in the United States, they are subsumed under the rubric of 'African American', accepted as fluent in the cultural codes of African American life, and read as members of the African American community. However, the US mainstream white media's description of these artists often works to manipulate their simultaneous national contexts in order to use their nationality and ethnicity to reframe them as 'exotic' and 'differently' Black from other African American performers. Such cosmopolitan worldviews that do not theorize the vulnerability of Black subjects to violence and oppression, no matter what class, ethnicity or location, seem inadequate. A critical cosmopolitanism, on the other hand, identifies sites of Black cultural production, specifically Black music, and performance, which encapsulate the struggles for freedom for Black people around the world. Drake and Minaj remind us that being cosmopolitan is not escaping the hood, but squarely identifying with it as a site through which collective freedom is won. To be a diva for Drake and Nicki Minaj is more about demanding cultural competency and legibility for the simultaneity of the Blackness they live in hip-hop, asking us to resist essentialisms and to remake the world as a space where Blackness and hip-hop are integral to reimagining the world as we know it.

Note

1 As of 2020, Lil Wayne sold his catalogue to the Universal Music Group for a reported $100 million. This sale is presumed to include parts of catalogues of others on the Young Money label, including Drake and Minaj; see Vaynshteyn (2020).

Reference

Benhabib, S. (2002), *The Claims of Culture: Equality and Diversity in the Global Era*, Princeton: Princeton University Press.

Benhabib, S. (2004), *The Rights of Cultures: Aliens, Residents, and Citizens*, Cambridge: Cambridge University Press.

Benhabib, S. (2008), *Another Cosmopolitanism (The Berkeley Tanner Lectures)*, Oxford: Oxford University Press.

Cummings, J. (2010), 'Drake on Overexposure, Staying Off The Internet and Playing Obama', *PaperMag* 2010, 19 July. Available online: https://web.archive.org/web/20170316052521/http://www.papermag.com/drake-on-overexposure-staying-off-the-internet-and-playing-obama-1425697894.html (accessed 5 November 2022).

DeFrantz, T. F. and A. Gonzalez (2014), *Black Performance Theory*, Durham: Duke University Press.

Delanty, G. (2006), 'The Cosmopolitan Imagination: Critical Cosmopolitanism and Social Theory', *British Journal of Sociology*, 57 (1): 25–47.

Elam, H. J. and K. A. Jackson (2005), *Black Cultural Traffic: Crossroads in Global Performance and Popular Culture*, Ann Arbor: University of Michigan Press.

Featherstone, D. (2008), *Resistance, Space, and Political Identities: The Making of Counter Public Global Networks*, Hoboken: Wiley.

Fishkin, S. F. (2005), 'Crossroads of Cultures: The Transnational Turn in American Studies: Presidential Address to the American Studies Association, 12 November 12, 2004', *American Quarterly*, 57 (1): 17–57.

Fleetwood, N. (2010), *Troubling Vision: Performance, Visuality and Blackness*, Chicago: University of Chicago Press.

Gilroy, P. (2004), 'It's a Family Affair', in M. Forman and M. A. Neal (eds), *That's the Joint: The Hip-Hop Studies Reader*, 87–94, New York and London: Routledge.

Hall, S. (1980), 'Race, Articulation, and Societies Structured in Dominance', in *Sociological Theories: Race and Colonialism*, 305–45, Paris: UNESCO.

Hobson, J. (2014), 'The Sexual Geopolitics of Popular Culture and Transnational Black Feminism', *The Feminist Wire*, 13 January. Available online: https://thefeministwire.com/2014/01/popular-culture-and-transnational-black-feminism/ (accessed 5 November 2022).

Kondo, D. (2021), *Worldmaking: Race, Performance, and the Work of Creativity*, Durham: Duke University Press.

McGarry, K. (2009), 'The New Queen Bee: Meet Nicki Minaj', *New York Times Style Magazine*, 4 June. Available online: https://archive.nytimes.com/tmagazine.blogs.nytimes.com/2009/06/04/the-new-queen-bee-meet-nicki-minaj/ (accessed 5 November 2022).

Neal, M. A. (2010), '"A Man Without a Country": The Boundaries of Legibility, Social Capital, and Cosmopolitan Masculinity', *Criticism*, 52 (3): 399–411.

Nwankwo, I. K. (2014), *Black Cosmopolitanism: Racial Consciousness and Transnational Identity in the Nineteenth Century Americas*, Philadelphia: University of Pennsylvania Press.

Raphael-Hernandez, H. (2003), *Blackening Europe: The African American Presence*, New York: Routledge.

Rolling Stone (2012), 'Drake: I Want to Play President Obama', *Rolling Stone*, 26 January. Available online: https://www.rollingstone.com/politics/politics-news/drake-i-want-to-play-president-obama-242661/ (accessed 5 November 2022).

Saeed, S. (2015), 'A Look at Drake's Rise to Fame Ahead of His Dubai Concert', *The National*, 7 March. Available online: https://www.thenationalnews.com/arts/a-look-at-drakes-rise-to-fame-ahead-of-his-dubai-concert-1.35863 (accessed 5 November 2022).

Vaynshteyn, G. (2020), 'Since Lil Wayne Sold Young Money to Universal Music Group, Does Nicki Minaj Own Her Own Masters?', *Distractify*, 17 December. Available online: https://www.distractify.com/p/does-nicki-minaj-own-her-masters#:~:text=So%2C%20does%20Nicki%20Minaj%20own,masters%20%E2%80%94%20Universal%20Music%20Group%20does. (accessed 5 November 2022).

Welteroth, E. (2010), 'Nicki Minaj: Crushes the Competition', *Ebony*, 66, no. 2/3 (December): 96.

Section three

Diva cultures

12

Curating the diva

Harriet Reed

Introduction

What happens to a diva when he, she or they enter a museum? This chapter explores how museum exhibitions have transformed our concept of the diva, using three examples from the Victoria & Albert Museum, London: *Kylie – The Exhibition* (2007); *The Supremes – From the Mary Wilson Collection* (2008); and *The House of Annie Lennox* (2011–12). While these exhibitions did not intend to present the artists as 'divas', nevertheless they provide a compelling framework for an examination of the female performer within a museum context. Exhibitions at their core communicate and define the legacy of a performer, explain an artistic vision, prompt enjoyment and nostalgia and reveal crucial truths about our society in the process. *Kylie* could be said to be a somewhat superficial exhibition that revealed the hard work behind the image. *The Supremes* began to appraise the female performers within their social and political context. And *Annie Lennox* was an experimental and process-driven installation which combined objects with performance art. The three are vastly different in their concepts. And through these varied exhibitions, and the wider field of cultural heritage, this chapter will reveal diverse layers of divahood in museum spaces.

The V&A museum's collections span from ancient history to the present day, across paintings, sculpture, decorative arts, textiles, furniture, costume and digital material. Across collecting departments, it is possible to trace the history of the diva from its etymological origins in deity figures, via classical sculptures of goddesses, to a costume worn by drag performer Danny La Rue. These objects in the V&A collection are the material culture of a diva's career – placing her or him in context, revealing notions of power, image, sexuality and fame.

Often considered a quasi-religious site, the museum is by extension complicit in the worship of the diva by both displaying and elevating their celebrity and becoming a site of pilgrimage for fans. Gilbert B. Rodman, in his study of the Elvis phenomenon, reasons:

> There are, after all, just enough plausible parallels between the two to suggest that stars are the closest thing that contemporary US culture has to living gods and goddesses: they're highly charismatic, larger than life figures; they're deeply embedded in cultural myths and legends (one could in fact argue that a crucial part of what transforms an 'ordinary' celebrity into a star is the articulation of his or her public image to one or more major strand of cultural mythology); and the behaviour that fans exhibit towards them is often nothing less than worshipful in its adulatory and awestruck quality.
>
> (1996: 111)

This in turn has led to associated objects and places being imbued with the same sacred-like quality. The 'music exhibition', now accepted as an integral part of the V&A museum exhibition portfolio, not only educates and entertains, but holds a deep emotional and often spiritual meaning for visitors – arguably more so than any other subject genre. Music uniquely creates a sense of memory, identity and place, and within the nuanced contextual display of 'celebrity' artefacts, assumes a powerful aura through the lens of the visitor.

Institutional worship

From the nineteenth-century prima donna to the twenty-first-century r'n'b superstar, the diva is defined by the adoration and worship of live audiences. But how does this worship translate to an institutional context? Their representation, through objects such as costume, has traditionally been staged in industry-motivated sites such as Halls of Fame (e.g. the Country Music Hall of Fame in Nashville) or small historic house museums (such as the Tina Turner Museum, or the permanent Dolly Parton exhibition at the Chasing Rainbows Museum, both in Tennessee). However, there has been growing attention to the subject within broader cultural institutions, in parallel with scholarly recognition of the historical significance of popular music, as Istvandity and Cantillon note:

> Although often undervalued in comparison to traditional, older forms of heritage, popular music is historically significant in that it constitutes a core

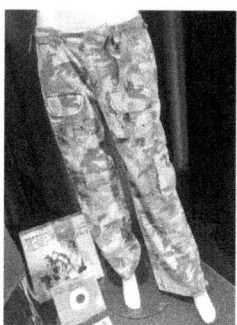

Figure 12.1 Spice Girls items from the *Spice Up Manchester* exhibition. (Photo by Benjamin Halligan).

element of everyday life and cultural expression across the globe in the twentieth and twenty-first centuries. These histories are in a precarious position, at risk of being lost if not recognized as significant and adequately protected.

(2019: 4)

While museums are slowly embracing this philosophy, the Hall of Fame model has been dedicated to this mission for decades and has been mimicked by the commercial sector (with difficult results) in respect of the Spice Girls; see Jackson (2018) and Small (2019) (Figure 12.1).

The American phenomenon of the 'Hall of Fame' can be viewed as the purest form of quasi-religious worship of the diva. While it could be argued that the concept itself is European (as with Westminster Abbey in London, the Panthéon in Paris, and the Walhalla in Germany), it has been an American preoccupation to adopt this moniker to celebrate the achievements of two entertainments: music and sports. It is now estimated that 90 per cent of 'Halls of Fame' in the world are in the United States, including those that exist intangibly and those that have dedicated museums (Danilov 1997: xi). Jan Armstrong, former director of the International Tennis Hall of Fame, Rhode Island, wrote in 1992:

> While not generally religious institutions, halls of fame and museums partake in the sacred character of holier shrines. Although not blessed with the legitimizing power of religion, both types of institutions derive a similar power from their contents. And interestingly enough, while each is intended to guard its contents from the corruptibility of time, neither halls of fame nor museums seem to consider the other worthy of the responsibility.

(1992: 14)

Armstrong makes an arresting point in legitimizing both types of institutions as sites for celebrity worship and the canonization of individuals. However, while the museum model contextualizes and largely remains curatorially independent, Halls of Fame often have vested interests.

At the Rock and Roll Hall of Fame in Cleveland, Ohio, and the Country Music Hall of Fame in Nashville, costumes and artefacts are displayed with very little contextual information. There is a lack of interpretation of how and why performers have reached such a level of success, but a singular focus on chart success. While Halls of Fame are becoming increasingly engaged with the wider museum world, their myth-making and almost religious curation of their subjects clearly prioritize commercialism. This is due to their institutional existence depending on the success of their respective music industry, such as the Country Music Hall of Fame. This tourist landmark in Nashville was founded, managed and supported by the Country Music Association (an organization founded to 'heighten the awareness of country music and support its ongoing growth').[1] It is not in their interest to explore the perhaps controversial aspects of their artists that may jeopardize the operation both critically and financially. No mention, for example, is made of the blacklisting of female artists on country music radio (Willman 2005: 36), nor of the troubling and complicated sexism in country music lyrics (Rasmussen and Densley 2017: 188–201). However, this does not undermine the purpose of such attractions as a celebration of performance heritage, and the preservation of musical material culture.

Conversely, named museums often prioritize a simpler interpretation situated within a local history. In Charles Fairchild's (2019) study of the Tina Turner Museum in Tennessee, he classes objects such as her personal letters as primarily 'mundane' or 'generic'. He argues that

> the objects in this museum are possessed only with precarious meanings and must have what we might call 'expressive' qualities inscribed on them by their settings and circumstances to maintain their aura as objects of interest, if not fascination.
>
> (2019: 102)

Fairchild disputes the idea that Turner's costumes, records and ephemera are not 'art objects' but indirect references to her work as a singer. He classes the 'mundane' as personal items such as her yearbook, personal correspondence and tour itinerary, and the 'generic' as the contextual objects: the desk, school books and wall map arranged in her former schoolroom. Fairchild asserts that these only gain significance to the visitor by their physical nearness to the 'star objects':

> The charge of meaning invested in the mundane objects is only produced by their proximity to the famous ones ... We are asked and expected to link the known and the unknown and test the limits of what we can know about the person whose life we are there to revisit. Finally, we are constituted as believers. We are there to accept an ideal so thoroughly acceptable that its repeated expression is made entirely without any form of apparent self-awareness: The American Dream.
>
> (2019:112)

This assessment underlines the importance of sound interpretation and curation in dismantling hierarchal structures of objects and imbuing them with insightful meaning.

Broader social, art and design museums, however, have taken an increasingly multidisciplinary and interrogative approach to the curation and display of music. As well as working in collaboration with ongoing scholarship of the subject, music displays and exhibitions have played important roles in recalibrating museums for the twenty-first century. The co-editors of *Sites of Popular Music Heritage: Memories, Histories, Places* assessed recent V&A music exhibitions such as *Kylie* and (eventually touring) *David Bowie Is* (2013–18) as initiatives that have provided

> sites of spaces of representation inviting critical reflection on the multidimensionality of popular music heritage as an affective, material, symbolic, or performative site of memory ... each revealing key issues relating to the way in which popular music heritage is constructed and mediated.
>
> (Cohen et al. 2014: 2–3)

In recent years, the music diva has also, and quite specifically, been a subject of focus. From the famous (*Vestiaire de Divas, de Maria Callas à Dalida*, 5 June to 31 December 2010 at the Centre National du Costume de Scène, in Moulins, France) to the less well-known (*Asian Diva: The Muse and the Monster*, 14 July to 19 October 2017 at the Seoul Museum of Art; *The First Indian Diva – The Courtesan and the Recording Industry*, 10 to 29 April 2018 at the Omnibus Theatre, London; *Divas from Oum Kalthoum to Dalida*, 19 May to 25 July 2021 at the Institut du Monde Arabe, Paris). *Asian Diva* blended contemporary art with 1960s and 1970s Korean pop music, focusing on Kim Chooja, the well-known 1970s singer. The exhibition examined the postcolonial era of Asia through the lives of women, celebrating the liberated sexuality of Chooja's music. *The First Indian Diva* examined the career of India's first recording artist, Gauhar Jaan, who contributed powerfully to world music and the Indian music industry in the twentieth century. Jaan, who recorded hundreds of songs in more than ten languages between 1902 and 1920, popularized Hindustani classical music through her commercial recordings. *Divas from Oum Kalthoum to Dalida* celebrate Arab actresses and artists from the 1920s to the present who have not only pioneered their own art forms but have also contributed to social, political and cultural movements. In this context, the historic diva takes on a positive and empowering public meaning.

Peter Doyle, reflecting on a raft of new music exhibitions and museums in the past decade, cited biographical shows as being of particular importance: '[b]iography can be judiciously used to shine light on *habitus*, on class and gender relations, on sexuality and cultural geography. Provided the storytelling is of sufficient finesse . . . biography can be both compelling and intellectually innovative' (2019: 126, his italics). The success of this model has led music exhibitions to now compete with post-Impressionism, couture fashion and contemporary art, for the highest audience figures. In *The Art Newspaper*'s audience figure survey for 2017, the V&A exhibition *Pink Floyd: Their Mortal Remains* (2017–present) was ranked in the top ten for ticketed shows in London that year, alongside *David Hockney* at Tate Britain, *Abstract Expressionism* and the annual *Summer Exhibition*, both the Royal Academy of Arts, (Art Newspaper 2018). Rightly elevated to the celebrated status of artists, designers and makers, performers in popular music are now the subject of canonic retrospectives, incorporated into local or social histories, and their artefacts re-interpreted as art objects. Their stories are now seen as vital narratives in our collective historical memory.

Contextualizing the diva

These curatorial narratives, uniting the personal, collective and local social histories of a performer, reveal private networks, personal interests and motivations. They promote the historic legacy and preservation of divas' careers, inspiring future performers and legitimizing their success and impact. From archival letters, account books and photographs, to costumes, music sheets and stage designs, objects can powerfully communicate the complex work of a

Figure 12.2 Catwalk costume display, from *Kylie – The Exhibition*. Photo copyright Victoria and Albert Museum, London.

performer and draw new parallels across centuries and musical disciplines. Over the past fifteen years, the V&A has worked in collaboration with artists to stage the exhibitions *Kylie – The Exhibition, The Supremes – From the Mary Wilson Collection* and *The House of Annie Lennox* (Figure 12.2).

Kylie – The Exhibition was promoted as the first exhibition about a performer at the V&A, transferring from its original venue, the Arts Centre in Melbourne (Fox 2007). Its retrospective approach celebrated the enduring popular image of Kylie Minogue, the highly successful Australian pop singer, and her widespread popularity with fashion designers and photographers. In the Preface to a 2002 photobiography, *Kylie: La La La*, her then-stylist William Baker wrote: '[e]verything is fleeting: maximum impact, maximum exposure, the ultimate triumph of style over substance' (2002: 3). In this manner the exhibition prioritized the display of costumes and photographs as a testimony of Kylie's role as muse and 'pop princess'. While her natural singing voice, arguably, does not qualify her as a true diva (in the sense of uniquely musically gifted), her seemingly supernatural likeability and commercial appeal has won her a diva-like global success. In collaboration with the Arts Centre Melbourne, and Minogue herself, the show was a significant first for the V&A. Reporting on the preview event, *The Guardian* wrote

> the [V&A] museum has been criticized for dumbing down with this exhibition, but Vicky Broackes, head of the theatre collection at the V&A, insisted

yesterday that it had cultural relevance[:] 'If it were just about fashion it might be questionable, but the exhibition is about collective collaboration, the work that goes into creating a performer's image, and how this comes together with contemporary culture.'

(Fox 2007)

The beauty and ostentation of Minogue chimes with the earliest conceptions of the diva, as crafted by male poets and writers. As derived from the feminine form of the Latin 'divus' (god), the term 'diva' became a term of homage, in Italian literature, to a beautiful woman within mythological imagery (Rutherford 2016: 40–1). However, this beauty has also drawn criticism, and further objectification, from the media due to the sexualized imagery. Baker reflects too on this paradox:

> For Kylie, the status of sex symbol is clearly a double-edged sword. We owe so much to an eroticized image of her. The hot pants, for example, were unveiled at a crucial point in Kylie's musical career as an attempt to emphasize what by her own admission is her most popular asset and to create the most desirable package possible – we always attempted to use her sex appeal as an enhancement of her music and to sell a record. But now it has become in danger of eclipsing what she actually is: a pop singer.
>
> (2002: 211)

The Minogue exhibition therefore served as another crucial point in her career: crystallizing a credibility and cultural impact on the world of fashion, design and performance that transcended her stereotypical media image. Objects on display included costumes designed by John Galliano, corsetier Mr Pearl, and milliner Stephen Jones for her *Showgirl* tour (displaying her high fashion influence), and an installation of her dressing room, which showed her hairpieces, make-up, 'good luck' tokens, travel cases, and performance schedule (revealing her hard work, sacrifice and spectacular ambition). And those notorious gold lamé hot pants were displayed in a bespoke case, in contrast to the majority of the fashion shown on open display. This simultaneously paid tribute to their iconic status and memorialized them, placing them behind museum glass as a historic piece: a full stop separating them from Kylie's current identity. The exhibition was, unsurprisingly, an immense success, attracting around 270,000 visitors across its four-month run.[2]

Just two months after the closing of *Kylie*, the V&A museum announced the upcoming exhibition *The Supremes – From the Mary Wilson Collection –*

a decision that once again sparked controversy for bowing to 'populism'. The *Evening Standard* reported:

> The director [Mark Jones], who will mark the V&A's 150th anniversary this year, said the institution had to attract a broader range of visitors and that the Kylie exhibition adhered to founder Henry Cole's mission to bolster the best of British design . . . Mr Jones revealed next summer will see a similarly glitzy and costume-led exhibition focusing on The Supremes (the celebrated Motown girl group), fronted by Diana Ross, who recorded number ones such as 'Where Did Our Love Go?' [1964] and 'Baby Love' [1964].
>
> (Razaq 2007)

In an interview with *The Times*, Jones defended the Kylie show against its critics, arguing that the show did not focus on the Australian singer herself but on the brands, design and street style that were spawned around her. He also likened her phenomenon to the creation of an artificial persona around Louis XIV at Versailles: 'I want to show beautiful things beautifully so that people can enjoy them. I'm bored with the idea that people should only go to a museum to be better educated. Why shouldn't they go for pure pleasure?' (cited in Binyon 2007) This was a rebuke to articles such as 'What is Kylie Minogue doing at the V&A?', which posited the idea that 'the V&A's remit is to celebrate the finest of arts and crafts, and on that criteria these flimsy and outrageous costumes just about make it.' (Bakewell 2007). This spat proved that in terms of the exhibition research and interpretation of performers, museums had yet to convince all critics.

The Supremes – From the Mary Wilson Collection curated by Geoffrey Marsh and Victoria Broackes was marketed as a cornucopia of glorious costumes but also served a nuanced social history narrative. The interpretation touched on identity, politics and race, including sections on 'Urban Protest', 'Racial Segregation', and 'The End of a Dream' (on the assassination of Martin Luther King Jr). Sections explored music production, the history of Motown and the impact of new media and technology. It also made an explicit link between the Supremes as pioneers of Black girl groups in American popular culture and the later success of Destiny's Child. A set of costumes, photographs and a poster for the film *Dreamgirls* (Bill Condon, 2006) were displayed with a label describing the costumes (designed by Beyoncé's mother, Tina Knowles-Lawson) as conveying the 'originality, image and polished elegance' that defined pop divas.[3] Destiny's Child, who disbanded in 2006, had modelled not only their close harmonies on the Supremes but also their uniform approach to movement and style. Knowles-Lawson, who took on the role of stylist, looked to the bold, dazzling and coordinated looks of Motown girl bands that would garner attention. However, as with the Supremes, these costumes would also be battlegrounds for mainstream success and acceptance by white audiences. Knowles-Lawson stated in a 2020 interview that their record label expressed concern that she herself would limit their crossover appeal:

> Because they were just a little too flashy, a little too Motown, but what they really meant was that they were a little too Black . . . I was told that they should look like Britney Spears and Christina Aguilera . . . At the time they were big pop stars, and in order for the girls to cross over, they said they needed to wear jeans and t-shirts. I took offense to it because I felt like the girls, in their splendor, were different, they were unique, they were unapologetically Black.
>
> (Cited in Johnston 2020)

Knowles-Lawson stood by her vision for the group, and they became a global success in due course. By contrast, the Supremes, clothed in the uniformity of the Motown brand, had been styled expressly for this purpose and were subsequently criticized by some members of the Black community for this reason (Figure 12.3).

The accompanying exhibition catalogue, *The Story of The Supremes*, written by Daryl Easlea, acknowledged the grit, talent and PR management of this 'socially subversive' group. They are described as bridging 'white conservatism

Figure 12.3 Destiny's Child costumes on display, for *The Supremes – From the Mary Wilson Collection*. Photo copyright the Victoria and Albert Museum, London.

and black radicalism', and Easlea positions the 'uniform' of the Supremes as work clothes: 'the dresses that helped make history' (2008: 26). The dresses themselves (around fifty were on display) clearly demonstrated the Supremes' style – refined, glamorous and conservative – but, placed within their social and political contexts, these objects also articulated the remarkable achievement of three Black women operating across tense racial barriers.

In her autobiography, Mary Wilson talks of the changing perception of musicians and their treatment by the press:

> Though we'd never shunned political or social issues, we were starting to take a beating for being glamour girls in a 'relevant' age. The press would accept some other pop stars' cries for revolution at face value, never bothering to note that these stars lived as lavishly as we did. But the Supremes were right out there and before long we'd be attacked in the press for not being black enough.
>
> (Wilson 2000: 211)

As women, and as members of the Black community, the Supremes were underestimated. Their image alone broke barriers, appearing on television screens across the United States as three dazzling and talented Black women, defying prejudice and discrimination. During their appearance on *The Tonight Show with Johnny Carson*, on the night that Martin Luther King Jr was assassinated, Diana Ross pleaded for peace and understanding despite her own anger: 'I'm Negro, and I respected and loved Dr Martin Luther King very much. And I know he lived and died for one reason, and I want all of us to be together. Not just the Black man but the white man and everybody. I think we should walk together.' (Cited in Adrahtas 2006: 81). Ross in effect acted as one spokesperson for the Black community before an audience of millions (and James Brown acted as another see McArdle 2018). This exhibition looked past the surface glamour of the group and the solo success of Diana Ross to their challenging and inspiring truth: as pioneering political artists, during times of profound social upheaval.

The House of Annie Lennox was staged in a smaller exhibition space: the V&A Theatre and Performance Galleries. With curators Victoria Broackes and Anna Landreth Strong working closely with Lennox (the Scottish singer-songwriter and activist, who had previously performed in the band Eurythmics before a successful solo career), it was entirely conceptual, centring on a large model house built in the middle of the gallery. The house, both replicating and symbolizing Lennox's creative process, comprised one room large enough for visitors to enter and sit. Visitors could interact in the space, opening drawers to reveal manuscript material. Surrounding the house were more traditional displays of costumes, photographs, awards and handwritten lyrics in cases and on mannequins. In a ground-breaking move for the museum, Lennox would occasionally visit the house during opening hours and interact with visitors. It traversed the existing lines of museum curation: to situate the living artist in the space itself, eliminating any final barrier to their private process. Similar to the performance art of Marina Abramovich, Lennox's presence allowed her to communicate her self-expression and creativity as artist and writer (instead of singer) through interactive live performances. Fascinating and truly 'immersive' for the visitor, the exhibition celebrated the creative autonomy of Lennox, placing her physically in the centre of her achievements (Figure 12.4).

While contextualizing each specific artist within a contemporary sphere, these exhibitions also amplify existing notions of the diva (e.g. vocal dexterity, transgressive behaviour and ostentatious dress) from earlier centuries. Lennox, who has experimented with different genders and identities throughout her career, echoes the 'genderless' concept of the diva, explored by Wayne Koestenbaum (1993) and Kimberly Nichele Brown (2010). Koestenbaum credits the origin of the diva in the sixteenth-century castrato, biological men who were castrated in order to retain their high voice. Heather Hadlock, in a review of Koestenbaum's work, encapsulates his position: 'The biologically male body of the castrato, a

Figure 12.4 Installation image of *The House of Annie Lennox* (house model interior). Photo copyright the Victoria and Albert Museum, London.

deviant, stigmatized body producing a soprano voice of magical potency, has become the body of the diva, now biologically female but still singing deviance and stigma.' (1993: 267) Brown interprets the diva in Black revolutionary terms: the diva 'serves as the ultimate archetype of the assertion of the female voice in the public sphere. Her staged androgyny partially derives from her position on the stage – the diva occupies the public domain usually reserved for men' (2010: 17). In contrast, Vanessa Knights asserts that the distinction of the diva (in this context, the Cuban singer La Lupe) lies not with gender or sexuality but with their power of 'rumour, innuendo and myth' and 'identification with the marginal and vulnerable combined with survivalist aesthetics of strength . . . with resilience in the face of emotional suffering and intense pain, with risque eroticism and excess, with the semiotics of glamour' (2013: 98). Lennox, who has used the term 'diva' in a tongue-in-cheek manner as the title of her first solo album, revels in the interchangeable nature of gender in print and on stage, as an artistic or deliberately transgressive act.

Piya Pal-Lapinski's work (2005), exploring the exotic and ostentation in the nineteenth-century opera singer, makes links with the solo career of Diana Ross. Pal-Lapinski argues that the excesses of opera (from jewellery to dress) foreground the 'vocal fireworks' of the singer, tying ornamentation with stage exoticism. The negative treatment of such ostentation is underlined by Susan Rutherford's (2016) assessment of nineteenth-century prima donnas Giulia Grisi and Adelina Patti:

> Grisi, 'La Diva', brought a more human passion, the suspicion of temperament, and the element of sexual transgression; Patti, simply the *diva*, contributed aspects of social brilliance, conspicuous display, eccentricity and excess. Such attributes combined with the loaded (and often hostile) meanings already prevalent in the broader image of the prima donna.
>
> (2016: 52; author's italics)

After years of similar chastisement of her behaviour, Ross was forced to address the divisive mantle in a television interview. Answering journalist Barbara Walters if she liked being a diva, Ross replied:

> Yes. I do actually, right now. I like the idea that women are able to take responsibility for their lives . . . and have the strength of character to say . . . I did this, I want credit for it . . . It takes a long time to get to be a diva. I mean, you got to work it.
>
> (ABC 2000)

Eccentricity and excess are not symptomatic of vocal dexterity but are now seen as the rightful rewards for strength, talent and hard work.

Most strikingly, it is the nineteenth-century divas' transgressions or willfulness that have the strongest resonance. Susan Rutherford (2016) calls them 'passionate, willful and proud'; for Koestenbaum (1993) their difference is 'perverse, monstrous, abnormal and ugly'; for Melissa Bradshaw it is 'egotism, arrogance and tempestuousness' (2016: 4); for Laura Miller and Rebecca Copeland, they are 'unruly', 'transgressive' and created from 'the friction produced when female genius meets social stricture' (2018: 8). Nineteenth-century divas have left a legacy of media attention, branding and typified characteristics that place an even more pressing demand on cultural institutions to re-address the realities of their lived experiences.

Conclusion

As music exhibitions engage and inspire wider audiences across the globe, the diva becomes increasingly integral to their development. The contemporary diva epitomizes the amalgamation of design, politics, social history and an auteur-like vision that can instil an exhibition experience with a powerful meaning. Divas, not only important as subjects, must also increasingly turn co-curator. At the V&A, Kylie Minogue and Diana Ross (or their management) did not exercise creative control in the same manner that Annie Lennox did, who immersed herself in the design, concept and experience of her exhibition. This does not denote ambivalence but reflects different artistic approaches and changes in the processes of exhibition-making. An exhibition can now be seen as 'total work', equal to a conceptual album or a concert film. The parameters between art installation and live show are increasingly overlapping in tandem with audience expectations.

Aside from the commercial benefits of exhibition-making, museum-endorsed shows can reaffirm critical respect and canonization. Artists who wish to be examined, understood, interpreted and even theologized can take opportunities to invite fans into their worlds to understand their creative process. Similar to social media channels, which balance an arms-length relationship with unprecedented intimacy, exhibitions can puncture mystique while still retaining an otherworldliness and inscrutability to their subjects. Exhibitions at their core communicate and define the legacy of a performer, explain an artistic vision, prompt enjoyment and nostalgia and reveal crucial truths about our society in the process. As shown by musician Nick Cave's autobiographical exhibition *Stranger Than Kindness: The Nick Cave Exhibition* (and as tied in with his book: Cave 2020), staged at the Black Diamond in Copenhagen, an exhibition can faithfully evoke the essence of an artist, rise above the canonical reinforcement of the artist's own mythology, reach audiences beyond a fanbase, and ask sincere questions about our culture and society. The success of this exhibition can be attributed to Cave's close collaboration with curators Christina Back and Janine Barrand, as well as his devised soundscape with Warren Ellis, and a clarity of curation goals: 'what shapes our lives and makes us who we are, and celebrates the curiosity and the power of the creative spirit'.[4] However, despite an increasing number of successful artistic collaborations, Peter Doyle argues that the balance remains a delicate one, between the populist and the urgent:

> Formal researchers of popular music may generally applaud its appearance in museum and heritage cultures over the past 25 years, and its widespread acceptance as worthy of further public culture work ... It could be said that now, two decades into the new century, the easy stories have mostly been told, and that the task at hand is to tell the not so easy, the more complex, more nuanced, but potentially even more rewarding stories.
>
> (2019: 127)

It is imperative that both musicians and museums work collaboratively to address this challenge as we enter the third decade of the twenty-first century.

Notes

1 For the Country Music Association's Mission Statement, see https://www.cmaworld.com/about/
2 For further on Minogue, including Baker's role in the construction of her diva persona and image, see Manghani and McDonald (2013: 219–34) and Manghani (2015: 247–67).
3 The quotation is from the V&A Curatorial and Interpretation exhibition label text for *The Story of The Supremes*, 2008.
4 Text from https://www.nickcave.com/news/stranger-than-kindness-the-book/

Reference

ABC Network (2000), '20/20 with Diana Ross', 5 August. Available online: https://www.youtube.com/watch?v=eOGdhMf2hK8 (accessed 7 May 2021).

Adrahtas, T. (2006), *Diana Ross: The American Dream Girl: A Lifetime to Get Here*, Bloomington: AuthorHouse.

Armstrong, J. (1992), 'Does the World Need Another Hall of Fame? Another Museum? Another Shrine?', *History News*, 57 (2): 14–17.

Art Newspaper, The (2018), 'Ranked: The Top Ten Most Popular Shows in their Categories from Around the World', 26 March. Available online: https://www.theartnewspaper.com/feature/top-10-exhibition-and-museum-visitor-figures-2017 (accessed 7 May 2021).

Baker, W. (2002), *Kylie: La La La*, London: Hodder and Stoughton.

Bakewell, J. (2007), 'What is Kylie Minogue doing at the V&A?', *The Independent*, 9 February. Available online: https://www.independent.co.uk/voices/commentators/joan-bakewell/joan-bakewell-what-is-kylie-minogue-doing-at-the-v-amp-a-435613.html (accessed 7 May 2021).

Binyon, M. (2007), 'Why Shouldn't Museums be for Pure Pleasure?', *The Sunday Times*, 1 August. Available online: https://www.thetimes.co.uk/article/why-shouldnt-museums-be-for-pure-pleasure-twj3c3b5ng2 (accessed 7 May 2021).

Bradshaw, M. (2016), *Amy Lowell: Diva Poet*, Oxford: Taylor and Francis.

Brown, K. N. (2010), *Writing the Black Revolutionary Diva: Women's Subjectivity and the Decolonizing Text*, Bloomington: Indiana University Press.

Cave, N. (2020), *Stranger Than Kindness*, Edinburgh: Canongate Books.

Cohen, S., L. Roberts, R. Knifton and M. Leonard (2014), *Site of Popular Music Heritage: Memories, Histories, Places*, Oxford: Taylor and Francis.

Danilov, V. J. (1997), *Hall of Fame Museums: A Reference Guide*, Westport: Greenwood Publishing Group.

Doyle, P. (2019), 'Showing Off: Taking Popular Music Research into the Museum', in L. Istvandity, S. Baker and Z. Cantillon (eds), *Remembering Popular Music's Past: Memory-Heritage-History*, 115–30, London: Anthem Press.

Easlea, D. (2008), *The Story of The Supremes*, London: V&A Publishing.

Fairchild, C. (2019), 'The Continually Precarious State of the Musical Object', in L. Istvandity, S. Baker and Z. Cantillon (eds), *Remembering Popular Music's Past: Memory-Heritage-History*, 101–14, London: Anthem Press.

Fox, I. (2007), 'Kylie Overwhelmed by V&A Show', *The Guardian*, 7 February. Available online: https://www.theguardian.com/music/2007/feb/07/kylieminogue (accessed 7 May 2021).

Istvandity, L. and Z. Cantillon (2019), 'The Precarity of Memory, Heritage and History in Remembering Popular Music's Past', in L. Istvandity, S. Baker and Z. Cantillon (eds), *Remembering Popular Music's Past: Memory-Heritage-History*, 1–10, London: Anthem Press.

Jackson, D. (2018), 'The Spice Bus Arrives in Manchester as the Spice Girls Exhibition Extends its Stay', *Manchester Evening News*, 19 September. Available online: https://www.manchestereveningnews.co.uk/whats-on/whats-on-news/spice-girls-exhibition-bus-manchester-15172578 (accessed 4 November 2022).

Johnston, B. (2020), 'Tina Knowles-Lawson Says She Faced Pressure to Change Destiny's Child's Look', *The Washington Post*, 4 August. Available online: https://www.washingtonpost.com/video/washington-post-live/wplive/tina-knowles-lawson-says-she-faced-pressure-to-change-destinys-childs-look/2020/08/04/ef92b518-7e2c-4e8a-9c29-3d66082f0b24_video.html (accessed 7 May 2021).

Knights, V. (2013), *Queering the Popular Pitch*, New York: Taylor and Francis.

Koestenbaum, W. (1993), *The Queen's Throat: Opera, Homosexuality and the Mystery of Desire*, London: Poseidon Press.

Manghani, S. (2015), 'Performing Kylie: Looks Divine', in R. Edgar, K. Fairclough-Isaacs, B. Halligan and N. Spelman, *The Arena Concert: Music, Media and Mass Entertainment*, 247–67, London: Bloomsbury.

Manghani, S. and K. McDonald (2013), 'Desperately Seeking Kylie! Reflections on William Baker's *White Diamond*', in R. Edgar, K. Fairclough-Isaacs and B. Halligan, *The Music Documentary: Acid Rock to Electropop*, 219–234, London: Routledge.

McArdle, T. (2018), 'MLK was Dead. Cities were Burning. Could James Brown keep Boston from Erupting, Too?', *The Washington Post*, 5 April. Available online: https://www.washingtonpost.com/news/retropolis/wp/2018/04/05/mlk-was-dead-cities-were-burning-could-james-brown-keep-boston-from-erupting-too/ (accessed 4 November 2022).

Miller, L. and R. Copeland (2018), *Diva Nation: Female Icons from Japanese Cultural History*, Berkeley: University of California Press.

Rasmussen, E. E. and R. L. Densley (2017), 'Girl in a Country Song: Gender Roles and Objectification of Women in Popular Country Music across 1990 to 2014', *Sex Roles*, 76: 188–201.

Razaq, R. (2007), 'First Kylie, Now the V&A turns to The Supremes', *Evening Standard*, 1 August. Available online: https://www.standard.co.uk/arts/first-kylie-now-the-va-turns-to-the-supremes-6602558.html (accessed 7 May 2021).

Rodman, G. B. (1996), *Elvis After Elvis: The Posthumous Career of a Living Legend*, London: Routledge.

Rutherford, S. (2016), 'Divining the "diva", or a Myth and its Legacy: Female Opera Singers and Fandom', *Schweizer Jahrbuch für Musikwissenschaft - Neue Folge*, 36: 39–62.

Small, N. (2019), 'Spice Girls Super Fan Left £420,000 in Debt after Memorabilia Show is a Total Flop', *The Mirror*, 26 January. Available online: https://www.mirror.co.uk/news/uk-news/spice-girls-fan-left-420000-13910682 (accessed 4 November 2022).

Willman, C. (2005), *Rednecks & Bluenecks: The Politics of Country Music*, New York: New Press.

Wilson, M. (2000), *Dreamgirl and Supreme Faith: My Life as a Supreme*, New York: Cooper Square Press.

13

A Diva on the Iranian stage

Ali Akbar Alizad's remix of Jean Genet's *The Maids*

Rana Esfandiary

Despite depicting Iran as a barbaric, backward and anti-Western Islamic state, the theatrical stages of the city of Tehran are among its busiest cultural sites, where art becomes a means of activism and artworks turn into an emotional archive storing lost promises, broken dreams and sometimes faint hopes for the future. Coping with myriad sociopolitical and cultural problems has pushed Iranian directors and playwrights to work and compose in order to cultivate an understanding of what life can be, what liberty can be and what equality and inclusion can be. Ali Akbar Alizad, the founder of 84Theatre Company,[1] is one of those directors – and has dedicated the entirety of his professional life to creating works that reflect the society in its most naked manner. This chapter delves into Alizad's 2018 staging of *The Maids* in Tehran in the context of the contemporary political situation of the country, and with the Islamic regime in the ascendency, which significantly affected the reception of the gender-fluid performances of Claire and Solange in relation to the divadoms of their Madam. The chapter also unpacks the directorial choices that Alizad incorporated to realize, alienate, and (re)introduce the characters of Claire, Solange and the Madam to his audiences. My analysis here is based on my use of the concept of the diva, and the performativity of the diva figure in unlocking the nuanced power play at the core of the play. I interrogate the wretchedness of the Madam's divadom and the construction of her character as an apathetic and supreme 'bitch'. In relation to the Madam's divadom, I then analyse the complexity of the characters of Solange and Claire alongside their performance of fakeness or their performative act of falsification/play-acting. I use the term *aesthetic of abjectness* to analyse the performance of two cis-male actors (re)presenting the characters of Claire and Solange, and their attempts to maximize their (wo)manpower in order to navigate the dynamics of the plays: that is, the play written by Genet, and the play designed by the characters themselves to dismantle the Madam's divadom. In this power play dynamic, divaness, for Madam, is a state of being, or a maintaining of supreme control over her world. For the maids, however, re-enacting/faking Madam's divaness is a way of finding liberation from, and so subverting, modes of oppression. In the context of such a paradoxical interpretation of divaness, the pressing question that I invite readers to reflect upon is: to what degree do the identities of dissidents, such as Claire and Solange, remain authentic, or become constructed, manufactured or hybridized, when faced with the oppressive ideological position of a power figure (Figure 13.1)?

In tandem with a critical analysis of the play's central concept, in the context of its staging in Iran, I also examine the inspiration that Alizad took from Reza Abdoh, the subversive Iranian-American director who is mostly known for his large-scale, unconventional and remarkable productions in the United States. Despite a short artistic life, divided between Los Angeles and New York City (where he died of AIDS at the age of thirty-two, in 1995), Abdoh produced an impressive oeuvre, comprising works that were among the sharpest critiques posed against a culture bathed in capitalism, blatant racism, homophobia and

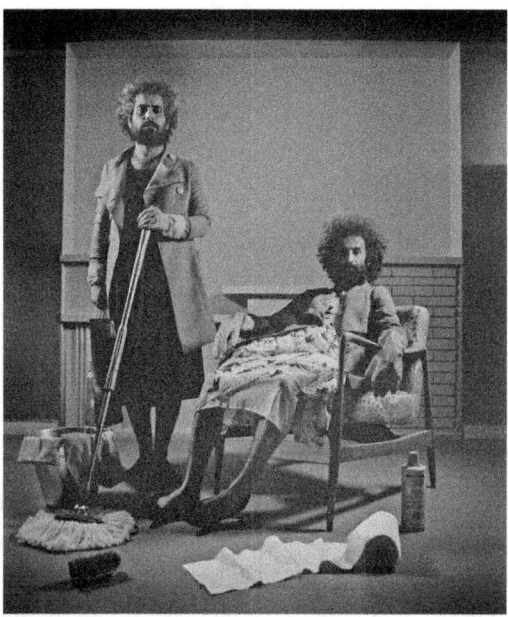

Figure 13.1 Photo by Siavash Tasaodian.

exclusionary rhetoric. After studying Abdoh, Alizad too aimed to expose the compliancy in a social culture that crushes its more vulnerable members in order to exert a hegemonic grip on society. Alizad was greatly inspired by the ways in which music, including hip-hop, folk and classical, assisted Abdoh in shaping a new and subversive vocabulary with which to denounce the homophobic and consumerist attitudes found in America.

As well as unpacking Alizad's take on Abdoh, my concern is also with Genet and his queerness, his marginalization and, as a consequence, his insistence on centring the narratives of the oppressed. I focus both on the 2018 staging and the streaming of this play, via YouTube, during the summer of 2020, amid the Covid-19 lockdown in Iran. How were Alizad's artistic choices, including privileging the story of workers, the casting of two cis-males in the two key roles of the play, and the cross-dressing and gender-fluid performances, critical to the production's reception by audiences? I identify Alizad's approach to *The Maids* then an artful act of (re)mixing Abdoh's Theatre of Cruelty with Genet's narrativization of violence. In this, both actors and audiences were challenged to revisit their most foundational beliefs in regard to their senses of their cultural and sociopolitical identities.

Fast-forwarding through the year 2018

For Middle Easterners, the year 2018 was marked by seismic sociopolitical and economic turmoil. These included the Gaza border protests (the so-called Great Gaza March of Return); then US President Donald Trump pulling the United States out of the Barack Obama-era Joint Comprehensive Plan of Action (known as the Iran Nuclear Deal); the provocative relocation of the United States embassy from Tel Aviv to Jerusalem; shifting alliances between Arab worlds and Israel; the premeditated murder of the journalist Jamal Khashoggi; wider ongoing crises for the Islamic State of Iraq and the Levant (ISIL); the availability of driving licences for Saudi women for the first time; and the mass protests of working-class people in Iran. All these events, good or bad, prompted those affected to reflect critically and adapt accordingly. Once again, Palestinians, Iranians, Yemenis, Syrians, Arabs and Israelis were forced to act quickly, collectively and individually: to redefine national identity and boundaries violated through domestic, regional and international threats. And yet interrogating Middle Easterners' coping mechanisms within their volatile political, social and cultural systems has been historically dominated by Western scholars and external ideological optics, typically presented as shorn of the region's historical actuality. The most jarring feature of such Western-calibrated analyses of Middle East upheavals is the noticeable absence of any localized historical contexts or perspectives. As Edward W. Said argues of this tendency, in *Covering Islam: How the Media and Experts Determine How We See the Rest of the World*:

> Whatever Iranians or Muslims say about their sense of justice, their history of oppression, their vision of their own societies, seems irrelevant; what counts for the United States instead is what the 'Islamic revolution' is doing right now, how many people have been executed by the Komitehs, how many bizarre outrages the Ayatollah, in the name of Islam, has ordered. Of course, no one has equated the Jonestown massacre or the destructive frenzy produced at the Who concert in Cincinnati or the devastation of Indochina with Christianity, or with Western or American culture at large; that sort of equation has been reserved for Islam.
> (Said 1981: 8).

The lack of nuanced representation and fair analysis of the Middle East and North African (MENA) region within Western cultural and political discourse has, it is typically argued, fuelled the rise of extremist policies – policies fuelled or even proactively promoted by countries with the goal of exploiting the region at the concomitant cost of impoverishing its citizens. One thinks, for example, of the ways in which the Iranian people have been left to wrestle with astronomical economic inflation, due to the rising crisis of currency and the scarcity of food and medical supplies, in the context of US sanctions, aimed directly at destabilizing the economy further to engineering a regime change; see (BBC 2018), (Borger and Wintour 2018), (Gladstone 2018). In this, it is the people who – caught between their unrest and misery, and a ruling class determined to retain their power at all costs – are pushed to their limits.

Thus, in 2018, in response to the collapsing economy of the country, the workers at the Haft Tapeh sugar cane plantation in the city of Shush, in southern Iran, coordinated their months-long strikes and protest. The outpouring of dissent by the Haft Tapeh workers then quickly spread to other peripheral towns, and ultimately to major Iranian cities, with people assembling en masse to show their frustrations with the ruling class. In support of the protesters and their demands, four independent labour organizations – the Free Union of Iranian Workers, the Association of Painters of Alborz Province, the Labor

Defenders' Center and the Committee for the Pursuit of the Establishment of Labor Organizations – issued a statement, declaring:

> It should be self-evident that ignoring the demands of workers and toiling people of Iran by resorting to demagoguery or crackdown or attempts by governmental factions or the opposition that is driven from power before to base itself on the wave of popular protests will not bear any fruit. This time, it is us, the workers and people of Iran, who will write our own destiny, with unity, solidarity and continuation of protests.
>
> (Various 2018)

The majority of the middle- and upper-class Iranians, who maintained belief in the strategies and moderate policies of the reformist president, Hassan Rouhani, failed to join the coalition of workers, robbing it of momentum. The Iranian Revolutionary Guard regained control of the streets and returned the country to its status quo. And so, with their demands unmet, the working class became once again the victim, both of the machinations of their country's crude sociopolitical and economic system, as well as its own courageous act of defiance. Asef Bayat, after surveying this defeat, asked:

> Who speaks for these disenfranchised people? In other times and in other countries ... segments of this class turned to nationalist and Islamist movements before resorting to street politics before and during the Arab Spring. In Tunisia, the center-left Tunisian General Labor Union seemed to give them a voice, if the Islamic State did not lure them first. But in Iran, they have had no representation – neither Islamists, who are preoccupied with building an ideological community, nor reformists, who are concerned with 'political development' and a post-Islamist project, nor the leftists, who have mostly disappeared.
>
> (2018)

At the same time as this uprising, and despite the wider society's indifference to the struggle of the working classes, the Molavi Theatre Hall in Tehran welcomed audiences for the opening night of a production of Jean Genet's *The Maids*, directed and staged by Ali Akbar Alizad.[2] The production quickly became of note, and a matter of discussion for three distinct reasons. First: in intentionally low ticket prices, and Alizad's refutation of the culture of commercialism and celebrity (which has plagued most theatre productions in Tehran). Second, with Alizad's decision to cast two cis-male performers in the roles of Claire and Solange caused a stir among audiences accustomed to the highly heteronormative cultural discourse of the country. And, third, in the way in which the production intentionally integrated elements of the struggles of the working class. Alizad, ever careful not to turn the production into a political statement in support of the uprising, curated a storytelling event through which – despite the stifling cultural discourse of the country – he could echo or amplify the voices of the marginalized and the most vulnerable people.

The Maids Remixed

In *Saint Genet: Actor and Martyr*, Jean-Paul Sartre argues that '[f]or Genet, theatrical procedure is demoniacal. Appearance, which is constantly on the point of passing itself off as reality, must constantly reveal its profound unreality. Everything must be so false that it sets our teeth on edge' (Sartre [1952] 2012: 612). While this passage concerns Genet's view of theatre's essentially artificial nature, Sartre's claim could not be more appropriately used to describe the chaotic conditions of daily life in a city like Tehran. When passing through the hustle and bustle of Tehran, one encounters moments of incongruous emotions, ranging from kindness and empathy to hatred, repressed desires, silences and bottled-up anger – and all accompanied by a cacophonous mix of the call for prayers, hip-hop songs and the anxious horns of cars. In the context of such a chaotic scene, and in the light of the myriad domestic and international pressures to which the city is subjected, nothing is as it seems, and nothing can be as it seems: everyone is performing, in disguise or as an ideal version of themselves that they think or hope will help them to survive the challenges of the day.

Although from another era, and of another (and Western) nationality, and preoccupied with different sets of concerns and ideologies, Genet is the perfect narrator for the drama underway in Iran. As an outcast himself, Genet's life was filled with incongruous events: arrest for petty acts of thievery; finding himself acknowledged as one of the most promising French novelists and essayists; camping with Palestinian fighters; siding with the Black Panther Party; and entering the United States illegally.[3] While Genet's experiences varied widely in nature, his obsession with death and solitude, his predilection for showcasing or exploring violence and his instinctive urge to mount challenges to systematic oppression, coalesced into a cohesive and characteristic theme, across both his life and literary works. For instance, regarding his insistence on placing the voices or emotions of the oppressed at the centre of his work, Genet shared the pain of Palestinian fighters when (in his lengthy text, 'Four Hours in Shatila'), he narrated his observations of the 1982 massacre which unfolded in the alleys and streets of Beirut. When encountering black and blue corpses, Genet writes:

> Love and death. These two words are quickly associated when one of them is written down. I had to go to Shatila to understand the obscenity of love and the obscenity of death. In both cases the body has nothing more to hide: positions, contortions, gestures, signs, even silences belong to one world and to the other.
> (Genet 1983: 5)

Whether narrating the reality as-is, or dramatizing reality in a form of a play or a novel, Genet's insistence on retelling and re-enacting violence, oppression, repressed emotions and the interconnectivity of life and death, remained at the heart of most of his writings.

Maids

The Maids, loosely based on the infamous 1933 French Papin crime case (in which the sisters Christine and Léa Papin were convicted of murdering their employer's wife and daughter), dramatizes Claire and Solange's diabolical plan to kill their mistress is referred to as Madam. Every day, in the absence of Madam, Claire becomes Madam and Solange becomes Claire. Within the context of this complex relationality to themselves, to their borrowed identities and to each other, Claire and Solange diligently refine their plan and, through it, a realization of their conditions, and identities. But as 'good' as the maids' murderous plan may be, Madam comes out unscathed in the end. In despair and exasperation, the maids see no point in carrying on. So, for one last time, Claire plays Madam, and Solange becomes Claire; (s)he brings out a special concoction for 'Madam' to drink and die.

The idea of staging *The Maids* occurred to Ali Akbar Alizad as he was working on the production of Harold Pinter's 1988 *Mountain Language*, which was staged in Tehran in 2016. Spurred on by the idea of critiquing the processes of the marginalization and oppression of minority ethnicities in Pinter's play, Alizad began to mull over the possibility of interrogating the adversarial effects of class violence, dysfunctional value systems, the rise of patriarchy and the economic crisis in Iran. In collaboration with his dramaturg, Reza Soroor, Alizad decided that the time was right to work on Genet, whose unique position on theatre could hold the potential to unlock new ways of criticizing the construction of reality within Iranian society. As Sartre notes, '[t]he most extraordinary example of the whirligig of being and appearance, of the imaginary and the real, is to be found in one of Genet's plays. It is the element of fake, of sham, of artificiality that attracts Genet in theatre. He turned dramatist because the falsehood of the stage is the most manifest and fascinating of all' (2012: 611). Genet did not appreciate theatre per se, as he considered the art form an untruthful expression of emotions – be those emotions love, hate, rage or violence. Such an outlook suited Alizad's interpretation of a society where all he saw appeared to him as a questionable 'reality', as carefully coordinated in relation to, and in contention, with itself.

In order to maximize the full potential of Genet's piece, Alizad decided to cast two cis-male performers, Alireza Keymanesh and Morteza Hossienzade, in the roles of Claire and Solange. As he argued:

> The clash between three women in a domestic space of a house appeared to me as an exhausted idea that I had no interest in exploring. I knew I needed to come up with a strategy capable of defamiliarizing these characters and their relationships for the actors and audiences alike. Brechtian alienation technique came across as an ideal solution where I could unpack the core concept of the play focused on dramatizing the disenfranchisement of the working class in a highly imbalanced bourgeoisie society.[4]

After the streaming of the production in the summer of 2020, via YouTube, Alizad confirmed to me that, in hindsight, his choice of casting two cis-male performers as Claire and Solange was among one of the best artistic decisions he felt he made, 'as casting two women would not have unlocked the intensity of emotional and sensual repression embedded in the play'.[5]

Alizad's production opens with Claire, played by Alireza Keymanesh, sitting in front of a mirror, applying heavy and exaggerated makeup to her/his face while Solange, played by Morteza Hossienzade, is diligently calculating where to tape down the floor. As the sound of folk music from the southern Iranian city of Bushehr fades out, Claire stands up, starts walking in a hyper-feminine manner towards a couch positioned on stage right, where (s)he sits, flexes muscles, and paints her/his toenails red. (The choice of music here is of paramount importance as the southern part of Iran is the home to the majority of the labourers who comprise the middle- to lower-impoverished classes of the country) (Figure 13.3).

In the meantime, Solange keeps marking the floor with tape in a laborious, mechanical manner. Audiences get a full view of the seated Claire's rough and bulky muscles, dark body hair, black beard and dark hair covered with a blonde wig. After (s)he has finished polishing her/his toenails, Claire stands up and

Figure 13.2 Photo by Ehsan Zivaralam.

Figure 13.3 Photo by Ehsan Zivaralam.

starts dancing flirtatiously to the music which gradually gets louder and faster. As Claire thus puts her/his (wo)manhood on full display, Solange puts on her/his bright green dish-washing gloves to mop the floor obsessively. Claire, too, picks up her/his red dish-washing gloves, but only to then use them as an accessory for dancing, which slowly morphs into self-flagellation. Upon noticing Solange, Claire turns to him/her, shouting:

> Claire: I have told you one thousand times that these gloves belong to the kitchen. Now get lost.

[Solange stands there, dazed with the performance that Claire has put on. Claire throws the gloves at Solange while shouting in a more masculine tone:
Claire: Why are you staring at me? We are losing time!
[Claire then restarts her dancing until (s)he gets to the couch.]
Claire (yelling): Claire!!⁶

From this moment on, it becomes clear that the maids are rehearsing/playing a game that they have designed to free themselves. Through an act of gender and identity 'transgression', Claire and Solange disenfranchise themselves from their imposed roles, of being male and maids, to two rebels who narrate their violent exclusion from the society. It is in the relationality between these maids' 'true' selves, and their play-acting, that we get a chance to glimpse the dissonance associated with reclaiming one's identity against or from the internalization of society's dominant ideology. In performative acts of falsification or re-enacting Madam's divaness, we see Claire desperately searching for her/his identity – the one that is free from humiliation and repression. And we see Solange, having internalized her/his inferiority to the point of no return, revealed to be in a situation in which (s)he cannot now be anything but a maid. The *aesthetic of abjectness* comes into full display when these maids are rehearsing their desire to be the 'other' – that one that is free and revered. But the juxtaposition of the reality and the ideal turns the two into 'freaks' (i.e. seemingly existing or being outsides norms or codes of acceptable behaviour): Claire entertains her/his femininity but her/his excessive body hair turns her/him into a subject beyond the pale of sociocultural redemption. Solange tries to become Claire, but her/his conservativism and inferiority block her/him from being more audacious.

Objects

Through a circular transformation, from maids to rebels and then back to maids, Claire and Solange not only use their own identities, physicality, mortality and gender as vehicles of storytelling but also cling to quotidian objects such as gloves, mops, shoes and blouses to reveal their love/hate relationship to their status, their mistress and their world. The role of objects in revealing someone's sorrowful condition is an integral aspect of Genet's life, as he was accused of petty acts of theft, in the stealing of objects such as handkerchiefs, bottles of spirits, books and clothes throughout his life. Following his own strange obsession with luxurious 'stuff', Genet's works elevate objects to the level of metaphors in which the intersection of power, status, societal values and consumerism is explored and satirized. In *The Maids*, Claire uses the red dish-washing gloves to symbolize the superiority that (s)he yearns for, as well as the inferiority that (s)he despises, by retooling the gloves as both a pleasurable object for dancing and torturous means of self-flagellation. The maid's dualistic attitudes towards Madam's objects are articulated by Solange when (s)he professes, 'Madam "loves" us just like how she loves the chairs in her house; how she adores her bathroom's tiles; how she appreciates that toilet plunger. The truth is we cannot even love ourselves for who we are.'

The fetishization of quotidian objects, cross-gender performances, the re-enacting of violence towards oneself and others and assailing the hearing of the audience through the playing of loud music, as well as actors' intentionally cacophonous and earsplitting moaning, groaning, laughing and screaming, are among the features shared by both Alizad and Reza Abdoh to a varying degree and quality. Alizad's fascination with the theatre of Abdoh started when he hosted Abdoh's brother, Salar Abdoh, at his house in Tehran, and the two watched rarely-seen footage of the legendary director's works and life. After watching this footage, Alizad began to study Abdoh and his oeuvre, to the ends of adapting his aggressive-yet-lyrical directorial style for the production of *The Maids* – a production that in fact, Alizad had been planning for at least three years. During my interview with Alizad, he remembered finding himself mesmerized by Abdoh's stage production, where 'normal' oscillated with the abnormal, harmony swerved into cacophony, tranquillity to mayhem and sanity to frenzy. Alizad's gravitation towards Abdoh comes as no surprise; Abdoh's theatre is a space in which those whose voices have been silenced have found themselves with a platform to talk, to be audible and to be noticeable. Abdoh's theatre, as Alizad understood, was an individual and a collective act of growing attuned to the volatility of society's shifting sociopolitical and cultural discourse.

Abdoh, just like Genet, put a startling emphasis on the showcasing of violence as a merciless, cold-blooded, poetic act, reenacted within high-tempo verbal and physical exchanges. For instance, in *The Hip-Hop Waltz of Eurydice*, which premiered at the Los Angeles Theatre Center in 1990, Reza Abdoh takes the myth of Eurydice and Orpheus to an unknown and imaginary place so as to narrate the story of sexual repression, the brutality of oppressive power and the power of love.[7] The core concept of the production, which is seemingly based on the idea of a lack of an organized homonormative movement in the United States, is then unpacked within the frenzied interactions among Eurydice, Orpheus and the Captain. Among these three characters, the Captain, whose presence is felt by audiences only through his assertive voice at the beginning of the production, symbolizes an authoritative and abusive source of power, incapable of showing empathy towards those whom he wishes to conquer. However, Abdoh mocks this authoritative figure as, upon the Captain's entrance, the audience encounters a person who appears distorted, hysterical and covered in warts and wounds. Both Alizad and Soroor, his dramaturg, found the power of Abdoh satirical and exaggerated violence appropriate for their approach to *The Maids*; as Soroor argued, 'Genet's dramatization of violence happens in an absurd situation where his characters are isolated and pushed to adopt a clownish performance.'[8]

Madam

To follow the trajectory of the maids, from their dissident position to the point where they seem to find themselves with no option other than entertaining their own mortality, necessitates an evaluation of Madam's role. For almost the entirety of the play, we see the two maids in a state of rebelling; in this, they are perfecting their plan to kill their mistress and free themselves from their pathetic conditions. In the absence of Madam, and in the context of the maids' performance, we feel Madam's larger-than-life presence looming over the house and the maids' existence and identities. Madam metaphorically exemplifies a utopia that Claire and Solange are desperately yearning to destroy in order to reconstruct as their own. Claire plays at being Madam and Solange plays at being Claire and, in their play-acting, we get to know a Madam who is powerful, flamboyant, arrogant, seductive, spoiled, bitchy and demanding. In Madam, Solange and Claire essentially see a diva and, in her house, a divadom that they plan to conquer. They then move to a rehearsed state of becoming diva.

Historically, the diva is taken to be an acclaimed female opera singer – one who has a flair for drama and is almost impossible to please, control or even ignore. However, in Alizad's *The Maids*, the concept of divaness, and its normative applicability to a female celebrity, is substantially complicated through the cross-gender performances of Solange and Claire. 'The diva represents dislocation', Laura Hein argues in 'Transnational and Time-Traveling Divas', which is

> something that presupposes a stable historical or geographic past and so is an excellent entry point into understanding social and political tensions in a specific time and place. Divas identify dissonance in a generalizable way but they always do so by capturing unexpressed aspects of specific experiences. Moreover, by showing their perspective to rapt audiences, they wittily and theatrically make themselves impossible to ignore. Divas convey the point that their pain was unfairly inflicted; without social injustice, there could be no divas. As Miller and

Copeland put it, 'divas are not born,' but rather, they are 'generated' from 'the friction produced when female genius meets social stricture.'

(Hein 2018: xi)

Hein's eloquent definition of divaness can be applied to the constructed identities of both Madam and her maids. In a patriarchal society like Iran, women are expected to dress modestly and act humbly. Amid the imposition of dress codes and the promulgation of a polity derived from one conservative reading of Islamic ideology, many women have had to find safe havens within the confines of domestic spaces. Against this conservative backdrop, Madam provides a counterhegemonic narrative to the norms of femininity as well as to those of gender roles and behaviours reified by traditional and patriarchal cultural discourse. As a rampaging, feisty and outgoing woman who does not shy away from adoration of her lover, Madam mocks the veneration of the ideal female icon which is so integral to the Islamic polity that dominates the country's cultural and social value systems. Madam has diva credentials as she 'often refuses to behave, to follow the rules, to act with decorum' (Hein 2018: xi). Her divaness symbolizes a forceful liberation and courage that everyone yearns for – including her two maids. And, as Miller and Copeland argue:

> We therefore have no choice but to acknowledge the diva. She is already there, thrusting herself in our faces and troubling us with her stories and provocative representations. The diva does not simply survive, she flourishes. She is ripe for expansion, fantasy, eroticization, and playful reinvention, yet her unavoidability also makes her a special problem. She may be memorialized, celebrated, or demonized, but she will not be ignored.
>
> (Miller and Copeland 2018: 2–3)

While being a diva provides Madam with a licence to behave freely, to live lavishly and to act petulantly, it is through re-enacting her divaness that her maids find themselves existentially viable and so worthy of existing. In short, for Madam, divaness is a state of being, while for Claire and Solange it is a mechanism to survive the cruelty of an ideological system that Madam represents.

Maids, objects and Madam: The remix

Divaness has myriad meanings and applicability: for Claire and Solange it is a performative act of surviving, becoming then what Beyoncé identifies (on her 2008 album *I Am . . . Sasha Fierce*) 'a hustler' – 'diva is a female version of a hustler'. Beyoncé pinpoints this new attitude towards being a diva, in that divaness, for her, in Al Horner's interpretation '[is] not a moment of self-criticism, but self-celebration' (Cited in Newland 2018). In Madam's absence, the maids hustle to piece together their fragmented individuality by taking apart their mistress's identity; they renounce Madam's superiority as a way to define their own positionality in a world that has (r)ejected them as dispensable objects. By imitating Madam, these two maids satirize the supremacy of totalitarian power while honouring the freedom of which they have been deprived. Being a diva, or re-enacting it, empowers these maids to be bold and rebellious; this is embodied by Solange who, despite her/his timid nature, points an axe towards Claire-as-Madam and declares: 'I hate everything about you. Maybe Madam has thought her luck will help her to avoid death. For sure, Madam has underestimated the workers' revolt. Watch our revolt as it will spoil your life and love story.'

Through their play-acting, the maids manage to preserve their hope, which is a hope that narrates their struggle and carries them forward towards their goal of emancipation. These maids wholeheartedly believe that by playing the game of falsification, emulation and copying Madam, they will be able to usurp her status once and for all. However, when Madam – due merely to her good fortune – comes out of the maids' sacrificial plan unscathed, the maids' hope turns to despair. Towards the end of the play, in the light of their defeat, Claire is exhausted and aghast; (s)he walks around the room mumbling:

> Madam loves me and Solange, or, she loves one of us or both of us. She always mistakes us, doesn't know who is who. Madam lets us go to the park that she goes too, to walk where she walks, because Madam is good, Madam is kind, Madam is beautiful. And in return, and as per Madam's order, we pray for Madam every night. We never raise our voice in her presence. Madam overwhelms us with her kindness, poisons us through her empathy because Madam is good, Madam is kind, Madam is beautiful. There is no decayed flower that Madam has failed to give to us because Madam is good, Madam is kind, Madam is beautiful.

Repeating the phrase 'Madam is good, Madam is kind, Madam is beautiful' is the maids' concession speech after their well-fought battle against the tyranny of their mistress. While desperate, Solange and Claire encourage each other to play their sacrificial games one last time; Claire plays at being Madam and Solange plays at being Claire. They sit on the edge of the bed and smoke marijuana. Left high and dry, Solange brings the poisoned tea. The Doors' 'The End' (1967) fades

Figure 13.4 Photo by Ehsan Zivaralam.

in while Claire drinks the tea and kisses the Solange on his/her lips. With bloody mouths, both maids die (Figure 13.4).

While watching the *The Maids*, in the summer of 2020 via YouTube, during the Covid-19 lockdown, it was difficult not to think of the massive workers' uprising, which spread throughout the whole country, simultaneous to the production's 2018 staging, as noted earlier. The staple slogan of those protesters was 'Death to the Worker' which, in retrospect, sounds perfectly aligned with the production's grim epilogue. The maids made it clear, repeatedly, that they cannot continue living as maids: they cannot go back to their shared bedroom and their beds, wearing the beautiful dresses that their mistress has given them. As Solange professes: 'I, too, cannot tolerate this excruciating condition', and (s)he moves downstage and addresses the audience directly:

> Don't wear this; don't eat that; don't say this; listen; don't go to street like this; don't raise your voice; don't protest; just suffer and suck it up; just suffer and die, so everybody can live comfortably; I cannot tolerate this anymore.

Naively, the maids fail to recognize that Madam, in her very divaness, achieves a behavioural mode through which the sociopolitical and cultural system materializes and extends its hegemonic rule into the very domestic spaces and interpersonal dynamics of its people. As Staci Gem Scheiwiller argues:

> The State exists only as a fetish, because the State is not a living, breathing entity, although in the modern world it has become understood as such. Moreover, the State is not an actual thing, but an abstract concept. Its power structures then become instilled in people, things and signs, which creates an aura of

omnipotence, even in one's own mind; hence, [Michael T.] Taussing calls this relationship between a person and the State, 'the nervous system,' because the body internalizes the concept of the State as a personal panopticon that continually surveys the subject.

(Scheiwiller 2013: 6)

By showing that they have nothing in common except their repression and loneliness, Claire and Solange embolden each other's abjectness, ugliness and un-assimilability. They dream about becoming someone other than themselves – the empowered diva tyrant, rather than the disempowered worker-maid; they believe eliminating Madam, as well as the Solange and Claire that they have known their whole lives, is the path towards salvation. What they fail to acknowledge is the futility of exchanging roles when the game and its rules are the reason for the promulgation of oppression. The game will go on with or without the maids who constantly equate themselves to 'shit that is rotten'.

Notes

1 Alizad found 84Theatre Company in 2006 in Tehran with the goal of staging works written by famous playwrights such as Samuel Beckett, Anton Chekhov, Sarah Kane and Harold Pinter. The group is mostly comprised of Alizad's past and current students from the Art University of Tehran, where he teaches acting and playwriting. For more information, see: http://84theater.com
2 The production opened in November 2018. Genet's play was first produced as *Les Bonnes* in 1947.
3 For a life of Genet, see Barber (2004); Genet's own memoires, *Prisoner of Love*, was first published posthumously in 1986.
4 Ali Akbar Alizad: Skype interview with the author, 25 September 2020. All further quotations from Alizad are from this interview.
5 The online streaming of *The Maids* started on 9 May 2020, and has attracted more than 2,600 views at the time of writing. This can be accessed here: https://www.youtube.com/watch?v=mENvx5Tp00I&t=2577s
6 This is the author's transcription of the streamed performance. All further citation from the play comes from the author's transcription.
7 The full production of *The Hip-Hop Waltz of Eurydice* is available via https://vimeo.com/156807696
8 Reza Soroor; WhatsApp interview with the author, 2 October 2020.

Reference

Barber, S. (2004), *Jean Genet*, London: Reaktion Books.

Bayat, A. (2018), 'The Fire That Fueled the Iran Protests', *The Atlantic*, 27 January. Available online: https://www.theatlantic.com/international/archive/2018/01/iran-protest-mashaad-green-class-labor-economy/551690/ (accessed 8 September 2022).

BBC (2018), 'Trump Administration to Reinstate All Iran Sanctions', 3 November. Available online: https://www.bbc.co.uk/news/world-us-canada-46071747 (accessed 8 September 2022).

Borger, J. and P. Wintour (2018), 'Trump Administration Unveils Full Extend of US Sanctions on Iran', *The Guardian*, 6 November. Available online: https://www.theguardian.com/world/2018/nov/05/iran-launches-military-drill-response-return-us-sanctions (accessed 8 September 2022).

Genet, J. (1983), 'Four Hours in Shatila', *Journal of Palestine Studies*, 12, no. 3 (Spring): 3–22.

Gladstone, R. (2018) 'Iran Sanctions Explained: U.S. Goals, and the View from Tehran', *New York Times*, 5 November. Available online: https://www.nytimes.com/2018/11/05/world/middleeast/iran-sanctions-explained.html (accessed 8 September 2022).

Hein, L. (2018), 'Transnational and Time-Travelling Divas', in L. Miller and R. Copeland (eds), *Diva Nation: Female Icons from Japanese Cultural History*, xi–xvii, Berkeley: University of California Press.

Miller, L. and R. Copeland (2018), 'Diva Seductions: An Introduction to *Diva Nation*', in L. Miller and R. Copeland (eds), *Diva Nation: Female Icons from Japanese Cultural History*, 1–12, Berkeley: University of California Press.

Newland, C. (2018), 'A Cultural History of the Diva', *Vice*, 1 March. Available online: https://www.vice.com/en/article/bj5a8q/pop-culture-history-diva-mariah-carey-beyonce-barbra-streisand (accessed 4 November 2022).

Said, E. W. (1981), *Covering Islam: How the Media and Expert Determine How We See the Rest of the World*, New York: Pantheon Books.

Sartre, J.-P. (2012 [1952]), *Saint Genet: Actor and Martyr*, trans. B. Frechtman, Minneapolis: The University of Minnesota Press.

Scheiwiller, S. G., ed. (2013), *Performing the Iranian Stage: Visual Culture and Representation of Iranian Identity*, New York: Anthem Press.

Various (2018), 'Statement by a Number of Independent Labor Organizations about Recent Protests', *Human Rights Activists News Agency*, 2 January. Available online: https://www.en-hrana.org/statements/statement-number-independent-labor-organizations-recent-protests (accessed 2 May 2021).

14

Recasting diva culture

Performative strategies of fourth wave Black feminist stand-up comedy

Rachel E. Blackburn

Introduction – Who is a diva?

The term 'Diva' in its original form was an opera-singing 'goddess', who emerged in late nineteenth-century Italy, captivating audiences with her presence and musicality (Kooijman 2019: 7). While divas would eventually be revered in cinema as well, the contemporary trope returns us to popular music . . . and connotations of someone who is narcissistic, demanding, high maintenance, yet high performing (Bernstein 2013). Kimberly Springer refers to the 'dual nature of divadom' (cited in Kooijman 2019: 256), meaning that a diva carries all the cultural baggage of previous incarnations: 'a talented female star who enthralls and inspires her audience', while simultaneously is 'unreasonable, unpredictable, and likely unhinged' (Kooijman 2019: 7). Patriarchy benefits from reducing women's power around strength, into hysterics: this method denigrates successful divas, and we cannot ignore the ways in which Black women specifically are stereotyped in these terms, inextricably affixed with white supremacy. Jaap Kooijman notes, when discussing musical superstar and Black artist Beyoncé:

> Although 'diva' has been applied to female stars of various ethnicities, there is a specific connection between the diva and Black female performers, based both on the positive connotations of strength and survival within a white-dominated entertainment industry, as well as on the negative connotations of excessive and unruly behavior, often based on racial stereotypes.
>
> (Kooijman 2019: 7)

One need not look further than the *Wall Street Journal* for an example of this duality: they placed a large photograph of Beyoncé above the article 'Why Divas Need Make No Apology: Demanding People Get a Bad Rap, But Behind the Tantrums and the Drama Lie Lessons in Success' (Bernstein 2013).

Current fourth wave feminism (2008–present; Baumgardner 2011: 256) has waded into diva discourse, calling out the label as sexist. Fourth wave feminism coordinates internet-born street protest, hashtag awareness movements (such as #MeToo), utilizes comedy significantly and has expanded its ideology to include the term 'intersectional identity'. Intersectionality was coined by critical race theorist Kimberlé Crenshaw when she observed egregiously high rates of incarceration for Black women in the United States who were subject to overlapping oppression through racism and sexism (Crenshaw 2012: 1424). Intersectionality refers to the ways in which oppression and/or privilege are manifest across facets of identity, such as gender, race, sexuality, class, (dis) ability, neuroability, immigrant status and so on. Fourth wave feminism does seek to be more inclusively intersectional. However, even this most recent wave frequently reveals its own shortcomings regarding the legibility of race. As regularly documented, white feminists have created protests around causes without bringing women of colour into the discussion, such as the organization of the Women's March of 2017 (Tolentino). Even the Black Lives Matter movement, founded in 2013 by three queer Black women, Alicia Garza, Opal Tometi and Patrice Cullors, tends to erase its founders' methods and women-led ethos within the operations of its local chapters (Garza 2016).

Given these recent histories around divas and fourth wave feminism, it is no surprise that Black feminist stand-up comics are underrepresented in any mainstream measure of renown: fame, mic time, press coverage, comedy specials and so on. In 'The Fourth Wave of Feminism: Meet the Rebel Women', Kira Cochrane describes intersectionality, protest and comedy as intrinsic to fourth wave feminist movement, discussing white stand-up comic Bridget Christie, but cites no comics of colour (Cochrane 2013). This chapter seeks to explore artists of colour whose voices are frequently omitted and uncover the many performative strategies in which Black women stand-up comics – here, Sommore and Gina Yashere – recast the diva through onstage acts of performative self-actualization. There is scant scholarship on the subject of intersectional feminist stand-up comics of colour (that said, this has been the primary focus of my own work; another notable exception is the work of Katelyn Hale Wood (2021), whose book *Cracking Up: Black Feminist Comedy in the Twentieth and Twenty-First Century United States* examines Black feminist comic performance over the past sixty years). However, this chapter will examine intersectional Black feminist stand-up comedy in conjunction with diva citizenship and how Sommore and Yashere, two markedly different comics, perform ownership over their diva citizenry through their relationships with their audiences.

When Lauren Berlant observes, 'Diva citizenship occurs when a person stages a dramatic coup in a public sphere in which she does not have privilege', this can be ascribed to women of colour on any stage (Berlant 1997: 223). Sommore and Gina Yashere captivate through jokes over songs, however, insist their audiences see them in the wholeness of their intersectionality and possess their Black feminism in subverting a historically white, male space – in two very different stylistic and personal ways. Utilizing Kimberly Nichele Brown's definition of the 'Black Revolutionary Woman who cultivates Diva Citizenship through appearance as performance', Sommore and Gina Yashere recast their diva citizenry as craftswomen of comedy, garnering their adoration from the public sphere in the form of laughter (Brown 2010: 117).

Sommore: Recasting the Diva and Chandelier Status

Sommore, an African American, cisgender, heterosexual comic, created an introduction for her Netflix comedy special *Chandelier Status* (Kevin Layne, 2013) that features a voice-over recording of herself speaking to her audience, introducing a chandelier metaphor.[1] This metaphor begins with her observations of a current cultural phenomenon: those who are famous simply for being famous, regardless of talent and/or intellect. An excerpt from this introduction follows:

> We are living in a celebrity-obsessed society, and I believe there are very few stars. You see a star has a unique talent that's undeniable. Whereas, nowadays, a celebrity is someone who's popular. You can have a million Twitter followers and be considered a celebrity. There are no shortcuts to becoming a star. Now I won't get ahead of myself and call myself a star. But what I will call myself is a chandelier. A chandelier is a constant fixture; in this ever-changing world, it remains the same. It shines no matter what. Yeah, it gets older, but that just increases the value.

The chandelier becomes an extension of Sommore herself, and the first image we see is an opulent chandelier hanging over the stage. It sparkles and gleams, radiating pink tones; a great big, steady fixture that shines upon everything below. Suddenly, entrance music begins to play, and the chandelier lights up brighter than before, illuminating more chandeliers around it, complete with shimmering drapes and fabric. Theatrically designed and thematically uniform, the chandelier becomes a part of everything you see; and, when Sommore emerges onstage, it becomes clear that the chandelier is in concert with her dress, jewellery (chandelier-style earrings) and even her microphone, which is encrusted with black diamond-shaped jewels. Sommore wears a long, flowing black dress that contains the same jewels as her microphone. In a Diva Citizen act of self-actualization, Sommore has recast herself as a chandelier.

The first thing Sommore does is thank her audience for coming out to support her, despite the ways in which Hollywood has not been inclusive of her: 'For some reason Hollywood don't fuck with me like that and have me do a whole lot of movies, so most of the time I'm on my own protest: they don't put me in their shit, I don't put 'em in my shit. Any movie I ain't in, I bootleg that bitch.' She goes on to say that despite this, she's humbled she's been doing stand-up for more than twenty years.[2] Sommore's introduction of the chandelier, followed by the discussion of her career's longevity over decades and pointing to her invisibility rendered by Hollywood, speaks to the ways in which her talent persists against the comprehensive forces of racism.[3] She proceeds to spend the body of her television special dissecting the ways her class, Blackness and womanhood intersect. Sommore speaks to the larger notion that these intersections are what have prevented her from gaining a stronger foothold in Hollywood: she is not a star per se, but a chandelier. This act of self-definition is Sommore's foundational strategy for performing intersectionality in *Chandelier[4] Status*, and a core strategy of Black feminism (Collins 2000: 4). It is a 'dramatic coup' of the audience's expectations, and a recasting of the Star turn – in this instance, a Chandelier diva.

Sommore paints a picture of the intersections of Blackness, womanhood and class in her comedy both according to class distinctions among levels of wealth, as well as class distinctions of behaviour, drawing a line between the two. In so doing, Sommore's performative strategy demonstrates the social construction of race as dependent upon multiple intersections, and not limited to skin colour or ethnicity only. We encounter one of the first examples of this when Sommore describes 'n***er shit' – a term she uses to describe classed behaviour, while careful to note that this categorization lies outside of Blackness:

> One thing I ain't spending my money on is n***er shit. Oh . . . you know what n***er shit is. Now n***er shit ain't got nothing to do with you being Black. N***er shit is when you do something that's so fucked up, you've got to look at your damn self in the mirror and be like, 'Really? Really . . . ' Here's an example: my neighbor keeps trying to get me to invest in his rap career. This motherfucker is 47 years old with grey braids. I'm like, 'Really . . . are you going to be Grey-Z?'

In using the *n* word here, Sommore reclaims and reappropriates this word which has such toxic history as a derogatory, racist slur, in order to illuminate distinctions based on behaviour, not Blackness. In doing so, she takes power away from the word and reassigns its meaning.

Further on, Sommore addresses different behaviours which result from her intersections of class and Blackness, stemming from an economic position within US culture. She tackles the realities of living with her single mother, who would send her kids to the movies with pre-made tuna sandwiches instead of money to purchase popcorn. Sommore then complicates her discussion of class and race in reviewing her grade school years:

> But she [Sommore's mother] did make sacrifices to send me to some of the best schools she could afford. Most of my childhood years I went to predominantly white schools. So I didn't know the difference as a child in being Black or white. I really didn't. Until one Christmas holiday, I went home with a little white girl friend of mine. Saw some shit at the white people's house I hadn't ever seen in my life. They had their Christmas tree up – they had these things on the Christmas tree called popcorn balls. This was some of the jazziest shit I'd ever seen in my life . . . as soon as I got home: 'Get some popcorn, Mom, I've got something to show y'all!' We popped the popcorn, put the food colouring on it, put the syrup on it, rolled it up into a ball and hung it on the tree. We woke up the next morning . . . the roaches were stuck like *The Matrix* [acts out a roach sprawled onto the popcorn ball].[5]

Sommore comments on how the systematic, economic disenfranchisement of Black Americans has created two disparate realities for white and Black housing. The houses may be decorated similarly for the Christmas holiday, with trees and ornaments, but those similarities extend only so far: the physical realities of forced economic disenfranchisement reveal themselves anyhow within the living space. Sommore's performative strategy of showing how class and race intersect challenges pre-conceived race-based notions of education, family and more, by demonstrating how economic disparity can signify race.

While many comics have discussed cultural nuances of Black culture and white culture onstage, Sommore spends a great deal of her special discussing the nuanced distinctions between white women's culture and Black women's culture – noting, for example, that 'Black women work to keep their man ... white women work to keep their man happy.' Such observations highlight the privileges that white women hold in contrast to Black women. In so doing, Sommore distances herself from a catch-all feminism of women, making an argument for how Blackness shapes her experience and feminist concerns as a woman in North American culture. The comparison Sommore makes early on as 'not a star, but a chandelier', is one that reflects her attempt to define herself in a framework as not only a Black woman but a woman whose career is forced to remain outside of white-dominant, mainstream Hollywood, due to her Blackness. Black feminist scholar Patricia Hill Collins, writing in *Black Feminist Thought*, notes: 'Maintaining the invisibility of Black women and our ideas not only in the United States, but in Africa, the Caribbean, South America, Europe, and other places where Black women now live, has been critical in maintaining social inequities' (2000: 5). Sommore utilizes this point in her performance, using herself and her lack of inclusion by Hollywood as prime comparison examples, next to the likes of someone else who *has* achieved star status, despite lacking Sommore's own level of talent: celebrity Kim Kardashian.

Halfway through her comedy set, Sommore returns to discussing the idea of fame within contemporary North American culture, while sustaining her performative strategy around notions of visibility as the thematic through-line for *Chandelier Status*: 'We're living in a society where motherfuckers are famous with no talent. The next time you watch TV, look at it and ask, "Now how is this bitch famous?". . . My favorite untalented famous person is Kim Kardashian . . . she was known as the white girl with the big ass.' Sommore frames Kardashian as an example of a figure who has become a 'star', according to white mainstream entertainment, without the years of hard work that Sommore has invested in her own career as a comic performer. It is by no means coincidence that Sommore highlights Kardashian because Kardashian has been criticized for capitalizing on the fetishization of a stereotyped, hypersexualized Black woman's body. The exploitation of this stereotype dates back hundreds of years in white women's fashion (Victorian-era 'bums and rumps') and, ever more violently, to the forced display of Black women's bodies.[6] Saartjie 'Sarah' Baartman, for example, was a South African woman who was kidnapped and involuntarily positioned on display in touring circus 'freak' shows during the late eighteenth and nineteenth centuries – thus denigrating her body and features as that of someone outside Eurocentric, mainstream beauty standards (Chandler 2014).

It is not lost on critics that Kardashian, a non-Black woman, has used her posterior to help propel her to stardom, which only further exploits and reifies the stereotypes of Black women's bodies and their subjection to hyper-sexualization. Sally Kohn, a CNN political commentator writing for *The Washington Post*, stated: 'For centuries since (and likely before), Black women and their bodies have been smeared by stereotypes of hyper-sexuality simultaneously displayed and denigrated, their individuality and self-determination suppressed by the whims of the white male gaze' – also citing the life of Baartman (Kohn 2014). Therefore, when Sommore references Kardashian in *Chandelier Status*, her performative strategy draws attention to the fact that non-Black women are catapulted into fame, for reasons which do not seemingly derive from talent or hard work. Paradoxically, it is the exploitation of this very same Blackness which has kept Sommore on the margins.

Patricia Hill Collins cites Maria W. Stewart as an early Black feminist intellectual in the nineteenth century in North America, and who advocated for Black women to create their own self-definitions as a means of resistance. Collins notes: 'To Stewart, the power of self-definition was essential, for Black women's survival was at stake' (2000: 4). In *Chandelier Status*, Sommore creates her own self-definition as the ultimate Diva Citizen: a chandelier of the comedy stage. In so doing, the set, lights, microphone, costume – and, indeed, the ultimate theatre of *Chandelier Status* – all work to elevate Sommore's stand-up comedy, by focusing her audience's attentions on her intersectionality, as a Black woman who grew up classed as poor. Despite white-dominant sector entertainment holding her on the margins, Sommore's talent shines through – as visible to all. In this manner, Sommore owns her Black feminism to self-define the nature of her sparkle, not as a star but as a chandelier – disrupting the already-dominant white space in which she is performing, and so making her a true Diva Citizen (Brown 2010: 117). Sommore asserts: 'When you're a chandelier, you know you're a chandelier . . . and, believe me, they see you.'

Gina Yashere: Recasting the diva and hip-hop queerness

Another comic who creates diva citizenry through performative strategies that highlight her intersectional identity (across the Anglophone world, and parts of

Asia), and who also performs her identity within a unique, hip-hop expression, is Gina Yashere.

Yashere is a first-generation Black, British, queer comic, born to her single Nigerian mum in London, and who now lives in North America. In 2017, she released a comedy special titled *Ticking Boxes* (Paul M. Green). The marketing artwork for this tour, recording and so on, featured a picture of Yashere next to a series of boxes which have all been check-marked. These boxes read:

> Female
> Black
> British/Nigerian
> U.S. Legal Alien
> Ex-Vegan
> Gay/Queer

Her fashion is borne of hip-hop, as legible from portraits supporting the special: she sports large gold chains around her neck and left wrist, a large watch on the right, spiral sagaris ('tribal') earrings, and matching ink across her arms, which are placing a trendy, brimmed-hat upon her head.[7] The messaging is clear: this is a hip-hop comic with a unique voice, embodying an intersectionality which is not often seen on stand-up comedy stages. Yashere's positionality as a queer, Black woman who straddles multiple national identities not only informs her writing and self-curated style but also speaks to fans who can relate to and embody aspects of her persona. These fans frequent her performances, resulting in Yashere's 'divafication' (in Lister's terminology) and a recasting of the contemporary 'diva's' negative connotations into positive meanings:

> In particular, female fans seem eager to identify role models both to deify and emulate . . . women celebrating the parts of themselves that they can see in their chosen idols . . . this practice of 'divafication' seems to have removed the derogatory connotation of 'diva' . . . Diva worship appears to enable both the worshipped and the worshipper.
>
> (Lister 2001: 8)

This relationship is seen in action in the bonus footage of fan interviews, shot after a *Ticking Boxes* performance at the Brixton Academy, London. One fan, clearly divafying Yashere as she sports similar hip-hop fashion and close-shaven hair, approaches the interviewer. She points a fake finger gun at the sky, grabs the microphone, and fires off a few mock shots while shouting in a Caribbean accent: 'Bleeaap, bleeaap, bleeaap! Gina you were so excellent, and I like to joke about the same, yo – that was great . . . 'cause being a lesbian . . . what, I'm a lesbian . . . I'm single! You need to be hooking me up, bitches!' In point of fact, Yashere had also been previously interviewed by *Diva* magazine (billed as 'Europe's Leading Brand for LGBTQI Women and Non-Binary People') where she spoke of her experiences as a Black, queer, hip-hop and transnational figure (Czyzselska 2014).

Yashere's comedy includes sharp observations of American culture, told from the perspective of a woman navigating her sexuality, gender and a diasporic understanding of Blackness born outside of North America. When Yashere discusses race onstage, one of her performative strategies is to use her transnational otherness to satirize North American politics. In her 2014 special, *Laughing to America*, Yashere engages this strategy by calling attention to the Black diasporic community living within North America, disrupting the ways we perceive and stereotype aural Blackness (see Carpenter 2014: 24). While riding the subway in New York City, Yashere encounters a group of men from the Dominican Republic and affects confusion when they begin to speak Spanish: 'What? I couldn't believe what I was hearing. Black people have their own language here?!' When Paul Gilroy discusses an Afrocentric diasporic community, he notes that '[t]he distinctive historical experiences of this diaspora's populations have created a unique body of reflections on modernity and its discontents which is an enduring presence in the cultural and political struggles of their descendants today' (1995: 45). Gilroy's portraiture of the Black Atlantic is intrinsic to Yashere herself, with roots in both Nigeria and the UK. The humour in this particular joke points to the fact that not all Blackness is homogenic – nor is all Blackness tied to the same nation-state – and so the racial categorization of anyone remains subject to the hegemonic, cultural assumptions on the part of the observer undertaking such categorization. The intersections of nation-state, accent, ethnicity and so forth, create different possibilities for that which constitutes racialized 'Blackness'. In this instance, Yashere's joke plays on her faux ignorance of American Blackness, which itself is a diasporic community within North American borders.

Yashere deepens her audience's understanding of her intersectionality through these multiple, transnational lenses and is a branch of her performative strategies. In *Ticking Boxes*, she describes four separate sets of experiences upon entering a country while Black: in Indonesia, Australia, Malaysia and China. Each experience is radically different and wholly dependent on the ways she is intersectionally classed, raced, gendered and nationalized by her observer. In

Indonesia, she realizes she is the only Black person in the airport. She becomes detained and harassed by a customs worker until the worker's boss intervenes upon hearing Yashere's British accent. The boss tells the customs worker to let Yashere go 'because she is British,' and Yashere jokes: 'I've never in my life been so happy to be British . . . my African pride went out the window.' The implication is that British Blackness is classed above African Blackness, and likely other Blacknesses, due to class/wealth and nation-state wealth differences.

Yashere intersects her gender and sexuality into this composition when she discusses how, in certain cities across Asia, she is often the first woman to perform there – confusing the promoters with respect to how to entertain her in her off-hours (when they typically take male performers to brothels). In relating these conversations, she quotes a conversation she had with a promoter:

> We'll take you to four floors of whores . . . oh wait, sorry Gina!

Yashere responds:

> No, that's okay . . . let's see the 'four floors of whores' . . . you see: I'm not a fan of the penis.

This amusing response challenges gendered assumptions on the part of the promoter (and audience) around Yashere's sexuality and attitudes towards sex for pay. Brown, in *Writing the Black Revolutionary Diva*, deliberates '. . . the multiple consciousnesses of [Black] women, the psychological battle to come to terms with the interrelated pressures of sexism, racism, and oftentimes classism' (2010: 69). Again, Yashere has challenged us to view her in the fullness of her intersectedness, as per Brown's reading: her Blackness and transnationality, her gender, her class as a high-earning performer and her sexuality.

Another of Yashere's performative strategies includes decoding cultural practices that are normatively white. In effect, Yashere reflects whiteness back to white audiences, so that the absurdity of racial categorization is apparent to those who are privileged enough to never know discrimination through that lens. When Faedra Chatard Carpenter comments that 'theoretical concepts of white visibility and invisibility [offers white spectators] the opportunity to experience this paradoxical construction of whiteness for themselves' (2014: 81), this is the very experience that Yashere gives to her white audience members. In her performance in Brixton, for example – an area of London known, historically and currently, for its primarily Black and multinational population – she leans over to a white couple in the front row, and asks: 'Are you from Brixton? No, I know you're not.' By calling attention to the raced expectations of a white couple, we are reminded of the absurdity of placing socially constructed assumptions onto raced bodies – and, in conjunction with this, the horrific continued practice of forcing raced expectations onto Black bodies and bodies of colour. Tellingly, Yashere has established and maintains a large demographic of white women who divafy her as well, and so has become a performer who can toy with members of her audience as objects of her ridicule while retaining their admiration. Yashere's divadom is multi-faceted in this manner, recasting the diva as holding layered interactions with audiences – something the original Italian divas could not have shared with their (typically) racially homogeneous, Italian audiences.

When exploring the comedy of Yashere, a consideration of how she is intersectionally racialized, gendered and classed by some of her UK-based male critics is critical for a true perspective on how Blackness and womanhood intersectionally position Yashere. Their criticism attempts to diminish Yashere's Diva status by masculinizing her (a traditional practice of sexism and white supremacy). In the words of Yashere's kinder reviewers, she is often noted for her 'brash charm', something which Yashere herself has embraced as part of her comic persona (Casey 2017). Yashere affects brashness by employing vocal techniques which reflect the emphases of her word choices, particular syllables, the repetition of words and phrases, and an overall rhythm of expression for comic effect. She is not altogether vocally dissimilar from that of Lewis Black, for example – an American, white, cis-male comedian who has built his career on the comic persona of an angry man, who expresses a perpetual frustration with American politics. It would be reductive to call Yashere an 'angry' comic, however; at most, her vocal patterns reflect a comic indignation with her subject material at times, but they are also an effect through which she moderates her vocal timing, in order to enhance and punctuate her jokes at key moments. Simply put, she is no louder in volume than Lewis Black; or for that matter, the majority of white, male comics. Uniquely, however, Yashere is often the recipient of a twofold negative critique from reviewers, which these other comics are spared: both that her 'in-your-face style is more appropriate for American audiences', and the application of masculinized ('laddish') terms of reference for her. Both of these are utilized in performance reviews as a means of criticizing and reducing her work – see, for example, Hardy (2015: 11), or, with respect to her 2012 London show at the Underbelly Festival, Clive Davis in *The Times* wrote that it was '[n]oisy, laddish, and the comic equivalent of six pints of lager and lime, [and] she obsessively pursued the lowest common denominator' (Davis 2012: 12).

These responses are also related to the intersection of Yashere's queerness and Blackness; white female comics from the UK, such as Bridget Christie and Josie Long, use similar vocal patterns and gendered presentation without experiencing this kind of critique. Additionally, the masculine characterization is intrinsically tied to queer and Black histories, wherein Black women and gay women are continuously, derogatorily painted as masculine – to the benefit of white supremacist patriarchal hegemony (which maintains power through the suppression of anyone other, such as Black and gay women) (Butler 1990; Covington 2011). In his writing for *The Times*, reviewer Alex Hardy suggested that Yashere's style might be appropriate for North America, but is 'not sure that it excels here [in England]' – denoting a transnational layer of further disparagement (Hardy 2015).[8]

The language used by Yashere's critics is a disappointing reminder that no matter the content of her comedy, she will continue to be measured in relation to her Blackness, gender, sexuality, class and even transnational subject. In grappling with Yashere and her criticism, it is important to consider the ways in which bodies of comics are read according to the very same hegemonic ideology to which Yashere draws our attention – an intentional, performative strategy aimed at inviting her audiences to understand her more fully. This understanding, arguably, is what has prompted Yashere's fans to crown her a diva – not, as previously noted, the white, Italian diva of opera performance, but a diva reborn as a queer, hip-hop, Black woman, stirring her audiences with laughter rather than music.

Conclusion

Both comics explored in this chapter utilize their own performative strategies to convey their identity in wholeness, generating profound diva worship from their audiences. Sommore's work self-fashions and controls the terms of her intersectional Black feminism by performing her self-defined divadom, and by providing audiences with a metaphor to understand the enormity of her presence through her own terms. Yashere's work negotiates her intersectional identity across national borders, but consistently maintains her spirit of hip-hop, queer diva – no matter how Blackness, womanhood and sexuality may be read onto her body. My aim in this chapter is to demonstrate that while white feminism has the privilege of believing it fights for all women, these two women have created a more inclusive feminism on the stage, and one that performs in the spirit of hip-hop and its subversion of the status quo. Sommore and Yashere are not divas in the Italian tradition, or even as aligned with the image of the contemporary diva, akin to powerful pop singers such as Mariah Carey and Beyoncé, who both emanate vocal and financial power. Sommore and Yashere recast themselves as a different kind of diva: the Black woman stand-up comedian, whose prowess on the stage demands the audience understand her personhood fully. They are the comic diva who demands that you laugh with her and not at her, who captures your diva worship and divafication and who makes an unseen Black woman be seen, in her true image.

Notes

1. Sommore and Wayne Baxley have writing credits for *Chandelier Status*.
2. Sommore is known for having been one of four comics featured in *Queens of Comedy*, a filmed performance showcasing the stand-up comedy of Sommore, Laura Hayes, Adele Givens, and Mo'Nique (Steve Purcell, 2001).
3. Mike Epps, in his 2015 special *Don't Take it Personal*, express a similar sentiment about his long-time consistency working in Hollywood, while never gaining mainstream, widespread visibility due to racism.
4. The punchline here is a word play joke, referencing the popular rap artist Jay-Z.
5. The film *The Matrix* was written and directed by the Wackowskis (Lana and Lilly), and released in 1999.
6. Bums and rumps were clothing accessories which accentuated the derriere in European/North American, Victorian-era white women's fashion, placed underneath dresses. These were rooted in white women's jealousy of the fetishized sexualization of Black women's derrieres; see Gordon-Chipembere (2011).
7. The use of terms 'tribal' or 'ethnic' to describe jewellery design is, I note, problematic; these words frequently refer to multiple distinct ethnicities and cultures, primarily of Bali, Kenya, Tibet, Thailand, Ethiopia and others. As noted in *Jewelry Making Journal*: 'The problem is that "tribal" is a loaded term . . . to socio logists/anthropologists/prehistorians it's either a group with a specific type of kin structure or the level of civilization two or three places below the city-state. It also refers to Native American ethnic groups in the United States' (Clarey, no date). I infer a hip-hop style from Yashere's fashion choices based on well-documented hip-

hop fashion descriptions, as often incorporating '. . . thick gold chains, retro-style coats and eccentric headwear, a hat tip to hip-hop's early days in the 1970s and early '80s' (Berlinger 2018).

8 To unpack this statement further would lend itself to another chapter's worth of study comparing the North American and UK experience, and epistemological investigations of 'lowbrow' versus 'highbrow' humour. Stereotypes still abound, correlating one's level of education or nationhood with personal taste in comedy and other entertainment. For such a discussion, see Claesenns and Dhoest (2010).

Reference

Baumgardner, J. (2011), *F'em: Goo, Gaga and Some Thoughts on Balls*, New York City: Seal Press.

Berlant, L. (1997), *The Queen of America Goes to Washington City: Essays on Sex and Citizenship*, Durham: Duke University Press.

Berlinger, M. (2018), 'How Hip-Hop Fashion Went from the Streets to High Fashion', *Los Angeles Times*, 26 January. Available online: https://www.latimes.com/entertainment/la-et-ms-ig-hip-hop-fashion-streets-couture-20180125-htmlstory.html (accessed 1 November 2022).

Bernstein, E. (2013), 'Why Divas Need Make No Apology: Demanding People Get a Bad Rap, But Behind the Tantrums and the Drama Lie Lessons in Success', *Wall Street Journal*, 8 April. Available online: https://www.wsj.com/articles/SB10001424127887323550604578410522536037666 (accessed 1 November 2022).

Brown, K. N. (2010), *Writing the Black Revolutionary Diva: Women's Subjectivity and the Decolonizing Text*, Bloomington: Indiana University Press.

Butler, J. (1990), *Gender Trouble: Feminism and the Subversion of Identity*, London: Routledge.

Carpenter, F. C. (2014), *Coloring Whiteness: Acts of Critique in Black Performance*, Ann Arbor: University of Michigan Press.

Casey, V. D. (2017), 'Gina Yashere: A Queer Queen of Comedy Brightening the World', *Tagg Magazine*, 19 October. Available online: https://taggmagazine.com/gina-yashere/ (accessed 1 November 2022).

Chandler, D. L. (2014), 'Little Known Black History Fact: Sarah "Saartjie" Baartman', *Black America* Web. Available online: https://blackamericaweb.com/2014/11/17/little-known-black-history-fact-sarah-saartjie-baartman/ (accessed 1 November 2022).

Claessens, N. and A. Dhoest (2010), 'Comedy Taste: Highbrow/Lowbrow Comedy and Cultural Capital', *Perceptions: Journal of Audience & Reception Studies*, 7 (1): 49–72.

Clarey, C. (no date), 'What Does "Tribal Jewelry" Really Mean?', *Jewelry Making Journal*. Available online: https://jewelrymakingjournal.com/what-does-tribal-jewelry-really-mean/ (accessed 1 November 2022).

Cochrane, K. (2013), 'The Fourth Wave of Feminism: Meet the Rebel Women', *The Guardian*, 10 December. Available online: http://www.theguardian.com/world/2013/dec/10/fourth-wave-feminism-rebel-women (accessed 1 November 2022).

Collins, P. H. (2000), *Black Feminist Thought*, London: Routledge.

Covington, J. (2011), *Crime and Racial Constructions: Cultural Misinformation About African Americans in Media and Academia*, Washington DC: Lexington Books.

Crenshaw, K. W. (2012), 'From Private Violence to Mass Incarceration: Thinking Intersectionally About Women, Race, and Social Control', *UCLA Law Review*, 59: 1418–72.

Czyzselska, J. (2014), 'She's Hustling: Out Lesbian Comic Gina Yashere on How New York Celebrates Ambition and Why She Loves UK Audiences', *Diva*, October, 58–9.

Davis, C. (2012), 'Gina Yashere: Comedy', *The Times*, May 3, 12.

Garza, A., P. Cullors and O. Tometi (2016), 'Black Lives Matter: Official Website'. Available online: http://blacklivesmatter.com/about/ (accessed 1 November 2022).

Gilroy, P. (1995), *The Black Atlantic: Modernity and Double-Consciousness*, Boston: Harvard University Press.

Gordon-Chipembere, N. (2011), *Representation and Black Womanhood: The Legacy of Sarah Baartman*, New York: Springer Publishing.

Hardy, A. (2015), 'Review: Gina Yashere', *The Times*, March 10, 11.

Kohn, S. (2014), 'How the Kardashians Exploit Racial Bias for Profit', *The Washington Post*, 18 November. Available online: https://www.washingtonpost.com/posteverything/wp/2014/11/18/the-kardashians-arent-just-trashy-theyre-dangerous/?utm_term=.3a6c06c0d19a (accessed 1 November 2022).

Kooijman, J. (2019). 'Fierce, Fabulous, and In/Famous: Beyoncé as Black Diva', *Popular Music and Society*, 42 (1): 6–21.

Lister, L. (2001), 'Divafication: The Deification of Modern Female Pop Stars', *Popular Music and Society*, 25 (3–4): 1–10.

Tolentino, J. (2017), 'The Somehow Controversial Women's March on Washington', *The New Yorker*, 18 January. Available online: http://www.newyorker.com/culture/jia-tolentino/the-somehow-controversial-womens-march-on-washington (accessed 1 November 2022).

Wood, K. H. (2021), *Cracking Up: Black Feminist Comedy in the Twentieth and Twenty-First Century United States*, Iowa City: University of Iowa Press.

Independent women

The impact of pop divas on stand-up comedy

Ellie Tomsett and Nathalie Weidhase

Introduction

This chapter will focus on the ways in which the enduring cultural fascination with the pop diva can be witnessed within contemporary stand-up comedy performed by women. Comedy requires shared understanding upon which to base joking – without awareness of the underpinning cultural or societal concepts being subverted in joking, access to the humorous meaning is impossible. During a period of heightened awareness of popular and celebrity feminisms, and the dominance of neoliberal female empowerment narratives, comedians have been able to draw on more direct intertextual references to the lives and work of pop divas within their routines. Beyoncé is perhaps the most referenced pop diva on the comedy stage, and references to, critiques and celebrations of her work and performance persona have been included in sets by comedians such as Bridget Christie, Miranda Hart and Katherine Ryan. In this chapter we argue that references to Beyoncé's diva performances may exist on a spectrum from admiration to critique, and we look at an example from each end of this spectrum. We highlight the ways in which these references to Beyoncé's work are often not just straightforward but also reveal the problematic racial blind spots in mainstream white feminism and forms of appropriation. Finally, we consider some of the commonalities of the career trajectories of women in both the music and comedy industries.

Our arguments are based on the textual analysis of recorded performances of two established female contemporary UK stand-up comedians, Jayde Adams and Luisa Omielan. Both comics had worked on the live comedy circuit for many years before their performances were recorded and disseminated to wider audiences (e.g. on the BBC and Amazon Prime). Close attention has been paid to the ways in which Beyoncé is not only discussed but also how visual signifiers from her music videos and performances are utilized on the comedy stage. We argue that this intertextual referentiality is one of the many ways in which diva performances make a lasting impact on popular culture. At the same time, we acknowledge that this approach to analysis does not capture the full artistic experience of each complete stand-up set. Multilayered comedic engagements with feminism and femininity are evident in both sets, which we take into account as context, but cannot analyse fully in the space of this book chapter.

Originating from the Italian 'diva', meaning female deity, the term diva in popular culture is usually used to describe a female star, originally in opera, but also the theatre stage, film and popular music. Transforming her personal suffering into art, the diva transgresses normative configurations of womanhood (Bradshaw 2008; Doty 2007; Weidhase 2015a). In contemporary popular culture, diva, when directed at Black women in particular, often has negative connotations (Springer 2007) and Beyoncé has remarked on the ways in which the term is instrumentalized against her (Kooijman 2019). Beyoncé's career trajectory – starting out in the mid-1990s with girl group Destiny's Child and focusing on her solo career after the band's final album in 2004 – has regularly been framed 'within the narrative of the black diva leaving her singing group behind to achieve superstardom' (Kooijman 2019: 6).

Beyoncé is a hip-hop and pop icon. Her cultural and artistic significance lies in the ways in which she embodies and performs gender, race and sexuality in popular music (Kooijman 2019). While her performance in front of a large, illuminated 'FEMINIST' sign at the MTV Video Music Awards in 2014 is often seen as her coming out moment, her work with Destiny's Child and early solo work are equally important for the ways in which she performed and spoke 'to Black working and middle class sensibilities while fulfilling her dynamic roles as both a hip hop belle and a US exotic other globally' (Durham 2012: 25). At the same time, she must

> negotiate the commodification-empowerment divide along gender lines... and also along racial lines, moving between a position of the politics of respectability on the one hand, which prescribes the 'acceptable' way black women are to present themselves in public, and a position of sexually [sic] provocativeness, yet without reinforcing persistent stereotypes of the sexually unrestrained black woman, on the other.
>
> (Kooijman 2019: 13)

The diva is also often seen as an object of gay white male imagination and worship (O'Neill 2007), a potentially outdated notion (Kooijman 2019). Beyoncé, too, is considered a gay icon (Kooijman 2019) and is noted for her devoted fandom, the Beyhive. While the diva thrives on and cherishes the adoration of her audience, divas also offer their audience inspiration on how to live a life that transcends normative conceptions of gender, sexuality and race (O'Neill 2007). This chapter, too, is concerned with the diva audience, in this case, the ways in which female comedians engage with Beyoncé's work on stage. We will focus on the ways in which female comedians incorporate the diva spectacle and diva worship into their performances, and how Beyoncé in particular is mobilized as both inspiration and 'danger' to the feminist project.

Divas in comic material

An initial question to consider might be why divas are of interest to comics when preparing their material? Fundamentally, humour requires a shared understanding or collective awareness between performer and audience to be in place, as 'in order for an audience to laugh, some form of identification (or disidentification) must occur' (Gilbert 2004: 163). Unless both parties have all the information needed to interpret the joke *as a joke*, it is going to fail to provoke the intended laughter. Comedians develop their routines by trying out jokes with live audiences and deciding, based on the humour responses they evoke, whether a topic is a fertile ground for humour and to keep or scrap the material. Choosing an obscure or niche reference point when a performer is unaware of the audience's cultural backgrounds is a risky business. As divas are well-known public figures whose behaviour fills column inches and whose music and performance styles are widely (though not universally) recognizable, they are a relatively safe bet. This could of course be said of any person or group holding a celebrity status, however, the stereotypical hyperbolic behaviour associated with divas (as considered in the introduction to this volume) means that the opportunity for ridicule is inherently ingrained in their public personas. Some divas themselves are aware of this and perform self-parody in relation to their diva-like behaviour. An example here is Mariah Carey's inclusion in a 2019 UK Walkers Crisps advert, the narrative for which is contingent on awareness of her 'demanding' and 'irrational' behaviour.

Double contends that in addition to the intention to provoke laughter, stand-up comedy 'puts a *person* on display in front of an audience ... involves *direct communication* between performer and audience . . . like a conversation' and finally that it 'happens in the present tense, in the here and now. It *acknowledges the performance situation*' (Double 2014: 19, our italics). Thus, for a woman performing solo on stage, in the traditional stand-up comedy performance mode outlined by Double, bringing a well-known diva character into the routine can be achieved fairly easily. Mimicry through impressions or replication of performance behaviours such as singing voice or dance moves, along with costumes referencing the diva in question, are all relatively easy to achieve with low/no budget as a solo performer.

The contemporary UK live comedy circuit includes a significant number of women comics dealing in explicitly feminist or postfeminist comic material (Tomsett 2018). Divas have clear links to celebrity feminisms, and therefore the inclusion of rhetorical positions taken by divas is an obvious choice. Pop stars who fall into the diva category are among the most well-known self-identified feminists of the present day (e.g. Taylor Swift, Beyoncé, Miley Cyrus). To provide clear examples here we will focus on the work of two women comics currently working on the live circuit in the UK. Both have recorded their shows for media outlets and incorporate references to Beyoncé into their material.

Our first example is Jayde Adams, a comedian, actress and presenter from Bristol, UK. Adams is, in addition to her solo work as a comic, a self-taught singer and co-presents live comedy night (and podcast) *Amusical* with Kiri Pritchard-McLean and Dave Cribb. The premise for *Amusical* involves comedians celebrating their favourite musicals by singing (with varying degrees of professionalism) songs from West End/Broadway shows. Adams' show *Serious Black Jumper* was recorded for Amazon Prime in 2019 (released in 2020). The show was originally entitled *The Ballad of Kylie Jenner's Old Face* when on tour live but was changed for legal reasons for the recording. Prior to this particular solo show Adams, a comic vocal about her working-class identity, was known for spectacle in terms of costume and staging. Notably, Adams' first solo show in 2016 entitled *31* directly referenced pop icon Adele's album *21* (2011), a nod to Adams' work as an Adele impersonator. Adams' time performing in sequins and glitter aligns her performance persona in many ways with diva traditions through allusions to drag performance, with many reviewers of her earlier work citing cabaret performance (e.g. Ensall 2016). Adams is associated with body-positive comedy, as typified by her contemporary, Danish comic Sofie Hagen. Adams is also therefore aligned with the operatic divas of the past who also embodied performance talent but were stereotypically known for being fat.

Our second example, Luisa Omielan, is a critically and commercially successful comic who developed *What Would Beyoncé Do?* in 2013. Omielan toured the solo show for several years nationally and internationally before finally recording the performance for dissemination via BBC3 in 2017. When advertised by the BBC, much was made of Omielan being the 'voice' of millennial single women and the romantic comedy themes of the show were foregrounded. The performance strikes a postfeminist tone in that 'the context of postfeminist humour is the world of leisure and consumption rather than politics or work' and the focus is on 'sexuality as a means of empowerment and goal achievement' (Shifman and Lemish 2010: 875). To set the scene for audiences in the auditorium (which Ellie experienced as an audience member for Omielan's show) a hen-night feel was deliberately created (think pink, glitter, loud sing-alongs to pop music and group dancing) to bond the predominantly female spectators into a coherent group – repeatedly referred to throughout the performance as Omielan's 'bitches'. Omielan's Polish heritage is often explored through the inclusion of routines about her family, especially her mother, whose broken English accent she affectionately mimics.

As noted in the introduction, comedy performed by women that include references to divas is relatively commonplace. The solo shows of these two performers were selected as examples as we believe they exist at two ends of the spectrum of engagement with Beyoncé in current comedy by women stand-ups. Independently we watched the shows several times and made notes in relation to the performance style, content and inclusion of feminist positions. We then discussed our findings and worked towards synthesizing an argument which included an identification of the spectrum we discuss here. It is worth noting that our interpretation of the humour of these performances varied, but our overall analysis of the performances as indicative of wider tropes did not. We have a very critical reading of Beyoncé's star text at one end, and at the other uncomplicated hero worship. Both these positions are complexified when held by those who do not share the lived experiences of Black women, and (despite other intersectional dynamics such as class) undoubtedly benefit from white privilege. This inclusion of Beyoncé within comedy is of course a reflection of wider media discussion or Beyoncé's work, body, branding and business decisions in relation to contemporary understandings of feminism. As Gilbert reminds us, comedy 'is a cultural barometer, revelatory and liberating' (2004: xvii). Thus, we present these examples as indications of what the cultural weather is like in relation to pop music divas in the UK.

Jayde Adams

Adams can be seen to exist at the 'criticism' end of our proposed spectrum. The premise of Adams' show is an exploration of the way high-profile women (Beyoncé, Jameela Jamil, Kylie Jenner) use their platforms to espouse certain views. The humorous critiques of these women centre on the discrepancy between their lived experiences or behaviours and the principles they claim to embody. Beyoncé's feminist credentials are questioned in light of her sexualised performances. Jamil's I Weigh (@i_weigh) campaign for body positivity is mocked as Adams highlights that Jamil typifies many mainstream body and beauty norms. Lastly, Jenner (the titular character of the original show) is ridiculed for being promoted as the 'youngest self-made billionaire' when she is from one of the most famous and wealthy families in America.

Adams' inclusion of Beyoncé into the routine rests solely on a take-down of the diva's complex relationship to feminism and the seeming contradiction between her sexualized performances and the political principles of the feminist movement. Beyoncé is introduced into the routine through Adams recounting a trip to a Beyoncé concert. She admits that she was 'not into it initially, but I liked the hand song' – a reference to the track 'Single Ladies (Put a Ring on It)' (2008) and its accompanying choreography. As the story continues Adams considers how she tried hard to appreciate the concert but was aghast at the discrepancy between the heavily made-up and spectacularly costumed Beyoncé, and her husband Jay-Z's appearance on stage in an anorak. When the singer revealed the now well-known giant 'FEMINIST' sign Adams explains that she was glad she took a friend with her to the concert as 'had I not taken him along I would have been like that one guy in Germany in 1936 thinking "something's not right here"'. Here Adams is, for comic purposes, comparing Beyoncé's brand of feminism to Nazism. She continues to clarify that 'the images and message aren't matching up with each other . . . I could stand in front of a sign saying Weight Watchers, wouldn't mean I am doing it though'.

While Adams' show is more recent than Omielan's, this particular line of criticism of Beyoncé in comic material, and popular culture more broadly, is not new. Comedian Bridget Christie made similar (albeit notably less contentious) points about Beyoncé in her Edinburgh Comedy Award-winning show *A Bic For Her* in 2013. Christie compared Beyoncé to the late UK Prime Minister Margaret Thatcher, highlighting that both openly rejected the term feminism (Thatcher famously referring to it as poison, Beyoncé rejecting the label initially

– in a time before *Beyoncé* [2013]). Christie made the point that while both women were incredibly successful in their fields and we can respect them for that, we do not need to claim them for feminism – not all women by default are feminists (Tomsett 2017). Our argument is not that Beyoncé should be above criticism, more generally or within comic material. Both of us have concerns about her role in Uber, a company with appallingly bad working conditions for a majority Black and minority ethnic workforce, for example (Butler 2021), and we acknowledge that Beyoncé's performances always also operate within and profit from capitalist modes of production (hooks 2016). However, critiquing Beyoncé's feminism based on her supposedly hypersexual performance on stage reveals a lack of intersectional thinking in white mainstream and celebrity feminism (Weidhase 2015b).

Western mainstream feminism has consistently foregrounded the needs and views of white cisgender women as explored extensively by Alison Phipps (2020). It has actively and passively excluded Black women and women of colour and often presented a homogenized view of women's lives that did not take account of the differences in women's experiences (Crenshaw 1991). Critiques of Beyoncé, who did not explicitly embrace the term 'feminist' until 2013 (but did engage with feminist topics such as financial autonomy in songs like 'Independent Woman Pt. 1' [2000]), often focus on the tension between supposed feminist beliefs and perceived hypersexual performance on stage. Here it is necessary to account for both the particularities of the pop stage, which has always been a space for supposedly outrageous expressions of sexuality (Whiteley 2006) and Beyoncé's embodiment on stage as a Black woman. White mainstream feminist thought may thus be an insufficient intellectual framework to critique Beyoncé. Black feminist approaches such as hip-hop feminism refuse 'easy and essentialist political stances about what is right or wrong or who or what gets to be called feminist' (Durham, Cooper and Morris 2013: 723) and reject respectability politics, while talking about 'both the pleasures and pain of sex and sexuality outside a singular heteropatriarchal lens while also looking at the nexus of hierarchical structures that shape our sexual selves' (Durham, Cooper and Morris 2013: 724). Thus, they offer both a critique of white feminist mainstream approaches and provide a more intersectional analytical framework suitable to make sense of diva performances on the pop stage.

When Adams critiques the way in which Beyoncé dances with Jay-Z (her husband) in the live performance, mimicking sexualized dance moves, the argument being made is that this presentation is not compatible with women's empowerment. When we consider the way in which Black women's bodies have long been sexualized to produce capital for others (Collins 2004), the very opportunity for a Black woman to control the way her body is seen and sexualized is in and of itself political. There are plenty of examples of white popstars displaying similar behaviours to Beyoncé, yet we can see Adams' comedy as symptomatic of social handling of Black women, in that they are held to a higher standard. Therefore, in addition, the lack of balance with white examples (see Snapes [2020] on Lana Del Rey's recent example of this phenomenon) further enhances the critique's problematic nature. Potentially the show becomes another media portrayal that is disproportionately negative about Black women. Thus, these critiques often reveal more about the whiteness of mainstream feminism than the actual performance of the diva.

Luisa Omielan

Omielan's solo show *What Would Beyoncé Do?*, as the title suggests, exists at the other, drastically less critical end of this spectrum. Within the show, Beyoncé is held up as an inspiration to Omielan (and by extension the audience) and portrayed as a universally aspirational model of womanhood. Omielan thus reproduces deifying elements of diva reception and mirrors some of the common fandom receptions of Beyoncé's work (Toone, Edgar and Ford 2017). The show intersperses more traditional stand-up routines (direct address and storytelling) with musical sing-alongs to Beyoncé's back catalogue, dance routines and audience interaction. Similar to Adams, Omielan's own performance borrows from the diva's dramatic embodiment on stage, and a close relationship with her audience. The content of this show is highly sexual, both in terms of the language choices and narrative joke-work (which involves detailed description of [hetero] sexual acts) and physical performance (which includes lap-dancing on members of the audience and miming sexual positions). Omielan makes full use of the comic licence afforded to stand-up comedians to engage with cultural taboos. In some ways, then, Omielan's work mirrors hip-hop feminism's (and Beyoncé's) embrace of messiness and performance of femininity and female sexuality. However, as we detail as follows, this often veers into problematic territory and the appropriation of Black femininity.

Beyoncé is introduced into the narrative of the show early on when Omielan reflects on the difficulties of moving back in with her mother and brother following a relationship breakup. Omielan describes considering how Beyoncé would act in the situation she finds herself in (in this case searching in the garden for an appropriate stick with which to unclog a toilet). Thus, Beyoncé's arrival within the narrative of the show is in relation to notions of overcoming adversity in hard times. Omielan uses Beyoncé as a cultural touchstone through which to discuss the need to develop resilience and self-reliance in order to deal with various emotionally challenging events. Omielan refers to her breakup and her brother's suicide attempt in relation to this. This neoliberal self-actualization is in line with the empowerment messages contained within 'Independent Women Pt. 1', a track included in the show and used for humour when positioning Omielan as a modern independent woman, yet one not paying rent, living at home and thus to some extent still financially reliant on her mother. It is in this way, as well as through the inclusion of the song 'Single Ladies (Put a Ring on It)' that the contradictions of mainstream postfeminist personhood are included in this show without systematic critique. Beyoncé's self-proclaimed independence is foregrounded in Omielan's routines (alongside Omielan's wish to emulate this) while the contradictory need to engage with capitalism through ownership of possessions/property and (arguably) people through heteropatriarchal norms of marriage, are presented as uncomplicated, universal and framed as aspirational.

The issue at the god-like worship end of the spectrum of Beyoncé's inclusion into stand-up comedy by women is that Beyoncé is presented without nuance or critical examination of her work. Omielan presents Beyoncé as a hero-like figure that inspires imitation, and this occasionally tips over into what could be considered cultural appropriation when done without reflection on Beyoncé's Black identity, or the specific racial context of Black women in the United States. One of the ways in which this show can be seen as trading in racial stereotypes is Omielan's use of comic accents. An example early on in the routine is when she mimics an East Asian beauty therapist (no specific country is mentioned, but it is clearly coded in this way) by saying with a pronounced accent 'ahh you want your chin done too?' Yes, of course, comedy is a form within which boundaries of acceptable behaviour and taboo language can be explored (as part of comic licence, see Double 2014) but moments like this, within a show so connected to the work of Black performer, whose race is being ignored, is problematic.

Omielan's use of American accents is particularly concerning in the way that she seems unaware of some of the connotations of these voices. Her use of a southern US accent when *pretending to be Beyoncé* (who is from Houston, Texas), for a section with dialogue that is overtly humble and grateful for success, is arguably evocative of the Black mammy stereotype (Sewell 2013). Putting on a southern American accent, in general, is clearly not offensive, however, when a white comic is performing in the character of a Black woman, the southern US context and its history of segregation and slavery is relevant. A very similar Americanized accent is also deployed when portraying an interaction with a job centre official when 'signing on' for benefits (although in this instance, despite the accent, Omeilan is playing a version of herself). In this job centre section the low-status character (Omielan) is evoked through an Americanized pleading twang as well as stooping and submissive postures.

It is notable that Omielan has been accused of culturally appropriating aspects of Black culture in relation to this show. The imagery produced for the poster for the original tour shows Omielan with big curly afro-like hair and hoop earrings clearly emulating a hip-hop aesthetic. Comedian Dane Baptiste has been very critical of the way comedians cherry-pick aspects of Black culture while not engaging with the political struggles of Black people. Without directly naming Omielan, during the 2020 Black Lives Matter Protests across the globe, following the killing of George Floyd, Baptiste argued that comedians

> co-opt Black culture when it suits them – whether its talking about pop stars du jour, or they want to be like Whitney or Mariah, or I guess Beyoncé being the star du jour. They'll co-opt that or they'll co-opt hip-hop music . . . but when it comes to issues that are a plague and the plight of Black women they now become strangely silent, or they are waiting for the green light from their agents or managers.
>
> (Radio 5 Live 2020)

Therefore, Omielan's approach to incorporating Beyoncé into her work is arguably just as problematic as being overly critical (as is evident in the work of Adams). Even though a significant amount of *What Would Beyoncé Do?* is about overcoming challenges and barriers to success, the fact that there are specific challenges that are unique to Black experience (e.g. having to deal with structural racism) remains totally unacknowledged. The attraction of the audience to this show, especially in the early days of its run when Omielan was little-known, is linked to the success and name recognition of Beyoncé as a Black diva. In many ways then this could be seen as indicative of the way that white women have used or co-opted the work of Black women for their own commercial gain – it is certainly no surprise that others within the comedy industry have picked up on the racial dynamics of this marketing strategy.

Conclusion

In this chapter we have analysed the work of two comedians and discussed how this comic material can be seen as part of a wider cultural referencing of Beyoncé (and diva figures more broadly). There are, however, wider similarities between the careers of women comics and pop divas than a simple content analysis may demonstrate and it is to these broader ideas that we now turn as part of the conclusion of our argument.

Both stand-up comedy performance and pop music performance (as a solo artist) are similar in that they are examples of embodied art forms, where a body is placed before an audience to demonstrate a specific skill (e.g. musical or comic talent). In this way both the positive opportunities for self-definition, as well as the negative challenges/ barriers that women face in these professions (such as gendered aesthetic scrutiny, policing of feminine behaviours, sexualization) are comparable. When performing as either a stand-up comic or pop diva there is no fourth wall between the stage and the audience, and interaction is a key part of the experience of seeing these performances live (explored in relation to arena concerts by Spelman 2016). This close performer-audience relationship enabled by the performance space mirrors the diva's close relationship with her fans. The interaction in the current digital environment is also part of the building of fan communities. Omielan provides a good comic example of this as she makes use of social media platforms such as Facebook Live, Twitter and Instagram to connect with fans outside of the live environment to maintain a presence.

In this way both roles require performers to put a version of themselves on display for audiences (especially when undertaking 'traditional' stand-up comedy as our two examples evidence) and to embody and manipulate specific identifiable traits, but in different ways. Diva status is arguably contingent upon being 'exceptional' in some way (there is only one Houston, Franklin, Turner, Carey etc.). Comedians however rely on their similarities to their audiences, physically and experientially, for their comic material. There needs to be an element of recognition with the content of a comedian's jokes, similar to the themes of popular music being overwhelmingly related to shared human experiences such as love/relationships and so on. However, this recognition may also result in the reproduction of problematic tropes about Black women, reflecting and feeding into existing inequalities in comedy and the creative industries.

It is understandable why women comics might see their own experiences reflected in the treatment and challenges experienced by their musical counterparts and thus decide to integrate these into their material. Both comedy and popular music as part of the wider creative industries are still dominated overwhelmingly by white men in positions of power. It is therefore no surprise that these industries have similarities in their treatment of up-and-coming talent (especially young women) and established artists who are not immune to these gendered and raced power dynamics. Both the comedy and the music industries in the wake of the #MeToo movement have had high-profile scandals involving abuses of power and sexual assault. At the same time, the popularity of diva performances in stand-up comedy demonstrates the lasting impact divas such as Beyoncé have on popular culture. While we appreciate these engagements are framed as comic in our examples, they are symptomatic of wider engagements with Beyoncé across the spectrum we have identified.

This chapter has demonstrated that these similarities between women comedians and musical artists are not only individual but also structural and industrial. The reception of a Black diva such as Beyoncé in a sphere of mainstream, white-dominated aspect of popular culture reveals not just problematic forms of cultural appropriation in the creation of comedy performance, but arguably is also indicative of the continued lack of intersectional thinking in mainstream popular feminism.

Reference

BBC Radio 5 Live (2020), [radio broadcast], BBC Radio 5, 2 June. Available online: https://twitter.com/bbc5live/status/1267848452626505728?s=20 (accessed 21 July 2020).

Bradshaw, M. (2008), 'Devouring the Diva: Martyrdom as Feminist Backlash in *The Rose*', *Camera Obscura*, 23 (1): 69–87.

Butler, S. (2021), 'Uber Facing New UK Driver Claims of Racial Discrimination', *The Guardian*, 6 October. Available online: https://www.theguardian.com/technology/2021/oct/06/uber-facing-new-uk-driver-claims-of-racial-discrimination (accessed 8 November 2022).

Collins, Patricia Hill (2004), *Black Sexual Politics: African Americans, Gender, and the New Racism*, London: Routledge.

Crenshaw, K. (1991), 'Mapping the Margins: Intersectionality, Identity Politics, and Violence against Women of Color', *Stanford Law Review*, 43 (6): 1241–99.

Doty, A. (2007), 'Introduction: There's Something about Mary', *Camera Obscura*, 22 (2): 1–8.

Double, O. (2014), *Getting the Joke: The Inner Workings of Stand-up Comedy*, second edn, London: Bloomsbury.

Durham, A. (2012), '"Check On It": Beyoncé, Southern Booty, and Black Femininities in Music Video', *Feminist Media Studies*, 12 (1): 35–49.

Durham, A., B. Cooper and S. M. Morris (2013), 'The Stage Hip Hop Feminism Built: A New Directions Essay', *Signs: Journal of Women in Culture and Society*, 38 (3): 721–37.

Ensall, J. (2016), 'Jayde Adams: 31', *The List*, 19 August. Available online: https://edinburghfestival.list.co.uk/article/83742-jayde-adams-31/ (accessed 17 July 2020).

Gilbert, J. R. (2004), *Performing Marginality: Humor, Gender and Cultural Critique*, Detroit: Wayne State University Press.

hooks, b. (2016), 'Moving Beyond Pain', *bell hooks Institute*, 9 May. Available online: http://www.bellhooksinstitute.com/blog/2016/5/9/moving-beyond-pain (accessed 17 July 2020).

Kooijman, J. (2019), 'Fierce, Fabulous and In/Famous: Beyoncé as Black Diva', *Popular Music and Society*, 42 (1): 6–21.

O'Neill, E. R. (2007), 'The M-m-mama of Us All: Divas and the Cultural Logic of Late Ca(m)pitalism', *Camera Obscura*, 22 (2): 11–37.

Phipps, A. (2020), *#MeToo Not You: The Trouble with Mainstream Feminism*, Manchester: Manchester University Press.

Sewell, C. J. P. (2013), 'Mammies and Matriarchs: Tracing Images of the Black Female in Popular Culture 1950s to Present', *Journal of African American Studies*, 17: 308–26.

Shifman, L. and D. Lemish (2010), 'Between Feminism and Fun(ny)mism', *Information, Communication and Society*, 13 (6): 870–91.

Snapes, L. (2020), 'Lana Del Rey's Swipes at Her Peers of Colour Undermine Her Feminist Argument', *The Guardian*, 21 May. Available online: https://www.theguardian.com/music/2020/may/21/lana-del-rey-criticising-peers-undermines-feminist-argument (accessed 17 July 2020).

Spelman, N. (2016), '"Sing It With Me Now": Audience Participation in Arena Concerts', in B. Halligan, K. Fairclough, R. Edgar and N. Spelman (eds), *The Arena Concert: Music, Media and Mass Entertainment*, 231–46, London: Bloomsbury.

Springer, K. (2007), 'Divas, Evil Black Bitches, and Bitter Black Women: African American Women in Postfeminist and Post-Civil-Rights Popular Culture', in Y. Tasker and D. Negra (eds), *Interrogating Postfeminism: Gender and the Politics of Popular Culture*, 249–76, Durham: Duke University Press.

Tomsett, E. (2017), '21st Century Fumerist: Bridget Christie and the Backlash against Feminist Comedy', *Comedy Studies*, 8 (1): 57–67.

Tomsett, E. (2018), 'Positives and Negatives: Reclaiming the Female Body and Self-deprecation in Stand-up Comedy', *Comedy Studies*, 9 (1): 6–18.

Toone, A., A. N. Edgar and K. Ford (2017), '"She Made Angry Black Women Something That People Would Want To Be": Lemonade and Black Women as Audiences and Subjects', *Participations: Journal of Audience & Reception Studies*, 14 (2): 203–25.

Weidhase, N. (2015a), 'Ageing Grace/Fully: Grace Jones and the Queering of the Diva Myth', in D. Jermyn and S. Holmes (eds), *Women, Celebrity & Cultures of Ageing: Freeze Frame*, 97–111, Basingstoke: Palgrave Macmillan.

Weidhase, N. (2015b), '"Beyoncé Feminism" and the Contestation of the Black Feminist Body', *Celebrity Studies*, 6 (1): 128–31.

Whiteley, S. (2006), 'Popular Music and the Dynamics of Desire', in S. Whiteley and J. Rycenga (eds), *Queering the Popular Pitch*, 251–64, London: Routledge.

Contributors

Rachel E. Blackburn is an artist, pedagogue, writer, PhD., MFA, consultant, and content strategist for academia and corporate organizations. She has been teaching in higher education since 2011. Rachel is a member of the Young Vic's Genesis Director's Project (London, UK) and the American Humor Studies Association (AHSA). She has published works on intersectional identity, acting, performance and humour with Bloomsbury, Routledge, ABC-CLIO, and others. Rachel currently resides in Atlanta with the love of her life, her husband Neil. And, she loves to laugh.

Timmia Hearn DeRoy is a practitioner and scholar of social justice-based theatre and film. She directs, writes, produces, draturgs, and teaches. She holds an MA and a PhD in Theatre & Performance Studies from the University of Kansas, and a BA in Theatre Studies from Yale University. She was a founding member of the Trinidad and Tobago PRIDE Arts Festival, former Director of the School for the Arts at the Trinidad Theatre Workshop and former Marketing Manager at the Caribbean Tales International Film Festival. Timmia's directing credits include Victoria Taurean's *10,000: A One-Woman New Play Development* (2020), *In the Blood* by Suzan-Lori Parks (2019), collectively authored *Buss de Mark* (2016), *A Midsummer Night's Dream* by William Shakespeare (2013–14), *Two Can Play* by Trevor Rhone (2013–14), and *An Echo in the Bone* by Dennis Scott (2012). www.timmiahearn.com

Rana Esfandiary is an assistant professor of Design & Technology at the University of Kansas, USA. She holds a PhD in theatre studies and an MFA in Scenography and has designed multiple shows in both professional and academic settings including *Twelfth Night, Chasing Gods, Sunset Baby, Mascot, The Curious Incident of the Dog in the Night-Time, The Wolves, Urinetown, Summer and Smoke, Dog Sees God, Adding Machine: A Musical* and *The Mousetrap*. Rana's research areas are race and performance studies, ritual and religious studies, Middle Eastern theatre studies, scenography and eco-scenography.

Mark Duffett is an associate professor at the University of Chester, UK, and his research interests include popular music studies and fan studies. His publications include *Counting Down Elvis*, *Understanding Fandom*, *Elvis: Roots, Image, Comeback Phenomenon* and *Scary Monsters: Monstrosity, Masculinity and Popular Music* (co-written with Jon Hackett).

Kirsty Fairclough is Head of Research and Knowledge Exchange, and Reader in Screen Studies, at the School of Digital Arts (SODA) at Manchester Metropolitan University, UK. She has published widely on popular culture and is co-editor of *Pop Stars on Film*, *Prince and Popular Culture*, *The Music Documentary: Acid Rock to Electropop*, *The Arena Concert: Music, Media and Mass Entertainment*, *The Legacy of Mad Men: Cultural History, Intermediality and American Television* and *Music/Video: Forms, Aesthetics, Media*. Kirsty was the curator of *Sound and Vision: Pop Stars on Film* and *In Her View: Women Documentary Filmmakers* film seasons at HOME, Manchester, and is the Chair of the Manchester Jazz Festival.

Dorothy Finan is a Lecturer in Cultural Industries at the School of Performance and Cultural Industries, University of Leeds, UK. She researches youth, gender, and virtuality in East Asian cultural industries, particularly the transmedia and transnational dimensions of popular music. She is interested in how popular music figures in national identity, and has published research on the "global" dimensions of J-pop and K-pop music, as well as on video games and popular music.

Gwynne George received his PhD in English and American Studies from the University of Manchester, UK, in 2021. His thesis was a cultural history of the early careers of Whitney Houston and Janet Jackson and explored their emergence as two of the most commercially successful popular music stars of the 1980s.

Benjamin Halligan is the Director of the Doctoral College of the University of Wolverhampton, UK. His publications include *Hotbeds of Licentiousness: The British Glamour Film and the Permissive Society*, *Desires for Reality: Radicalism and Revolution in Western European Film* and *Michael Reeves*. He has co-edited the following books: *Mark E. Smith and The Fall: Art, Music and Politics*; *Reverberations: The Philosophy, Aesthetics and Politics of Noise*;

Resonances: Noise and Contemporary Music; *The Music Documentary: Acid Rock to Electropop*; *The Arena Concert: Music, Media and Mass Entertainment*; *Stories We Could Tell: Putting Words to American Popular Music* by David Sanjek; *Politics of the Many: Contemporary Radical Thought and the Crisis of Agency* and *Adult Themes: British Cinema and the X-Rating in the Long 1960s*.

Nicole Hodges Persley is Vice Provost of Diversity, Equity, Inclusion & Belonging, and Associate Professor, at the University of Kansas, USA. She is an award-winning professor, director and community leader in diversity, equity and inclusion work between academic and creative communities. She is the author of *Sampling and Remixing Blackness in Hip-Hop Theater and Performance*; *Black Matters: Lewis Morrow Plays*; and *Hip-Hop in Musical Theater*. She is the co-author of *Breaking it Down: Audition Techniques for Actors of the Global Majority* (with Monica White Ndounou). She is a professional director who specializes in race and performance in American theatre and is a member of SAG/AFTRA and the Stage Director and Choreographers Society. She is the Artistic Director of KC Melting Pot Theater and co-founder of CreateEnsemble.com.

Shara Rambarran is a senior lecturer in Music, Business, and Media at the University of Brighton, UK. She is a musicologist in the award-winning Spotify music podcast, *Decode*, co-runs the Art of Record Production conferences and is an editor on the *Journal on the Art of Record Production*. She is the author of *Virtual Music: Sound, Music, and Image in the Digital Era*, and co-editor of *The Oxford Handbook of Music and Virtuality* and *The Routledge Research Companion to Popular Music Education*.

Harriet Reed is Curator of Contemporary Performance at the V&A Museum, London. She has co-curated the exhibitions *Censored! Stage, Screen, Society at 50* (2018), *Re:Imagining Musicals* (2022), *Alice: Curiouser and Curiouser* (2021) and contributed research towards the exhibition *Diva* (2023). She is part of the curatorial team behind The David Bowie Centre for the Study of Performing Arts, set to open at V&A East in 2025. She is a Committee Member of the UK Society for Theatre Research and the Membership Secretary for SIBMAS (International Association of Performing Arts Collections).

James Reeves is a PhD candidate at the University of Wolverhampton, UK, where he is currently researching the representation of women in the works of

Dolly Parton, in part through the analysis of lyrics as poetry. James is originally from Atlanta, Georgia, and has a deep love and admiration for Dolly and country music. He has taught at universities in China and the United States and has an abiding passion for teaching literature. His other interests include playing the piano, young adult fiction, environmentalism, mythology and animal activism.

Gina Sandí Díaz is an assistant professor of Theatre at California State University, USA, where she specializes in Latinx theatre, devised theatre, acting, and directing. Recent credits with the University Theatre include *Electricidad* by Luis Alfaro, *The Agony of Ecstasy* by Sabina Berman, and *Lydia* by Octavio Solis. She has written on Augusto Boal in *Fifty Key Figures in Latinx and Latin American Theatre* and Ebano Teatro in *Seeking Common Ground: Latinx and Latin American Theatre and Performance*. She currently runs the ArteVism Fellowship in collaboration with the Pan Valley Institute of AFSC in California and serves as the National Chair of Representation, Equity and Diversity for the Kennedy Center's American College Theatre Festival (KCACTF).

Shawna Shipley-Gates is a health educator, sexual wellness influencer and Black feminist scholar whose research places eroticism in conversation with Black feminism, critical health psychology and digital humanities. Her work explores digital erotic content production as a form of resistance against sexual oppression to address sexual health disparities among Black women. She is currently pursuing her doctoral degree in Women, Gender, and Sexuality Studies at the University of Kansas, USA.

Hannah M. Strong is a PhD candidate in Musicology at the University of Pittsburgh, USA. Her research interests focus on intersections between rap and hip-hop, social movements, and feminism. Strong earned a Masters degree in Music History from Temple University and completed her Bachelor of Arts in classical voice performance at Westminster Choir College. Her article 'Expanding the Limits of Protest: Rap and Social Media in the Wake of George Floyd's Death' was published by *Music & Politics in the Moment*. Strong frequently presents at these conferences: American Musicological Society (AMS), International Association for the Study of Pop Music (IASPM), Society for American Music (SAM), and the Cultural Studies Association (CSA).

Ellie Tomsett is a senior lecturer in Media at Birmingham City University, UK, and co-founder of the Mixed Bill Comedy and Gender Research Network. She is the author of *Stand-Up Comedy and Contemporary Feminisms: Sexism, Stereotypes and Structural Inequalities* and has written on feminist comedy, self-deprecatory humour and media representations of women's paid labour.

Nathalie Weidhase is a lecturer in Media and Communication and the Programme Director of the BSc Media and Communication at the University of Surrey, UK. Her research focuses on (post)feminism and femininity in popular culture, and she has published on women in popular music, celebrity feminism, Brexit, and the royal family. Her current work is concerned with the intersections of populism and gender in popular culture and media.

Index

Note: Only artists with relatively conventional given or persona names are listed by surname first.

2Pac   34
9 to 5 (Colin Higgins, 1980)   63, 64, 67

Aaliyah   15, 16, 97–105, 108, 109 n.2, 109 n.4, 109 n.6, 110 n.8
Aaliyah Live in Amsterdam (Pogus Caesar, 1995)   97, 101
Abdoh, Reza   231–2, 240–1
acid house, raves   107, 110 n.8
Adams, Jayde   262, 265, 267–9, 271
Adichie, Chimamanda Ngozi   116, 118
Afrofuturism   15, 90, 141–4, 147, 152–4
After School   134
AI   134
Alice in Chains   27
All You Need is Love (television show)   73
Amerie   8, 15, 105–9
Amnesty International   17 n.2
Amuro, Namie   15, 125–37
Antebellum (Gerard Bush and Christopher Renz, 2020)   144, 145, 149
apartheid   17 n.2
Armstrong, Louis   7
Ashanti   105–6
Austin, Dallas   132, 133
Awich   135

Baartman, Saartjie 'Sarah'   252, 253
Baker, Josephine   25
Baldwin, James   89
Bambaataa, Afrika   7
Bangs, Lester   73, 74
Banks, Azealia   164
Barthes, Roland   36–7
Beyoncé   3, 4, 15, 18 n.4, 38, 48, 89, 105, 113–24, 131, 136, 166, 180, 221, 242, 247–8, 259, 262–73, *see also* Destiny's Child

Beyond the Valley of the Dolls (Russ Meyer, 1970)   6
Bikini Kill   18 n.10
Black, Lewis   257
Black Lives Matter (movement)   153, 177, 248, 271
Blackpink   9
Blige, Mary J.   34
Bone Thugs-n-Harmony   27
Bowie, David   8, 73, 86, 217
Brown, Foxy   97, 123, 162, 165
Brown, James   77, 142, 223
Burke, Tarana   120

Caesar, Pogus   97, 109 n.4
Callas, Maria   105, 217
Cardi B   15, 16, 113, 116, 158–61, 164–73
Carey, Mariah   1, 2, 6, 9, 14, 25–39, 110 n.8, 259, 264, 272
Carpenter, Karen   99
Cassie   104
celebrity feminism, *see* feminism/feminists
Chandelier Status (television comedy special)   249, 252, 253, 259 n.1
Chapman, Tracy   150
Chepp, Valerie   114, 123
Christie, Bridget   248, 258, 262, 267–8
Ciao! Manhattan (John Palmer and David Weisman, 1972)   5–6
City Girls   164
Clinton, George   142
Coachella (music festival)   15, 113–14, 120–4
Collins, Patricia Hill   49, 161, 163, 172, 250, 252, 253, 269
colonialisms   16, 72, 77–9, 82, 129, 134, 143, 153–5, 177, 179, 182, 186, 217

commodification 83–4, 87, 169, 173 n.1, 183, 206, 263
consumerism/consumer culture 50, 75, 104, 232, 239
cosmopolitanism 16, 78, 87, 190–9, 201–4, 206–7
costume 37, 57, 59, 61, 67, 84, 146, 203, 213, 214, 216–22, 224, 253, 265, 267
Crenshaw, Kimberlé 178, 179, 248, 268
Crunk Feminist Collective (CFC), the 97, 163, 173 n.2
cultural appropriation 270, 273

Da Brat 97
Da Pump 129
Dash, Damon 101
Davis, Betty 6
decolonialism, *see* colonialisms
Degrassi: The Next Generation (television series) 199, 200
Des'ree 102
Destiny's Child 2, 105, 221, 222, 263
Devo 74–6, 80
disco 2, 63, 70, 73, 75–7, 79, 89
Dogg, Snoop 27, 34, 168–9
Dolce Vita, La (Federico Fellini, 1960) 5
Dollywood (theme park) 64–5
Doors, the 243–4
Dr. Dre 33, 34, 39 n. 7, 169
Drake 16, 190–4, 197–205, 207, 207 n.1
Dupri, Jermaine 27
Dyer, Richard 28, 48, 53
Dylan, Bob 75, 81

Ekberg, Anita 5
Elba, Idris 194–6
emceeing 17, 97, 102, 105, 106, 109
Eminem 33–7, 39 n.5, 39 n.7
Estefan, Gloria 1
Everyday Sexism Project 13
Extras (television series) 83

feminism/feminists 4, 5, 7, 8, 10, 12, 13, 15, 16, 43, 49, 51, 63, 88, 105, 113–20, 123–4, 155, 163–6, 168, 180, 205, 252, 259, 262–9, 273,
  see also the Crunk Feminist Collective; intersectionality
  antifeminism 3, 49, 50, 118, 163
  Black feminism 43, 49, 50, 52, 161, 163, 164, 166, 168–73, 247–50, 252–3, 258, 268
  celebrity feminism 262, 265, 268
  feminist killjoy, the 3
  fourth wave 3, 13, 14, 177–8, 248
  hip-hop feminism 12, 16, 97, 105, 160, 163, 164, 166, 168, 170–3, 268, 269
  postfeminism 4, 10–11, 13, 15, 43, 45, 50–2, 133, 134, 265, 266, 270
  second wave 10, 12, 13, 16, 25, 60, 89
  third wave 3, 4, 9–11, 13, 103–4
Ferry, Bryan 73–4, 80, 87
fierceness, fierce 3–4, 6, 8
Fischer, Wild Man 99
Fleetwood Mac 9
fourth wave feminism, *see* feminism/feminists
Franklin, Aretha 1, 2, 28, 180, 272
Fyre Festival (2017) 106

G8 summits 15, 132
Gabriel, Peter 17 n.2
Gaye, Marvin 155
Genet, Jean 17, 230–2, 234–45
Gilbey, Tom 84, 86
Gilroy, Paul 76–8, 193, 255
Girls Aloud 10, 11
glam rock 73, 74
Goldin, Nan 98
Goude, Jean-Paul 87–8
Grande, Ariana 39 n.8
Grundy, Bill 70, 82, 83
Gudda Gudda 204

Hakim, Catherine 5, 9, 11
Hall, Stuart 78, 198
halls of fame (curation tendency) 214–16
Hanna, Kathleen 12, 18 n.10
Happiness 135
Harlem Cultural Festival, the 7
Hawkins, Sophie B. 9

Hayes, Isaac   2, 6, 17 n.1
Heard, Shawnette   131
Hendrix, Jimi   61
Hill, Lauryn   27, 97
hip-hop feminism, *see* feminism/feminists
hood, the   192, 194–6, 200, 202, 204
hooks, bell   3, 10, 18 n.4, 78, 118, 161, 162, 169–70, 268
Houston, Whitney   14, 42–53, 180, 271

icons, religious   107–8
Imajin   132
intersectionality   13, 16, 45, 49, 167, 177–9, 183–6, 204, 248–51, 253–8, 266, 268, 273, *see also* feminism/feminists
Isley Brothers, the   100, 109 n.3

Jackson, Janet   131, 137 n.6
Jackson, Michael   47, 77, 99, 102
Jagger, Mick   81
Jay-Z   27, 114–15, 117, 119, 176, 187 n.4, 204, 259 n.4, 267, 268
jazz   7, 39 n.1, 81, 129, 251
Jimi Hendrix Experience, the   155
Johnson, Daniel   99
Jones, Brian   102, 110 n.8
Jones, Grace   25, 38, 70–90, 137 n.6
Joy Division   80

Kaepernick, Colin   31, 176, 186 n.3, 187 nn.4–5
Kardashian, Kim   252–3
Kelly, R.   98–101, 109 n.2
Keys, Alicia   101, 103, 105
King, Carole   1
Kožená, Magdalena   104
K-pop   9, 39 n.8, 134

Labelle, Patti   25, 28
Latifah, Queen   97, 162, 170
Latto   167, 173 n.3
Left Eye (Lisa 'Left Eye' Lopes)   97
Lennox, Annie   118, 213, 219, 223–6
Lewis, Martin   17 n.2
Lil' Kim   97, 123, 134, 162, 165
Lil Miquela   9

Lil Wayne   199, 200, 204, 207 n.1
Lilith Fair Festival   2
Lloyd, Marie   25
Lopez, Jennifer   16, 107, 178–9, 181–2, 184, 186 n.1
Lorenz, Trey   27
Los Angeles Memorial Coliseum   1–2
Love, Courtney   9

MC Lyte   97
McRobbie, Angela   43, 50–1
Madonna   2, 38, 57, 131
Mahogany (Berry Gordy, 1975)   48–9
Markle, Meghan   6
masculinities/masculinity   81, 85, 160–2, 166–9, 172, 194–6
Matrix, The (The Wachowskis, 1999)   142, 251
May'n   135
Mean Girls (Mark Waters, 2004)   31, 39
Megan Thee Stallion   15, 16, 160–1, 164–73
MeToo (movement, also presented as #MeToo)   13, 15, 100, 109 n.4, 114, 120–1, 123–4, 138, 248, 273
Metropolis (Fritz Lang, 1927)   142, 146, 148
Mezzrow, Mezz   81
Michico   135
Migos   173 n.3
Miku, Hatsune   9
Milano, Alyssa   120
Minaj, Nicki   16, 113, 116, 164, 166, 190–4, 196–200, 203–7
Minogue, Kylie   8, 219, 221, 226
Misora, Hibari   128–9, 136, 137 n.1
Missy Elliott   27, 101, 109 n.6, 134
Monáe, Janelle   141–57
Montezuma, Magdalena   105
Morissette, Alanis   9
Morley, Paul   79
Morrison, Jim   81
Mothersbaugh, Mark   75–6
MTV   2, 7, 18 n.7, 26, 29, 30, 42–6, 52, 53, 104, 263
   MTV *Cribs*   30

MTV Unplugged   26–7, 38–9
Munford, Rebecca   10, 11, 13, 18 n.9

Nakamori, Akina   128
Nas   27
Nate Dogg   27
Neptunes, the   27
new jack swing   97
new jill swing   98
Nicks, Stevie   9
Nirvana   27, 99

Obama, Barack   194, 201–3, 232
objectification   87, 115–16, 119, 169, 205, 220
O'Day, Anita   7
Okinawa   129, 132, 137 n.3
Omielan, Luisa   262, 266, 269–72
Oprah (television show)   26, 70

Paris is Burning (Jennie Livingstone, 1990)   7, 18 n.6
Parton, Dolly   14, 56–68, 214
Pearl Jam   27
Playboy (magazine)   31, 62
Pop Art   73, 76, 78, 80, 88
Porter Wagoner Show, The (television series)   59, 60
postfeminism, *see* feminism/feminists
postmodernity   77, 78
Poucher, Walter   84, 85
Prince   110 n.8, 142
punk and post-punk   12, 74, 76, 77, 80, 82
pussy (slang), *see* vagina
Pussycat Dolls, the   104

Queen Latifah   97, 162, 170

racism   14, 28, 30–1, 78, 87, 88, 120, 123, 143, 146, 154, 172, 176–8, 182, 183, 200, 207, 231, 248, 250, 251, 256, 259 n.3, 271
Rapsody   164
Reagan, Ronald   43, 45, 48–50, 52
Red Velvet   9
resistance, practices of   3, 89, 155, 160–1, 165, 168, 171, 173

Riot Grrrl   9, 10, 12–13
RiRi   135
r'n'b   7, 26, 29, 31, 214
rock music   9, 10, 26, 29, 44, 71, 73–4, 76–7, 81–2, 147, 153, 184, 216
rock'n'roll   72–3, 80–2
Ronstadt, Linda   11
Rose, Axl   81
Rose, Rubi   167, 173
Ross, Diana   38, 48–9, 106, 221, 223, 225–6
Roxy Music   73–4
RuPaul   2
Russell Harty Show, The (television show)   70–1, 79, 82–7

Sade   102
Salt-N-Pepa   162
Sanjek, David   44, 98
Sartre, Jean-Paul   235–6
Saweetie   164
Schroeter, Werner   105
science fiction   142–3, 152
Sedgwick, Edie   5
Sex Pistols, the   70, 82
Shakira   16, 176–89
Shepp, Archie   102, 110 n.8
Sheth, Fulgani   82
Showgirls (Paul Verhoeven, 1995)   8
Sill, Judee   99, 103
Simon, Carly   11
Ski, Frank   168
Sommore   248–59
Sonic Youth   12
Spears, Britney   99, 107, 222
SPEED   129, 133
Spice Girls, the   9–11, 215
Springsteen, Bruce   81, 179
stand-up comedy   17, 249, 253–4, 259 n. 2, 262, 264–5, 270, 272–3
Static Major   101
Stax Records   1
Stonewall Riots   3, 18 n.3
Studio 54 (nightclub)   70, 78, 86
Sukihana   167, 173 n.3
Summer, Donna   2, 53 n. 4
Sun Ra   142

SUNMI   39
Super Bowl, the   16, 174, 176, 178, 180–2, 184, 186, 186 n.2
supermodels   74, 79, 85
Supremes, the   213, 219–23, 227 n. 4
Surviving R. Kelly (television series)   98
Swift, Taylor   9, 265

teens/teenagers   28, 109 n.1, 200
Tetsuya, Komuro   130, 132–3, 137 n. 5
Ticking Boxes (comedy special)   254–5
Timbaland   101–3, 107, 109 n.2, 109 nn.5–6, 110 n.8
Timberlake, Justin   110 n.8
TLC   9, 132
trap music   31
Treacy, Phillip   85
Tsai, Jolin   134
Tsuchiya, Anna   134
Turner, Ike   7
Turner, Tina   7, 53 n.4, 214, 216

Utada, Hikaru   128

V&A Museum   213–14, 217–21, 223, 226, 228 n.3
vagina, the   16, 103, 165, 167, 169
  as termed 'pussy'   162, 165, 167, 170
Viola, Bill   102
voguing   7

Warhol, Andy   5, 88
Wattstax (1972 concert)   1–2, 17 n.1
Welles, Orson   107
Wilson, Mary   213, 219–23
Wire, The (television series)   194–6
Wogan: Now and Then (television show)   70, 88
Working Girl (Mike Nichols, 1988)   50–1
working girl, the   43, 49–52, 62

X-Factor, The (television show)   5, 83

yacht pop   104
Yashere, Gina   248–61
Young M.A.   5

www.ingramcontent.com/pod-product-compliance
Lightning Source LLC
Chambersburg PA
CBHW070019010526
44117CB00011B/1638